TRAUMA

www.**transworldbooks**.co.uk

TRAUMA

From Lockerbie to 7/7:
How trauma affects our minds and
how we fight back

PROFESSOR GORDON TURNBULL

BANTAM PRESS

LONDON • TORONTO • SYDNEY • AUCKLAND • JOHANNESBURG

TRANSWORLD PUBLISHERS
61–63 Uxbridge Road, London W5 5SA
A Random House Group Company
www.transworldbooks.co.uk

First published in Great Britain
in 2011 by Bantam Press
an imprint of Transworld Publishers

Copyright © Gordon Turnbull 2011
Diagrams on pp. 78, 93, 290 and 293 © Patrick Mulrey

Every effort has been made to obtain the necessary permissions with reference to copyright
material, both illustrative and quoted. We apologize for any omissions in this respect and
will be pleased to make the appropriate acknowledgements in any future edition.

Gordon Turnbull has asserted his right under the Copyright,
Designs and Patents Act 1988 to be identified as the author of this work.

A CIP catalogue record for this book
is available from the British Library.

ISBNs 9780593061947 (cased)
9780593061954 (tpb)

This book is sold subject to the condition that it shall not,
by way of trade or otherwise, be lent, resold, hired out,
or otherwise circulated without the publisher's prior
consent in any form of binding or cover other than that
in which it is published and without a similar condition,
including this condition, being imposed on the
subsequent purchaser.

Addresses for Random House Group Ltd companies outside the UK
can be found at: www.randomhouse.co.uk
The Random House Group Ltd Reg. No. 954009

The Random House Group Ltd supports the Forest Stewardship
Council® (FSC®), the leading international forest certification organization.
All our titles that are printed on Greenpeace-approved FSC® certified paper carry
the FSC® logo. Our paper procurement policy can be found at
www.randomhouse.co.uk/environment

Typeset in 11/14pt Sabon by
Falcon Oast Graphic Art Ltd.
Printed and bound in Great Britain by
Clays Ltd, Bungay, Suffolk

2 4 6 8 10 9 7 5 3 1

With all my love to Alison,
my wife and my very best friend

Be brave enough to live creatively. The creative is the place where no one else has ever been. You have to leave the city of your comfort and go into the wilderness of your intuition. You can't get there by bus, only by hard work and risk and by not quite knowing what you are doing. What you'll discover will be wonderful. What you'll discover will be yourself.

Alan Alda

A Note to the Reader

In order for us to understand how a person's experiences may lead to psychological trauma, and how that trauma can be treated depending on a person's circumstances and personality, we must be given sufficient detail of their lives and the events that occurred in them. At the same time, it is important to ensure that the secrets and histories of individuals I have met in the consulting room are not set out in a manner that would enable people to recognize them. To be true to both requirements, I have, with the exception of names that are in the public domain, protected the identities of the people I write about by changing names and altering a number of details when describing case histories.

However, every case is real; no dramatic strands have been added or embellished for effect. Of course those cases which are a matter of public record are reported in their original detail, in the accepted manner, and I would like to thank John McCarthy, Terry Waite and Johnson Beharry for allowing me to use their experiences in this book. I hope that a growing insight into PTSD will lead to greater acceptance and awareness of the condition, and will help reduce the torment of those who have already suffered so greatly.

Contents

Acknowledgements

I first met Mark Lucas at Lyneham during the McCarthy family debriefing. Once the dust that blew in from the Middle East had settled and the last of the British hostages had been released and the initial re-entry work had been done, he asked me if I would write a book about what had happened from the rescuer's point of view. For several years I declined. In truth, I didn't know what to write because I wasn't sure what had happened, but I had a feeling that, one day, I would have the opportunity to reflect and hopefully get a glimmer of understanding I could put down on paper. Throughout that time, which lasted for 16 years, I was constantly nagged by the lines from W. H. Davies's well-known poem:

What is this life if full of care,
We have no time to stand and stare?

The hurly-burly of clinical work makes life very busy. There were a lot of people out there to listen to who had experienced psychological trauma and the field was moving fast, with new discoveries in neuroscience making the connections between our inner wiring and our thinking patterns, emotions and behaviours. I identify the time I started to 'stand and stare' as the period when I was given the opportunity to help Stuart McNab, Rebekah Lwin, Tony Parnell and Anne

Boran to develop the MSc in Psychological Trauma at the University of Chester. I cannot thank them enough for broadening and deepening my intellectual landscape. This also extends to all the students on our course, from whom I have learned much more than I have given them since 2005. This chance to reflect on my own journey through the twists and turns of the trauma maze led directly to the determination to write this book. Fortunately for me, Mark Lucas remained keen to go ahead and he has been an inspiration; truly one of my Merlins.

You will find in these pages that I am unashamedly curious by nature. There were a lot of clocks in our house in Edinburgh when I was growing up that needed replacing! My curiosity to find out how things worked led me to dismantle them but, unfortunately, I didn't know how to put them back together again! My father and my mother, who was probably the greatest armchair explorer the world has ever seen, were able not only to accommodate this curiosity but also to provide the essential surroundings to kindle it. This applies equally to my brother Derek, whose wisdom has often kept me on the path, and to members of our extended family and friends.

Returning to that wonderful home environment provided relief from my first experience of school and a sense of security and safety, maintaining my optimism that life was not all about being forced to conform and that there was indeed a realistic prospect of individual development and being curious was all right. I will never be able to thank Katharine Sprunt enough for setting me free at school to bring both worlds together. This led to a wonderful, inspirational time with Jim Ireland and then at George Heriot's School, which brought me through to university with the burning appetite for learning about the world undimmed.

However, after almost a quarter of a century in Edinburgh and half of that in one street, it felt right to spread my wings and joining the Royal Air Force was just the ticket. I want to thank certain people in the RAF Medical Branch who opened opportunities and introduced new ideas during my twenty-two years in the service: Brian Kelly for helping me into general medicine and later into neurology, Rex Fitzgerald, John Hill and Fredoon Amroliwalla, Bob Chappell and 'Big Al' Johnston for their Wisdom; David Johnstone (and his eyebrow), Angus Black, John Rollins, Bob Merry, David and Dea Price and all of my psychiatric colleagues for the experiences we shared at a time of exciting advances in the field. For me, the most exciting development was the setting up of a new treatment service for Post-Traumatic Stress Disorder (PTSD). This could not have happened without the enthusiasm and hard work of Walter Busuttil, Bert Venman, David Stevens, Chris Cook, Leigh Neal, Adrian West, Nick Blanch, Jackie Hall, Ron Herepath, Dick Hilling, Alvin Cranmer and others involved in what became a very successful project. This was also a time when the three services worked together and close relationships with Morgan O'Connell and Alan Lillywhite from the Navy and Jonathan Bisson and Mike Srinivasan from the Army proved invaluable. I will never forget the open and friendly reception I had when I was allowed to go to the National Center for PTSD in Palo Alto, California, to study the management of psychological trauma in 1990 before deploying to the First Gulf War. Matthew Friedman, Dudley Blake and the others out there in California and Charlie Clark in Florida did more to shape the British reaction to military psychological trauma than they can imagine.

The link with the RAF was not lost when I left in 1993 because it was a retired RAF psychiatrist who offered me a job at Ticehurst House Hospital. Appropriately, this oldest psychiatric hospital in England also had a 200-year reputation for innovative psychiatry and Tony Goorney, the medical director, wanted to set up a traumatic stress service. With the help of Margaret Cudmore, Louise Orpin, Bill Balthazar, Pat Young, Anne Davies, Penny Long and Beau Cackett, this became a reality and Ticehurst grew to be a centre of excellence for treating survivors of trauma. The successful transfer of a treatment method that worked in a military hospital setting was the result of the imagination, experience and efforts of Bo Mills, Margaret Egner, Ian Dennis, Christine Miller, Tosin Clairmonte, Stu Johnson, Sheila Davidson, Heather Robyn, Jayne Gibb, Sue Pittman and Coli Hanbury-Aggs.

I would like especially to mention Pat Young, who has been my guiding spirit and my rock right through from the very beginning at Ticehurst to the present. She has truly been a wise and inspirational sounding board for me, and also epitomizes that atmosphere of curiosity and thinking out of the box that I found at Ticehurst.

The link between Ticehurst and The Sanctuary, which was the oldest psychiatric hospital in the United States and currently developing a trauma programme, was forged by Sandra Bloom, who has continued to be an inspiration throughout this time, as have Bessel van der Kolk, also from the USA, Sandy McFarlane and Mark Creamer and the Army Psychology Corps from Australia and Atle Dyregrov and Lars Weisaeth from Norway, all of which emphasizes the global quality of the work. It extended also to the north of Scotland, with inspiring ideas on trauma management from David Alexander and Alastair Hull.

From time to time one encounters kindred spirits. This might not be unusual in one's own field but it is exceptional, in my experience, to discover a truly affinitive connection in another discipline. Such a bond has developed over the years with Mark McGhee, one of the country's leading personal injury lawyers with a special interest in military psychological trauma. I have learned so much from knowing him and also Sally McGhee.

The launching pad that created the space to free my imagination early in life has fortunately been recreated very skilfully by my wife Alison. The harmony has been extended into our own family life with our three splendid sons, Iain, Stuart and Robert, who have been a joy to bring up, and is now further strengthened by their own families, by Hannah, Pebbles and Katy and our grandchildren Violet, Florence and Matilda and, God willing, the safe arrival of 'le bump' in August. An extra advantage of family life has been the philosophical sparring with my father-in-law, Noel Fisher, who was another Merlin.

I would like to thank all of the above for their help in making this book possible and all others who know that they have helped but are not mentioned, especially my extended family on both sides. Their contribution is no less appreciated.

The support from Transworld Publishers has been invaluable. To Sally Gaminara, Vivien Garrett and Laura Sherlock, to copy-editor Deborah Adams, and to the army of proofreaders at Transworld, many, many thanks for helping me to transform my experiences into a book.

And last, but very definitely not least, to Nick Cook and Ali, Lucy and Will, without whom this book would almost certainly never have been written, and their friends Giles and Clare Daubeny.

To all colleagues in the world of psychological trauma, 'May the process be with you.'

Prologue

Princess Alexandra Hospital, RAF Wroughton, Wiltshire

23 December 1988

The distant strains of Slade's 'Merry Christmas' wafted into the room and a tinsel-decked, cone-shaped hat appeared as my secretary, Carol, poked her head round the door.

'Gordon,' she said, 'there's a phone call . . .'

I could sense the restlessness of the doctors and nurses around the room. Surgeon Lieutenant Commander Price let out a groan. On loan to us from the Navy, David was one of the most experienced psychiatrists on the ward. I respected him hugely – we all did. He was also one of my best friends. But patience didn't feature among his virtues, especially when he'd planned an afternoon's golf.

'An RAF flight sergeant,' Carol continued. 'David Whalley. Says he knows you.'

I had to delve into the memory banks a bit before it came to me. I remembered a bull of a man, but couldn't recall whether we'd met in the UK or Cyprus, where I'd been stationed for a while. Either way, it had been years ago. Whalley was a mountain rescue wizard.

But I couldn't think why he should be contacting me now. The look on Carol's face gave a hint of urgency.

Out of the corner of my eye I could see David Price glancing at his watch.

'Can't it wait?' Surely a call from a man I hadn't seen in a decade couldn't be that important.

Carol removed her paper hat and I realized she was close to tears.

'He's calling from Lockerbie . . .'

The atmosphere in the room changed in an instant.

Carol's office was 20 yards down the corridor. I'm tall – six foot two – and had to duck beneath loops of paper chains to get there. Christmas is not an easy time for the mentally ill and we tried to strike the right balance on the ward. A nod to the festive spirit can lift the mood; too much of it and we ran the risk of reminding people of things that might have brought them to us in the first place.

The phone was off the hook. A newspaper sat on the desk beside it. The photograph below the headline had already assumed a terrible, iconic status: taken from the air, it showed the nose section of Pan Am 103, the *Clipper Maid of the Seas*, lying crumpled on a Scottish hillside.

I put the receiver to my ear and sat down. 'David?'

'Gordon, thank Christ.'

He explained that there were only a handful of phones working in the town. There was a queue a mile long for the one he was using. He would have to be quick.

Mountain rescuers are the SAS of the RAF: tough beyond belief and generally blessed with a healthy measure of cynicism. David was no exception. He'd seen everything – from fingers and toes blackened by frostbite to chunks of RAF jets and their occupants strewn across the most inhospitable landscapes.

He was in charge of the four RAF mountain rescue teams combing the area around Lockerbie for survivors. He happened to be based at RAF Leeming in North Yorkshire, my first ever posting in the RAF.

'But there's no rescuing to be done, Gordon.' He sounded utterly exhausted. 'It's over, hopeless, a complete mess.' They weren't finding anything except bodies and bits of bodies.

He told me he was worried about his boys – especially the younger ones. He was rambling now, almost incoherent at times, but I listened without interrupting.

There was something happening up there, something he'd never encountered in 25 years on the hill. He said it over and over, like a mantra.

'What do you mean?' I asked.

'Please, Gordon . . . I need you to come and see for yourself.'

It wasn't easy for David to articulate much beyond this. All he'd say was that people were seeing things – the same things – and the things they were seeing wouldn't go away.

Even if David didn't know what forces had conspired to make him pick up the phone and call me, I thought I did. I felt my throat constrict.

'How do you want to play this, David?' I said. 'How many people are we talking about?'

One hundred and twenty, he replied. They were dispersing; going back to what they were meant to be doing when they got the call from Lockerbie, deploying from their bases into Britain's mountain regions for the holiday season, because there was always some idiot, no matter what the weather, who decided to go rock-climbing in his pyjamas and trainers.

The RAF had four mountain rescue bases: St Athan in Wales, Stafford in the Peak District, Leeming in North Yorkshire and Leuchars in Scotland. David asked if we could visit each in turn when the teams come down from the hills on 3 January. He asked me if we'd debrief every member of his team.

I was writing notes as he spoke. One hundred and twenty people. Jesus . . . I was trying hard not to give away what I was thinking. *We've never done anything like this before – not on this scale.*

A significant proportion of those in his team – hard men conditioned to withstand extremes – were in dire need of help. And by the sound of it, David was one of them.

Chapter 1

The Legacy of the Wee Red Box

Leith, Scotland
1955

Leith, the run-down port on the south shores of the Firth of Forth and the northernmost district of Edinburgh, was where my road to Lockerbie began. I lived there with my mother, my father and my little brother Derek in a small tenement flat in Dalmeny Street, just off Leith Walk, which used to be the main artery between Edinburgh and its port.

My pre-school years were blissfully happy. Our flat was at Number 11 and one set of grandparents lived at Number 21 in Dalmeny Street and the other in Easter Road, very close to the hallowed ground where the Hibs played. Further afield, on the rarefied outskirts of Edinburgh, which I occasionally saw from the top of a bus, there were bungalows and villas with neat front lawns and houses with high walls and hints of well-tended gardens beyond. We had no car – we walked or took the bus, the tram or the train if we ever needed to go anywhere. But in those days I had little need. The criss-cross maze of streets and alleyways that surrounded Dalmeny Street was adventure enough.

My two best friends were Johnny Hughes and Raymond Brown,

who lived in the block opposite. Occasionally, we played in our 'back greens' – the courtyards, strung with lines of washing, that were the cored-out hearts of the tenement blocks. But whenever we could we went exploring. Everyone in our street knew each other and it was accepted that children would be out all day playing, even those under five. The worst threat that we faced, Johnny, Raymond and I, was running into another gang. We were the Dalmeny Street Gang and our bitter foes were the Balfour Street Gang. The rivalry was intense – we loathed each other. Never mind that our average age was four, maybe five. This was the real thing; life or death.

The main object of our loathing was a kid called Callum. Callum, who had bright red hair and freckly cheeks, owned a bike with inflatable tyres and stabilizer wheels, which was the envy of us all. He also happened to be the leader of the Balfour Street Gang and was bigger than Johnny, Raymond and me put together.

On our street, there was usually plenty to keep us occupied. We had Mr Marshall's, the newspaper shop, Mr Scott's, the ice-cream parlour and Mr Turkington's, the sweet shop (which also sold the best and biggest bangers on Guy Fawkes Night).

And on Saturdays, there were Hibs matches.

My grandpa used to work on the gates at the Hibernian stadium on Easter Road. Once the match had started, he used to lift us over the turnstiles, ostensibly to watch the football. But Johnny, Raymond and I weren't there to watch football; we were there to make money.

When the match was over, we collected the beer bottles from the terraces, put them into string bags and lugged them back to Mr Turkington's, which, aside from selling sweets and fireworks, was also the local off-licence. We'd pick up a full penny per bottle, and with a couple of dozen bottles between us our trips to the stadium usually netted us a small fortune.

The Balfour Street Gang was on to this lucrative wheeze and we needed all our stealth and guile to avoid them, knowing that we'd have to fend them off with sticks and conkers if our route back was discovered. Whenever this happened we came into our own: protecting our stagecoach from attacks by marauding Apache braves; becoming merchant seamen shooting back at Jerry aircraft trying to bomb our convoy; or Roman legionaries fending off barbarian hordes. It was intense, thrilling stuff.

The other place we could count on running into the Balfour Street Gang was at Saturday Cinema and it was after one such session that I had my first encounter with trauma.

It had been a great morning. We'd watched a Flash Gordon short followed by the main feature, a full-length Lone Ranger adventure in which our hero and Tonto had prevented a lynching. None of us had seen a lynching before. The word had not even entered our vocabulary. Some poor, hapless – and wholly innocent – victim, a Mexican in a giant sombrero, had been nabbed by a gang of angry ranchers who were determined to drive him off his land. At the precise moment he was set to swing, the Lone Ranger shot through the rope. He and Tonto then mopped up with a few well-aimed shots and the day was saved. We were still yabbering excitedly about the lynching outside the cinema, when I heard someone mention the time: close to twelve o'clock.

Johnny and Raymond had some money to spend and they were all for spending it on a threepenny 'poke of chips' at Mr Scott's. But my mother had told me I had to be home by midday, because our friends the McKenzies were coming over for lunch. I was already late.

Normally I would have gone back the safe way, but today I cut through Balfour Street. This didn't make me any less careful. I stopped and surveyed the enemy's domain from the safety of an alleyway before tearing across the street, breathing a sigh of relief as I rounded a corner, free from pursuit, and spotted the cut-through, another alley, that would take me past the Dalmeny Street church and from there to home.

I was skipping past the side door of the church when I heard a sound. I stopped and turned. In the doorway, skulking in the shadows, I saw four familiar figures, one much taller than the other three.

I was still rooted to the spot, wondering for the life of me what they were doing on our patch, when Callum barked at his henchmen: 'Get 'im!'

They fell on me. I tried to fight them off, but it was useless. Within moments, they had both my arms up behind my back. Somebody then tied some string around my wrists.

Callum stared at me, his jaw pounding on some bubble gum. He was sat astride his bike.

'What are you doing here?' I yelled at him.

'Shut yer face,' he spat back, a moment before one of his hench-men delivered a clip to the back of my head.

Callum pointed to the back wheel of his bike. 'You did this, I know you did – you or one of yer grubby pals.'

'Did what?'

'That.' He pointed again. 'We left our bikes outside the cinema. I know it was you. You did it, didn't yer?'

As my eyes grew accustomed to the light, I could see that his rear tyre was flat.

The accusation wasn't true and I told him so.

'I don't like liars,' Callum said, propping his bike against the wall. Again I tried to break free, but his pals had done a good job on my hands.

'What do we do about this, boys?' There was swagger to the way Callum walked up to me, and a strange twang to his voice, and suddenly I knew where I'd heard it before.

From behind his back he produced a length of rope. It had a big knot in it. My eyes widened. I knew what it was the moment I saw it.

I yelled, but one of his mates clamped his hand around my mouth and the sound died in my throat.

Callum walked back to the doorway and looked up. I followed his gaze. Above his head, across the top of the doorway, was a beam. It took Callum a couple of swings to get the end of the rope over.

I looked at the noose, twisting in the breeze that was blowing up the alley, and I looked at Callum. He beckoned me to him.

Images of the man I'd just watched in the cinema sprang into my mind. I tried to yell again, but Callum's mate had his hand clamped firmly around my mouth.

They tried to stand me on Callum's bike, but I kicked out and managed to send it crashing to the ground. Unperturbed, they lifted me up; and this time, they managed to slip the rope around my neck.

Panic rose in my chest and throat. The rope bit into my neck.

They let go and for a terrifying second I swung free.

Then Callum yelled and I caught a fleeting glimpse of him and his mates running off down the alley, back to Balfour Street.

The rope snapped and I fell to the ground.

As I dropped, I hit my head on the step of the church, but I felt no pain. Somebody – the Lone Ranger, it had to be – had saved me.

I looked up into the unsmiling face of Constable Meekie.

He shook his head, picked me up and set me back on my feet. Gently, he removed the rope from my neck. I coughed a few times. Constable Meekie was our local bobby. He told me to hold still while he undid the string behind my back.

I rubbed my eyes. When I opened them, Constable Meekie was studying the rope that had been biting into my neck. He was still shaking his head. 'Kiddies,' he muttered under his breath.

It dawned on me that this wasn't the Wild West after all.

He proceeded to tell me that you couldn't possibly harm anyone by hanging them with rotten gardening string. He pulled at the ends to make the point. It snapped again.

But I had been there. I had been convinced that I was going to die.

That night, as I tried to get to sleep, images of Callum and the lynch mob that I'd seen in the film played in my mind's eye over and over again.

I was born just the wrong side of the start of the academic year, which meant that while Johnny and Raymond went off to primary school, I was left alone to fend for myself. The streets, my playground, suddenly seemed deserted – until the magical hour of 3 pm when school finished and we could resume our adventures. But it wasn't the same. I longed to go to school so I could join in the fun. I also wanted to learn about the world I'd glimpsed through the Saturday Cinema Club.

When I finally arrived at school, I talked a lot – not because I was trying to cause trouble but because I wasn't getting answers from my teachers. I'd ask anybody I thought might know, mainly the kids around me.

Of course, this was never going to endear me to teachers intent on keeping order in the classroom. For one teacher in particular, Miss Roberts, a grey-haired spinsterish type with winged glasses, a bun on her head and a prominent wart on her chin with hairs sprouting from it, it was such an affront to her authority that I was constantly in her sights.

Day after day, I'd find myself climbing the stairs to the

headmistress's office. It was always the same. At the top, I'd turn and there would be the door at the end of the corridor, its paint peeled away and the wood worn where generations of boys' shoes had scraped against it.

Miss McGregor's name was spelled out in black letters on a sign hanging from a pair of hooks.

'Come, come!' she'd say.

On this particular day, I twisted the knob and pushed. The headmistress of Lorne Street School worked with the window open and the air in the room was icy. The Wee Red Box, an old biscuit tin, was waiting for me beside a pile of books on the edge of Miss McGregor's desk. A miserable feeling raked through my stomach. I gulped, but the feeling wouldn't go away.

Miss McGregor glanced up. Her glasses were balanced on the end of her nose. She looked at me with a mixture of pity and disappointment.

'Gordon Turnbull,' she said, shaking her head. 'What do you have to say for yourself?'

I had no idea.

'Come closer and hold your head up, child, your hands behind your back.'

I did as I was told.

'What do you have to say for yourself?' she asked again.

'I was talking in class, Miss McGregor.'

The long hand of a wall clock, its face as big as a plate, clicked on a minute. Miss McGregor continued to stare at me.

'This is the second time today,' she said eventually, turning to look at the clock, 'and it isn't yet lunchtime. How often have I had to tell you, Gordon Turnbull, that there is a time and a place for talking? I won't have bad behaviour in my school. Do you understand?'

I nodded.

'Speak up, child. Do you understand?'

'Yes, Miss McGregor.'

But the truth was, I didn't; not really. Had I thrown something at Miss Roberts, that would have been naughty. Had I called her a silly cow, or stuck my tongue out, that would have been really naughty. But I'd done none of these things. All I ever did was ask questions, because my head was full of them. I was six years old. I wanted to learn and when Miss Roberts didn't know the name of the third star on the right in the night sky above Leith or how far beyond it Neverland lay, I'd ask my friends Campbell Tucker or Jennifer Traynor and that's what landed me in trouble.

Miss McGregor pointed to the red box and told me to take it.

I picked it up and retraced my footsteps.

As I went back into class, a hush fell. When the Wee Red Box was in the room, it was always the same: you could hear a pin drop.

Miss Roberts was standing on the stage in front of the blackboard. Unlike Miss McGregor, there was nothing soft about her face. I wondered how she came into the world. She had taught my father and I knew she was old then.

'Open the box, laddie.'

I removed the lid and placed it on her desk. Inside, the belt was coiled like a snake.

She asked me to take the belt out of the box and hand it to her.

The tin was as cold as Miss McGregor's room. The buckle rattled as I passed the belt to her. She took it from me and let it unfurl.

I had red welts on my skin from the last time. I bit my lip. The pain would be unbearable, but whatever happened I would still refuse to cry.

There was a ritualistic aspect to the ceremony of the Wee Red Box that would never have been tolerated in more enlightened times. And thank goodness, because its effect on me was profound. Sometimes I would be sent to Miss McGregor two or three times a day and it generally ended in a thrashing. The worst part about it was that I genuinely did not understand what I was doing wrong.

The freedom I'd experienced on the streets of Leith, where curiosity about what lay beyond the next corner and the notion that the horizon contained wonders beyond my wildest imagination were encouraged, had been suddenly and viciously withdrawn. It had been replaced by a regime in which, to my young mind at least, teachers were punishers.

If my early experience was to teach me that the outside world, away from home, had a darker side, it was soon reinforced by other, covert dangers.

My brother, Derek, who was three years younger than me, went down with poliomyelitis when I was six. Immediately after the diagnosis he was admitted to the Edinburgh City Hospital, which was the place chosen to treat infectious diseases. I was placed in quarantine. I wasn't able to go to school.

At the time I needed my friends most, I couldn't gain access to them.

Fortunately, Derek went on to make a full recovery.

One night, some weeks after he was brought home, I was trying to get to sleep, listening to the sound of my brother's breathing and trying not to think of the two occasions I'd seen him in hospital. I hadn't been allowed to visit him more often because of the risk of infection. I had been terrified that he might have to be hooked up to something my parents had called an 'iron lung'.

I became aware of my parents' hushed voices in the next room. They were talking about Derek. I crept out of bed and tiptoed down the corridor until I had my ear pressed to the door of the room off the kitchen – the room where we ate and where we gathered as a family to listen to the radio.

My mother was talking about the chocolate and raspberry sauces at Mr Scott's and blaming them for Derek's illness.

I was at once horrified and fascinated by this. Horrified that a place as innocent as Mr Scott's ice-cream parlour could have inflicted such suffering on my brother; fascinated that a place I actually *knew* could have been responsible for something my mother had termed – her voice catching as she said it – an 'epidemic'. It had made all the newspapers and we'd even heard it talked about on the radio.

I had no idea what an epidemic was, but, as soon as I was allowed to return to school, I'd ask.

Miss Roberts retired when I was eight years old and was replaced by a young, energetic teacher straight out of training called Miss Sprunt. If Miss Roberts was responsible for introducing me at an early age to trauma, it was Katharine Sprunt who introduced me to something just as influential: the notion that inspiration can be found in things that exist all around us; and, as importantly, that these, too, can imprint themselves on us in a most extraordinary way.

Soon after she became our form mistress, Miss Sprunt took us on an expedition to the Kelvingrove Art Gallery and Museum. This was a truly big adventure, involving a train journey from Waverley station all the way to Glasgow.

When we got to the museum – as big as a palace, with towers and high, arched windows – Miss Sprunt divided us into groups and packed us off in different directions. Our task was to find a picture that we really, really liked and write about it in class the following day.

She was right about one thing: the museum was an exciting place, filled with stuffed animals and complicated pieces of machinery. The exhibits were set out in long corridors with high ceilings. Other corridors led this way and that and I soon became lost in them, separated from the others.

I realized very quickly that I didn't share Miss Sprunt's taste in art. The only pictures I could see were large portraits of stern-looking men. Some were lairds, some were Scottish kings. They looked as bored as I felt. I soon gave up on our assignment and went hunting for the glass cases filled with weird-looking insects.

Just then, I stopped dead in my tracks, in front of the strangest painting I'd ever seen. It was huge – taller than my father, even – and as wide as I was tall.

It showed Jesus on the cross, but the cross wasn't stuck in the ground; it was hanging in a sky that was as black as ink and I was looking down on Jesus's head, as if I was floating in the sky with him. Below his feet was a lake with a rowing boat on its shoreline. In the background were mountains and a sliver of pale sky. As I stared at it, it was almost as if the cross and Jesus were moving – soaring into the black sky. I'd never seen anything like it. I couldn't take my eyes off it.

'Is this the picture you're going to write about?'

Miss Sprunt was standing behind me.

'Why is the cross floating in the sky, miss? Why are there no nails in Jesus's hands? Why isn't there any blood on him?'

She smiled and told me it was by a Spanish artist, a man called Dalí, whose paintings often came to him in dreams. In this one, Dalí didn't want blood or nails or thorns to spoil his vision of perfection – of a perfect Jesus in a perfect world. His dream also told him how the cross should be painted – not in the ground, but floating in the sky.

'I think it's about freedom,' she said. 'The freedom to be whatever you want to be.' She knelt down in front of me. 'What does it say to you, Gordon?'

I looked at her strangely. 'Say, miss?' We'd been reading about St Paul and his vision of Jesus on the road to Damascus. Was this what Miss Sprunt meant? Should Jesus have spoken to me from the painting? I hoped not. I liked it very much, but it didn't make me believe in him any more than I had when I left home that morning. It certainly didn't talk to me.

I stared at her. I was afraid that whatever I said next, I was going to disappoint her.

'I'm sorry, Miss Sprunt, I don't understand.'

'It's all right,' she said. 'This isn't a test. How does it make you *feel*?' She smiled again and I realized how much I liked her.

I closed my eyes and the weight of my two years in Miss Roberts's class fell from my shoulders. I felt something else in its place.

Freedom.

Freedom like I'd known in the streets before I attended Lorne Street School. Before I had the misfortune to run into Miss Roberts. 'Like I can do anything,' I told her. The words tripped off my tongue, as if I was also in a dream.

When I opened my eyes, Miss Sprunt was still smiling.

'That's what I hoped you'd say.'

I bought a postcard of the picture and took it home with me. Whenever I looked at it, Miss Sprunt's words came back to me.

Freedom.

Imagination was a good thing, she'd told me. Dalí's picture of Christ on the cross had come from his imagination and somehow, with it, he had inspired me.

I never set out to be a psychiatrist. They say that medicine is the most artistic of the sciences and the most scientific of the arts and this lay at the heart of my dilemma when it came to a choice of career. I'm a polymath – I like to know about everything. If I'd been as laissez-faire in deciding my future as a lot of other people were in the Swinging Sixties, I'd have studied a combination of arts and sciences at senior school.

I enjoyed learning foreign languages, Spanish especially, the language of Dalí, because of the tantalizing possibility of being able to travel abroad and actually talk to people. But instead I was encouraged to focus on the sciences. And this, in turn, led me into medicine.

I enrolled as a medical student at Edinburgh University in 1967. I'd spent six years at a terrific establishment in Edinburgh called George Heriot's School, where the staff put a great deal of effort into making pupils curious about life – nirvana for an irritating polymath like me. I went on to do the statutory six years at university – three of them dedicated to theory, the remainder to clinical learning – that were required of med students prior to graduation to houseman status in a hospital.

During the clinical phase, like all medical students we were introduced to general medicine and general surgery and then to ever more specialized disciplines, a short psychiatry course among them. On the first day of my six-week placement in psychiatry at the Royal Edinburgh Hospital, I was standing in line at the canteen to get a coffee, when I turned and noticed a vaguely familiar face in the queue behind me. This guy was quite a bit shorter than me, around five foot nine, with black, wavy hair and piercingly dark eyes. I don't generally talk to people in queues, but I had one of those moments, based, perhaps, on the paltry amount of sleep we students seemed to be getting, what with study, work and the inevitable partying. I knew the face but couldn't place it. It was driving me nuts.

I tucked my tray under one arm and held out my hand. 'Gordon Turnbull,' I said, smiling hesitantly. 'Have we met?'

'In a manner of speaking,' he replied, shaking his head in wonderment. 'I'm one of your classmates. The Yank?'

The conversation at this point could have gone either way. Indeed, had Greg Vagshenian been a different kind of person that might have been the moment when our relationship began and ended. There were, embarrassingly, only ten of us in our group – small wonder I recognized the face.

Luckily, Greg didn't hold it against me and he shook my hand warmly, nipping my apologies in the bud.

Based on the little I already knew about psychiatry, I had never thought of it as a career path. My fellow med students who were drawn to the field tended to grow their hair long and wear the 'wannabe-psychiatrist' uniform of tan corduroy jackets with leather patches on the elbows and a Sartre or Camus novel in a pocket with the front of the book facing outwards for all to see. I was more the beer-swilling, rugby-playing kind and had already set my long-term sights on surgery.

Greg, from the 'get-go', as he told me, knew that he wanted to be a psychiatrist. He was at Yale Medical School but had chosen to do his elective – his study period away from campus – at Edinburgh. He was first-generation American, the son of Armenians who'd escaped persecution in Turkey. In the short space of time that we chatted in the canteen line, I realized I'd never met anyone quite like him. He was animated, open and full of enthusiasm.

'So how do you like it so far?' he asked me, as we walked back to the department clutching our coffees.

'Too early to tell on day one, really, but I don't think it's going to be for me.'

'Oh? Why's that?'

'Too many poseurs.'

'Poseurs?'

'You know, the Jean-Paul Sartre brigade.'

He laughed. 'So what do you want to do?'

Surgery, I told him, nothing else for it.

'Psychiatry really doesn't do it for you then, huh?'

I shook my head.

'OK, let me ask you something,' he said. 'How long have we known each other?'

I rather absently looked at my watch. Around ten minutes, I told him, not quite sure where this was heading.

He nodded. 'And how would you say we were getting along?'

I'd heard Americans were to the point, but this was something else. His dark eyes studied me intently.

'I'd say we were getting along rather well, wouldn't you?' Then, suddenly realizing how pompous I sounded, I checked myself. I stopped walking. Greg stopped too.

The weird thing was, I'd only been chatting to Greg a few minutes but it felt as if I'd known him a lifetime – like we were kindred spirits. It was actually one of those occasions when you feel an affinity for someone right away, before the usual social interplay. I felt like I was in the presence of an old friend, someone I'd known for years.

Later, I found out there was a reason for this. Greg's parents had been highly protective of him and, when he was a child, scarcely let him out of their sight. Even in his early twenties, they checked on him constantly – a product, he explained, of their experience in the old country, where Armenians would always be looking over their shoulders to see where the Turks were.

Partly to break free of this confinement, he'd leapt at the opportunity to study abroad. It didn't take a psychiatrist to point out the parallels between Greg's confinement and my early experiences at the hands of Miss Roberts, whose attempts to shut down my freedom of expression represented a confinement of a different though related kind.

'Well,' Greg said, staring at me over the top of his coffee, 'it looks like you *do* have something else to say.'

I did. And this time I told him the truth. I told him that deep down, I had always admired the wannabe-psychiatrists because they represented the ability to think in a liberated and curious way that reminded me of the free era of my pre-school days before going to primary school and meeting Miss Roberts. But it was a dark and dangerous thought.

'Aha!' he said. 'That's interesting.'

'It is?' We carried on walking.

He nodded and started gesturing between him and me with vigorous and slightly mad movements of his free hand. 'I felt it, too, the moment we started talking. A connection.' He smiled. 'Let's hope it's not a "reaction formation".'

'What's that?'

'Psychologists talk about it. Basically, it's a self-protection mechanism. Say you walked into a party with your girlfriend and after a while you wandered off and started talking to a beautiful girl in a red dress with a stunning figure and then your girlfriend turned up and, to your surprise, you found her being incredibly friendly to this girl . . . That's a reaction formation.'

'You mean disguising unpleasant feelings towards someone by being effusively nice? Sounds like basic human nature to me.'

'It *is* basic human nature. And it happens most of the time at a deeply subconscious level. When you meet someone for the first time, your subconscious is weighing up the other person on many levels and it's all happening in an instant. But you're assessing *every-thing* – the tone of the person's voice, their mannerisms, the way they look at you, the whole shebang, and at a subconscious level you've already made your mind up. If your subconscious decides that actually you don't like this person, it might also lead you to disguise the fact by over-compensating.'

'And you thought that that might explain why we . . . connected?' It sounded a little weird and Californian to me. But part of me was reeled in, intrigued.

He risked a slurp of coffee while we were still on the move.

'Here's what I think, Gordon. You look like a regular guy to me. You're built like a quarterback. You clearly like your sports and it wouldn't surprise me at all if you spent most of the little spare time we have walking up and down the bumps that pass as mountains around here. But beneath that bluff, hayseed exterior there's an inquisitive, sensitive side that you're not so sure about. The poseurs clutching their copies of Sartre and Camus? That's a classic reaction formation, my friend.'

He cocked an eyebrow at me. 'You still set on becoming a surgeon?'

We had reached the lecture theatre. Our fellow students were already settling into their seats.

I looked at my new-found friend and shook my head. Then I burst out laughing. 'Are you actually trying to tell me you think I have a career ahead of me in psychiatry?'

Greg cocked that eyebrow again and looked me straight in the eye. 'I don't think it,' he said, 'I know it. You've got "shrink" stamped across your forehead.'

Chapter 2

To See Ourselves As Others See Us

One of my medical tutors at Edinburgh was Tony Gunn, a man of considerable renown in the medical profession, who seemed to me to be the ideal role model for what I wanted to be: a top surgeon. I enjoyed studying under Gunn enormously. He worked us hard, but was so full of enthusiasm we didn't care. We worshipped him. It seemed only logical, therefore, when casting around for my first surgical house job to put in an application to work on his 'firm' – his surgical unit – at Bangour General Hospital in West Lothian.

The hospital was a collection of prefab huts that had been erected during the war as a temporary gesture, but, 25 years on, as I turned up for my first day's work, the huts were still there. Yet, despite the dingy appearance, I couldn't have been more excited. I'd joined the Royal Air Force as a cadet officer after my first three years at med school and the way ahead seemed bright and clear: I was relishing the challenges and opportunities that would come with being an RAF surgeon.

But things didn't turn out quite as I expected.

In the operating theatre Tony Gunn could behave like a monster. Every now and again, when we least expected it, he'd erupt. These explosions weren't always directed at me, but more often than not I was the one in Gunn's immediate firing line. Usually the causes of these eruptions were so slight as to be unnoticeable to anyone else; and quite often there was no discernible reason for them at all.

To say this all came as a shock was an understatement. If, as a medical student, I could have aspired to be anyone it was Tony Gunn. But ten weeks into my housemanship at Bangour, Gunn's behaviour was taking the shine off my ambitions. It made me so angry and frustrated, I decided to go and do something about it. I went to see the Dean of Medicine at my alma mater, Edinburgh University Medical School.

This took me right back to my old school stamping ground: Heriot's was on one side of Lauriston Place as you looked towards the castle, and Edinburgh Royal Infirmary and the Medical School were on the other. It was the realization that I would spend six years in each – 12 years in total – that prompted me to join the RAF; it was the best way I could think of to decouple from these institutions. Via the RAF, I reckoned I could achieve my dream of seeing the world.

Prior to going to see the Dean I'd made enquiries and discovered that I could split the statutory six months required of a houseman into two lots of three months – a move that freed me to go elsewhere, away from the oppressive atmosphere that surrounded Gunn. The problem was the short notice: there were no vacancies anywhere else. I needed the Dean's advice and, ultimately, whatever I decided upon, his blessing.

The Dean sat behind a large Victorian desk. He stared at me languidly over his half-moons as I began the long march across the room to his desk. The smell of polish was suddenly replaced by the dust and must of old books lining the shelves on the four walls.

The Dean consulted some notes and announced in a dour, monotonous voice that he understood there to be a bit of a problem with Mr Gunn. He asked if I could elaborate on the nature of the problem.

I coughed nervously. I felt awkward about dishing the dirt on Gunn, but I also felt trapped and I told him so.

'Trapped?'

I nodded. 'I feel the need to get away. I want to be a surgeon, but I need to recapture my enthusiasm. I don't understand where these bursts of irrational anger are coming from. Nobody does.'

'Irrational?' the Dean said.

I told him that was the way it seemed to me – to all of us.

'What would you like me to do about it?'

I told him my predicament. While I wanted to transfer at the earliest opportunity to another houseman job, I couldn't, because all the positions were taken. If I stuck with it and then went on to another houseman position for a further six months, I'd run up against the wrath of the RAF, which was champing at the bit to get hold of all of its cadets because it was short of medical manpower.

'Medicine is not a job you should do unless you enjoy it,' the Dean announced, as he removed his spectacles and tucked them with an air of finality into his top pocket. 'It's a vocation. You need to be sure what branch of medicine you want to go into, Turnbull. There's no easy option. You have to enjoy hard work, otherwise you'll find yourself in a terrible predicament – the demands will prove excessive. You're saying that Mr Gunn's . . . behaviour is causing you uncertainty. Is that it?'

My face remained mask-like, but inside I was screaming hallelujah. He'd got it.

'Yes,' I said simply.

'Then let me think about it,' the Dean said. He got to his feet and placed an avuncular hand on my shoulder. 'Don't worry, laddie. We'll think of something.'

I drove back to Bangour, which was about halfway to Glasgow, full of hope. I was suddenly reminded of Dalí's painting on display at the Kelvingrove Gallery. The signposts to Glasgow as I pelted along the road seemed to be a good omen.

Back at the hospital, however, as I navigated my way through the prefab huts an announcement went out over the tannoy: would Dr Turnbull please report to Mr Gunn's office. That's funny, a part of me thought, if only he knew what the Dean and I had just been talking about . . .

Gunn did know. He knew the moment I stepped out of the Dean's office, because what I hadn't counted on was that Gunn and the Dean had been lifelong friends.

The moment I stepped into his office, Gunn exploded. 'How dare you embarrass me!' he shouted, his face so red I thought it might burst, along with numerous internal organs. 'If you leave me,' he said, shaking his finger at me, 'I will ensure – in fact, I will make it my mission in life – that no hospital in the land will touch you. Do you hear? Now get out!'

So, things had suddenly gone from bad to worse. And still with no explanation as to what I'd actually done.

My ambition to be a surgeon was rapidly becoming a pipe dream.

I went from being mystified and anxious to becoming white-hot with anger. How dare *I*? How bloody dare *he*, more like.

I had no idea why he didn't like me, only that it was visceral, something he couldn't help.

Why had this man taken so violently against me?

After I left Edinburgh and Bangour I managed to persuade the RAF that I should do a further six months in casualty to solidify what I'd learned during my first house job in medicine on the island of Jersey, which turned out to be something I really enjoyed. My second house job in surgery was at Bangour. I was hoping that a stint in casualty would help me find a suitable new direction. The choice was whether to pursue my desire to become a surgeon or to change tack and become a physician.

Physicians are diagnosticians. Surgeons are technicians – the people who wield the knives. I'd always viewed them as sitting on the summit of the entire medical profession. Now I wasn't so sure and my uncertainty was killing me.

Having always been convinced that surgery was the course for me, my experience at the hands of the master had proved so bruising that it left me feeling unsure, rudderless. I decided to keep moving, hoping I'd find some answers.

I applied for senior house officer jobs in Northampton, Brighton and at St Bartholomew's and the Westminster Hospital in London. Things were very different in those days. If you were brought up in Scotland you didn't have many opportunities to go south to England. As a family we'd always taken our holidays north of the border. When we visited my uncle, auntie and cousins in Coldstream, I used to gaze at England from the banks of the River Tweed and feel that I was looking at a strange land. As a child, I half believed that Redcoats would suddenly emerge from the trees and fire their flintlock rifles at me.

Soon I was offered a series of interviews down south. During my first, at Northampton General, I was offered a job. My interviewer, a consultant surgeon, told me he had been very impressed by my reference from Mr Gunn. Somehow I managed to suppress a smile.

The same thing happened at Brighton. Here, I was offered the tantalizing prospect of three months in casualty and then the option of a further three months in the plastic surgery unit at East Grinstead, where the RAF had developed its cosmetic surgery skills during the Second World War. RAF aircrew who underwent plastic surgery there under the redoubtable Archibald McIndoe were known as the Guinea Pig Club.

To resume the surgical trail was a great temptation, but I decided to see what was on offer in London first. St Bartholomew's was a fine place with a great reputation, but there was something very special about the Westminster Hospital, something that immediately struck me, so I elected to take their offer instead. Four offers from four interviews. Not bad going, I thought. I only hoped I'd chosen the right one.

Westminster Hospital proved the perfect antidote to life under Tony Gunn in Scotland, where part of me had been waiting the whole time for a bomb to detonate.

At the Westminster casualty department I was exposed to the mentally ill on a scale I'd not encountered before. I found myself regularly treating people with schizophrenia and manic depression, conditions far less well understood then than they are today, and I was intrigued. There were also people with acute stress reactions as a result of some of the first terrorist attacks on London – the wave of bombings that swept the city and other mainland targets of the IRA in the seventies and eighties.

At the Westminster, the diagnostician in me kicked in. I wanted to know what had made my patients ill in this way. It seemed to me, intuitively, that many mental conditions had an organic basis – a biological route; and if that was so, the pathways to understanding them, as with any disease of the body, ought to be identifiable.

I grew a beard, wore corduroy jackets and fell in love with a student nurse called Alison. I slipped readily into the role of the easy-going doctor, until the call came from the consultant adviser at

Kelvin House, the Central Medical Establishment for General
Medicine in the RAF.

Kelvin House was where all the consultant advisers across the
whole range of medical specialties gathered. It was the consultant
adviser in medicine who had invited me to meet him, to discuss my
application.

Air Commodore Kelly, a very distinguished-looking man, welcomed me into his consulting room, a large airy office on the third
floor.

I suddenly wished I'd shaved off my beard. I was wearing a
corduroy jacket with leather elbow patches, although it was
green, not tan. I just remembered to tuck a volume of Sartre's *The
Roads to Freedom* in my pocket as I walked into the interview
room.

I instinctively warmed to Brian Kelly. He rose from behind his
desk and asked, cheerily: 'So you want to be a physician in the Royal
Air Force?'

'Yes,' I told him, 'I'd very much like to.'

I explained that I wanted to follow a specialist career and that I
used to think I wanted to be a surgeon, but that now I'd thought it
through thoroughly and come to a decision while working in the
casualty department at the Westminster. 'You can never predict what
sort of problem is going to come through the door next. I've discovered that I enjoy the diagnostic challenges medicine throws at
you and would like to be better at it.'

'Well then, let's see,' he said and pushed an electrocardiograph
tracing that was on his desk towards me. He explained that it was
the ECG of a Danish Air Force fast-jet pilot who had been experiencing extra heartbeats (extrasystoles) and had been referred for
investigations.

I looked at the tracing and could easily pick out the extra beats.
I'd had a lot of experience of looking at ECGs in the extremely busy
coronary care unit during my medical house job in Jersey where my
consultant, Dr McInnes, had a special interest in cardiology. Much
more recently, it had been a daily part of my job as a casualty
officer at the Westminster.

There was nothing for it but to plunge in. 'I think that these are
the non-pathological kind,' I said. 'The P wave is normal, the P-R

interval a normal length and the QRS complex takes off at the right point and is the right width.'

I was explaining in medical language that the extra heartbeats were coming from the normal spark points and were normal in form and shape; it was just that they were 'extra'.

I heard the words, 'Good, good.'

Then came the next question: 'Would you allow him to fly?'

It wasn't quite like flicking a mental coin because I was pretty sure what I'd do next, but I still felt anxious. This was the most senior physician in the RAF and my future career depended on my answer.

I said that I would like to see an exercise ECG and, hey presto, on cue, his technician knocked on the door and wheeled in an exercise ECG.

'Take a look at that and see what you think now.'

I studied the graph. 'Well, the extra beats have gone, which means that the heart muscle is healthy and, yes, I would allow him to fly.'

Kelly sat back in his chair and smiled. 'When would you like to start?'

Here was the lesson. If the rapport was good and encouraging then people tended to perform well. Take the pressure off and they would tell you the things you needed to know. They usually knew already what was going on and just needed an opportunity to tell the right person. No need for guessing or esoteric interpretations.

And the right person was going to be trusted, because they made you feel safe, were not trying to be in control and would not make judgements.

I realized, thankfully, that I was in a place that was a world away from Tony Gunn.

In Jersey, Dr McInnés used to ask me what, given 30 minutes to evaluate a medical patient, was the best way to divide the time between taking a history and examining them? In other words, how much time should you devote to each?

I told him that I thought equal amounts of time should be dedicated to the history and the examination.

He told me that his experience had taught him to spend 25 minutes taking the history of the patient's condition, really *listening* to their description, and only five minutes confirming the diagnosis, because by then, somewhere inside you, you would already know it.

This apprenticeship style really appealed to me. It taught me something else, too. There would be 'Merlins' who would come along in life and the trick would be to recognize them and listen to what they had to say, because they knew an awful lot more about their field of expertise than you did. Listening, I told myself, that was the secret.

I passed my interview and was formally accepted into the RAF Medical Division.

I completed my six-month stint at the Westminster casualty unit, said goodbye to my new friends and headed back to Edinburgh to collect my uniform and other bits and pieces. The long journey north would be followed by a much shorter one south to RAF Leeming in North Yorkshire, where I was due to be purged of all the bad habits I'd picked up in civilian life.

Quite sensibly, the RAF Medical Branch liked its doctors to be introduced to the Air Force properly. I was sent to a flying training base for about a year before moving into the more rarefied medical atmosphere of a hospital.

At Leeming, they flew Jet Provosts for SORF (the School of Refresher Flying) and piston-engined Bulldogs for RNEFTS (the Royal Naval Elementary Flying Training School). SORF was used to reintroduce senior pilots to aircraft after a spell flying a desk. RNEFTS was there to introduce naval officers to a career in the Fleet Air Arm.

My senior medical officer, a squadron leader, painstakingly took me through the protocol for my initial interview with 'the Boss' at Station HQ. We rehearsed again and again how I should wait outside his door with my hat on and gloves in my left hand for him to call out, 'Enter.' I was then to open the door with my right hand, walk into the room, close the door, swing round, approach the Boss's desk, snap off a smart salute (in the RAF this took the form of 'longest way up, shortest way down') and stay at attention until invited to sit down.

There was a way of doing this, too, I learned. This was to take off the cap with the right hand, place the gloves from the left hand into the upturned hat, move backwards on to the chair in front of the desk, sit down, fold the right leg over the left and hold the hat with gloves in the lap. There was no flinging the hat on to a convenient hatstand as in the movies and I was nervous, wondering if my hair was short enough.

'Turnbull,' the Boss opened, 'when was the last time you saluted?'

I noted there was no menace in his voice, but that didn't altogether fool me. The Boss had been a fast-jet pilot and I knew already that pilots were able to exert a lot of control over their feelings.

'Well, sir, to be honest, I think it was when I was in the Scouts.'

'Thought so,' he said. 'Haven't seen that three-fingered salute since I was in the Scouts myself. Welcome aboard.'

After about a month at Leeming I was sent on the first part of my initial medical training course at RAF Henlow. Professionally qualified and re-entrant RAF personnel (PQRE) did not go through the much longer initial training course at Cranwell; we went on the one-month course at Henlow instead. So I joined a bunch of doctors, dentists, nursing sisters and chaplains. It was a very worthwhile course. I learned about the rank structure, protocols and systems and how to march and press my trousers.

It was 1975 and computer technology hadn't yet arrived. It seemed that we were forever filling in forms by hand wherever we went, often repeating the process with the same forms over and over again. Bored with this, I somewhat impishly listed among my interests and hobbies 'ichthyology'. I had, in fact, always been fascinated by fish and kept aquaria when growing up at home. I had even considered making a career of it – training as a marine biologist. Now I thought, if I have to fill in these forms over and over again, at least I'll have the satisfaction of knowing that the bloody admin people will have to look up 'ichthyology'.

The person who did just that was a delightful chap – our flight commander. Despite the fact that he had developed high-tone deafness as a result of flying Vulcan bombers and had been grounded permanently, he remained remarkably well disposed towards doctors.

He called me into his office. He was excited because he had the current issue of Defence Council Instructions (DCIs) in his hand. DCIs were published monthly and carried announcements about changes in uniform and other essential but rather dull items of RAF life. Very occasionally, however, DCIs came up with something really exciting. This announcement definitely fell into that category. It was a call for volunteers to go on a joint service expedition to Elephant Island in Antarctica the following year. He had been browsing through the announcement, picked up on the keyword 'ichthyology' and remembered that it featured on one of my forms. One of the reasons I'd joined the Air Force was to travel and I just knew I had to get on that trip. My flight commander showed me how to complete the application.

After completing my stint at Henlow, I went on a two-week course at RAF Halton, then returned to Leeming, where Air Commodore Kelly told me he needed a junior physician in Cyprus at the RAF hospital in Akrotiri. I began to realize how small a world the RAF actually was when in the searing heat of the Mediterranean I was greeted off the VC10 by a chap I'd got to know at Leeming: a freckle-faced Scot by the name of Eric Henry who had been promoted to flight sergeant and was now running the mountain rescue team in Akrotiri.

A decent job as an RAF physician, sunshine and a fun bunch of people. I couldn't think of a better way to spend the next three months.

Eric Henry had been in charge of the mountain rescue unit at Leeming. I had no idea he was even in Cyprus, much less what my role there would be. My transfer had happened with bewildering rapidity. But that, I was discovering, was one of the curious delights of the RAF. Often, nobody seemed to know what was going on. The eccentricity of the set-up suited me better than I could ever have imagined.

'Eric,' I said, 'what on earth are you doing here?'

He shook my hand and told me.

'Next stupid question. What am *I* doing here?'

'You, Mr Turnbull, are the new mountain rescue team doctor. It looks like we'll make a mountaineer of you yet.'

For me, a 27-year-old travelling abroad for only the third time in his life, Cyprus was every bit as exotic as I hoped it would be. It also gave me an insight into the minds of men who were as tough as any you are ever likely to encounter. I'd got to know a few mountain rescuers at Leeming.

The RAF set up its Mountain Rescue Service in 1943. RAF mountain rescuers are based wherever the RAF and British Armed Forces are stationed or on operations. The MRS is manned entirely by enthusiastic volunteers – men and women who give up their private time and risk their lives to rescue people who get into trouble on mountains, sometimes through outright stupidity. They are from all ranks, and are not paid for the considerable amount of training they regularly have to undertake to maintain their effectiveness.

Much of their emergency work involves recovering and rescuing people who aren't aircrew, as originally intended, but civilians who have underestimated the harshness of the weather you get in the mountains. MR teams turn out in all conditions, 24/7; hence the motto on their crest: 'Whensoever'.

Soon after I arrived in Cyprus, I was given the opportunity to go on weekend exercises with them. One weekend consisted of travelling into the Troodos Mountains from Akrotiri by truck, camping overnight, getting up very early the next morning and walking round a circular range of hills for the whole day. Good fun, but the weather was sweltering.

The ring of hills did not have a natural ridge. So, having climbed a hill, we found ourselves descending all the way to ground level before going all the way back up again to the top of the next hill. I was rugby-fit and determined to make it, but after eight hours of this I actually seized up on my last ascent. My legs went into painful cramps and simply wouldn't work. I had to be rescued myself.

My MR team mates poured water and salt down my throat and I can still remember the eerie feeling of the strength coming back into my legs. Heatstroke can often be fatal. On that particular day, I'd really pushed the boat out.

That was my baptism of fire with the Akrotiri MR team. We also took part in a major exercise in Pakistan while I was with them. We flew from Akrotiri to Karachi in a Hercules loaded up with our kit. There was a spot of drama at Karachi Military Airfield when one of our loadmasters cut his thigh on a jagged piece of metal while unloading the kit. The wound required suturing. The job called on all my plastic surgery skills and earned me the nickname The Butcher of Karachi.

In its official history, *Whensoever*, the MRS is described as appearing to be very unmilitary: 'But beneath its apparent casual attitude lies a code of conduct refined over the past 50 years.' (The book was written in 1993.) 'MR rank and status replace the normal RAF rank structure. Respect is gained through actions, not words. Junior members are expected to work hard. All members are expected to work as a unit, mix and contribute towards team spirit.'

All MR personnel love the mountains, but mountaineering skill and enthusiasm are not always their most important charactersitics; selflessness is also required. 'Those who cannot integrate easily, whilst retaining an almost constant sense of humour,' *Whensoever* says, 'will not stay long in RAF Mountain Rescue.'

Perhaps that's why I enjoyed their company so much. Team spirit was everything and, unlike other people I'd encountered in the RAF, no one individual was remotely interested in dominating another. They looked after their own. Outsiders had to prove themselves before they were accepted. In a word, they were tough – incredibly so – which was what, thirteen years later, made Lockerbie all the more shocking and significant. It would prove a true turning point in my understanding of what traumatic stress was and how it could be treated.

After returning from Cyprus, in January 1976 I did another short stint at Leeming and then was posted to the RAF hospital at Ely in Cambridgeshire. I had been so focused on becoming a surgeon and then moved away from that ambition. I was on a different career path and had a sense that 'something' would happen and that it would be good. It did, but not remotely in a way I could have guessed at. By that time I had been selected on paper for the Antarctic expedition. During the first year at Ely I was very busy learning a new trade, although I'd had a good start in Cyprus with my consultant, Wing Commander Rex Fitzgerald, an extremely accomplished physician.

At Ely, I found myself under the wing of another eminent consultant, again a wing commander: Fredoon 'Fred' Amroliwalla. Fred, the father of the BBC news correspondent Matthew, was extremely thorough and I liked his approach because it appealed to the curious side of me – the diagnostician, detective, call it what you will.

A lot of consultants operate in the vein of Lancelot Spratt, the irascible surgeon played by James Robertson Justice in *Doctor in the House* and its follow-on movies in the 1950s. These consultants make a virtue of being as brief as possible as they sweep through wards passing judgements on the notes of hapless, bewildered patients awaiting operations. But not Fred. Fred was meticulous. As I accompanied him on his rounds, I noticed that he'd not only study every aspect of a patient's notes, but would also spend a considerable amount of time talking to them. He derived a lot of additional, pertinent information from these discussions and I could see that he put the patients at their ease too. All of this made a deep impression on me and reminded me of the adage I'd become familiar with when entering medical practice:

Surgeons know nothing and do everything
Physicians know everything and do nothing
Psychiatrists know nothing and do nothing, and
Pathologists know everything but it's too bloody late to do anything
about it!

One day, Fred pulled me into his office to discuss my Annual Confidential Report – an unavoidable routine for anyone in Her Majesty's armed services. The ACR covers every aspect of a service-man or -woman's personal development, from his or her professionalism to the way he or she behaves in the mess.

Unlike the other two services, the written part of an RAF ACR – during my time – was withheld from its subject. I've often wondered about this behaviour and have come to the conclusion that the RAF, as the adolescent of the three service branches, is quite capable of emulating some of the behaviour traits of its teenage counterparts in the real world – lack of confidence in its own abilities being one of them. Fred, however, was happy to tell me that my ACR of 1976 was very good and I shouldn't worry about a thing. I felt pleased to have received such a fulsome pat on the back from someone I admired so much, especially since I'd spent so much time studying plankton instead of swotting for my medical membership exams.

Then I found myself transferred somewhere very far away from Ely: the Antarctic. Over a hundred service personnel – Navy, Army,

Air Force and Marines – had applied to go on the Elephant Island expedition. But ultimately only 16 men boarded the plane at Heathrow on 20 November 1976 on the first leg of the journey, to Rio de Janeiro, and I was lucky enough to be one of them. I had been awarded a Winston Churchill Memorial Scholarship to make a study of plankton around the Elephant Island group of satellite islands. There was intense interest in 1976 in the survival of the krill population, which feed on plankton, Sir Peter Scott told me at my interview at the Trust headquarters in London; so off I went.

Frank Worsley, one of the survivors of Shackleton's ill-fated 1916 expedition, had written of our destination: 'It is impossible to describe accurately the violence of the atmosphere of Elephant Island: the screech of the wind and the driving storms, the cannon-like reports of the glaciers calving masses of ice as big as the dome of St Paul's.' Sixty years on, I was one of the two expedition doctors who were being shipped out to Elephant Island on the *Endurance*'s namesake, the Royal Navy's ice patrol vessel. We were to spend three months on the ice.

The expedition leader was a Royal Navy lieutenant commander, a big, decisive man and an engineer to boot. Chris Furse was cut, in many ways, from similar cloth to that of Shackleton. He liked many of the things I liked. He was a great artist and he knew a lot about wildlife, birds in particular. Furse was an interesting, deep-thinking bloke, a polymath, and I saw him as something of a kindred spirit.

One afternoon, on the first leg of our passage from Buenos Aires, a trip of several days bound for the Falkland Islands, I was standing at the stern, watching the wake, when Furse came to join me. We spent several moments in silence, each of us watching the water and the albatrosses following the ship.

We were in a part of the southern ocean called the Antarctic Convergence, which is a curve encircling Antarctica where cold, northward-flowing Antarctic waters meet the relatively warmer waters of the sub-Antarctic. It forms a natural zone of mixing currents very high in marine productivity, especially for Antarctic krill. There is no Arctic equivalent due to the amount of land surrounding the northern polar region. The colour of the water was unbelievably beautiful – on one side of the convergence the deep blue of the Atlantic and on the other the pale blue of the cooler Antarctic seas – and to top it all, a school of killer whales was porpoising in and out of the water beside us, as if to show us the way.

But the Antarctic Convergence was also notorious for its fickle weather – it could turn in an instant – and as I looked skyward, I could see roiling clouds gathering off our port bow. As we made a move to go inside, I turned to Furse and asked him a question that had been troubling me ever since we'd stepped on board.

'I know penguins live exclusively at the South Pole, but is there an equivalent bird for the North Pole?'

Furse stopped dead in his tracks, turned and looked at me. 'If you don't know the answer to that, then you shouldn't be on this bloody expedition.'

And with that, he stormed inside.

Things thereafter went from bad to worse.

After we had tested our equipment, tents and canoes in a two-week shake-down on the Falklands we packed up again and set off for our final destination, the Elephant Island group in the South Shetlands. Our team of 16 split into two groups to mount expeditions to two neighbouring islands to begin with, Clarence Island and Gibbs Island. Chris Furse was the overall leader of the expedition and had actually been to Elephant Island previously, a few years beforehand. He led the group heading to Gibbs Island while the deputy leader, Lieutenant Commander John Highton, was in charge of the second group, destined for Clarence Island. Fortunately, given the *froideur* between me and Furse, I was in Highton's team. The plan was to transfer the groups, along with our provisions, by helicopter. *Endurance* carried two Wasp helicopters aft and these were going to be used to ferry us ashore and then to carry our gear out in underslung nets to establish caches of food and equipment on the islands.

On the morning of the transfer, the weather was auspiciously lovely: the sea was flat calm, the sky an azure blue. The islands, their mountain peaks encrusted with ice and snow, sparkled like diamonds.

Chris Furse had tasked me with hauling our kit out of stowage in the forward hold, a job that required a block and tackle, some strong rope and plenty of welly. For those of us working on the job there was a sense of urgency, because the weather was set to turn and we had only a narrow window to load up and launch the helicopters.

Suddenly, our efforts were interrupted by the bosun, a man none of us was inclined to disobey, who announced that the rope we were using wasn't thick enough. He told me to call a temporary halt while he went off to find some rope of appropriate thickness.

I was balancing a 100-lb box of provisions on the lip of the hold, waiting for him to come back and catching my breath in the lull, when Furse appeared. He was walking quickly along the waist of the ship and had come from the stern where the helicopters were waiting to ferry the equipment ashore.

He took one look at the scene and ran straight up to me till our noses were damn near touching.

'When I tell you to do a job . . . you bloody well do it!' he yelled, the sinews of his neck straining.

He grabbed me by the shoulder and spun me around. It was a miracle the box didn't tumble into the hold. I careened across the deck and thudded into the bulwark.

I had only ever experienced the 'red mist' previously on the rugby pitch but this was of a totally different magnitude.

As a 27-year-old flight lieutenant I was significantly junior to Furse, but I didn't care – I didn't even think about it. I got up, walked back to where he was standing, grabbed him by the shoulder and flung him across the deck. He was very shocked.

Not so many moons ago, striking one's senior officer on a ship would have been a keel-haulable offence, but that didn't bother me either. I was that far gone.

Furse picked himself up and strode purposefully towards me, his face full of anger. I grabbed the box that was still balancing on the lip of the hold and threw it on to the deck at my feet and between him and me. It was a signal: thus far and no further. Both of us had lost it; we'd pared right back to the basest of instincts – anger and aggression. We squared off, like a couple of prowling tigers.

I pointed my finger first at Furse's face, then at the box and said: 'Get out of my sight or it will be the worse for you, I swear to God.'

To my amazement, he did.

Later, when we were on Clarence Island, our eight-man team's home for two months, I had a chance to reflect on what had happened. What gnawed at me was the existence of a pattern. Tony Gunn, and now Chris Furse . . . was it them or was it me?

I had been particularly shaken by my encounter with Furse. It was the most direct confrontation I had ever had with anybody – even Miss Roberts had failed to stir up as much ire in me as Furse had; I'd never previously lost my temper – not to the degree that I had on the ship, anyway. Just as worrying was the knowledge that there must have been something in me that these people had all reacted against. What was it? It made me introspective. I felt my future slipping away from me; like it was no longer in my hands. I needed to regain control.

One evening we were eating dinner in our base camp, a huddle of tents close to the shoreline, doing our best to ignore the howling South Atlantic wind outside. We often shared meals and had 'dinner parties' – each tent trying to outdo the others with whatever imaginative hoosh we could throw together from our provisions. I remember one of our team light-heartedly raising the subject of my contretemps with Furse, who was safely tucked many miles away on a different island. He asked whether I'd ever done anything to annoy him and I told him I didn't think so. Then I recalled the moment when we'd been out on the fantail of the *Endurance* watching the wake and talking about penguins.

I told them about our somewhat quaint exchange – my question about whether the penguin had a counterpart at the North Pole – and how for some reason this had really got under Furse's skin.

'That's an orc,' someone said. He spelled it: 'O-R-C.'

I laughed. 'There's no such creature. Not outside Middle Earth, anyway. You mean an auk: A-U-K.'

A furious debate ensued about auks, orcs, penguins and whether, indeed, there was a denizen of the North Pole to rival the penguin in Antarctica. In the midst of it all, John Highton took me quietly to one side to tell me something: people like Furse, he said, people who knew a lot about a lot of things, were very protective of their knowledge. Maybe it wasn't me, strictly speaking, he'd taken against, but my enthusiasm, John said.

This was the first time I'd ever stopped to consider this. I'd seen Chris Furse as a fellow polymath; someone who, like me, enjoyed knowledge for its own sake – someone, too, who liked to share it.

Back in Ely, when I returned there a few months later, I remained mindful of what I had learned. By that time Chris Furse and I had become the best of friends. People like Gunn and Furse were at the top of their profession. They were forceful, highly knowledgeable characters; they did not like to be challenged. I wasn't remotely interested in challenging them but I was interested in learning. I felt exactly as I'd felt all those years earlier in Miss Roberts's class. I was being penalized for my curiosity and it didn't feel right. In fact, it made me downright furious. Ultimately, though, any awkwardness or criticism that I experienced with these figures led to improved self-insight on my part.

I wondered where in medicine could I find a discipline that allowed me to remain a square peg in a round hole – an enthusiast in a world of characters who would inevitably interpret that trait as a challenge?

Chapter 3

Beating *la Belle Indifférence*

The Antarctic adventure over, I settled down to 'real life' and my job as a trainee hospital physician in the RAF. I could have passed my exams in marine biology before going south, but now I had to put all of that to one side and get down to remembering the hundred-plus possible causes of atrial fibrillation.

Working in the military hospital system, I began to notice just how fine it was. It was a small enough world for me to get to know all the other doctors, right across all the specialties, in my own hospital, and in my own specialty across all the hospitals.

The purpose of the military hospitals was to maintain the fitness of service personnel and their families. Military doctors had to wear two hats, one covering the needs of the individual and one looking after the service. A great deal of attention was given to rehabilitation. In those days a fast-jet pilot cost about £3 million to train and we tried to fix them properly so that, if they were injured, we could get them back in the air as soon as possible.

There were several RAF hospitals at that time in the UK, a number of Army hospitals and two Royal Naval hospitals, one at Haslar in Portsmouth, the other in Plymouth. In 1976 only the RAF and the Army maintained hospitals overseas: the RAF in Germany and Cyprus and the Army in Germany and Hong Kong. The Navy had only recently given up its hospitals in Mauritius and Malta. There was also a wonderful tri-service unit at RAF Headley Court in Leatherhead, Surrey, which was dedicated to rehabilitation.

Some of the hospitals ran specialist units for the whole network. For example, the Princess Alexandra RAF Hospital at Wroughton, near Swindon in Wiltshire, was the neuropsychiatric centre for the whole RAF.

When military hospitals were not operating in times of emergency or war they took in civilian patients, which helped maintain contact between doctors in the military and their civilian counterparts. The RAF, Army and Royal Navy wanted their medical personnel to retain general medical skills, such as being able to assess patients presenting as emergencies and put up drips, and ran a system of residential medical officers (RMOs) or orderly medical officers (OMOs) so that specialists in whatever field would revert to houseman or casualty officer duties for 24 hours, including keeping an overnight watch on the hospital. The Navy would deploy hospital specialists on sea duties for a tour to sharpen general medical skills. This was one big difference between military doctors and civilians.

Military hospitals were commanded by senior doctors and nurses and specially trained medical administrators who all had considerable experience of medicine. There were regular conferences to keep up professional coordination and regular mess functions to promote social cohesion. Military hospitals were based on teamship. Personnel were posted to other hospitals every three years or so, which maintained the cohesion throughout the system.

Gradually, from 1976 onwards, the number of separate military hospitals was reduced. This reduction accelerated after the end of the Cold War, 'the peace dividend', and the growing belief that the reservist medical units would be sufficient to cope during emergencies and that the NHS would be able to cope with veterans. So, hospitals were closed and military wings of civilian hospitals were introduced. Maintaining general medical skills in hospitals shared between the military and civilians increasingly depended on attending specific training courses rather than through the natural spin-offs that resulted from the old system.

Territorial Army and Reservist medical units lacked the quality of cohesion throughout their systems that the regular full-time hospital personnel enjoyed.

When I returned from the Antarctic, I was sent to a general hospital strategically situated in East Anglia to look after the many RAF stations nearby, RAF Hospital Ely. At least that was the official name for the hospital, though it was affectionately known to the local population as 'Ely's RAF hospital'. We took in local people who had strong connections with the RAF or the military such as veterans, people who had no connection whatsoever with the military and sometimes people with very tenuous connections, such as a pleasant elderly gentleman whose GP claimed that his brother had served in the Royal Flying Corps in the First World War.

One day, not long after I got back, we had a patient come in with severe chest pain which radiated down his left arm, accompanied by shortness of breath. These were classic symptoms of a heart attack. However, my patient was only about 30 years of age.

Working with the same consultant with whom I'd first worked in Cyprus, Wing Commander Rex Fitzgerald, I ran the usual cardiac enzyme blood tests and serial electrocardiograms (ECGs). Cardiac enzymes indicate heart muscle damage detectable in the blood and there is a typical ECG pattern to be seen when someone has had a heart attack.

By the third day there had been no change in the blood tests to indicate a heart attack and the ECG, which had showed slight changes on the day of admission to our coronary care unit, had reverted to and remained normal ever since. My consultant saw Mr Smith on that day and told him that he was fine, there was nothing wrong with him and he could go home.

I looked at Mr Smith's face. There was a flicker of doubt, then disbelief. Then, when the realization kicked in that he wasn't going to die, his face lit up. He'd been given a clean bill of health; the doctors had said he was going to be fine.

How could this be? I thought. Mr Smith had come into the hospital with severe symptoms indicating that he was having a heart attack, and genuine respiratory problems. I'd been a witness to them – we all had. OK, there was nothing unusual in the tests that we ran on him, but that, for me, didn't answer the question: what was it that had led Mr Smith to come to the hospital? I never found out.

A few weeks later, we had another case: a lady in her fifties who was admitted with breathing problems. X-rays were taken and the radiological evidence seemed to suggest she had pulmonary tuberculosis (TB). This was because the shadows in the lungs were at the top of both lung fields. (Interestingly, bats develop shadows at the other end of the lungs, in the lower lobes, because they spend so much time upside down.) The tuberculosis bacteria thrive in areas that are less well aerated and most humans under-inflate the upper parts of their lungs. I took an in-depth social history because it looked as if we were going to have to trace her contacts over at least the past year.

So I started to talk to her; spent time getting to know her – just as Fred Amroliwalla had done with his patients. And what I found intrigued me. The woman was a landlady of a small B&B close to the coast and over the years she had played host to many guests from far and wide, some of them from overseas.

We always used to do our big weekly ward round in two parts. The first part was shared with our consultant radiologist because it was useful for him to tell us about our patients' X-rays. After that was finished we went round the wards to see our patients.

I started to present this lady's story to Rex and made a case for going into her social background because the bacterial cultures had not yet come back from the lab to confirm my diagnosis. TB bacilli take a while to grow in the lab and they require special culture media.

Rex waved his hand and said: 'Look, you're not writing a bloody novel, Gordon. Just show me the X-rays and let's be done with it, shall we?'

I stood there looking at him. Where was this man's sense of curiosity? Why wasn't this data important to him?

As it happened, our patient did not have TB. She had a plain, straightforward pneumococcal pneumonia, the ordinary kind, but the patches of consolidation were in an unusual position. She made a full recovery on penicillin.

Talking to the patient – getting to *know* the patient – seemed to me to be an essential part of a physician's job description. The psychological condition of a patient clearly had an important bearing on his or her physical health, as I was finding out more and more.

At Ely, we had quite a few people come in with duodenal ulcers. We had a new-fangled flexible fibre-optic endoscope and were able, for the first time, to actually visualize any ulcers in the stomach and the duodenum. The diagnosis was much more precise than using the older method of barium meals and clinical examination on the outside of the abdomen.

We also had a relatively new, breakthrough drug called cimetidine – which blocks the production of gastric acid – and then as now it proved very effective. After prescribing cimetidine for a month, we'd carry out another endoscopy to see if the ulcers were still there. In the vast majority of cases, the ulcers had disappeared. However, it was often only a temporary relief because at least 50 per cent of the patients would re-present with the same symptoms within six months. The trick, we discovered, was to identify which 50 per cent would re-present and then provide them with low doses of cimetidine for longer. Since in most of the cases stress was clearly contributing to the problem it seemed only sensible, when trying to ascertain which patients were likely to re-present, that we should seek out the underlying causes of the stress.

Knowing the role the mind played in the general well-being of the patient – I only had to remember Mr Smith's face upon being told he was fit and well, when clearly he wasn't – I began to spend more and more time on my ward rounds talking to my patients, just as Fred had.

I'd made a commitment to being a physician, but there were hints that I wasn't thinking like one. A lot of doctors made a virtue of doing their rounds in double-quick time. I, on the other hand, found it important to discover the mental state of my patients.

The nurses liked it, because the longer I spent with my patients, the happier they seemed to be and this contributed to a better, happier ward. This wasn't universal, because sometimes they didn't like the length of the ward rounds and I got ribbed for it. But then nurses, I had discovered at first hand, were wonderfully mercurial creatures.

Not long after returning from Antarctica, I'd proposed to Alison on the top deck of a London bus. We were married in a military wedding with all the trimmings: uniforms, white gloves and a 'sword party' – an 'avenue' of service colleagues, their swords raised over the bride and groom as they walk underneath – to see us out of the church.

I kept thinking of my old friend Greg Vagshenian. He still signed his letters to me with the old wind-up about when I was going to become a shrink. At Ely, I found it harder and harder to shake his words from my head. Thinking differently from my colleagues didn't make me feel comfortable – quite the reverse. I felt out of place and didn't like it at all.

At Ely, I had a case that became hugely influential on the way I began to see things. In the parlance of yore, she was deemed to be a 'malingerer'. I had formed a typical physician's view of malingerers and would-be suicides – the latter especially. They were seen to occupy valuable bed-space and drew resources away from more deserving patients who hadn't harmed themselves; people who bore their lot with great dignity, who hadn't asked to be ill. I'd heard similar arguments expressed by the RAF mountain rescue team. They bore no resentment to people who took precautions before climbing mountains and then found themselves in trouble – because of an accident or perhaps because, against the run of the weather forecast, the conditions had suddenly deteriorated. They did have a problem with the reckless kind: the idiots who went out and climbed mountains dressed in their pyjamas. It was about making work for people who were already up to their eyebrows saving others who genuinely needed help, through no fault of their own.

In the medical profession, doctors aren't alone in thinking like this about people who harm themselves. Being on the front line, many nursing staff do too. It's not fair, because people who attempt suicide are inevitably in great pain and distress, but we saw some, too, who might simply have been trying to manipulate a situation or a relationship. The irony for me was that the psychiatrists examining these people would often be quite perfunctory in their analysis and diagnosis. They would ask basic questions to see if they were truly suicidal, but to my mind they rarely got to the heart of the issue. This served to reinforce my view that, for all my feelings of alienation on the ward, psychiatry was largely a waste of time. I made a point of telling Greg this in my next letter to him.

Our 'malingerer' was a woman of 35 who'd been admitted to the hospital because she couldn't walk. One moment she was apparently fit and well; the next she couldn't move her legs. What could have caused this? One possibility was that she'd had a bleed into her spinal cord, but the X-rays came back negative. Physically there was nothing wrong with her. But still she professed to be unable to move her legs.

Soon after the consultation, I happened to walk into the ward sister's office as a group of nurses were talking about this person.

'What's up with her?' a nurse called Kerry was saying. 'I mean, there's nothing visibly wrong with her – not according to her X-rays.'

'It's as if she doesn't care,' a second nurse said. 'I mean, if that had been me – fine one minute, paralysed from the waist down the next – I'd have been terrified. But this one takes it all in her stride.'

Another nurse nodded vigorously as she stirred milk into her coffee. 'I think she's putting it on,' she said. 'If you ask me there isn't anything wrong with her at all.' She looked up as I closed the door behind me. 'What do you think, doctor? Is she putting it on?'

The woman hadn't been admitted long enough for me to have had time to examine her, although others had. With the X-rays and the tests all showing normal, it was inevitable that this person would be thought of as a malingerer. It's a word I have come to detest, but when the physical signs are absent and you deal in what you see, what else are you led to conclude?

In medical terms, there was a name for what this woman exhibited: it's called *la belle indifférence* and I started to explain it to Kerry and her friends. This woman wasn't weeping or beside herself with anxiety or fear. She just told anyone who'd listen the same thing, quite matter-of-factly: 'This morning I woke up and I couldn't walk.' It was, literally, 'a beautiful indifference' to her situation.

I had read about *la belle indifférence* in textbooks, but I never thought I'd come across a case. They were extremely rare. Or so I had been led to believe.

When I told Kerry and her two friends that I found the whole thing rather interesting, I could see them looking at me strangely. Having found myself in the nurses' good books for the care and attention I lavished on their patients, I could now see myself about to undo all that good work.

But there was something about this patient – a look, something behind the eyes, perhaps – that said she wasn't lying. I had seen it once as I'd passed by her bed. 'This woman can't walk,' I told Kerry. 'For the moment, I think we should take her story at face value and try to find the reasons why she can't walk. It may be there's a good reason for it – a reason we haven't got a handle on yet.'

'Well, best of British,' she replied. 'But we're all agreed. She's pulling the wool over our eyes. She's looking for attention.'

That afternoon, I had to perform a lumbar puncture on her.

I found her sitting up in bed as I walked on to the ward. Her name was Carrie and, according to her notes, she'd lived in the Ely area most of her adult life. Although it was an RAF hospital, there had been space available so she had been given a bed.

For a moment, as I approached, I wondered whether the nurses weren't right after all and I had made a considerable misjudgement. Carrie was nonchalantly tapping her teeth with a Bic biro while she pondered the clues of a crossword.

I pulled up a chair and checked her charts. Then I asked her how she was feeling – whether she'd recovered any sensation in her legs. She smiled and told me she hadn't.

'I know other doctors have been over this before with you, but do you have any idea how this might have happened?' I asked.

She shook her head and gave me the same answer she'd given everybody else: when she went to bed two nights ago, she was fine; when she woke up the previous day, she couldn't move her legs.

She spoke in a flat, monosyllabic voice; a little like she'd been hypnotized.

What bothered me was this: if Carrie was putting it on, as everybody else seemed to think she was, if this was just a cry for attention, why hadn't we seen her before? She'd lived in the area long enough. I would have expected her to have some previous, but she didn't. This had all come out of the blue. She'd made infrequent if regular visits to her GP, but for all the things you'd expect: check-ups, inoculations, treatment for a persistent cough.

I checked her notes again. She was single, no children. One of the nurses told me she worked as a PA to the managing director of a local firm that repaired and maintained tractors.

I tried engaging her in conversation, but she didn't seem remotely interested in small talk. She glanced up every so often as I rambled on about the weather and the attractive architectural features of the market town where she lived. All I got back was a weak smile.

A lumbar puncture can be incredibly painful. I got Carrie to lie on the bed in a foetal position to open up the spaces between her vertebrae at the back, creating a good aperture for the needle to go through. As I punctured her skin and slowly slipped the needle in, I expected her to wince at the very least, but she didn't. I glanced at her face. It remained a mask of indifference.

I thought back to my training. The textbooks said that you'd expect somebody who'd developed a sudden and alarming physical disability to be distressed, but she wasn't. She was totally indifferent to it. All the tests thus far had concluded that her paralysis had no physical basis and, studying her now as I tapped a small amount of lumbar fluid from her spine, my instincts said that she wasn't trying to pull the wool over our eyes; she wasn't, I suspected, remotely capable of it, even had she wanted to attempt such a thing. Perhaps because by now I'd excluded all the physical possibilities, my mind suddenly jumped to Freud.

Freud, I remembered, said that if somebody was struggling with a huge emotional conflict that couldn't be resolved, then the only way the mind could deal with it was to convert it into a mental state of dissociation – a state of denial. Dissociation, in its extreme form, could make the patient act, to all intents and purposes, like a zombie, totally detached from reality. This clearly wasn't the case with Carrie, who chatted quite amiably to anyone who'd listen – her indifference was reserved purely for her own condition.

But Freud, I remembered, also said that mental conflict could be transposed into a physical disability; plus a condition that exhibited a bit of both: dissociation, in the form of a kind of mental numbness, combined with some sort of physical disability – which, to my mind, was what Carrie had. A conversion disorder.

I was still thinking about this when, later that afternoon, the lumbar puncture results came back from the lab. It confirmed all the other data: Carrie had nothing physically wrong with her.

I decided to go back and see her. I found her, as before, sitting up in bed doing the crossword. She was frowning heavily.

'What are you stuck on?' I asked.

She drew breath to speak, then stopped.

'Go on. I promise I won't bite.'

'This one,' she replied, passing me the newspaper. 'Second brightest star in a constellation, four letters.'

Her voice was not local to the Fens. There was a nasal quality to it. A Birmingham accent, perhaps. The Midlands, certainly.

It was one of those rare, gratifying moments when the answer popped straight into my head. 'It's Vega,' I said.

She looked doubtful, but when I passed the paper back it fitted.

She asked me how I knew something like that and I told her I'd always been interested in the stars, right from when I was little, and that recently I'd had the chance to see them in all their glory, without a trace of light pollution, when I'd been in the southern ocean, close to Antarctica.

She frowned again.

'You think I'm pulling your leg?' When I realized what I'd said, I couldn't help it; I smiled. Fortunately, so did she.

'I'm sorry,' I told her, 'but I'm fascinated by your case.'

'Then you believe me?'

'Why do you say that?' I asked.

'Because I know some of the people around here don't. I can tell by the way they look at me.'

'The staff are concerned about you. They want to find out what's wrong with you. They want you to get better.'

'What do you think is wrong with me?' she said.

I didn't know how to answer that, so I told her that the key, in my opinion, lay in something that she hadn't told us yet.

'But I've told everyone everything,' she said defensively.

'Everyone except me,' I said.

I waited for her to come back at me, but she didn't. I asked if I could take a few notes.

It turned out she'd moved to the area from Wolverhampton more than ten years earlier to come and live with a boyfriend who'd got a job as an accountant in a firm near Cambridge. The relationship soured and when they split, she decided to stay. I noticed she hadn't had any visitors and asked whether she had any family locally, but she didn't. What about a boyfriend, I asked. Was she in a relationship now?

Now, for the first time, I got a reaction. 'Not every 35-year-old woman has to be in a relationship, you know.' She stared at me defiantly.

'I'm sorry,' I said, holding my hands up. 'These are just questions, Carrie.'

She continued to scowl.

'Sometimes things happen in a relationship,' I prompted as gently as I could, 'things that—'

Just then, Kerry appeared. She must have noticed the change in Carrie's expression, because she looked at me and asked if everything was all right. I thanked her and signalled as best I could that I was fine.

When we were alone again, I looked at Carrie and asked her why she'd been upset by this line of questioning. 'Have you been hurt by someone in a relationship?' There were no bruises on her body, but that didn't mean that this woman hadn't been hurt in the past; sometimes all it needed was a threat of violence.

Carrie looked down at the crossword again. This time, however, there were tears in her eyes.

'Not *in* a relationship . . .'

She told me then that she had been raped.

It rapidly became clear to me that Carrie's inability to walk was due to the fact that she had suffered a massive trauma – she had been raped by someone she knew. She had been unable to come to terms with what had happened and had sought to suppress it by blocking the memory. But in so doing, she had become so stressed that it had triggered her paralysis. In neurological terms, the electrical current in her brain had nowhere to go. It was supposed to relay via two sets of neurones, the second neurone firing the signal commanding her legs to walk. It was, to my mind, like a glow-plug in a diesel engine. The glow-plug has to have a certain heat in it before it will ignite the fuel that powers the engine. In Carrie, that glow was absent because of the trauma of her rape ordeal.

It was 1979 and I'd recently passed the exams that allowed me to write 'MRCP' after my name – Member of the Royal College of Physicians. I now began a four-year phase of higher professional training that would lead to my becoming a consultant. It was a time of excitement, change and uncertainty – not least because I found myself utterly intrigued by what I had personally witnessed: a trauma – a shock to the system – having a demonstrable, debilitating effect on the body.

Adolf Hitler, I recalled, had to be taken out of the trenches in the First World War because he'd become suddenly blind. He was seen by one of the top psychiatrists at the time, who recognized that he was suffering from hysterical blindness, not physical blindness from mustard-gas poisoning as the doctors who initially treated him had believed.

Throughout the First World War, Hitler had never risen above the rank of corporal. He was nondescript and taciturn and before the war he'd been a hand-to-mouth drifter. He wasn't a particularly energetic person; he didn't speak a lot. Yet, within a few months of the end of the war, he had embarked on the path that was to lead Europe into years of war, terror and the Holocaust.

What had brought about the transformation?

David Lewis, in a book called *The Man Who Invented Hitler*, suggested that the answer lay in the treatment Hitler had received in 1918.

Edmund Forster, the doctor who treated Hitler, was professor of neurology and director of a nerve clinic in Pomerania. Forster's unorthodox methods included telling patients how only the strength of their will and personality could bring them to recovery. Once Hitler found he could cure his own blindness by sheer will he buckled down to the task and emerged a changed personality. Forster was worried about the way Hitler had responded to the treatment, because during his recovery he came to believe he'd been saved for a divine purpose. He interpreted the blindness, his treatment and his recovery as a gift from God that gave him a mission. The rest, unfortunately, is history.

I became fascinated by this idea – the idea that the emotions could be the key to physical effects witnessed in the body. If I hadn't actually witnessed it in Carrie, I might not have believed it possible. I had not been responsible for Carrie's recovery process, but I had witnessed it. When she told me she'd been raped, it had acted like a total catharsis. The floodgates had opened and she had become extremely upset. She poured out her story to anyone who'd listen, but since we weren't qualified to do the listening, to administer to her psychiatric needs, we pulled in a psychiatrist from Cambridge to channel the catharsis professionally.

Two days later, Carrie walked out of the hospital unaided. I realized that this was far too soon for her to have recovered from a mental illness; she had recovered because she had processed the memories of her trauma and this had begun when she started to talk about her terrible experience. I could not possibly have been provided with a more powerful example of how psychological trauma, and the emotions it stirs up, can dramatically affect body function. And yet, to begin with, she presented with her *belle indifférence* and not a sign of emotional distress.

In the end, after she had had several sessions with the psychiatrist, I was delighted to watch her walk out of our ward. How many other patients, I wondered, would I attempt to treat in the future who would present with physical problems but would actually be suffering from psychological stress?

In deciding what to do for my higher professional training, I had picked gastroenterology as my 'special interest subject'. I was not yet 30 and keen to get cracking, but under the RAF medical training system there were only a certain number of positions available in the key disciplines and I was informed that the gastroenterology slot had been taken. I had to choose another discipline and selected neurology. In medical terms, there seemed plenty to interest me. Neurology included an understanding of, and treatment for, diseases such as Parkinson's and Alzheimer's, as well as spinal cord injuries, meningitis and encephalitis. It would allow me, too, to study conditions such as Carrie's that were right on the edge of what was known and understood; and I found that prospect exciting.

In civilian practice at that time, neurologists did not have to train in psychiatry in addition to their main subject, but in the RAF they did. The RAF saw extensive psychiatric knowledge as an advantage within the neurology discipline, because the RAF had a key interest in so-called 'psychosomatic disorders' – conditions that had arisen for the first time primarily during the Second World War, when pilots were found to be burning out under the intensity of round-the-clock operations against Germany and Japan.

Air Vice-Marshal Brian Kelly, as he had become since I first met him at Kelvin House, confirmed my appointment as senior specialist in medicine. I would take over the neurology unit at my new place of work, Princess Alexandra's RAF Hospital Wroughton, in Wiltshire, close to one of the RAF's largest and busiest flying stations, the home of the Hercules fleet, RAF Lyneham, and near to the boom town of Swindon. This meant that I also had to take on new training in psychiatry.

I went and told Rex Fitzgerald. Despite my reservations about the psychiatry side of things, I was feeling pretty upbeat. The RAF didn't have any other 'double-membership' consultants at that time because the only other one had moved to Australia. I was looking forward to becoming a physician-neurologist with psychiatry on the side.

My CO at Ely had told me that he would hold my job open for a year and that if I contacted him during that time he would personally see to it that I got back into my physician role. What the heck did he know that I didn't?

Rex put it on the line for me.

'So, you're heading off to Wroughton and hanging out with all those pointy-heads,' he said when I told him the news. 'You know what they call it, don't you?'

With great glee, Rex informed me that the Neuropsychiatric Centre at Wroughton was known to every senior doctor in the service as 'the Snake Pit'.

Chapter 4

Down Among the Snakes

Princess Alexandra RAF Hospital Wroughton was, for me, like a home from home, at least as far as the appearance of the place was concerned. It was 1980.

It was the sister ship to Ely and the buildings had been constructed to the same plan, towards the end of the 1930s. One difference was that Wroughton was built on top of a ridge that looked out on to the Ridgeway, the hilltop path that extends from the Chilterns in Buckinghamshire to Bristol and the sea. It was windy and fresh. To tap into this, the RAF had built a separate building on the site, which they used as a sanatorium for patients with pulmonary tuberculosis. When the treatment for TB changed and new antibiotics were found to be effective, the building had become the Neuropsychiatric Centre for the RAF. It had 35 beds and was the main treatment centre for psychiatric inpatients worldwide.

The move to Wiltshire had been stressful, especially for Alison with young Iain clocking in at only three months. We had moved into married quarters and both of us were feeling a bit unsettled. We had left behind a fine bunch of friends and had liked being at Ely, close to Cambridge.

What I didn't communicate to Ali was that I was feeling gravely unsettled in my new place of work as well.

For the entire first week, I'd occupied myself by decorating my office. I'd quite literally barricaded myself in the room. There were photos of Ali and Iain pinned to the noticeboards, shots of large, beautiful icebergs I'd taken in the Antarctic, as well as photos of happy times in Cyprus – snapshots of moments when I'd felt either secure or safe in the knowledge I had things to discover.

I was packing up my briefcase ready to leave for home on the first Friday when I heard a knock.

My boss, Group Captain David Johnstone, popped his head round the door.

I'd met David briefly the day I arrived. He was ten or fifteen years older than me and exuded a quiet sense of authority. Although in his early forties, his round, chubby body and jowly face gave him a wise, almost avuncular air. This was reinforced by his soft but authoritative voice.

He apologized for not having been around more to welcome me in my first week, but between some delegations down from London and a trip he had had to make to the MoD, this had been his first chance to see me.

I knew this to be true because David's office was two doors down from mine and all week it had been conspicuously empty.

'It looks like you've been busy,' he said, pointing to the photos on the walls. He cast his eyes briefly along the titles on my bookshelf, then noticed the poem in a frame on top. 'What's this?' he asked.

I explained that it was by Goethe and that it had been given to me by an elderly patient in Ely. The poem was about commitment and the events that conspire to help you, seemingly out of nowhere, if only you'll take that first step towards whatever it is you believe in.

He scanned down the poem and started to read from it:

A whole stream of events issues forth from that decision,
Raising in one's favour all manner of unforeseen incidents and
*   material assistance which no man could have dreamed would*
*   have come his way . . .*

He put the frame back on the shelf. Then, out of the blue, he said: 'Tell me, what's your take on intuition?'

I didn't know what to say. Nor was I sure why he was asking me this. Was it some kind of test?

I stammered out the first thing that came into my head: that I'd read *The Naked Ape* by Desmond Morris and that in it he had written that intuition, our sixth sense, was a residue of survival instincts we'd forged as apes to protect ourselves in the wild. It was an interesting idea, but still too challenging for a good many doctors to accept. For most doctors it was nothing more than puff and magic.

'I'm interested to know what you think,' David said.

I told him I happened to believe in intuition, because I'd had my own experience of it.

At this, he shot an eyebrow into his hairline. 'Tell me,' he said, drawing up a chair. 'I'd like to hear.'

I put my briefcase down. Ali was expecting me home, but I still had a little time in hand. I started to tell David the story.

When I was 11, I was listed to sit bursary exams at two Edinburgh public schools, George Heriot's School and the Royal High School. The day I turned up at the Royal High, accompanied by my friend and academic rival, Sandy McFedries from Leith Walk Primary School, I knew the moment I stepped on to the school grounds that it wasn't for me. The weather was cold; the skies were grey. It felt all wrong. Sandy, on the other hand, loved it.

A week or two later, when I took the bursary exam at George Heriot's, I not only realized it was the place for me, I also knew – I mean, *really* knew – that I was going to go there; that the award of a bursary was a foregone conclusion, never mind that my chances of success were minimal. It wasn't arrogance. It wasn't confidence, even. I just felt it in my bones.

'And did you?' Johnstone asked. 'Go there, I mean?'

I spent six very happy years there, I told him.

His eyebrow shot into his hairline again, a characteristic that, when I knew him better, would let me know exactly what he was thinking. He could make it signal anything – from surprise to opprobrium.

'I know,' I said, apologetically, 'it's not very scientific, is it?'

'Science doesn't hold all the answers in a place like this,' he told me. 'With psychiatry, only one thing works and that's the truth.'

I asked him what he meant.

'In general medicine, there's a hit-or-miss element. In a great many cases, you can make an approximate diagnosis and prescribe a treatment and often it will work, because mostly people tend to get better. I mean, you can prescribe an aspirin for someone with a headache and it will go away. But it will also go away if you just let nature take its course.

'Psychiatry isn't like that. To the outsider, it might all seem a bit woolly, but when you're doing it you actually find that it's incredibly precise. You have to notice what people are telling you. You have to listen carefully. More importantly, you have to notice what they're *not* telling you. It isn't necessarily that the patient is trying to deceive you. More often than not they're actually deceiving themselves.'

He went on to tell me that it was an exciting time to be involved in psychiatry. There were a bunch of what he described as 'young Turks' at Wroughton who were bringing fresh approaches and new ideas with them into RAF psychiatry. A number of them had come from general practice medicine and, like me, from physical medicine.

David, true to the conversation we'd had, proved himself to be highly intuitive, a very good psychiatrist and a great mentor to the people who worked under him.

On Friday evenings, he told me, it was customary to head down to the mess for 'happy hour'.

I hesitated because I'd promised Ali I'd get home as soon as possible, but David insisted and it was right that he did. When I got to the mess, there was a buzz in the room. In 1980 the American Psychiatric Association had just published its third version of the *Diagnostic and Statistical Manual (DSM) of Mental Disorders* and it took up much of the conversation.

DSM-III identified for the first time the existence of a condition known as post-traumatic stress disorder. PTSD, the manual said, could strike anyone. It was not down to a flaw in the character of the individual, but a reaction to 'events beyond the usual range of human experience'; the very thing, in essence, that warfare and the RAF were all about.

This flew in the face of the conventional wisdom – forged in Britain from bitter experience in two world wars – that those who'd cracked in the face of the enemy had done so because the stress of combat had found and exploited flaws in their character; that it had, if you like, wriggled its way into weaknesses in their personality and broken it apart, much as ice does to rocks.

Although it didn't say so explicitly, *DSM-III* indicated that PTSD had nothing to do with the personality of the individual. PTSD could happen to anyone, and that included civilians exposed to trauma. It recognized that PTSD was not exclusive to military combat veterans. And this, to me, seemed intriguing, to say the least.

The *DSM*, which was responsible for all the controversy, had had a long and chequered history.

In 1917, a Committee on Statistics of what is now known as the American Psychiatric Association, together with the US National Commission on Mental Hygiene, developed a new guide for mental hospitals called *The Statistical Manual for the Use of Institutions for the Insane* that included 22 diagnoses of mental illness.

When the Second World War came along, the involvement of psychiatrists in selecting, processing and assessing soldiers who had fought in the conflict brought the US military better insights into mental conditions than any other medical body. This gave impetus in 1943 to the development of a new classification system in the US for mental illness.

The first edition of the manual, *DSM-I*, was published in 1952 and listed 106 disorders. With the horrors of the Second World War still uppermost in people's minds, particular attention was paid in *DSM-I* to combat veterans. It was acknowledged that some 'well-balanced' people had, under extreme circumstances, developed reactions to overwhelming fears of death on the battlefield; a phenomenon *DSM-I* identified as 'catastrophic stress reaction'.

The first revision, *DSM-II*, was published in 1968 and this listed 182 disorders. Not to be confused with psychotic illnesses, such as schizophrenia, these newly recognized disorders were characterized as reflections of broad, underlying life problems – neuroses – that included conditions such as anxiety and depression.

During and after the Vietnam War, when large numbers of veterans came home exhibiting stress symptoms – symptoms that became known initially as 'post-Vietnam syndrome' – the US military did an extraordinary thing: it excluded the diagnosis of catastrophic stress reaction from *DSM-II*. All references to the existence of catastrophic stress disorder sank without trace.

This was denial on a grand scale, something that Western societies do from time to time, especially in moments of crisis. Schizophrenia is acceptable because it is a 'flaw' in a person's make-up, a fault in the way they were constructed – an accident of birth. Stress-related disorders, on the other hand, are an admission of human frailty and particularly frightening to authorities in the context of a war because they can happen to anyone – and, *de facto*, during the Vietnam War and its immediate aftermath, the US military clearly thought this was best suppressed. How conscious this denial is is a matter for debate. It seems entirely possible that a collective form of unconscious denial, seeking to protect the population at large, might play a significant role.

Anti-war activists protested bitterly against the censorship of *DSM-II*, because it affected the ability of a great many veterans to receive benefits for the treatment of their illnesses. It was partly thanks to their efforts that *DSM-III* emerged with the condition reinstated and rebranded: this time, it was referred to as 'post-traumatic stress disorder'.

PTSD, as laid out in *DSM-III*, was recognized as having to satisfy certain identified criteria. The first was that the 'victim' – someone I have since preferred to refer to as the 'survivor' – should have been exposed to an event that was 'outside the range of usual human experience'. The second was that the survivor persistently should have 're-experienced' the event in a number of ways. These re-experiencing factors included 'recurrent and intrusive distressing recollections of the event'; recurrent distressing dreams of the event; a sudden feeling 'as if the traumatic event were recurring' – the classic flashback syndrome; and 'intense psychological distress at exposure to events that symbolize or resemble an aspect of the traumatic event, including anniversaries'.

The third criterion related to the 'persistent avoidance of stimuli associated with the trauma or a numbing of the survivor's general responsiveness'. These characteristics included efforts to avoid thoughts or feelings associated with the trauma; efforts to avoid activities or situations that aroused recollections of the trauma; an inability to recall an important aspect of the trauma; and feelings of detachment or estrangement from others.

The fourth criterion related to persistent symptoms of increased arousal – symptoms that included difficulty in falling or remaining asleep; irritability or outbursts of anger; difficulty concentrating; hyper-vigilance; and an exaggerated response to being startled by something.

For a doctor to make the diagnosis of PTSD, *DSM-III* stated that the survivor needed to exhibit at least one of the re-experiencing symptoms within that cluster, at least four of the seven avoidance symptoms and three of the hyper-arousal symptoms.

For all its potential for controversy, *DSM-III* elicited little reaction in the UK. Outside of places like Wroughton, it was either seen to be an irrelevance or brushed under the carpet. In 1980, with the exception of a few low-intensity conflicts in far-flung corners of the former empire, Britain had experienced 35 years of peace.

The impression given by the medical hierarchy in Whitehall was that PTSD, as defined in *DSM-III*, was a unique American phenomenon defined by a unique American event. There was a prevailing view, too, that Britain's armed forces, being non-conscript-based, would react with corresponding professional sangfroid to traumatic events on the battlefield. We were, after all, the nation of the stiff upper lip.

Eight months after I arrived at Wroughton, I went to London to attend the annual Military Psychiatry Symposium at Millbank. As I was now a trainee military psychiatrist, alongside my main discipline as a physician-neurologist, this was very much a three-line-whip event, but I did not see it as a particular hardship. Given the controversy surrounding *DSM-III*, I was looking forward to some stimulating debate.

My new-found enthusiasm for psychiatry was largely down to David Johnstone, whose understated approach, so different from anything I'd experienced at Edinburgh and Ely, dovetailed neatly with the way I liked to learn. David's technique was to get his junior doctors to look at the cases that came into the hospital before he became involved. He would select which trainee would look after which patient and put the case-notes in the relevant pigeonhole in the secretaries' office where the post arrived.

When we assessed a new patient we created what was called a 'formulation', a multi-dimensional understanding of how the condition we had diagnosed, such as a depression, had developed over time. Dimensions included the biological, psychological and social aspects and the process of formulation was to try to make sense of them all as they interacted. It was about digging deep, getting to the nub of these issues, and was a far cry from what I increasingly saw as the relative superficiality of general medicine.

The great thing about David was that he said very little when the time came to present your formulation to him. As he sat behind his desk, the only thing that told you whether or not you were on the right track was that left eyebrow. A slight twitch denoted surprise, an indication that you should take another look at the evidence; an eyebrow raised somewhere around the hairline said you needed to completely rethink your approach. Essentially, it meant that I was teaching myself – except I wasn't on my own, because in David I also had a great mentor. I had met the first of my Merlins.

The previous year's symposium had served as my introduction to the field of combat stress. I had learned that the British military's understanding of combat stress still owed much to studies that had started during the First World War.

Early in the conflict it was thought that 'shell shock' had its origins in the concussive effect of explosions. But by 1915, when increasingly large numbers of men on the front line were diagnosed with the condition, the British Army started to distinguish between soldiers who had suffered from 'genuine' exposure to shellfire and those whose breakdown could not be attributed to enemy artillery.

In the former cases, casualties' reports were prefixed by the letter 'W' for 'wounded', which led to their entitlement to a wound stripe on their uniform; in the latter, their report was prefixed with 'S' for 'sick' – though some say it stood for 'shell shock' – and led to their being denied a wound stripe and sometimes even a pension.

By mid-1917, all British Army cases of shell shock were evacuated from the front line to a nearby neurological centre, where they were labelled 'NYDN' – 'not yet diagnosed nervous'. The thinking behind treatment of NYDN cases was summarized in a process that came to be known as 'PIE', for 'proximity', 'immediacy' and 'expectancy'.

Proximity meant treating the casualties close to the front line – within earshot of the fighting. Immediacy meant treating them with-out delay, while expectancy meant ensuring that all those treated were placed under no illusion of the outcome: that there would be no escaping a return to the trenches.

Under the NYDN/PIE process, a patient could only receive specialist attention when a form known as an AF3436 had been filled in by his commanding officer. This led to so many delays in soldiers receiving 'treatment' that medical officers by and large gave up referring cases to the centres.

Via this process the British Army concluded that only 4 – 10 per cent of sufferers were 'commotional' – i.e., 'genuine' cases. The rest it threw out as 'emotional' cases. This killed off shell shock as a valid condition, or disease, but questions remained, many of them raised in the aftermath of the conflict by the writings of the war poets.

In *Memoirs of an Infantry Officer*, Siegfried Sassoon wrote tellingly about a colleague called Jenkins:

> We left him in a corner, where he remained most of the day. His haggard, blinking face haunts my memory. He was an example of the paralysing effect which such an experience could produce on a nervous system sensitive to noise, for he was a good officer both before and afterwards. I felt no sympathy for him at the time, but I do now.

On the train from Swindon to London to attend the symposium in Millbank, I had all of this information in my head. The First World War had been a new kind of war, with more soldiers on the battle-field than ever before, wielding more powerful weapons than ever before and dealing destruction on a scale that could hardly be believed. It wasn't surprising, I thought, that such a large percentage of combat personnel presented with symptoms of shell shock. If the psychiatrists who'd drafted *DSM-III* were even half right, then avoidance was one of the four criteria you'd expect to find as a component of PTSD.

But could it really be possible, I wondered, that human beings were all hard-wired with the same potential 'trait' – I hesitated even to think the word 'flaw' – that under the right, or wrong, circum-stances could see them reacting to trauma in the same way?

In 1980, the medical community of the Ministry of Defence still held the traditional psychodynamic view that what happened to you in your early life, if it were sufficiently traumatic, marked you out later for potential difficulties.

This, too, was the basis of the teaching of Freud and, as a trainee, it was what I had been taught. I realized that I was interested in the heretical notion promulgated by *DSM-III* – that PTSD was a normal reaction to an abnormal event – but I wasn't yet ready to accept it.

And yet, from the way it behaved, it was as if the British establishment knew that something was not right. In 1916, confronted by the statistics – that, despite the firing squads at dawn, British troops were still running from the battlefield in large numbers – the use of firing squads as a deterrent to desertion began to be scaled down. After the war, in 1921, the major combatants – including the Germans – came together to share their knowledge of shell shock and in so doing realized that the experience was universal and that some kind of common phenomenon – something akin to the prognosis outlined in *DSM-III* – had to be at work. Then something odd happened. The British government formed a committee of inquiry into shell shock. Among its findings, reported in 1922, the committee stated that in 'forward areas' no soldier

> should be allowed to think that loss of nervous mental control provides an honourable avenue of escape from the battlefield; that when sending soldiers to neurological centres no case should be given an 'evacuation label' lest it fix the idea of a nervous breakdown as an opt-out from the fighting; and that when evacuation to base hospitals was necessary, cases should be treated in a separate hospital, or section of the hospital, and not with the 'ordinary sick and wounded'.

Finally, the committee said, good results would be obtained in the majority of cases by the simplest forms of psychotherapy, i.e., explanation, persuasion and suggestion, 'aided by such physical methods as baths, electricity and massage'. Psychoanalysis in the Freudian sense was 'not recommended'.

All the good work that had come out of the war, that had seen the participants come together to compare notes and draw enlightened conclusions, was quietly but comprehensively dumped. This was denial, I thought, on a large scale; and where there was denial, there was usually something to deny. But what? I still found it hard to believe that people could react in a uniform way to the horrors of war.

During the Second World War, the PIE principles were still regarded as the best way to treat traumatized soldiers, sailors and airmen. However, just as the First World War produced the term 'shell shock' with its clear implications of character weakness, so the 1939–45 war gave rise in British military circles to an equally notorious piece of terminology: 'Lack of Moral Fibre' or 'LMF'.

In the RAF, rules governing LMF were on the whole sympathetic to the sufferer – but much depended on the outlook of the individual's station commander. Men found to have physical or nervous problems were generally treated on the station, passed elsewhere for more specialized examination, admitted to hospital or sent on leave.

Between the early part of 1942 and the end of the war, around 8,400 aircrew were diagnosed as suffering from 'neurosis', which was distinct from LMF. Around a thousand, however, were diagnosed LMF and these individuals were usually removed instantly from the squadron. Many were put to work in the coal mines.

Even great leaders like Group Captain Leonard Cheshire VC dealt briskly with LMF for fear it might be contagious. 'I was ruthless with moral fibre cases, I had to be,' he said after the war. 'We were airmen, not psychiatrists.' On the whole, however, it was the thought of letting down comrades, and the idea, real or implied, that an LMF diagnosis would result in public humiliation in front of colleagues, that kept many aircrew flying.

As I took my seat at the symposium, I figured that *DSM-III* would crop up within the context of the talks or ensuing discussions. But in the run-up to lunch it scarcely rated a mention.

When it did, it was generally in the context I had heard it debated before: that 'post-Vietnam syndrome' was in all probability a 'disease' unique to the American armed forces because of the draft issue and other factors, not least the ready availability and use of narcotics by a great many conscript combatants. While that may well have been the case, what surprised me was that I heard PIE mentioned many more times than *DSM-III* and this made me curious. I kept asking myself why this should be.

After lunch I slipped out of the symposium unnoticed and made my way to the Tate Gallery, a few minutes' walk away, where I lost myself in its J. M. Turner collection. The Tate's Turners whetted my appetite for more, so instead of returning to the symposium I wandered over to the National Gallery, home of my favourite Turner painting of all: *Rain, Steam and Speed*.

The picture, first exhibited in 1844, shows an early steam train shooting out of a curtain of mist on a viaduct over the Thames. On my first viewing several years earlier, it had seemed to me to be a complete mess. The bridge and the train were barely distinguishable through the haze; and the sky seemed little more than a blur of whites, yellows and browns. But the more I looked, the more I saw. A hare, terrified, darting out from under the train's wheels; a farm labourer, seemingly oblivious to progress thundering by, ploughing in the field below.

What I loved about Turner, and this painting in particular, was his ability to capture the old and the new – England at a time of change.

That day, as I stared at the painting, instead of Turner's brushwork it was the symposium that pulled into focus. What I'd been confronted by, it seemed, was the same atmosphere of collective denial that had permeated the British medical-military establishment after the First World War. I found the implications of *DSM-III* extraordinary – it flew in the face of almost everything I'd learned about trauma reactions as a student – but that didn't mean I didn't find it interesting. *DSM-III* had made me curious. In place of the establishment, I saw Miss Roberts, gazing down at the contents of the Wee Red Box.

When it came to trauma reactions, there was no doubt at all that the British MoD remained firmly in the past. It would be a long time before any change in attitude emerged. But that process of change began two years after I arrived at Wroughton, when Argentina invaded the Falklands.

If the British establishment thought that PTSD was a phenomenon unique to America and the Vietnam War, the Falklands War of 1982 served as Mother Nature's way of informing Her Majesty's government that it wasn't going to escape unscathed.

Days after the Argentine occupation of the Falkland Islands, Margaret Thatcher's government announced it would send a naval task force to liberate them. Having some Spanish, I suddenly found myself on standby to join it, but for administrative reasons it didn't happen and like a lot of other people I watched the conflict unfold on the television.

In the patriotic fervour that had swept the country, and with the conflict so far away, it was difficult in the early stages to see it as real, Britain's first full-blown conflict since Suez. But after initial British victories – the retaking of South Georgia and the sinking of the *Belgrano* – came the hard, cold reality: the devastating Exocet strike on HMS *Sheffield*, the Battle of Goose Green, the bombing of the landing ship *Sir Galahad* . . . The list was long and painful.

Being close to RAF Lyneham, the RAF's main tactical transport base, Wroughton found itself far closer to the front line than I'd ever imagined.

The Princess Alexandra was the principal hospital involved in Casualty Evacuation (CASEVAC) operations: all the wounded arriving by C-130 Hercules and VC10 transport aircraft into Lyneham were immediately triaged through us before going on for specialist treatment at other military or NHS hospitals. All in all, we were pretty busy – busy, that is, treating some of the terrible physical wounds caused by Argentinian bombs, bullets and missiles. With one exception – a soldier who'd been shot on Mount Tumbledown in the final hours of the conflict – the mental anguish of the Falklands veterans remained, to us at least, a largely unknown quantity.

By all accounts, Tumbledown had been a nightmare. On the night of 13–14 June 1982, the British launched an assault on Mount Tumbledown, one of the heights dominating the capital, Port Stanley. The attacking British force consisted of the 2nd Battalion Scots Guards, with mortar detachments from 42 Commando Royal Marines and the 1/7th Duke of Edinburgh's Own Gurkha Rifles with support from a troop of Blues and Royals. They found themselves considerably outnumbered by an Argentine marine battalion that had recently been brought up to brigade strength.

The night of the battle, which saw the British tasked with taking the mountain, was witness to some of the most vicious close-in fighting of the war. The Scots Guards alone suffered nine dead and 43 wounded. But when the fight was over, the mountain was in British hands.

The soldier who ended up with us had been shot in the shoulder – a nasty wound that had affected the main nerve running down his arm. There were questions as to whether he'd ever be able to use it again, but the surgeons did a terrific job of patching him up and, in the end, he was expected to make a pretty good recovery. Because the RAF shared the Princess Alexandra with the Army, we decided to hold on to this particular soldier until he was better. But he didn't get better. Despite X-ray analysis that appeared to show a near-complete recovery, the poor chap's arm remained useless. And he was in a great deal of pain.

One day, Group Captain Bob Chappell, who was our CO at the time (but not a psychiatrist), called me in to discuss the case.

'I think we may be seeing our first case of post-Vietnam syndrome,' he told me.

'What do you mean?'

'There's little that's physically wrong with him, Gordon, but I tell you what: this poor guy had a pretty bloody ghastly war. There was hand-to-hand fighting all around him. He saw people bayoneted to death. He heard the screams of the dying in the darkness. He lost God knows how many of his colleagues. But the interesting thing is this: he's convinced he was hit at the exact same time they were announcing the ceasefire in Stanley.'

'You mean he believes he shouldn't have been shot at all?'

'Precisely. And that thought replays over and over in his mind – he can't shake it.'

Our COs often took an interest in patients in the hospital. They heard about their progress every morning at a start-the-day 'Prayers Meeting' at which they met Matron, the OC Administration Wing and the OC Medical Wing. The last was a senior administrative doctor whose principal task was to carry out medical boards to ascertain serving personnel's medical categories, which determined what sort of duties they were fit to undertake.

The CO was also convinced, from what he had heard, that the man's pain wasn't purely physical – that it was exacerbated by PTSD, a condition that until then had only ever been discussed as a theoretical possibility by our military, although it was considered a definite diagnostic entity in *DSM-III*. Our Tumbledown casualty gave us an opportunity to turn theory into practical reality.

Some time after this, I attended the Military Psychiatry Symposium again – the first such event since the Falklands. There, I heard about the experiences of a Royal Navy psychiatrist, Surgeon Lieutenant Commander Morgan O'Connell, who found himself deployed to the Falklands conflict on board the SS *Canberra*, known as the Great White Whale, which had been commissioned as a troop ship with the South Atlantic Task Force.

Morgan O'Connell modestly relayed how his terms of reference for the job were almost non-existent. He joined the Navy in 1965 and became a Member of the Royal College of Psychiatrists in 1976, having spent several years before that treating alcoholics. He went to the Falklands as psychiatrist to the surgical support team attached to 3 Commando Brigade and confessed that the 99-day cruise in the Great White Whale had changed his entire professional outlook. In emotional terms, he told the audience what he had seen among the battle-hardened professionals who had endured the horrors of the *Sheffield* attack, Goose Green, the *Sir Galahad* and Tumbledown. The trauma suffered by these men, he said, was, if you left aside the detail of it, little different from the suffering experienced by soldiers, sailors and airmen in the First and Second World Wars. What had changed was the sociological context. In years gone by, combatants and veterans could go to the pub, the British Legion – church, even – and be surrounded by people who had endured similar experiences to themselves; people who understood. Short of there being a third world war, that wasn't going to happen in the modern era. A tiny proportion of Britain's population had fought in the Falklands. The rest of us had watched it on television.

Thirty-seven years after the end of the Second World War, this was quite revelatory, but denial is a funny thing. After O'Connell's talk, I didn't hear the murmurs of assent that I'd expected among my colleagues in the room. There was more of an embarrassed hush. Had it not been for my CO's admission that our Tumbledown case might well have a connection to post-Vietnam syndrome, I might have had my own doubts. But what O'Connell was saying sounded right to me. Based on what I'd read – and my own intuitive response – I felt that the naval psychiatrist was on the money. Furthermore, he was the first qualified professional within the ranks of the British military establishment to stand up and make the point: PTSD wasn't a US phenomenon; it had arrived in the UK and here was the evidence.

Some months later, I heard that O'Connell had established a small PTSD unit within the Royal Navy. It came about not because of direction from on high, or with sanction from the MoD's senior medical hierarchy, but because officers and petty officers – administrators, essentially – had noticed changed behaviour patterns in sailors who'd fought in the South Atlantic.

Some things hadn't changed. Professional soldiers, sailors and airmen will always be reluctant to present – to unburden themselves, even to medical staff, of any mental difficulties they may be experiencing, and this remained true after the Falklands. Whatever *DSM-III* said about PTSD was yet to filter through to the people who'd suffered Exocet attacks or who'd watched their friends being bayoneted.

To a military man in the 1980s, the term 'combat stress' was redolent with echoes of shell shock and LMF. But stress, untreated, will always find a way through and Royal Navy administrators had begun to notice that incidents of drunkenness, brawling, violence at home – even marital break-ups – were far more prevalent among personnel who'd been in the South Atlantic than those who hadn't.

Because of its experience in the Falklands, it was the Royal Navy, therefore, that was the first British armed service to recognize the relevance of PTSD after the Second World War.

'The Royal Navy was ready and willing to recognize that, in spite of being the best Navy in the world, many of the lessons learned in previous conflicts had been forgotten in the intervening period, particularly in matters psychological,' O'Connell said years later.

While that might have been true of the Senior Service, it was certainly not true of the wider military establishment. In Whitehall, where the real decisions were made, many people remained convinced that in terms of mental health outcomes the Falklands conflict was a one-off.

Chapter 5

Jill and the Atomic Model

By 1983, I was 35 years old, had passed my psychiatry exams and was let loose, under supervision, to run a clinic at RAF Lyneham. I'd gone beyond wanting to make a go of this field of medicine – one a short while earlier I'd never envisaged getting into. Now I really, really wanted to become involved in it. I wanted to make a difference. It seemed to be so much more 'complete': a way of understanding the needs of patients and of helping them to come to terms with the suffering they were challenged by.

But it was a huge field for me to come to grips with. What I needed were some models to work with: templates that were sufficiently flexible to help me understand what the patterns of symptoms meant – patterns that might help me to help my patients understand what it was that confronted them.

One of the patients I met there was to have a profound effect on my professional development and future plans and she prompted the evolution of something I came to call the 'Atomic Model for Personality Development'. She proved to me an essential point: if you meet people with your sensors open, they will teach you more than any textbook can. It's great if what you see, hear and feel from people correlates with what the textbooks say, but it can be even more powerful, I discovered through this particular case, if what patients teach you doesn't fit the textbook at all.

Jill was a teacher in her thirties. The senior medical officer (SMO)

at Lyneham, who knew her socially, came to see me in my consulting room one day because she had been acting strangely, quite out of
character, and he was worried about her.

'She's a great girl,' he told me, 'life and soul of the party normally,
but lately . . . well, she's just not herself. I'd appreciate it if you'd
take a look at her.'

I asked him what kind of change he'd noticed.

The first thing, he told me, was her sense of humour – or rather,
her lack of it. It had completely disappeared. What everyone liked
about Jill, he said, was her sense of fun, particularly the way she
poked fun at herself. But that had all gone. He was convinced that a
depression had set in.

We went over the usual things. I asked whether there was any
possibility of marital difficulties, whether there had been any deaths
in the family recently, if she had a history of depression or alcohol
abuse, but the SMO shook his head. Ostensibly, everything was fine.

'Her husband was in the Falklands,' he explained, 'but he came
through it unscathed and anyway he's back now. They're an
extremely loving couple. Always have been.'

'You said there were other manifestations of uncharacteristic
behaviour.'

'Lately, she's become dithery and unable to make decisions. I
heard from another teacher at her school that she'd been turning up
late and skipping classes. A few days ago, she was put on sick leave.'

A lot of wives whose husbands had been in the Falklands had
developed the blues. Their partners had been away, some for long
periods of time, they'd felt lonely, maybe drunk a little more than
usual, and, burdened suddenly with all the responsibilities of
running a home and raising children, had lapsed into some form
of depression. I assumed that Jill was going to be one of those, so I
asked the SMO to persuade her to come to the clinic.

On form, she might have been bright and vivacious, but the girl I
saw, with her long, lank hair and lack of make-up, was a very long
way from being the life and soul of the party. I asked her how she
was feeling and she told me she was fine; a little tired, maybe, but
otherwise OK.

I think that was the first time I experienced what the textbooks
called 'cognitive dissonance' in a real clinical situation. This is an

uncomfortable sensation caused by a conflict between what one is feeling and what one is being told. For example, it is always important for a psychiatrist or GP to pay attention to instinct if a patient tells you that they are feeling well but you experience a powerful sense that they are not well, that they are exuding an atmosphere of depression or anxiety. This is not a conscious communication process and certainly does not mean that the patient is being deliberately deceptive or lying. I remember having that powerful feeling. I didn't believe her, but you can't make someone take antidepressants if they don't want to, so I asked her instead to come back and see me in a week's time.

When she returned, she told me she continued to feel fine (even though she clearly looked unwell), but when pressed, did confess to a change that she'd noticed in her behaviour: she told me that she couldn't stop cleaning the house; obsessively tidying things that didn't need tidying. She'd rearranged all the tins in the food cupboard into alphabetical order. She'd cleaned a bathroom that was already spotless and she'd cleaned it again and again. I asked her whether she was normally this obsessive about tidiness in the house and she told me she wasn't. At this point, my eyebrow, like that of my Merlin and mentor, probably drifted towards my hairline, because I sensed the beginnings of a pattern here. Although she maintained she didn't need them, I prescribed antidepressants to see if that would 'lift' her mood. By now, secretly, I was very worried about her. I asked her to come back and see me within a few days.

When she returned, my suspicions were confirmed. She told me that she'd started to have monumental arguments with her husband and her children, who were aged eight and ten, and that she had become utterly convinced that her husband was planning to leave her and take the children with him. By now, she was in a desperate state, her nerves shot to pieces, and I suggested that we admit her on the spot for treatment at Wroughton.

It was as well we did, because her freefall did not stop there. Soon after she arrived on the psychiatric ward at the Princess Alexandra, she regressed completely. She screamed at the nursing staff and tried to run away on several occasions. We managed to persuade her that running away from the hospital would delay her recovery and that staying was in her best interests. She seemed to accept this, albeit under sedation, but a day or so later one of the nurses told me that she would not stop wetting the bed. Soon afterwards, she became doubly incontinent. By the end of the week, she had lost the ability to speak and had to be spoon-fed. I had never seen anything like it – not outside the textbooks at any rate.

Jill's condition was known as 'involutional melancholia', a psychiatric condition that affects mainly elderly or late middle-aged people. It was classically described as 'depression of gradual onset' occurring during the involutional years – 40–55 in women and 50–65 in men – and was marked by anxiety, agitation, restlessness, hypochondria, insomnia, weight loss and a number of related symptoms.

What Jill had done was regress through various 'shells' of protection, literally crumbling down through layers of defence mechanisms, until she reached the very last one. When she regressed to the point where she could no longer speak, there was nowhere left for her to go, except death.

She needed emergency treatment and my boss was fully involved in her care by the time she was admitted to our ward. And it was there that we decided to administer electro-convulsive therapy, otherwise known as ECT. The prevailing theory governing the development of depression for several decades has been the chemical one – that there are certain neurotransmitter chemicals that are lost in the brain during the onset of a depression; that either they're not produced in sufficient quantity any more to allow a healthy mood-state or they're burned and used up very quickly. This view has been successfully reinforced by the use of antidepressants, which are thought to boost the production of chemicals – principally serotonin and noradrenaline – in that part of the brain where mood is created. But in certain dangerous depressions where rapid regeneration is required, because the patient has become deluded or suicidal, something more immediate is necessary – and that's where ECT comes in.

People have a horror and dread of ECT thanks to its depiction in movies like *One Flew Over the Cuckoo's Nest*, but ECT can be a saviour because it can get to work extremely quickly. And this was what was needed with Jill.

We wheeled her into the treatment room where she was given a general anaesthetic – a dose sufficient to knock her out for two or three minutes. Putting the patient under gave me the opportunity to let the tiny electrodes that had already been placed on her scalp get to work. The electrodes are designed to administer a shock to induce a convulsion – a convulsion at that time, in the early 1980s, being a measure of electricity sufficient to release the required chemicals into the brain. It is this aspect of ECT that instils thoughts of barbarism – the idea that plugging someone into the National Grid can possibly do them any good.

The other misconception is that the patient is awake when this happens, which they are not.

The third objection is that damage is inflicted to the patient's body by the convulsions, but thanks to muscle relaxants that are given beforehand this doesn't happen either. And while some people have claimed memory loss from ECT, when that has happened it would almost certainly be down to the anaesthetic, not the electrical current.

When Jill came round, the first thing I noticed was that her speech had returned. She asked me where she was, then promptly wet the bed. Her husband, who was beside her, was mortified, but I told him not to be. It might be a good sign. He gave me an odd look.

The next day, she stopped wetting the bed, but was still in a highly emotional state – so much so that one of the nurses reported back to me that she'd overheard Jill telling her husband, who'd remained by her bedside to watch over her during the night, that she was still convinced he was preparing to leave her.

'Keep a close eye on her and let me know when you notice the next change,' I told the nurse.

'The next change?'

'Yes.'

'What's going on?' she asked me.

I lifted both hands, showing her two sets of crossed fingers. 'I'll tell you when I'm a little more sure, but I'm rather hoping that the ECT is doing the trick.'

Fortunately, the process kept on working and within two more days she'd reversed back through the next shell: the obsessive-compulsive layer, in which she'd constantly asked the nurses to change her sheets – sometimes several times per hour – even though they were clean as a whistle, and had been ever since her incontinence had ceased.

I knew, then, that we'd seen Jill reverse back out of her clinical state and that the ECT had worked its magic: it had reversed the very sequence of her collapse; something the textbooks said was technically feasible, but which I never thought I'd actually witness. The process of resolution was the reverse of the process of evolution of the depression.

The disintegration had become a reintegration, a rebuilding, of her defence mechanism shells – layers we all have. These shells act as barriers to challenge stress. But when the stress is massive and un-relenting enough to overwhelm the ability of the shells to function as a defence, the shells corrode one by one. The interesting thing about Jill was that it appeared to be an intrinsic condition. It was not a reactive state to external stresses (any kind of stress build-up), but an internal or endogenous biological process, resulting in a depression that had come out of nowhere, as they occasionally do. The moment we stopped the slide – the moment we were able to reverse that biological change – she was able to reconstitute the defence mechanisms herself.

I had watched this lady go through every defence shell to the most primitive form of herself and then climb back through each one to wellness. The ECT had triggered the body's own 'happy drugs' and let them go to work – remarkably quickly, as it turned out. This, for me, was an amazing observation, because it would in time have huge implications on my appreciation of what a trauma actually does. In Jill's case, it allowed me to construct a model – the first of several that I have built during my career – for understanding and treating PTSD.

I called this one the Atomic Model, because of the way it looked when I first set it down on paper: a series of concentric circles built around a core.

Stephen Hawking it wasn't, but it helped me to get around the floundering feeling I often experienced with psychiatry. Applying the lessons of learned psychiatric papers and journals seemed very difficult to me. With medicine it was different. Somebody came in with a symptom and you already had a list built into the back of your head of how to identify the condition that was causing the symptom, and that led directly to effective treatment.

Psychiatry didn't seem to work like that – there appeared to be any number of ways of interpreting, let alone implementing, all the fascinating data that emerged from peer-reviewed literature on the subject. Sometimes it seemed to be a melting pot where one person's opinion was as good as anyone else's. And that was what the atomic model was designed to overcome – for me at least. I wanted to see what had happened to Jill clearly, so that next time I could take practical steps to implement a solution sooner.

The model I conceived for looking at psychological defence mechanisms – the Atomic Model – was based on the fundamental atomic structure I'd learned about during my first year at senior school, with a nucleus at the centre and orbiting electron shells.

Newborn babies appear to come ready equipped with the first defence shell and it's possibly the most powerful defence we are ever going to possess – one that is loud, demanding, dramatic, impossible to ignore, unrelenting, totally egocentric and gives no quarter.

The baby that's lying in its cot at two in the morning feeling hungry doesn't think, 'I'll just hang on till seven till Mum comes and feeds me'; there are no finer feelings about disturbing its mother, it just yells and screams and Mum comes running. The baby realizes that this yelling business is valuable stuff, allowing it to believe, for a while, that it is all-powerful.

The new baby concludes that it controls everything and that is its way of feeling secure. In this way, what has become known as the hysterical defence becomes our primary defence mechanism, the first shell, closest to the nucleus of the atom which represents the intrinsic part of the real self, what Sigmund Freud referred to as the 'id', an old German word meaning 'it': the basic, raw stuff which gives that extraverted or introverted quality to temperament.

But there comes a point when the mother decides that she must move on and start the weaning process to introduce the child to solids. This means that she has to 'declare unilateral independence', because the child has established a comfortable and secure routine for meeting all of its needs. Changing from an exclusively liquid diet to a mixture of solids and liquid will inevitably represent a threat to the child and it has only one way to register its protest: the hysterical defence. It doesn't have anything else in its repertoire. The mother doesn't consult the infant about this, of course; she just does it. And because the hysterical defence mechanism has worked so effectively before, the infant naturally tries it on with more of the same, furiously, but by now these episodes are perceived by the parents as tantrums.

The mother, if she is resolute, will be able to overcome the tantrums with quiet determination and gradually the infant is introduced to solid foods. All well and good, but because the infant has controlled everything up to now on its terms, including its mother's behaviour, it perceives the withdrawal of the mother's breast as a huge rejection.

Such a rejection is probably experienced as the worst possible event ever. Bear in mind that 'ever' is actually a short period of time for a baby because 'time' is an adult concept based on a conscious appreciation of the movement of events. In the earliest stages of life a baby depends on its carers to look after this concept of time on its behalf, while it gets on with the business of trying to make sense of a world of sensations that do not come equipped with defined marker posts such as the ones adults use to measure time: watches, clocks, etc.

Can you imagine the shock experienced by the powerful infant when it has used its tried and tested defence mechanism at full blast to try to bring its world under control again, only to discover that it simply doesn't work? It can, thus, be forgiven a few distress-driven tantrums.

However, Mother Nature, like a rescuing fairy godmother, has the answer. She helps the bewildered infant to develop a new defence mechanism now that the previous one, hysteria, has failed to bring the mother back in line. Nature does this by creating a dam against the world. The world may be capable of springing nasty surprises for which there doesn't seem to be an explanation. For example, the infant simply doesn't understand what it could possibly have done to deserve being rejected by its mother. Survival is at stake and this is such a massive event that the only thing to do is to shut down and deny that it is happening.

This psychological barrier, like a dam, can hold the anxiety back and protect the infant from the new and unprecedented awareness that it is not completely in control of its world. So the dam holds the anxiety back at least for the time being, until something better comes along.

But all dams have to have a sluice-gate – a release valve – otherwise they'd crack. The baby has to be able to release tension from time to time to protect the dam. This has been described as 'projection'. Just enough release from time to time will fulfil two purposes: first it will keep the internal level of pressure stable and not overwhelming; and, secondly, it isn't quite enough to drive the mother further away or risk total rejection. In this way the second defence shell is set up, a balance of denial and projection, which is known as paranoia (literally, from the Greek, 'seeing things in a parallel way'). The growing child's world settles down again nicely but there are still many challenges to face.

The third psychological defence mechanism starts to be built when the child accepts that there is a world out there that it has to develop a relationship with. This naturally follows the realization that it is not the controlling centre of the universe and that its mother is capable of making independent decisions. The antidote is to create a more sophisticated defence mechanism based on self-control and independence while at the same time developing skills to relate to other individuals in a safe and secure way.

In order to be able to do that, the child has to gain control of body function – potty-training comes into this – it has to learn how to dress and feed itself and it also has to interact with people. But a preschool child, between the ages of two and five, has not yet learned how to relate to other children, so it actually becomes obsessionally preoccupied with its own world – its own space.

You see this when you walk into a room that's full of kids aged around three. They don't socialize or play together much, because they don't yet know how to. What they do is play with their own toys individually in their own space – often quite obsessively and compulsively – and this becomes the third shell of the atom: the obsessive-compulsive defence.

But they'll still have the first two lines of defence – hysteria and paranoia – to fall back on as well.

From about the age of five, when the child goes to school, it develops increasingly sophisticated social skills and then, as rapid brain development takes place, it acquires better and better cognitive skills as well. This behavioural process matures in girls earlier than in boys and, by about the age of 10, girls are usually around two years ahead. Behavioural maturation depends on the evolution and growth of the central nervous system and there are probably several steps to be climbed to develop a good set of social skills, which could be regarded as the fourth shell of psychological defences.

Puberty is arguably a more defined stage in development for females compared with males. It marks the beginning of reproductive capability and females probably need the social maturity at an earlier stage than males to be able to deal with a world that has expanded into a new dimension – the capacity to reproduce themselves.

Along with the development of social skills, growing children start to think about the world in a more consciously aware style that used to be known as the acquisition of 'concrete thinking'. This depends on the power of thought and the ability to solve problems. Suddenly, algebra and the world of mathematics becomes comprehensible, at least for some.

The development of multiple layers of cognitive skills to make sense of the world and to keep safe and secure probably represents the fifth layer of defence shells. At least, it does in my Atomic Model. It's a doubly appropriate analogy, because an atom is at the beginning of everything and must form relationships with other atoms to become molecules and then bigger and more sophisticated structures.

The sixth shell is what I think of as the most sophisticated line of defence of all: humour.

To be able to parry an attack with nothing more than one's wit is a remarkable asset and has given rise to a good many comedians – the ones who attribute their careers to fending off the school bully with some well-directed jokes or impersonations. Humour is such a sophisticated form of cognitive defence that it merits a shell layer all on its own.

With Jill, I'd noticed something interesting where I'd not expected to see anything: in me.

Each phase of her mood-state she'd denied, but her mood-state was palpable – it left something in the room, as pungent as the smell of cordite. Perhaps it was in the way she looked at me, but mostly it was how she made me feel. This was when I realized how important empathy was as a diagnostic tool, although the technical term in this instance is cognitive dissonance: the idea that a patient's genuine mood-state is at odds with what they're telling you about it.

It was from this moment that I knew you had to pay a lot of attention to the way patients make you feel, because the impression they leave is 'dissonant': a polite way of saying they're lying, except they're not – it's denial at work. Sometimes this can be so strong that I've been left feeling the person's depression long after they've left the room. The pungent aroma of depression lingers on, only gradually creeping into the corners.

Jill had given us no clues in what she'd *said*, but the clues had been there nonetheless. Her humour, as the SMO observed, had been the first to go. Next it had been her organizational skills, then her social skills and then she had become obsessive-compulsive. When that defence mechanism hadn't worked – when that shell, too, had collapsed – she'd become paranoid and then hysterical and finally almost catatonic.

It was terrifying, but fascinating at the same time, especially, following ECT, when it became apparent that the shells were starting to repair themselves.

It was during this process of regeneration that the Atomic Model had come to me. I sketched it out graphically and then walked down the corridor to talk to David Johnstone about it, because it had disturbing implications for a big assumption made in psychiatry: the whole notion of what a personality disorder is.

'Conventionally,' I said, placing the model of the atom in front of him, 'this woman would have been labelled as having a hysterical personality disorder, but that's not how I see it at all.'

David arched an eyebrow – just enough to embolden me to continue.

'Take someone with OCD,' I said. 'Someone who counts up the letters in a word or who listens to the same piece of music over and over. Or someone who does compulsive hand-washing, because they have recurrent thoughts about contamination with germs. Instead of thinking of that as a disorder, maybe we should look on it as a survival tool.'

'What do you mean?'

A conventional psychiatrist – although, I joked, that was probably

THE ATOMIC MODEL:
Personality Development

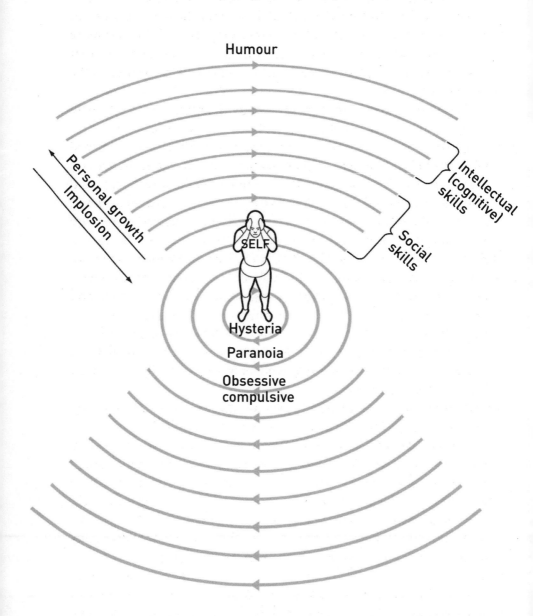

an oxymoron – would want to treat the symptoms of the OCD directly; to aim to modify or eliminate that phenomenon itself. I saw it differently. I saw the obsessional thinking and the compulsive rituals as extremely effective distractions from the core anxiety. So, before eradicating the symptoms of the compulsion, I'd be far more inclined to find out what the underlying anxiety was and help that to be resolved so that those mechanisms didn't have to be used in the first place.

'These symptoms are actually pretty helpful, David. They're a signal, a warning. Sticking with the OCD example, pound to a penny, nine times out of ten, it'll be about something that happened when the OCD developmental phase kicked in – between the ages of, say, three to eight or nine. If something really threatening and frightening occurred during that phase of personal development and the front-line response was to use the most powerful defence mechanism available and that happened to be to use obsessional thinking patterns and compulsive ritualistic behaviours, then it's entirely understandable that is what would be used. Then, it seems to me, if that strategy worked, it might be stored away as a method of dealing with challenges in the future, something that our protective brain might regard as a defence strategy that might come in handy. So, someone in middle age might select that defence mechanism as a starter, even though it wasn't actually their most highly evolved defence.'

David nodded. He glanced down at the atom. 'I've always been somewhat suspicious of the term personality disorder.'

'Me too,' I said. 'This is about people who, for whatever reason, have lost the ability to cope with challenges, powerful challenges, at a more sophisticated, everyday level. They have had to resort to using primitive defences that other people – our colleagues, mostly, I'm ashamed to say – label in a somewhat pejorative way.'

David continued to stare at my model of the atom. 'Personality disorder, character flaw, that kind of thing . . .'

'Precisely. Stick with OCD. To trace the underlying anxiety in someone, you'd need to ask what happened between the ages of three and nine. Most people will think back and say, "Nothing happened to me then." So you have to probe a little. Then, maybe, they'd say they had to go into hospital for an operation; or they'd started boarding school, or maybe their dad had had to up sticks because of his job and move to another part of the country – the other side of the world, even.'

'And you're saying this is normal?'

'I'm saying it's a defence mechanism, a survival technique. Some of our colleagues would say the opposite. That these people had flaws in their personalities that were revealed by a particular stressor. That, to me, is a throwback to the arguments used by the very people who said that shell shock and LMF were only to be found in people with character flaws.'

He arched an eyebrow again and this time I knew what it meant: this was mad, bad, possibly dangerous stuff. I knew that, too.

There was one final corollary to all of this – and I kept it to myself.

Jill's final line of defence had been a dissociative state that was almost catatonic in the way it manifested itself.

I'd read about that same dissociative state time and time again in shell-shock victims. What pertained to Jill ought, logically, to have pertained to them too. Dissociation – vanishing mentally from the source of the anguish – appeared to be the mind's very last line of defence; the kind of defence mechanism one would use, for example, when confronted with a life-threatening event on the battlefield or off it.

Chapter 6

The Pint Pot Theory

The 'Falklands Effect' led to an explosion of interest in PTSD in the UK among a core of psychiatrists who liked the idea of being at the cutting edge of what appeared to be a new psychological subject, but was really a phenomenon as old as man himself that had been suppressed. Those of us who embraced the concept felt that we were dealing with the most important medical development to have emerged out of the Vietnam War.

In the US, more papers were being written on PTSD than any other psychiatric condition. However, at senior levels of the military on both sides of the Atlantic – in medical ranks, as well as 'secular' echelons of the military – there remained a great deal of scepticism and denial about trauma reactions. It was not unlike the story of *DSM-II*, the second version of the *Diagnostic and Statistical Manual* that had abandoned the concept of catastrophic stress reactions during the Vietnam War.

Now I knew a little more about it, the changes made to *DSM-II* didn't really surprise me. Doctors are renowned for making very bad patients. When it comes to admitting psychological frailty, they – we – are even worse. In this respect, we are a little like fighter pilots. Both of us have to be high on denial, otherwise in the high-octane, rarefied world we live in we would not be able to function – that, at least, is how some see it.

Such people fear that when they crack, they'll crack completely and never be able to return to what they did before – a fear that in the early 1980s had more than an element of truth in it (at least as far as fighter pilots were concerned). As a result, at an establishment level, they simply refused to accept there was any basis of truth in the literature. PTSD was not real. It couldn't be. We could not *afford* it to be.

It explained to me why I'd come up against some cranky surgeons, particularly, in the course of my training. Surgeons live in a world of life and death; despite their best efforts, they see people dying on the operating table. But they have to carry on. In medicine, it's called 'professional distance'. A doctor has to condition himself to believe he is going to be objective at all times; that when he looks in his patients' eyes he is not like them.

In the early 1980s, it was the same with soldiers, sailors and airmen. In many ways, our decisive victory over the Argentinians had not helped. Napoleon had reputedly said: 'There is nothing more stultifying to progressive human thought than a successful war.' If he did say it, he was right. Society heaped a huge burden of expectation on its military in the same way that it did with doctors. Society needed to know that the military was not vulnerable; that if the Soviet tank divisions poured across the East German border our boys were not going to falter and crack. What was still being absorbed from the Falklands was, for the most part, being ignored or left unexplored.

It seemed a crazy paradox to me. My experience with Jill told me that, within us all, we had an innate capacity to survive extreme moments of stress; that stress reactions were a normal response to an abnormal event. And in that sense, if this was something built into us all, it couldn't be new.

I searched encyclopaedias and history books in any spare moments I had to see what evidence there was for PTSD prior to the First World War. The more I looked, the more I uncovered.

Traumatic stress reactions were clearly described by Homer in the *Iliad* around 850 BC. This was the era that gave rise to the word 'trauma', which means, from the Greek, to 'pierce' or to 'puncture'.

Herodotus, writing about the battle of Marathon in 490 BC, told of an Athenian soldier who went blind after witnessing the violent death of the soldier standing next to him, in spite of the fact that he was 'wounded in no part of his body'. Shades, I thought, of the hysterical blindness that had afflicted Hitler.

In *Henry IV Part One*, Lady Percy describes profound and disturbing changes in her husband Hotspur following his return from the Wars of the Roses:

> *O, my good lord! Why are you thus alone?*
> *For what offence have I this fortnight been*
> *A banished woman from my Harry's bed?*
> *Tell me, sweet Lord, what is't that takes from thee*
> *Thy stomach, pleasure and thy golden sleep?*
> *Why dost thou bend thine eyes upon the earth,*
> *And start so often when thou sitt'st alone?*
> *Why hast thou lost the fresh blood in thy cheeks,*
> *And given my treasures and my rights of thee*
> *To thick-eyed musing and cursed melancholy?*

Great authors and historians down through the ages had written about PTSD, I realized, because the psychological reaction to trauma is part of the human condition. It follows that, throughout history, war has generated such huge episodic increases in PTSD that it became impossible to ignore and was reflected in the literature of the times.

Shakespeare certainly lived through some turbulent years. He was obviously well aware of the capacity of trauma to produce stress reactions but it is remarkable that he also recognized the distinct pattern of symptoms that was described four centuries later as PTSD in the *DSM*. His plays contain many descriptions of psychological reactions to trauma which recognize that a trauma is a dangerous experience that does not only expose people to threat to life and limb: it also pierces strong psychological defences to produce a state of fear, helplessness or horror.

In *Henry IV Part One*, Lady Percy goes on to document the terrible changes she's perceived in her husband:

> *In thy faint slumbers I by thee have watch'd,*
> *And heard thee murmur tales of iron wars;*
> *Speak terms of manage to thy bounding steed;*

Cry 'Courage! To the field!' And thou hast talk'd
Of sallies and retires, of trenches, tents,
Of palisadoes, frontiers, parapets,
Of basilisks, of cannon, culverin,
Of prisoners' ransom and of soldiers slain,
And all the currents of a heady fight.
Thy spirit within thee hath been so at war
And thus hath so bestirr'd thee in thy sleep,
That beads of sweat have stood upon thy brow
Like bubbles in a late-disturbed stream;
And in thy face strange motions have appear'd,
Such as we see when men restrain their breath
On some great sudden hest. O, what portents are these?
Some heavy business hath my lord in hand,
And I must know it, else he loves me not.

Shakespeare might as well have been armed with a copy of *DSM-III*; but he was writing in 1598.

And then there was Pepys. 'It is strange to think,' he wrote, following the Great Fire of London in 1666, 'how this very day I cannot sleep a night without great terrors of fire; and this very night could not sleep till almost two in the morning through thoughts of fire.' Pepys wrote later about a huge swathe of society traumatized by what it had witnessed. 'So great was our fear, it was enough to put us out of our wits.' Although his own house was not burned down, Pepys was unable to sleep for quite some time afterwards. 'Both sleeping and waking, and such fear of fire in my heart that I took little rest.' Two weeks after this, the fear had not gone away. 'Much terrified in the nights nowadays, with dreams of fire and falling down of houses.'

DSM-III described a post-traumatic stress event as having four main components. Pepys had clearly experienced three of them. He had been exposed to an event that was 'outside the range of usual human experience'; he was 'persistently re-experiencing the event' by day and by night in the form of dreams and flashbacks; and the fact that he was having trouble sleeping demonstrated clear signs of hyper-arousal.

Shortly after the Great Fire, Swiss military physicians described, accurately by modern standards, a collection of symptoms – heart palpitations, loss of appetite, insomnia and melancholy, all wrapped in the banner term 'nostalgia' – that broadly mirrored the symptoms outlined in *DSM-III*. German physicians came up with similar conclusions to the Swiss at around the same time. In the years that followed, Swiss and Spanish military doctors, faced with almost identical symptoms amongst their own troops, came up with their own terminology: '*maladie du pays*' (homesickness) and '*estar roto*' (being broken).

The American Civil War was one of the first conflicts to be reported by official war correspondents, who brought the realities of war to the civilian population. The war itself threw up the terms 'soldier's heart' and 'exhausted heart' to describe combatants with the same symptoms as First and Second World War soldiers, sailors and airmen who'd suffered from shell shock and LMF: good old 'lack of moral fibre'.

The American Civil War coincided with the emergence of more 'psychological' explanations for traumatic stress reactions. 'Traumatic shock' was introduced as a term by Neal in 1882, 'nervous shock' by Page in 1885, 'fright neurosis' by Kraepelin in 1899, 'traumatic neurosis' by Clevenger in 1889 and 'anxiety neurosis' by Freud in 1894.

The Freudian concept was summarized by his observation that 'a primary psychological event leads to repressed memories which lead to physical manifestations which are known as "hysterical"'. Without the benefit of any kind of MRI-type scanning techniques, Freud had worked out that memory-processing systems in the brain played a significant role in the development of certain anxiety states and that reminders of the traumatic event could trigger an exact replay of it – not just in terms of a visual memory, but the whole gamut: the sights, sounds, smells, emotions, even, that hit the senses and psyche at the moment of crisis; the classic flashback, in other words.

David Johnstone was a great mentor of mine, but so too was John Rollins. Each was everything I'd come to want in a Merlin. After several years with the RAF in Germany, John returned to Wroughton in 1983 and became deputy to David, who remained the senior consultant.

The two of them couldn't have been more different. David, using that raised eyebrow to great effect, was softly spoken and a supporter of the premise that the best person to teach you is you. John, who had a big reputation in the world of psychiatry long before I met him, was the opposite: in your face, opinionated, abrasive and a big supporter of mentoring. His mother was Burmese and his father Scots-Irish, the result being he looked a little like Buddha. John took some getting used to, but it didn't take me long to see what an inspirational soul he was.

A patient came in one day – an inpatient of John's – and John asked me to take a look at him. The chap was in his early sixties and had a recent history of explosive irritability, outbursts of extreme anger that were directed primarily at his wife. He had been in the RAF, was now retired and lived locally, which was why he was referred to us. He had served in Bomber Command, on Lancasters, during the war and had been shot down and captured. He'd also been one of the poor souls forced by the SS to march from PoW camps in the east of Germany away from the advancing Allies as the war entered its final phase. In the winter of 1945, many had died during this terrible experience and those who hadn't had suffered terribly, including this man, whom I'll call Freddie.

During the march, an SS guard had rifle-butted Freddie in the head and it was thought that this might have some bearing on his behaviour changes. Basically, Freddie had become impossible to live with. His irritability had got worse and worse. To get by, he and his wife had moved into separate bedrooms. This had relieved some of the pressure, but recently things had taken a sinister and bizarre turn.

Freddie's wife would always wake him with a cup of tea. But in the last couple of weeks, whenever she had done this, he had begun jumping out of bed and attacking her.

Looking at him now, staring at me, with his sallow complexion and milky grey-blue eyes, Freddie didn't seem like someone who would beat anyone, let alone his wife.

I asked him why he did it.

'Because it's not her who wakes me.'

'Who is it then, Freddie?'

'A Gestapo officer.'

I leaned forward. 'I'm sorry?'

'It's not my wife who wakes me,' he repeated, slowly. 'It's a Gestapo officer.'

I asked Freddie to tell me what he saw. The guy he described sounded straight out of central casting: a tall, thin German wearing a long leather coat. I asked Freddie whether he'd encountered this person during the war and he nodded. The Gestapo officer had conducted his interrogation soon after he'd been captured.

'I'm only defending myself, doctor. When he was interrogating me the bastard used to beat me. But I'm not going to let him get the better of me this time. No, sir.' He held up his fists to make the point.

Later, I confronted John Rollins about this. What, I asked him, could possibly account for Freddie's behaviour?

'It's called Capgras syndrome, after a nineteenth-century French psychiatrist called Joseph Capgras, and it's pretty rare. I've never encountered a case of it before. Basically, Freddie thinks that his wife has been taken over by an impostor. It's a form of paranoid psychosis. He's hallucinating. Something his wife does, the way she opens the door, perhaps, or the way the door hinges creak, reminds him of this Gestapo officer who once interrogated him.'

I knew about Capgras syndrome, but hadn't thought of it as the underlying cause of Freddie's illness. Capgras was a paranoid syndrome made up of denial and projection. Bereaved people some-times exhibited a form of it: seeing the person they'd lost among faces in a crowd; or convincing themselves that someone they'd seen from the back was their dead loved one risen from the grave.

We treated Freddie with lots of vitamins to get his brain back up to scratch and also put him on antidepressants and tranquillizers. The antidepressants were a forerunner of Prozac called Zelmid. This was the conventional way of treating people who experienced hallu-cinations, but it left John and me feeling uncomfortable. There were echoes in Freddie's symptoms of everything we'd recently immersed ourselves in; a feeling that part of what Freddie was experiencing had been brought on by stress. But this thinking ran counter to what the textbooks said. And while the vitamins, Zelmid and tranquillizers all alleviated Freddie's symptoms, they certainly didn't cure him of them. His case made John and me more determined than ever to delve back into the causes and effects of stress, about which, at the time, remarkably little seemed to be known.

In the mid-1980s, the majority of psychiatrists, a number of them at senior levels in the British armed services, were still resistant to the validity of the concept of PTSD. At Wroughton, however, several of us began to treat patients according to the trauma theory laid down in *DSM-III*. This was the non-pathologizing model that said that the stress reaction was not due to a personality flaw, but that it had been a normal reaction to an abnormal event.

Firmly convinced that this was at least a more practical and scientifically valid way of looking at it, I now felt a great deal of guilt about the number of people I'd treated according to the pre-trauma, pathologizing model. This stated, in essence, that the trauma victim had to have had a personality flaw prior to the crisis. What is so terrible about this approach, with the clear benefit of hindsight, is that it's all about suspicion. The psychiatrist is looking for a flaw, a vulnerability in the victim right from the beginning; and when you start looking, you're always going to find something; some crack, some fissure, through which the trauma will have wriggled to do its work. The concept also relied on the victim – the survivor of the traumatic event – accepting that he or she had a predisposition and had to live with it. On this basis, of course, the pathologizing model says he or she is never going to fully recover.

My next patient was a case in point – an MoD policeman who was suffering from depression. He came to us from an RAF station up north, having been referred by his GP who asked if we'd see him because his depression wasn't getting any better; far from it, the man had been off work for months and had started to decline further and rapidly in recent weeks. After a quick chat with David Johnstone, it was agreed that we'd see him as an outpatient. If the guy was collapsing, I didn't want him to suffer the same fate as Jill.

I had a consulting room on the first floor of the Neuropsychiatric Centre. From the outside, its distance from the main hospital gave it an atmosphere of being out on a limb. By contrast, on the inside, all the rooms had big windows to let the air and light in and mine was no exception. This was useful when it came to treating patients with low mood-states. There was nothing remotely oppressive about the

Neuropsychiatric Centre at the Princess Alexandra; quite the reverse. It was a great place to work.

There was a knock on the door and the man entered. I'd already read his notes. I knew that he was married with children, in his mid-fifties and had no previous health issues to speak of, barring a car accident a year before. The notes also said he'd tried to shake off his depression by cycling a lot.

The first thing you do after carrying out a physical examination (though not in this case, because the policeman was an outpatient) is to conduct what's known as a Mental State Examination. The MSE is a formal thing, but it starts the moment a patient walks in the door. You assess the person's manner, how they're dressed, the pallor of their skin, the timbre of their voice, whether they smell of alcohol . . .

I could tell, right from the start, that this man was nervous. Although there was nothing untoward about his appearance – he was dressed neatly in a jacket, tie and slacks – his hands shook slightly as he shut the door behind him. When he looked at me, he could not hold my gaze.

'Mr Arun,' I said, already on my feet, 'please take a seat.' I shook his hand, noticed that his palm was moist, and gestured to the chair in front of my desk. He took it without saying a word.

To break the ice, I told him a bit about the Princess Alexandra and asked whether he'd had a pleasant drive south, to which I received a minimal response. Then I told him that he appeared to be a little ill at ease. 'Is that because of our meeting?'

He nodded, glanced up and looked away again.

I told him there was nothing to worry about. 'Most psychiatrists really aren't how you see them in the movies. In films, psychiatrists usually encourage the patient to lie on a couch and ramble on. In movies, psychiatrists say "Mmm" a lot and end up writing a report which you never get to see. I'm guessing you've seen those films too.'

He glanced up and gave me a wince that passed as a smile.

'I can assure you, Mr Arun, that today will be nothing like that. We're going to have a two-way discussion and I promise I'll give you my thoughts at the end so you'll be in full control of what happens. I'm going to listen very carefully to what you have to say.'

He began to relax a little.

I asked him a number of other questions, including a seemingly innocent one about the upcoming FA Cup Final – in actual fact, a stealthy googly designed to check if the chap was oriented in time and place, which he was.

Next I looked at his mood – an assessment of the level of his spirits and his energy-state. I asked him how he was feeling generally, then asked how he felt his spirits were and how he saw the future: a good lead-in usually to whether the patient was entertaining any suicidal thoughts. The MoD policeman didn't own up to any of these, but did tell me that his mood was low and repeated what his GP had written in his notes: that he'd tried to cycle his way out of his depression, but it hadn't worked; he continued to feel low, couldn't shake it and didn't know why.

I glanced down at his notes. 'I see that you recently suffered a road traffic accident. Can you tell me what happened?'

He told me in very general terms. At dawn he had been patrolling the perimeter of the base in his van. It had been misty and he hadn't noticed the tractor and trailer that had pulled out of a turning in front of him. He had hit it hard because he'd also been fiddling with the controls of the heater. He'd broken a few ribs and an ankle, but by his own assessment had got off lightly because the van had ended up totalled. I asked him whether he felt the accident had had any bearing on his mood-state, but he couldn't see a connection. All he knew was that he felt very, very depressed. He didn't use the word suicidal, but he didn't need to. This man was 'stuck' in time and didn't seem to have moved on since the accident. I was very concerned by what I saw. I thought the best thing was for us to admit him to the hospital so we could maintain a constant watch over him – he was too far away to treat as an outpatient – and he agreed.

A few days later he checked into the ward and we started to treat him with antidepressants and psychotherapy sessions. It was during one of these that he opened up about the accident. The details didn't change; there were just more of them. As he'd raised his eyes from the heater controls and realized he was about to hit the trailer, time, he said, started to slow right down. He felt completely helpless and his life flashed before his eyes. He was convinced he was going to die. He also described how he'd felt 'detached' at the time – as if he wasn't there.

After this, he spoke about the accident quite a lot and to anyone who'd listen. But talking about it, which might have been expected to be cathartic, didn't seem to help. He became a magnet for attention on the ward because he simply wouldn't respond to treatment. We debated this endlessly over the several weeks he was with us and in the end concluded, quite unjustifiably, that this was a man who didn't want to get better; that there was some 'gain' to his not responding to treatment.

In psychiatric terms, there are two types of gain. The primary gain is the resolution of the inner conflict by converting it into a physical condition such as the inability to walk or blindness, the psychological condition of dissociation which leads to disconnection from the real world and *belle indifférence* such as in Carrie's case. Secondary gain is the care and attention given by others who are concerned about the apparent disability, such as relatives, close friends and health workers. On our case discussions on a Thursday afternoon, which immediately followed our ward rounds, we concluded that this man had more to gain from being ill – i.e., secondary gain – than from being better. We thought that he was chronically depressed and that it had something to do with the accident, but there was no telling what. We had no choice, therefore, but to discharge him.

With Mr Arun and Freddie before him, John and I both felt that there was a piece missing in the jigsaw of evidence.

We were right. The missing piece was stress.

How I wish sometimes that I could turn the clock back.

Stress was something we had to be very familiar with in the Air Force. Occasionally we saw major mental illnesses such as psychosis, schizophrenia and intrinsic biological mood conditions like manic depression. But for the most part, the patients who came to us did so with stress-related problems. And just as there are formats for dealing with biological conditions, I felt I needed a format for dealing with stress-related issues – a format that would allow me to come up with treatment therapies.

Soon after John Rollins's return to Wroughton from our front-line hospital in Germany I showed him the Atomic Model. He told me he'd devised his own stress model and that it was based on a prism.

Stress, like white light, he said, would appear on one side of the prism, then split off, re-emerging the other side as a spectrum of dimensions rather than colours, with psychological, social and biological elements as the three dimensions of stress. He started to draw his 'stress prism'.

At one point in the conversation, the word 'narrative' cropped up and that struck a chord with me. To be meaningful, I thought, the stress 'story' had to have a beginning, a middle and an end. But how do you make a narrative out of stress?

'Maybe we should think of all the things that stress human beings and write them down,' I said.

John, hands together, his chin perched on the tops of his fingers, said nothing for several moments. Then he shook his head. 'You could write on every available piece of paper. You could write on the walls, the ceilings and the floor and you would never, ever come up with a complete list of stressors. And even if you thought you had, there's always some bright spark who'll come up with a stressor you hadn't thought of.'

He tapped his drawing. 'If we can split stress into dimensions, break down a stressful situation that's challenging a person, and then make a story out of it – a story that is meaningful to us and to the patient – then there's a good chance of coming up with a model that might work.'

Critics of psychiatry often complain that the way it is practised is *reductive*. They see the psychiatrist as a clinician who aspires to reduce a patient's problem to a psychological dimension. This could not be further from the truth. Psychiatry is an *expansive* discipline, not a reductive one.

John and I discussed how modern psychiatrists had the task of weaving together the psychological, social and biological strands of the development of a condition into a meaningful fabric. This is the *biopsychosocial* formulation. We talked about the dangers of seeing the way the mind and the body connect as merely *psychosomatic*, because this does not capture adequately the concept of a mind–body–brain continuum, which sees the organism as a whole machine that works in a harmonious way.

We thought that we had to look beyond dysfunctional behaviour to the underlying neurophysiological and autonomic nervous system

STRESS REACTIONS:
the Pint Pot model

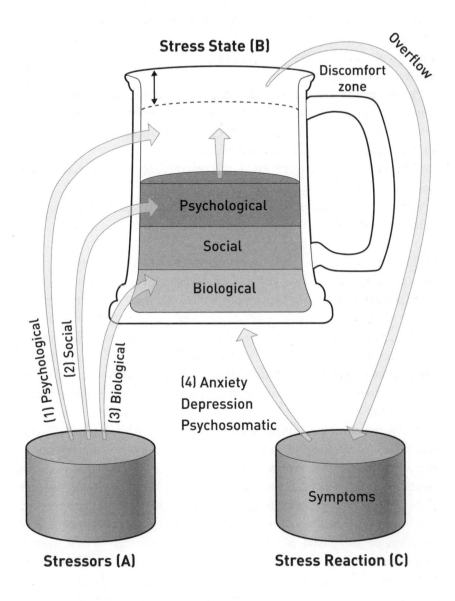

Stress State (B)

Overflow

Discomfort zone

Psychological

Social

Biological

(1) Psychological

(2) Social

(3) Biological

(4) Anxiety
Depression
Psychosomatic

Symptoms

Stressors (A)

Stress Reaction (C)

A → B → C: Evolution of stress reaction
A ← B ← C: Resolution of stress reaction

Interventions: C – Medication / psychotherapy
B – Self-regulation
A – Stress inoculation. Improving coping skills

disruptions that are the ultimate source of the symptoms and eventually lead to disease. We felt that medical science needed to shed the concept that a symptom which is not measurable by current technology is, by default, *psychological*, and therefore invalid.

Our stress model had to include three basic elements: (1) the sources of stress; (2) the amount of stress generated; and (3) the reaction to stress. In my mind's eye, I saw (2) as a kind of flask or container and in drawing it on the board – rather badly – it emerged looking like a bit like a toby jug. Perhaps inevitably, it ended up being called the 'Pint Pot Model'. Importantly, however, it had a beginning, a middle and an end. The Pint Pot Model was our narrative for stress.

In the Pint Pot Model, containers One and Three, the beginning and end of the narrative – the sources of stress and the reaction to stress – I represented as boxes. But Two, the Pint Pot, had to be open at the top in order to represent a container with a 'threshold' or 'limit'. The evolution of stress reactions, therefore, moved from One to Two to Three like a cascade. The *resolution* of stress reactions, I determined with John, moved in the opposite direction.

I got to work, taking John's three basic elements as the starting point of the narrative.

The 'stressors box' contained the personal (psychological), social and biological elements John had identified as the three-dimensional underpinnings of any stress.

The biopsychosocial model for psychiatric conditions was not an alien concept in our field. I had already discovered that it was not, or should not be, an alien concept in physical medicine. I had experienced the psychological dimension via the case of the young man who'd been admitted into the coronary care unit at Ely, only to be dismissed from the hospital by Rex Fitzgerald, and again in the case of Carrie, the young rape victim who suddenly couldn't walk, and the social dimension of the case of the lady with pneumonia.

But John and I knew we couldn't really start to stratify stress unless we had a good idea what stress was in the first place. I thought of Newton and his laws governing the physics of motion and mechanics.

The Newtonian concept of stress was that it was 'a force that moved or distorted objects'. That seemed to fit the bill, that stress in our context could be conceptualized as something 'real': a force that had an impact on the way individuals functioned, and an energy or pressure that was applied that had the capacity to distort function. A universal principle in biological science is 'homeostasis': the ability of an organism to maintain an internal state of balance or 'internal equilibrium' by adjusting its physiological processes. Stress, in whichever of the three single dimensions, or any combination of the three, puts pressure on this homeostatic balance and the struggle is to keep things on the button. A very important, life-preserving example is the maintenance of normal body temperature. Increased heat from the outside world leads to the body stepping up heat-reducing mechanisms such as sweating and, when the external environment gets colder, to increasing heat production such as shivering. Of course, the same corrective mechanisms operate when the source of the heat change comes from the inner environment of the body itself when a virus invades to produce a fever, for example. Thus, this pressure from stressors produces tension and distortion resulting in individual personal changes, social or relationship changes and biological changes, all three or any combination thereof.

The personal/psychological dimension of stress involved the generation of stress through personality factors, essentially through living with oneself or having to do a job against a background of self-underconfidence, for example. Individuals could 'carry' unresolved stress with them throughout life; or previous, unresolved traumatic experiences, for example, which might lead to underconfidence.

The social dimension involved forces generated by relationships in which the individual was involved – family life, marriage, work relationships, for example; any situation, in fact, that required rubbing shoulders with the rest of humanity. Underconfidence in interactions with others could have its roots in early development and be carried over into later life from background issues such as childhood trauma.

The biological dimension generated stress from the effect of medical conditions on biological function – conditions such as diabetes, the invasion of a virus or the taking of medication, for example. In the Air Force world this dimension would also include heat stress, cold stress, gravitational stress (pulling 'G' in fast jets), altitude stress and other stresses generated by flying.

The idea was that each of these dimensions of stress would make a contribution to the whole. It would be usual for each dimension to contribute a small amount of stress each day, but there would be times when one, two or, in the case of a 'bad hair day', all three dimensions would light up simultaneously.

Take the case of a businessman who arrives home in the UK after a flight from the Far East. He's already physically exhausted and jet-lagged so his biological stressor dimension is burning bright. Things are worse than that because he is phobic about flying and has had no choice but to fly, so the personal dimension is activated. And then he gets home to find that his wife has run off with her tennis coach, which will activate the social dimension. Such a person will be under considerable strain as a result of the impact of a great deal of stress from all three directions and will either be fully loaded up with stress or come close to the threshold.

The stress loading container has a finite capacity. It can only take so much. It helps to see the container as being filled up by a liquid stress medium – hence the Pint Pot as a suitable image. The pot represents the amount of stress hormones generated to meet the current challenges.

It is also important to see that the stresses generated by psycho-logical, social and biological dimensions are all the same when they are dumped in the stress loading container. One source can no longer be distinguished from another.

The level of stress will fluctuate, depending on circumstances. The level will rise if any single dimension, all three, or any combination of the three is activated. As the level rises there will be a sense of growing tension. Then the experience will enter an 'alarm zone' as the final threshold approaches. Eventually, the level will reach the top of the container and the stress will spill over the edge.

The stress reactions box itself represents the constitution of the individual and is the accustomed way for that individual to react to an over-accumulation of stress; as I'd seen with Jill and her step-by-step collapse – and my next patient, a girl who provided me with my first real test as to whether, so to speak, the Pint Pot Model held water or not.

Janine was a pretty girl in her mid-twenties, a corporal who worked as an air stewardess on the RAF's transatlantic route, usually on VC10s, and usually on the diplomatic flight between London and Washington. She had been referred to me by the senior medical officer at RAF Brize Norton in Oxfordshire, the RAF's hub for personnel transport aircraft, around an hour's drive from Wroughton. She had developed a sudden and very deep depression and the SMO had been unable to find any cause for it. The poor girl had descended into such a deep black hole that she had become utterly unable to function and had been taken off flying duties altogether.

The SMO was very worried about her. He rang me on a Friday to check if I'd be able to see her the following week. As it happened, I was free that afternoon so I asked him to send her over straight away.

She was in bad shape – so listless that she slumped down in the chair in front of me and then proceeded to stare blankly over my shoulder out of the window. Over her shoulder, on the whiteboard, I caught sight of my rather primitive drawing of the Pint Pot. I had already resolved to use it. Faced with Janine's very real distress, I only hoped it worked.

As in any other case, the beginning of Janine's stress narrative was represented by the stressors box in the model. John's prism analogy had been very helpful because it had enabled me to see that the stressors box could be split into psychological, social and biological components – the three primary colours that would determine the next part of the narrative: the middle of the story, the Pint Pot, the stress vessel itself.

I started off by looking for any psychological factors, therefore, that could have sent this girl into her spiral. I asked her what she could remember about her childhood, her schooldays, whether she enjoyed married life, her job in the RAF . . . but I turned up a blank. There were no anomalies at all. Her childhood had been happy, she loved her husband and she'd been supremely happy in her job. So I moved on to the social dimension, asking her how much she and her husband went out in a given week (they had no children), whether they had friends, whether she was ever lonely, if she played sports . . . But all I turned up was a healthy girl, who'd seemed perfectly happy prior to her depression, who had played lots of sports, had plenty of friends and who was at a complete loss to know what had turned her life upside down in this way.

So I moved on to the biological dimension, asking her about childhood illnesses (the normal range) or adult illnesses (none). The only vague factor was that she was on the pill, but as she had been on it for several years and hadn't developed any problems before I discounted this as the gremlin that could have caused her stress levels to cascade into the Pint Pot.

All of which seemed to point to an endogenous stress reaction: a reaction in someone who has a genetic predisposition towards depression, something that is hard-wired into only one per cent of the population and even then may never come out.

So I went back to the stressors box and probed again and this time, for some reason, I thought to ask her about her training.

'How,' I asked, 'as you trained for your present job, did you find the regime?'

'Easy,' she told me. 'Very enjoyable, in fact. We flew a lot, but it never bothered me. They were short hops mainly. Quite a few of them were to Deci . . .' Her voice trailed off and I suspected I knew why. Decimomannu was a base in Sardinia where NATO fighter crews practised their air combat techniques. Surrounded by beaches and bars, and kissed by clear blue seas and warm winds, the base was a highly popular destination for RAF personnel. To this girl, in her present state, Deci must have seemed like a lifetime ago; or a part of somebody else's life, not her own.

I brought her back to the here and now. A little voice was telling me I had missed something – something important. I rewound the clock and asked her about the nature of the flights she'd made. 'Short hops', she'd said.

She nodded.

'North–south mostly?'

Again she nodded.

And that, I realized, must have been it. The circadian rhythm, the way in which our body responds naturally to the 24-hour cycle of day and night, can be heavily disrupted by trans-meridian, east--west/west–east flight, the result being jet lag. During her training, Janine had flown north–south and had never had a problem. But when she had gone 'operational', her beat had been the transatlantic route.

I looked at her and smiled. 'Janine, I think we've cracked it.' I picked up the phone and dialled the number of her SMO at Brize. It rang and rang and I checked my watch, wondering if I'd missed him, but eventually he picked up.

'Colin, I want you to put Janine back on flying duties.'

There was a momentary pause on the other end of the line. 'But she's not well, Gordon.'

'I know.' I looked at Janine, who was staring at me in a bemused way. 'She needs to go back on to flying duties, but only on north–south routes. No more east–west flying for a while. Is that clear?'

'Doesn't she need to go on antidepressants?'

'No. Trust me. This is going to work.'

And it did. Janine went back on to short hop duties, flying north–south routes, and quickly made a complete recovery. As soon as we knew she was better, Colin and I discussed her case and agreed she could be tried out on east–west flying duties again. This time she coped fine and the depression never returned. I was delighted for her and I was delighted for us – John and me. The Pint Pot Model appeared to hold up fine, too. The vessel itself could be filled with all three types of stressors – the psychological, social and biological kinds – it could be filled with two of them, or, as in Janine's case, just one. Previously, when we'd asked the question of a distressed patient, 'Can you think of anything that might have triggered this depression?' a number of people would have been unable to think of any particular factor. This was certainly true with Janine. The temptation then for us as psychiatrists was to reach for the endogenous answer: that he or she had a predisposition towards depression, a statistically unlikely explanation. But here, in the model, we had a system that was far more scientific and which appeared to work. Not only that but, by reversing the narrative, we had a means of restoring the patient to full health as well.

*

John and I made two important discoveries after we started to use
this model.

First, the identified stress reaction in Box Three often became a
stressor in itself, sometimes because of its actual effect. A depression,
for example, can slow down memory-processing and this would
cause stress in an individual who has an occupation requiring speed
of thought and intact cognitive power. This was probably the reason
why Janine was able to muster the strength and motivation to get
back to flying, at first north to south. She was reassured that she was
not suffering from an irreversible illness and that the way she
was was not going to be a life sentence.

In the form of PTSD, a stress reaction would hamper the performance of a soldier in the field recurrently exposed to the dangers
of combat. There is always the stigma caused by the stress reaction
and this would generate further stress. This adds a fourth dimension
of stressors in the stressor box that forms the start of the stress
narrative. Furthermore, this secondary stressor-source could continue to fill up the Pint Pot, even after the original over-accumulation
of stress from the dimensions of psychological, social and biological
sources have waned and are no longer capable of filling up the pot
on their own.

This explanation for 'chronicity' – long-term suffering – can be
very helpful to patients who cannot understand why the symptoms
have not disappeared despite the reduced (or even absent) initiating
causes.

Second, we discovered that the model worked backwards.
Forwards was *evolution* and backwards was *resolution*. Resolving
factors associated with Box Three included identification of the
nature of the stress reaction and appropriate biological and psychological treatments.

For the Pint Pot, therefore, it might be possible to fit a tap which
would allow stress to drain away as it accumulated and might even
prevent the threshold being reached and breached in the first place.
This would involve training in stress-management techniques and
would include a wide range of activities. The best thing about learning how to 'open the tap' *oneself* when feeling tense and stressed and
under strain – without reaching for a pill or a beer or a doctor –

would be that it would boost self-esteem and a sense of being in control.

It would work, we surmised, mainly by stimulating the release of endorphins, the body's own opiates. Ideally, all individuals who operate in a stressful environment of whatever type should use a stress-busting activity as a matter of course to prevent becoming ill and to optimize performance. What coal miner doesn't have a shower at the end of each shift to wash away the accumulated debris of his job? What nuclear power plant worker would dream of avoiding the decontamination process after a day at work?

Box One offered therapeutic exploration of the three dimensions of stress.

For example, if a marital problem was generating stress then that could be identified and treated to reduce the overall stress loading.

The Pint Pot theory drew heavily on the General System Theory of an Austrian-born biologist called Ludwig von Bertalanffy, who died in 1972. Von Bertalanffy believed that a general theory of systems 'should be an important regulative device in science,' to guard against superficial analogies that 'are useless in science and harmful in their practical consequences.' This is to try to understand the parts in relation to the whole: in contrast to Descartes's scientific reductionism, it proposes to view systems in a holistic manner by examining the linkages and interactions between the elements that compose the whole system.

As far as I was concerned, it boiled down to one thing: what you had to do was listen, be curious and explore.

Whether help arrived in the form of medicine or psychological first aid, the important thing was to make the patient feel safe. As I had witnessed with Jill, when the patient felt safe – i.e., no longer in a place where he or she was in freefall, feeling out of control – the body's own remarkable defence systems would come alive and kick in.

Describing our stress model in terms of a pint pot might not have endeared us to the intellectual elite, but it enabled John and me to visualize stress and how to treat it.

'You know, GT,' John said one day, soon after we'd put the finishing touches to the model, 'your background in general medicine may actually be preventing you from becoming a really good psychiatrist.'

He laughed and so did I but something tugged at my thinking as soon as he said it and it took me a few moments to understand what it was.

Tony Gunn, my irascible mentor at Edinburgh, had once said the same thing to me – about my capacity to become a surgeon – but the difference was Tony had meant it.

I sat back in my chair and muttered softly under my breath: 'Bingo.'

John looked at me. 'What did you say?'

I glanced back at him, but by now I was miles away. I wasn't just in the operating theatre at Edinburgh. My mind was bouncing between images of Tony Gunn at Bangour and Chris Furse on Elephant Island.

Unlike Gunn and Furse, John Rollins hadn't reacted angrily when I'd let my curiosity run free. John had not seen the sharing of ideas as a capitulation; he hadn't seen me as challenging him.

John could be pretty frightening when he wanted to be, but somehow he'd taken my ideas, run with them, added to them, then used the result to inspire me to work harder and do better, until, between us, we'd come up with something really useful – a tool not only for understanding stress but, potentially, for treating it.

But that was just a part of my eureka moment. Miss Roberts and the Wee Red Box, I realized, had traumatized me – not in any hugely significant way, perhaps, but enough for me to have reacted in some manner to any kind of imposed learning; the kind espoused by the people I'd had my run-ins with. There was I thinking it was about *them* – and it was, in part – but it was mainly about *me*. These people had reacted, chemically almost, to *me*; and I had not seen this for what it was: a life lesson. It was almost as if Mother Nature, in her wisdom, had re-presented Miss Roberts to me in other guises – in the form of Gunn and of Furse – in a bid to get me to learn from these experiences.

And from this, I'd glimpsed something else.

The characteristic signature of PTSD was the flashback – a replay of the signature event that was so real it was as if the survivor was there, reliving the trauma all over again. It was such a full depiction of the event that it was accompanied by emotions, too – as if the terror that you felt during the time frame of the trauma was playing out for real as an accompaniment to the pictures.

Why, I wondered, did the mind do this?

The way I saw it, there were two clocks running for PTSD survivors: a real-world clock that continued to tick away, the same as it does for everyone; and one that had stopped because of the trauma.

Getting the survivor to a place of mental safety was the key to bringing these two clocks in line; to getting them to tick together.

But so, it seemed to me, was understanding. The flashback appeared to be the brain's way of saying: look at this, because I don't understand what has happened to me; what *is* happening to me.

Oh, and by the way, it adds, if you don't address this, I'm going to make you see this thing, experience it in all its horrors, over and over again.

In the same way that nature had allowed Jill to climb back through her protection shells one by one, the flashback seemed to have a purpose. I had no idea what that purpose was yet, but it appeared to be as much about a natural defence mechanism against PTSD as a symptom of it.

Chapter 7

Staring into the Unconscious Mind

Most of 1985 was taken up with a hard core of us at Wroughton, led by John Rollins, trying to get to grips with the central features of PTSD. For John, there was a deeply personal element to this: his son, who was an RAF fighter-controller, went AWOL after a helicopter he should have been on board crashed, killing all the occupants. When finally he returned to the fold, he was diagnosed as having a personality disorder. It wasn't us who saw him, so it was hard to be sure, but I didn't see it this way at all and John didn't either. A Norwegian psychiatrist had told me of a similar case involving a patient who should have been on board a South African Airways 747 that crashed into the Indian Ocean, killing all the passengers. The psychiatrist's patient was consumed with guilt about someone – a man he didn't even know – who'd got on to the flight instead of him. The intensity of this feeling manifested itself as PTSD – flashbacks, repeated over and over, of the plane going down, replete with all the terror of those final moments. With John's son, it must have been similar and I saw his going AWOL as a natural avoidance reaction straight out of the *DSM-III* manual.

It's hard to say whether knowledge of John's personal situation drove us harder to find a solution to PTSD, but there was a real sense of urgency to get to the root of it during the mid-eighties. Even after

DSM-III, it became, in British military circles especially, the great unspoken issue, the elephant in the room.

We got the distinct impression from some of the people we encountered in Whitehall that it was seen as a contaminant: who else, they seemed to think, might 'catch' PTSD, if we acknowledged it to be real? There were others, I'm sure, who denied it because it appeared to drive a stake through their selection criteria. The British armed forces pride themselves, and rightly so, on the way they recruit their soldiers, sailors and aircrew. In the 1980s, there were certainly those who seemed to think that PTSD undermined this process, when in fact, in my view, it did quite the reverse. If a trauma can 'pierce' anyone faced with an 'abnormal event', it had nothing to do with the selection process. But saying someone had a personality disorder because they'd gone AWOL was an awful lot tidier than acknowledging it might have been a natural way of reacting to an extremely traumatic event. While personality disorders were real enough, they did not provide a catch-all explanation for PTSD. The personality disorder label, applied incorrectly, was little different from the stigmatizing effect of the labels of 'shell shock' and 'LMF' bandied about by the military during the First and Second World Wars.

Up until the 1980s, psychiatry had been driven by psychoanalysis but our arrival at Wroughton coincided with the emergence in the UK of cognitive therapy as an effective treatment for conditions such as depression.

Psychoanalysis, as a form of therapy, is based on the understanding that human beings are largely unaware of the mental processes that determine their thoughts, feelings and behaviour and that psychological suffering can be alleviated by making those processes known to the individual. Sigmund Freud originally developed the theory and technique of psychoanalysis in the 1890s. Freud's ideas are still used in contemporary practice. However, many have been further developed or refined and some even abandoned.

The theory and technique of psychoanalysis continue to integrate new insights about human development and behaviour based on psychoanalytical research and discoveries from related fields. Different schools of psychoanalytical theory have evolved out of the original Freudian one, reflecting a range of ideas and perspectives.

Cognitive therapy, on the other hand, is all about helping the patient change dysfunctional thinking and behavioural and emotional patterns. It was first developed by American psychiatrist Aaron Beck in the 1960s. In simple terms, if a person comes to believe that they are useless at work on the basis of a single mistake, this can lead to thinking and behavioural activities that reinforce this view, thereby perpetuating the cycle and initiating or deepening a depression.

Cognitive therapy addresses the way the patient thinks and behaves in response to similar situations by developing more flexible ways to think and respond in future. This, done successfully, allows the patient over time to escape the negative behavioural and dysfunctional thought patterns and prompts the depression to lift. With PTSD, John Rollins saw a relationship between analysis and cognitive therapy in understanding and treating PTSD and encouraged us to use all the tools at our disposal to get to the heart of the condition.

One of the huge benefits of having two mentors at this time – 'tormentors', as I jokingly call them today – was that I could cherry-pick ideas from both of them.

David Johnstone, for example, was a strong proponent of hypnosis in the treatment of panic attacks. Hypnosis helped people revisit memories and impressions of events that their conscious minds had long forgotten, chosen to forget or had not fully known, perhaps because they weren't available to them in full consciousness. It allowed them to explore their unconscious – where there were secrets relevant to their condition that were hidden from them, or perhaps intentionally buried.

If someone has suppressed something, the golden rule is not to uncover things in hypnosis that the patient doesn't want uncovered. It's an entirely voluntary pact the two of you – doctor and patient – have entered into.

Hypnosis remains a valid tool available to the psychiatrist for finding out a patient's unconscious thoughts or impressions – as long as they are willing to share them with you. It relies on heavy measures of trust and empathy. It removes the paraphernalia of everyday existence to enable the patient to focus exclusively on the thing that is distressing them. Hypnosis is thus an interesting mixture of deep relaxation and heightened focus.

In his early career, David Johnstone had found hypnosis useful in the treatment of panic attacks because panic attacks have a starting point, but the starting point is often obscured by subsequent panic attacks.

Panic attacks are ferociously unpleasant adrenaline surges that have a strong psychological impact. The physical impact is pretty strong too, with heart palpitations, sweating and feelings of being out of control, to the extent that sufferers often describe *angor animi*, the feeling that one is about to die. These effects can be so unpleasant and debilitating that the sufferer will go to great lengths to avoid them and this is why the first panic attack – the only really legitimate one, in my opinion – can become obscured over time. As well as fear they can also become obscured by shame, guilt and anger.

David had stopped using hypnosis prior to my arrival at Wroughton, because, he said, it took an inordinate length of time and therefore interfered with other pressing matters in the course of a typical day. But when I talked to him about it, he swore that it worked. Encouraged that someone so unerringly professional could rely on what, on the face of it (certainly at that time), seemed a rather other-worldly technique, I decided to go and learn for myself.

The best place to go was a weekend course taught by dentists in Bristol who represented the British Medical and Dental Hypnosis Society. Dentists use hypnosis because quite a lot of patients have an irrational fear of the anaesthetic needle and the pain involved in dental treatment, and I knew that it was – and still is – often very useful in treating children. I turned up with a colleague, John Todd, a trainee RAF psychiatrist who'd recently arrived at Wroughton. John had come from general practice and was a fellow Scot, from Aberdeen. He was as keen as I was to learn this seemingly exotic technique.

The method was relatively simple. It was explained to the class that hypnotherapy was a way to use guided relaxation, intense concentration and focused attention to achieve a heightened state of awareness – the 'trance'. The patient's attention is so focused while in this state that anything going on around them is temporarily blocked out or ignored. Hypnosis is a naturally occurring state that we have all experienced from time to time ('A penny for your thoughts?'). But with the help of a trained therapist a person may focus his or her attention on specific thoughts or tasks. Hypnotherapy is usually considered to be an aid to psychotherapy rather than a treatment in itself, because the hypnotic state allows people to explore painful thoughts, feelings and memories they may have hidden from their conscious minds.

The word 'Hypnosis' is derived from the Greek word for 'sleep' and sleep it is definitely not! It was introduced into the psychiatrists' repertoire during the 1890s at the Salpetrière Hospital in Paris, while Freud and Jean-Martin Charcot, the leading pathologists and neurologists of their day, were practising there.

At that time, hypnosis had acquired a bad reputation in the medical profession in part due to the efforts earlier in the century of Franz Anton Mesmer, a German physician, who had developed some highly controversial and dramatic techniques for the treatment of insanity with his theories of Animal Magnetism. But Freud, Charcot and others, who were responsible for the first principles of modern psychiatry, believed that hypnosis could not only unlock the secrets of the unconscious mind, but that it had a strong role in unlocking buried trauma.

In Bristol, we were taught the 'eye-fixation' method to induce the trance, with the patient staring at the end of a finger or some other object such as the tip of a pen, while being coaxed to relax through the use of breathing exercises and muscle relaxation techniques. Once the trance was induced, we were taught how to use the 'arm-raising strengthening technique' to deepen the trance-like state.

The time soon arrived when we were told by our tutors to practise on a partner – mine being John. John's attempts to put me under were only mildly successful; I ended up feeling comfortably drowsy, but not remotely susceptible to his suggestions that my right arm felt so light that it would float off towards the ceiling – the raising of the arm being the sign that the subject was 'under'.

When it came to my turn, John kept asking me to try a bit harder, because nothing was happening. I felt frustrated we weren't getting anywhere, but our tutors explained that practice was key. So, fighting my impatience to carry on trying, we drifted back into the lecture theatre for another round of instruction.

A couple of minutes into the lecture, John gave me a nudge.

'What is it?' I kept scribbling, my mind already struggling with the note-taking process; half my brain trying to listen to what was being said, while the other half wrote down something that had been said moments earlier. Any intrusions and my rhythm threatened to unravel.

'Can you take notes for me, Gordon?' John whispered.

'Why can't you take them?' I shot back.

'Because my hand won't work.'

I stopped writing and looked at him. John had a reputation for joshing around, so I gave him the David Johnstone eyebrow.

'Seriously,' he protested. 'I can't move my arm at all.'

A month or so later, I saw a new patient (new to me, although he had already been seen by just about every other RAF psychiatrist). He was an RAF flight sergeant from St Athan in Wales who was suffering from intermittent panic attacks. They were severe and disabling when they struck and they happened when he travelled, not every time but with enough frequency for it to have seriously interfered with his work.

It didn't make any difference what form of transport he took, either; the attacks would hit him in cars and trains, as well as on aircraft. Flight Sergeant Thomas 'Tommy' Brown was also hampered in pursuing his main hobby, sea fishing from a boat, because he had experienced panic attacks on the water too.

This was intended to be a routine check, because Brown had already been seen by just about everybody else and the huge pile of notes proved the point. He had been permanently medically downgraded from flying and was restricted to duty within the UK only.

I looked at his notes, saw he was taking a drug called clomipramine to control the attacks, but noticed, too, that there was no mention of when the first attack had struck – and physicians, being pernickety, like to pinpoint the exact onset of an illness. As a physician by training, this attention to detail had never left me, thanks to my old boss, Fredoon Amroliwalla. I asked, therefore, if he could remember and he told me it was while returning to the UK from Aden, where he had served during the insurgency war in the 1960s. It had been quite a hairy posting and he had always attributed the first attack to the stress of the deployment. He was 18 at the time and had been serving in the RAF no more than a few months. I asked him for further details, but that was it: he'd told me all he could remember.

I had been very impressed by hypnosis and thought about what had happened to John Todd only a few weeks previously. It seemed to me that if Flight Sergeant Brown had been suffering from panic attacks for many years and he was vague about what had happened to him in Aden, then it was possible he might have suppressed a painful thought, memory or feeling; and that, as they had said on the course, it might be 'hidden from his conscious mind'.

To my surprise and delight he agreed to come back a week later when I set aside a Friday afternoon, a quiet, reflective time in our schedule.

I wasn't sure how long a hypnosis session would take, never having done one before. It might take only minutes to find out that it wouldn't work at all, but there was nothing to lose and my willing patient was very keen to get rid of the panic anxiety, not only because it had wrecked his career but because it was extremely frightening when it occurred, as the high levels of adrenaline surged round his body and he felt completely out of control. There were times when these feelings set in that he thought he might not survive.

If he was apprehensive, then he wasn't half as apprehensive as I was. But I recall that neither of us showed it. My main worry was that if I could induce the trance, would I be able to reverse it? I figured, however, that David Johnstone was in the building and could step in if I got myself into trouble.

'Have you ever been hypnotized before?' I asked him.

Brown shook his head. He looked petrified.

I told him that it wouldn't take him completely out of this world; that he would, to a large degree, be consciously aware of things going on around him. Finally, I reassured him that I'd be able to bring him back at any time if he became uncomfortable with any part of the process, and that he would be able to break the trance as well. I crossed my fingers that David was somewhere nearby if I suddenly had to call upon him.

I decided to use the eye-fixation technique I'd learned in Bristol and got Tommy to lie down while I sat on a chair next to him. I then asked him to follow the tip of my finger, which I placed six inches from his eyes.

Slowly, I raised my finger towards his forehead until, from his point of view, the tip disappeared into his eyebrows. I then brought it back until it was just visible at the uppermost point of his gaze. This had the effect of straining his upper eyelids.

'Your eyelids are becoming very heavy, very tired, Tommy. Try not to close your eyes. You'll get an opportunity to close them very shortly.'

As he gazed at the point of my finger, I could see the pupils of his eyes beginning to dilate – a sure sign that he was about to go under.

'I'm going to count to ten and then I'd like you to close your eyes.'

I started to count. 'Your eyes are getting very tired now.'

He closed them.

'Your head is sinking back into the pillow. And now your shoulders are feeling heavy . . .' I went through all the other areas of his body that were in contact with the couch, telling him that each – his back, his arms, his legs and his heels – was sinking into it. Then I repeated this a number of times, remembering to tell him every few seconds that he was perfectly safe and relaxed; that nothing untoward could happen to him.

I then moved on to the clincher. I told him that his right hand was feeling lighter than the left hand and because of this it was beginning to float away, as if pulled upwards by a balloon.

I got a bit of a twitch, which was evidence that he was resisting. So I began to say: 'You shouldn't take this to mean I'm controlling you, Tommy; quite the opposite. This is proof that you are perfectly safe and relaxed. The higher your hand goes, the more safe and relaxed you are.'

At this, his right hand began to lift into the air.

I felt like giving a whoop of joy. This, we were taught, was the moment the patient, via his subconscious, was giving you permission to continue.

'Now, Tommy, is it all right if I ask you a few questions?'

'Yes.'

There are no ghostly voices in hypnosis. Tommy spoke normally, albeit in a slightly dull, flat way. I knew he was now in a trance.

I asked him to go back to the first attack and in the same tone of voice, level and monotonous, he started to describe a train journey to his fiancée in Essex.

'I thought you said it was on your way back from Aden,' I interrupted gently.

'No, that's not right, not exactly,' Tommy said. 'This was after the flight landed.'

I asked him to take me back to the very beginning. What had prompted him to travel back to England in the first place?

Tommy, it transpired, had been allowed to go back to the UK on compassionate leave. His father, to whom he was devoted, had fallen ill and it was thought that he wouldn't survive. Tommy was woken up in the middle of the night and given immediate leave to travel to the hospital in Plymouth, where his father was being treated, but it was touch and go whether he would make it in time – his dad was that ill.

The way he described this, his face contorting with the memories of it all, I knew that this was real enough, but what about his recall?

I tried to get Tommy right back to the flight. I asked him what he had been wearing. He told me in precise detail, right down to the colour of his socks. I asked him what type of aircraft it was. It was a Viscount. I asked him if he was sitting next to someone. Yes, he told me, a major, and he recalled his name, what he was wearing and what they talked about.

Now this was really remarkable. I was truly astounded at the detail Tommy could recall. Any inkling of a thought that he might be putting me on, that it was an elaborate spoof on his part to take revenge on the psychiatric profession, was instantly and completely washed away on the tide of what happened next.

All I did was to ask Tommy if he had had anything to eat on the flight.

He suddenly sat bolt upright, spat and said: 'Yuk, those mashed potatoes were bloody awful!' He was still in a trance with his eyes closed.

I came as close then as I've ever come to having a panic attack myself. I was in no doubt about the power of hypnosis and I decided to move on in the story.

When he'd touched down at RAF West Drayton, he was presented with a dilemma. Should he head straight down to Plymouth, where his father was battling to stay alive, or should he go to his fiancée's home in Essex and pick her up before travelling to Plymouth? If he chose the latter course, his father might already have died by the time he got to Plymouth. Because he was in such an emotional state, he didn't want to confront his father on his deathbed alone. In the end, after debating this with himself endlessly, he decided to jump on a train and go to his fiancée's and it was there, on the train to Essex, that the first panic attack occurred. Being 'there', he was choked with emotion as he told me this.

It didn't take a genius to work out that at times of heightened stress these attacks would return, hitting him when he was most vulnerable: while he was travelling.

'The panic attack was an honest expression of how you felt at the time. Do you see that?' I said.

He nodded.

'What happened to your father?'

'He got better.' Tommy smiled. 'He's still alive. Loves his grand-children every bit as much as he loved me.'

'Do you think, now that you understand why you've been having these attacks, that you need to continue having them, Tommy?'

He shook his head.

'Shall we agree, then, right here, that you won't have them any more because you don't need to?'

Yes, he said, let's agree on that.

After this session, Tommy never had another attack. His medication was slowly discontinued because he had been on it for so long. His medical employment standard was readjusted. But there was an interesting twist to his story.

About six months later, I found myself running a fortnightly clinic at RAF St Athan. I was parking the car one day when the senior medical officer, whom I knew well, rushed out of the clinic waving his arms in the air. This wasn't like the usually unflappable Bill I knew. Something was up.

'Thank God,' he said, dragging me out of the car. 'There's a woman having a panic attack in the waiting room. Can you deal with her?'

It turned out to be Tommy's wife. She had been supporting him for so long after Aden that her tension had built and built. When she recovered her breath she told me that it was only recently that she had realized Tommy was 'cured' and she really could regard him as being fixed. All of that tension, not let go immediately after the hypnosis because of her fear of a false dawn, had just released itself that morning in a huge surge of adrenaline. It was like a catharsis, a massive panic attack; the kind where the four walls seem to be closing in on you and you can't breathe.

I did not need to hypnotize her, because this was her first attack and it's the first one that's key, the one that is an authentic expression of the stress being felt at the time. The series of panic attacks after the first one seems to be reminding the sufferer that they haven't yet understood why that first one happened. It would seem a rather harsh way of doing this, and it would be if no further exploration was undertaken. That's why hypnosis is so useful: it is a gentle way to unlock stressful memories so that they can be processed and not remain hidden in the unconscious part of the mind.

With Tommy's wife, it was enough simply to get her to understand that the panic attack wasn't some random assault on her normally well-balanced existence. It had come about because she had been experiencing referred anxiety from Tommy.

When she understood this, I told her that it was highly unlikely she would experience any more attacks, and this turned out to be the case.

Chapter 8

The Darkness before the Dawn

Treating Tommy and his wife was a stepping-stone to my under-standing of PTSD. In PTSD the flashbacks usually involved surges of adrenaline similar to panic attacks but elaborated by vivid re-collections of what was seen, heard, smelt, tasted and touched at the time of the trauma. To cause PTSD it was as if the surge of adrenaline was so enormous that it 'burnt' into the memory of the survivor the details of the entire event in order to leave its mark, so that it would not be forgotten. In Tommy's case, as in all other cases of panic attack, he re-experienced the emotion of fear that he'd felt at the time of the original attack: on the train travelling to his fiancée. Panic attacks are an emotional response to fear that is stored in the brain and subsequent stimuli will reproduce that fear, only without the important signature characteristics of PTSD: the smells, sights and sounds of the traumatic encounter. Panic attacks aren't usually dissociative either. With panic attacks, you remain fully aware of the here and now; with flashbacks, all the situational memories come back too – you are, in effect, so immersed in them it's as if you're back there, reliving the trauma in all its horrors.

Just as sufferers from panic attacks learn to avoid places where they have happened, because they fear the association will trigger off another panic episode if they return, individuals with PTSD learn to avoid reminders of their trauma. Perhaps a difference between the two conditions is the type of experience which triggers them. Panic-anxiety attacks are associated with exposure to highly stressful and frightening events. PTSD is the way that we respond to life-threat.

With the benefit of hindsight, the Cold War might seem static – a 40-year period in which nothing much happened – but that wasn't how it felt to a member of Her Majesty's armed forces serving in West Germany in 1985. The tempo of RAF operations at bases such as Wildenrath and Brüggen, where fighter crews mounted round-the-clock patrols in readiness against a Soviet invasion, was relentless and psychiatry was viewed as having an important role to play in easing the pressure in what could at times be a very stressful work regime.

In mid-1985, I was posted to the RAF hospital at Wegberg, close to Rheindahlen. I was an almost 'time-expired' senior specialist by then, 37 years old, and planning to wait another six months before putting in my application for consultancy.

Wegberg was viewed as a key posting because of its position and role in West Germany. When the RAF split the psychiatry and neurology roles a year or so beforehand, I'd already decided to concentrate on psychiatry. Bob Merry, my doubly qualified counterpart, luckily wanted to focus on neurology so there was no problem. Before I could become a consultant psychiatrist, however, I had to pass something known as the Armed Services Consultancy Assessment Board, ASCAB, a formal review that would entail my being grilled before a panel of senior military medics, who would assess my readiness to become a consultant. This is a somewhat different process from the National Health Service, where physicians, surgeons and psychiatrists have to earn credits before they graduate to consultancy. In the military it's more about earning ticks in boxes and a posting to RAF Germany was seen as a big tick. All being well, I would be qualified to sit the ASCAB in the latter part of the year.

RAF Germany was a good place to be all ways round in 1986. As professionals, we felt happy and valued and the psychiatric ward at Wegberg was a very well-run affair with a solid reputation for best practice. My expectation was that I would take over as the consultant psychiatrist in Germany as soon as my predecessor departed.

John Rollins had just left the RAF to work for the Royal Navy as a civilian. His departure had come as a shock to those who'd not been in the loop over what had happened to his son. His leaving created a ripple in our community, because John had long been seen as the heir-apparent to the post of psychiatric consultant adviser within the RAF.

He was the front-runner to replace Group Captain Angus Black, a fine man who had played scrum-half for the Scottish rugby team and had been a stalwart of the successful British Lions tours to New Zealand and South Africa in the early 1950s. My father told me that he had seen him play at Murrayfield and was very impressed that I had been working under his leadership at Wroughton, where he was consultant adviser in psychiatry.

Angus, in fact, had first introduced me to the team at the Neuropsychiatric Centre in 1976 when I was preparing for our Antarctic adventure. I had betrayed an early interest in his subject when I decided to run a study on resilience and the development of team relationships under expedition conditions. He and the rest of the team of psychiatrists at Wroughton had been very helpful in developing a strategy for the study. I also had another study in mind, more medicine-based, to look at the nutritional value of our compo rations by measuring key indices in the blood and vitamin levels before and after the expedition. This I hoped to do by taking blood samples from expedition members and having them analysed in our laboratory at RAF Hospital Ely, where I was based.

Consultant adviserships were supposed to go to middle-grade consultants – 'young bloods' – to give them experience of dealing with senior leadership. The job of the psychiatric consultant adviser was to advise the RAF's Director General Medical Services on psychiatric matters, having gathered opinions beforehand from his or her consultants. But the role had developed over time into a kind of kingship and people tended to hold on to it as long as possible.

Fortunately, none of the above had anything to do with me. I was happy simply to be in a posting that had a real buzz about it. I was also counting the days to my ASCAB and the prospect of becoming a consultant.

By now Alison and I had had two more sons, Stuart and Robert.

After an administrative cock-up that prevented Alison and the boys from joining me for the first six weeks of the posting, the five of us eventually settled into our married quarters in Rheindahlen in the late summer. Iain was six by now, Stuart five and Bobby, our youngest, just one.

For a family with young children, the northern part of West Germany, close to the Dutch border, was an idyllic place to be. Because the area was completely flat, people cycled everywhere and we tended to be out and about the whole time. After a couple of months, we were settled. I'd always liked the travel element of the job, but to be able to do so with the family was a real bonus. We were close to the centre of Western Europe and we did not waste the opportunity. We made frequent trips around West Germany, visited West and East Berlin and saw the Wall. We also made forays into Belgium and Holland and even as far as Spain.

One day, Rex Fitzgerald, whom I'd first encountered at Ely and who was now the consultant physician at Wegberg, came to see me. He was clearly at his wits' end over something and I asked him what the problem was.

'It's a patient,' he told me wearily. 'I can't make out what the problem is. He's an RAF policeman, been here a few months. Arrived here looking like Twiggy and has ballooned in weight bigger than Giant Haystacks—'

'You are kidding me.'

'Somewhat, but you get my drift. This guy has put on a lot of weight, GT. I mean a lot. And none of us can understand why.'

Rex went on to tell me that they'd put him on starvation rations – 500 calories a day – and had been keeping him on the ward under supervision for a month. But the bloke had hardly lost any weight at all.

I knew that Rex hadn't come to see me without good cause. 'What can I do to help?'

'There is no medical reason why this man is putting on weight. I wondered if you'd take a look at him.'

This was quite an admission from someone who'd once sent a man home who thought he was having a heart attack – ignoring any psychological explanations for the distress that had brought him to hospital in the first place.

'What do you think I might be able to do?' I asked Rex.

'Well,' he said, looking distinctly ill at ease, 'I heard you're a dab hand at hypnosis.'

I looked at him and Rex shrugged apologetically. 'Like I said, I'm all out of ideas.'

Whether Rex believed in hypnosis or not, it was actually a half-reasonable suggestion. I'd carry out a full psychological evaluation of the guy, of course, but if there was anything lurking in his background that might explain the weight issue, then hypnosis might be the way to find it.

The policeman came to see me and I saw what Rex meant. He was in his late twenties, should have been at the peak of fitness, but, while not quite the stature of Giant Haystacks, he had a couple of chins too many and was carrying a generous spare tyre.

We immediately got down to work and I asked him if he was troubled by anything.

The policeman scratched his stubble-length hair. 'No, sir. Although I'm not enjoying lying around in this place much.' His accent betrayed his Scottish roots. I knew from his notes that he came from the Borders.

'Well,' I said, 'let's see if we can get you out of here. But first I need to know what's wrong with you; why you're putting on weight. Can you shed any light on that?'

The guy shrugged. 'Wish I could, sir. But the truth is I have no idea.'

'Have you ever been hypnotized?' I asked him.

He shook his head. 'Can't say I have, sir.'

'Would you object to my hypnotizing you now?'

He hesitated a moment. 'No, sir. Not really.'

'You don't sound too sure.'

'That's because I'm not sure I believe in it.'

We got to work. We used the clinic room in our unit where there was a couch. Hypnosis was not used often in our unit and the GP trainee attached to us for six months' psychiatric training asked if he could sit in, as did two of our nursing staff. Our patient gave his permission and I used the same eye-fixation technique I'd used on Tommy, asking him to focus on the tip of my finger as I brought it to within six inches of his face. I raised my finger until, from his point of view, it would have disappeared into his brow-line, then told him his eyelids were getting heavier and heavier . . .

A strange thing happened to me at this point. My own vision began to tunnel in and I developed a negative image of his face:

lighter parts appeared dark and vice versa. This was perhaps evidence that I had entered some kind of mild altered state, but, whatever was happening to me, I could tell that my patient was in no such place at all. He never closed his eyes, he didn't get any dilatation of the pupils and at one point sat bolt upright and told me that we might as well stop because it wasn't working. Interestingly though, I remember glancing round at the audience and they were all asleep, three heads down in a row. I was feeling drowsy myself, so the only one in the room who apparently wasn't affected by my efforts was my patient!

But I'm nothing if not stubborn and decided to keep going, repeating the process over and over and even getting the guy to count backwards from 300. If nothing else, this will bore people into a hypnotic state. But none of these things worked on the RAF policeman, except in one respect. During my attempts to put him under, perhaps because he was so bored, he confessed to something; something that turned out to be the key to his weight gain. He was so miserable at being in Germany, so homesick, that he'd gorged himself on Coke and biscuits. And, despite the stringent diet Rex had put him on, he had secretly continued to gorge himself on these same high-sugar foods. His mates had been smuggling in an endless supply of Coca-Cola and chocolate digestives under the noses of the doctors and nurses on the ward. Part of me was quite amused by this, but I couldn't show it, of course, and told him that this wasn't a good idea and he should stop it forthwith. I suggested to him that instead of lying on his bed eating biscuits when he got bored or homesick, he should take some form of exercise, ride a bike or play squash. I always follow the advice of my hypnosis trainers to count back down from 10 to 0 and then snap my fingers and talk to my patient at the end of a session, irrespective of whether I think that they've only entered a light trance or not even been in hypnosis at all. And then I said goodbye to him. My audience woke up too.

Afterwards I went to see Rex, who was pleased, at least, that the mystery had been solved. And that, I thought, was the end of the matter.

A few months later, I was wandering through the orthopaedic wing of the hospital when I saw a wraith-like figure lying on a bed undergoing traction. He waved at me and I did a double-take.

'You don't recognize me, do you?' said the skeletal figure. 'Even though this is your fault . . .'

'My fault? Perhaps you'd better explain.'

'Whenever I was tempted to have a biscuit or a Coke, I went running or played a game of squash. I ended up slipping a disc, which is how I ended up in traction.'

It was the policeman, and another reminder of just how powerful a tool hypnosis could be in combating certain psychiatric conditions. Unknown to me, I had managed to hypnotize him after all.

After several happy months in the posting, I popped back briefly to the UK for a few days to attend the Royal College of Psychiatry's annual conference. During a break in the proceedings – in the toilets, standing at the urinals, in fact – I bumped into my boss, Eric Anthony. He had taken over from Angus Black as the current consultant adviser in psychiatry, and was a group captain to boot.

'Ah, Gordon,' he said, as we both stared at the tiles, concentrating on the matter in hand. 'How fortuitous. I was going to give you a call. Has anyone spoken to you about your coming back to the UK?'

I thought I must have misheard him. 'Coming back to the UK? But I've only just left.' The two older boys were in school and our dog had gone north to my brother, Derek, in Scotland and our two cats, Jimmy and Tiger, had been taken on by the chaplain at Wroughton. 'You mean in a year or two, I presume.'

'No,' he said, 'with immediate effect. You'd be back in three months.'

I confronted him outside the loos. I simply couldn't understand it. I thought he had to be kidding. But he wasn't. He told me there was a new rule – one that he had only recently implemented – that said a newly qualified psychiatric consultant was not allowed to serve his first post in Germany, because it was deemed to be 'strategically sensitive'.

Think about it, he told me. Suppose the Russians did suddenly flood across the border. A newly qualified consultant wouldn't have the depth of experience to cope.

I didn't know whether to laugh or cry when I heard this. If the Russians invaded, nobody would have the depth of experience to cope.

'Listen,' he said, 'your ASCAB is coming up soon and then you'll be a consultant. What does it matter whether you're here or in Germany?'

'We like Germany,' I said, pointedly. 'But if this is about my consultancy, I'll simply defer my ASCAB. I'll wait till the posting's over.'

Anthony set his jaw and shook his head. 'No you won't,' he said, 'because it's already been decided. You're coming back anyway.'

On my return to Germany, I refused to accept that my conversation with Anthony had ever taken place. I stopped taking calls from him – behaviour that with hindsight was not me at all. But then I had no idea of the storm that was brewing. Because everything that had happened seemed deeply unjust, I dug my heels in. This tactic seemed to work, because the calls from the UK soon stopped and the whole issue appeared to go away.

I concentrated instead on going for my consultancy and asked one of my colleagues – Alf Watts – if he'd endorse my ASCAB application form with a testimonial. Furthermore, after he'd written it, he said he'd send the form off to the board. I didn't have to do a thing.

Months went by without my hearing anything, but that wasn't so unusual, because ASCABs could take ages to organize. The important thing was that the application had been submitted because in purely fiscal terms, as soon as it hit the Director General's desk, your pay as a consultant was backdated to that moment.

Six months later, I happened to be in Alf's office and noticed what I took to be a copy of the form sticking out of a drawer in his desk.

'Why did you keep a copy of my ASCAB form?' I asked him.

He had his nose in a filing cabinet. He looked up. 'Sorry?'

I picked up the form and waved it at him.

I could tell by the look on his face that something was not right – not right at all. 'Surely that's not the actual form?'

Alf mumbled something about this not being the time or the place, but I stopped him right there. Why the hell hadn't he sent it?

'I didn't think you were ready,' he said, looking at the floor.

'Why on earth didn't you tell me any of this?'

He had no answer.

In disgust, I took the form and sent it myself. Rightly or wrongly, I felt strongly that this wasn't about new rules or not being ready, but more about politics.

I reasoned that perhaps Alf had got it into his head that I was lining myself up for the consultant adviser's job, when nothing could have been further from my mind. I was exactly where I wanted to be. I'd found my niche.

My decision to pack in surgery had been justified by my decision to enter psychiatry. Psychiatry had fulfilled every ambition I'd ever nurtured. It was about being a detective, solving problems, thinking outside the box. Done properly, there was more fixing to be done in psychiatry than ever there was in surgery.

I felt as if I'd been completely betrayed.

I continued to work with Alf, but it wasn't the same – and couldn't be ever again. The kindest explanation I could come up with was that he had just suppressed the matter of my application form – that is to say, it was tagged by his subconscious as 'lost' the moment he filed it in his desk.

If so, he would have lost the ability to see that it was there every time he came across it. Be that as it may, it was a bit more significant than just 'losing' a set of car keys or a pair of specs and it didn't make the betrayal I felt any easier.

Several weeks later, I attended the ASCAB at the Royal College of Psychiatry in Berkeley Square.

I walked into a large room to find myself confronted by three tables arranged in a horseshoe shape with my chair – a tiny bench-seat with a desk attached to it – set in the centre. The desk was very similar to the one I had first sat in when I was five years old in Miss Roberts's class at primary school.

Sitting behind the tables were the three psychiatric consultant advisers of Her Majesty's armed forces, accompanied by the three professors who were the civilian advisers to the RAF, Army and Navy, and the Dean of the Royal College of Psychiatrists, each clearly identifiable thanks to a huge brass plate with a name on it on the table in front of him.

I squeezed into the tiny desk and noticed that my nameplate was a folded piece of paper with 'G. Turnbull' written in ballpoint pen. I thought, Is this deliberate? Am I being made to feel that I'm not a member of the club?

They must have done their homework, because they asked me about a number of things I was interested in, including, I remember, circadian rhythms. I spent a while taking them over the case of Janine, the air stewardess, and how it had been the Pint Pot Model that had enabled me to isolate the biological cause of her depression, and how, in the end, merely putting her back on to north–south flights for a while had lifted her depression without recourse to anti-depressants. They then asked me for my views on the future of military psychiatry and for a moment I thought about diving into the whole subject of PTSD. I dismissed this because I knew about the tensions this question elicited. PTSD had split the British medical establishment, most of which still regarded it as an American phenomenon, despite growing evidence from the Falklands that it had affected a swathe of personnel who had fought in that conflict. I didn't, however, want to open the lid on this Pandora's box during my ASCAB, figuring it would be easier to fight the establishment from within than without and that would mean passing the board. Becoming a consultant would give me more power to help change the system.

Instead of PTSD, we talked about the contentious matter of community psychiatry. Community psychiatry was supposed to be a wondrous thing. As its name suggested, it was designed to cut down on hospital visits and rely more on community care – outpatient visits and visits by psychiatrists and psychotherapists to the patient. Of the three services, the RAF had embraced community psychiatry in a big way and the way we had handled it was supposedly the envy of the Army and Navy and, indeed, it provided an example for civilian pioneers. But I was not a big fan and I told them so.

'Why not?' growled the professor of psychiatry from King's College, a large man with half-moon glasses who plucked them from his face theatrically to give me a harsh stare.

'Because I think it makes psychiatry more of a social service than a medical service.'

The Dean glanced up from his notes. 'Do you now, Turnbull? Would you care to expand on that?'

I was keen for this not to become a gladiatorial contest, but at the same time I knew I had to stand my ground on what I believed to be right; they would expect it of me. 'Take, for example, a traumatized patient. Whether they are suffering from PTSD, a depression or both, they need a place of sanctuary, a place where they feel safe. For a great many people, that's what a hospital bed offers.'

'And you don't believe the community psychiatry programme offers that?' the King's College professor said, having replaced his half-moons.

'No, I don't,' I said. 'I think it's a false economy. A lot of these people need to get away from the community when they are ill. And please excuse me for saying so, but hang the expense.'

'You're very forthright in your views,' the Dean said.

'I believe strongly in them,' I replied.

My consultancy was approved and I was told that I would be returning to Wroughton, replacing David Johnstone as head of the Division of Psychiatry there because he was shortly to retire. Big things had happened in the world of RAF psychiatry since I'd been in Germany.

I should have felt elated, but I was still too upset by what had happened in Germany to feel anything other than anger and disillusionment.

Depression is too strong a word for what I had when I arrived back in the UK. I wasn't clinically depressed. I certainly didn't have suicidal thoughts. I wasn't losing weight and I wasn't suffering from insomnia. Malaise is probably a more appropriate term. I felt cut off at the ankles.

In Germany, you could be independent, you could think on your own and try things out in a front-line environment. It was what we'd joined the RAF for. Writing treatises on cutting-edge psychiatric developments seemed to me to be a complete waste of time if we weren't actually coming up with techniques that would cure people.

RAF Germany, with its tempos and pressures, was probably the closest I'd ever come to an environment where I could make that happen.

If we were ever faced with a hot war and hadn't in the meantime found a better way to treat stress reactions, I was terrified we'd be straight back to the Second World War and LMF: officers being demoted to the lowest ranks or sent down the late-twentieth-century equivalent of a coal mine. Forty years earlier, the Air Ministry had convinced itself that too lenient an attitude might lead to abuses of the system. I could hear echoes of that attitude in the corridors of Whitehall in the 1980s. All ways round, we were totally unprepared.

*

The low-lying cloud parted as I drove up on to the Ridgeway and there was RAF Wroughton, clearly visible a mile away, illuminated by a ray of sunlight piercing the overcast. I pulled into a lay-by and switched off the engine. I was suddenly filled with a strong sense of foreboding; dread, even. I was 37 years old, a recently promoted wing commander, about to take over my first command, and instead of feeling on top of the world I was feeling worse than I had thought I could ever feel. For a second or two, I thought about going AWOL and imagined the headlines: 'New Head Shrink at RAF Hospital Does a Runner'.

I stared at the hospital buildings for what seemed like hours, then the mist closed in again. I started the car up and eased it back on to the road.

Ten minutes later, I walked into reception at the Neuropsychiatric Centre, doing my best to look like nothing was wrong. It was my first day back, and my first day as head of the Psychiatric Division at the Princess Alexandra Hospital, Wroughton. Everyone was extremely welcoming.

'Good morning, Wing Commander Turnbull, welcome back.'

'It's good to see you again, Wing Commander.'

'Welcome home, Gordon.'

I passed friendly faces in the corridor. People waved and shook my hand.

I was stumbling through a nightmare. Voices sounded distant. I felt like an observer, not a participant. When I spoke, I was on automatic.

'Hello.'

'Thank you.'

'Good to see you, too.'

'Thanks. It's good to be back.'

I walked into my new office, David's old office, and closed the door behind me. There were marks on the walls where his prints had been; scuffs on the carpet where he'd stretched out his feet. Where were my tormentors when I needed them?

I didn't need to close the curtains, it was dark enough inside my head. I sat at my desk in the darkness.

Images played through my mind. Whenever I thought about the

little desk I'd squeezed into at the ASCAB hearing, all I could see in my mind's eye was my desk at Lorne Street School. The feelings I had about Germany had become indistinguishable from all the emotions I'd felt when I'd trudged up the stairs to fetch the Wee Red Box.

This is ridiculous, I told myself. Snap out of it. But I couldn't. I was no more capable of snapping out of my malaise than someone with clinical depression can get on with life by 'pulling their socks up'.

It was October and already dark. The next thing I knew, the lights came on and I found myself staring at the startled face of Dr Mike Waters, our clinical tutor, a delightful, wise and gentle man who had retired from the NHS and been a terrific help to us. He asked me how long I'd been sitting in the darkness and I honestly had no idea, because I'd dissociated – for the first time in my life. When I worked backwards, however, I realized I'd been alone with my thoughts, enveloped by darkness, for over two hours.

The malaise continued for a year. I functioned. I got on with life, but I wasn't much fun to be with. What made it worse was that I was perfectly well aware what a pain in the arse I was. But anger is a very destructive emotion. It's also very difficult to shake. Ali told me later that she needed to weigh my mood before bringing the kids and the dogs in to see me after I got back from work. She also told me that she'd been so worried about me during this period she'd thought about going to see David. The only thing that had stopped her was the thought that going to see my old tormentor might make things worse, not better.

In the end, however, the malaise did lift, but in the unlikeliest of ways.

We threw a small dinner party and Kate and Norman Hunt were invited. Norman was our GP as well as a close friend. I didn't know it then, but Norman had been part of a circle of confidants who'd been keeping a discreet eye on me at Ali's request.

During dinner, he started to tell me about his enthusiasm for horseracing. I had no idea he had this interest. We talked about it for two hours.

Why this conversation should have acted as a catalyst to lift a depression that had sat on my shoulders for the best part of a year, I don't know. But it was like shutters opening and light flooding in. Maybe it was because it opened up a new window into a personality I

thought I knew well and reminded me that there was always something new to discover about people and the world. Perhaps that
conversation rekindled my curiosity – a quality that had always been
so precious to me.

I hear this same metaphor about the shutters and the light today
from post-trauma survivors and in some respects what happened to
me is reflected in my PTSD work today. I know that PTSD doesn't
go gradually, but in jumps. I'd sat down at that dinner table feeling
bleak and by the end of the evening my malaise had gone – it had
completely left me. In psychological terms, the only real pointer I can
think of is this: when he told me about his interest in horseracing,
Norman gave me an insight into a part of his life I'd no inkling of
previously. When Alf had buried my ASCAB application form, he
too revealed a part of himself that had been hidden from me.

Good and bad; yin and yang. The good moving in to cancel out
the bad. Maybe it had been that simple.

Although my personal experience of a malaise that permeated
everything I did and thought was a very unpleasant one, it did give
me real insight into what my patients were feeling when they
described being depressed and unmotivated and without energy.

If there was one thing I had never been in my life before the malaise
struck, it was lethargic, and it was quite an insight to understand that
this was not just an attitude of mind. It truly was not possible just to
'pull oneself together'. The experience also taught me that it was stressful life events which caused such downturns in outlook and energy.

Later I was to learn about the Chinese attitude to crisis. Although
you need thousands of different characters (pictograms) to communicate in the Chinese language, there is no single character for the
concept of 'crisis'. The Chinese get round the problem by using
two characters together. One conveys 'danger' and the other
'opportunity'. So they see a crisis as a dangerous or risky time but
one which also offers opportunity, a bridge into the future.

It was a big lesson. My natural curiosity had been badly injured
by events in Germany but the new discovery about an old friend had
restored it. Goodbye Miss Roberts, hello Miss Sprunt.

I determined then that I would never again ask my patients: 'What
do you think is wrong with you?' Instead, I would always ask:
'What happened to you?'

This simple question became a critical tool in how I approached PTSD survivors.

Fate, in any case, intervened to throw me in at the deep end. In August 1987, a 27-year-old unemployed Wiltshire labourer called Michael Ryan drove into a petrol station on the A4 just outside Hungerford, a town barely 30 minutes' drive from my house, pulled out a Second World War-vintage M1 carbine and tried to shoot the cashier. He missed, attempted to shoot her again, but failed because the weapon wouldn't fire, most likely, investigators deduced later, because Ryan inadvertently hit the magazine release mechanism, leaving the weapon bulletless after the first shot.

Unfortunately, this was neither the beginning nor the end of Ryan's assault on innocent lives that afternoon. The first shooting occurred around midday – around 15 minutes before the garage incident – when he abducted a young mother in the Savernake Forest, just outside Hungerford. Susan Godfrey had come to the forest to picnic with her two small children. Ryan showed Mrs Godfrey no mercy, shooting her 13 times in the back. He then drove to the garage, where a motorcyclist was able to call the police, but it was several hours before the police turned up in force.

The headlines the next day reflected the fact that Hungerford, up to that point, was the worst criminal atrocity involving firearms in British history. Ryan, it transpired, was a local man, an only child with a father who was in his mid-fifties at the time of Ryan's birth. He died at the age of 80 two years before his son went on the rampage.

His mother worked as a dinner lady at the local primary school. The press rapidly speculated that his relationship with her was cloyingly claustrophobic and that she had spoiled him rotten. Inevitably, the papers branded him a 'Mummy's boy'. They also detailed his fascination with weapons and gung-ho firearms publications like Soldier of Fortune.

In a development that would become fatal, Ryan had been issued a shotgun certificate in 1978 at the age of 18. Eight years later – nine months before he went on the rampage – he was issued with a firearms certificate that enabled him to buy a vast arsenal of weapons, including several handguns and a Kalashnikov assault rifle.

These he used to terrifying effect. After the garage incident, his murder spree resumed after he drove to his home in Hungerford and picked up his weapons, which he bundled into his Vauxhall Astra. He then doused his home with petrol and set it alight. He shot dead his neighbours who were in the back garden of their house – Roland Mason six times in the back, his wife Sheila once in the head.

Ryan then proceeded on foot towards the town common, shooting as he went. After killing or injuring three more people, he walked back to his street, where his house was now blazing. The first policeman who tried to intervene was shot dead in his patrol car. After he had wounded several more people, Ryan's mother drove into the street, saw her house on fire and her son brandishing his AK-47 and several other weapons. Ryan shot his mother dead as she raised her hands to plead with him not to shoot. He then ran back to the common. There he shot and killed several more people before walking towards the town centre, where police were attempting to evacuate the public. Within minutes, three more people were dead.

More than an hour and a half after the first shooting in the forest, Ryan was still firing at everyone he encountered. On the day of the massacre there were only four policemen on duty, with the nearest armed response team 40 miles away. It later emerged that the telephone exchange could not handle the number of 999 calls that had been made by witnesses. This left Ryan to kill, maim and injure several more times before, at around 2.30 pm, he finally took refuge in the John O'Gaunt Community Technology College, where he had once been a pupil. The college was empty, thank God, because of the summer holidays. When police surrounded the building, negotiators soon made contact, but at seven o'clock in the evening a shot rang out. Before he died, Ryan reportedly told negotiators he wished he'd stayed in bed.

Including Ryan himself, 17 people died that day and 15 more were injured. It resulted in the Firearms (Amendment) Act of 1988, which led to a ban on ownership of semi-automatic rifles and restricted the use of shotguns with a magazine capacity of more than two rounds. This reflected the fact that Ryan's arsenal of weapons had all been legally owned.

The Hungerford massacre involved me in two ways.

The first was a realization that I could have easily lost four members of my own family. Alison and all three boys had been in the

Savernake Forest having a picnic with friends when Ryan shot his first victim, bringing the events of that day close enough to give me nightmares.

The second came six months later, when the survivors of Hungerford were assessed on their residual physical disabilities by a consultant surgeon, Group Captain Maurice Mahoney, the head of surgery at the Princess Alexandra. Maurice, who was aware of our PTSD work, approached us to see if we could assess whether they had suffered any psychological injuries. The wave of national sympathy elicited by Ryan's actions had resulted in the collection of a large public fund. It had been agreed that the way in which the fund was to be divided would depend on the degree of trauma suffered by each survivor.

The trouble was, there was no way at this point in time of measuring the impact of a post-traumatic event. Thanks to *DSM-III*, we now knew the *definition* of PTSD: that the survivor had to have been exposed to a 'recognizable stressor that would evoke significant symptoms of distress in almost everyone'; that re-experiencing what happened through dreams and flashbacks was almost always present; that the survivor usually went to great lengths to avoid any link to the trauma; and that the post-traumatic phase was generally marked by hyper-arousal symptoms – difficulty in falling or remaining asleep, outbursts of anger, difficulty in concentrating and so forth.

But no one as yet had devised a tool, as far as we were aware, to *measure* these symptoms directly.

Shortly before Ryan went on his rampage, *DSM-III* had been re-issued as *DSM-III-Revised*. This updated edition tweaked the original definition of the first criterion of PTSD – the definition of what a traumatic event is – so that it became exposure to 'an event that is outside the range of usual human experience . . . that would be markedly distressing to almost anyone'. The wording might have altered, but the definition was essentially the same: anyone exposed to a traumatic event of sufficient severity was capable of suffering from PTSD.

Hungerford certainly fell into that category.

Measuring PTSD somehow seemed demeaning to the survivor, but the payout conditions of the fund demanded it. We decided that the best way of coming up with a measurements scale was to take the 17 core symptoms defined by *DSM-III-Revised* within the four main PTSD criteria and rate them as 'mild', 'moderate', 'severe' or 'extreme'. We also had to define what we meant by these terms and decided that the guidelines should be: *Mild* – 'little functional impairment'; *Moderate* – 'satisfactory functioning but with effort'; *Severe* – 'limited functioning even with effort'; and *Extreme* – 'pervasive impairment/little function'.

Within the 're-experiencing cluster', therefore, we were able to ask questions like: 'If you are experiencing recurrent distressing dreams of the events of 19 August 1987, how would you rate their severity?'

In the course of working with the Hungerford survivors, we made an interesting discovery: there was an inverse relationship between physical injury and psychological disability. This seemed to me to be important, because it appeared to contradict experience from the First and Second World Wars, Vietnam and the Falklands, where there seemed to be a direct relationship between physical and psychological injury.

In the case of the Hungerford survivors, I thought I understood the dynamics at work. Those who had sustained significant injuries received a lot of medical attention, clearly, whereas those whose trauma wasn't visible received little by comparison. In the process of this attention, even though it was focused on the survivors' physical injuries, the survivor was able to unload to a degree. There would have been no doubt about what they had been through – their injuries alone would have attested to it. There would have been lots of sympathy. People with little to show, on the other hand, would not have received so much sympathy or care – by comparison, they would have been seen almost as malingerers. This, in many cases, would have actually compounded their trauma.

I hoped the scale that we had devised for the Hungerford survivors had gone some way towards dispelling this myth. It was crude, but it represented a start. And thank God we had something, because the following year, 1988, was when it all kicked off, starting with what we thought of back then as the terrorist event to end all terrorist events: Lockerbie.

Chapter 9

The Turning Point

After getting the call from David Whalley, I handed over the ward round to David Price, the highly experienced Surgeon Lieutenant Commander on loan to us from the Royal Navy, and got on with the job of organizing the response.

There was no point in going to Lockerbie there and then. The RAF mountain rescuers were dispersing as the phone call was made. It was their leaving the scene that had alarmed Whalley, I reckoned. He was worried about what was going to happen to his people once they had all gone their separate ways.

He probably sensed that an opportunity to debrief them was vanishing before his eyes and had wanted to communicate that to someone. That someone had been me and, I reckoned, for a simple reason: I was most probably the only shrink Whalley knew. We'd never actually worked together, but he must have known about me from the time I'd climbed with the mountain rescuers – become one of the team, so to speak. On such simple choices sometimes the world turns.

I contacted Air Commodore Bob Chappell, my CO at Wroughton, to tell him what had happened. Time was very short. In just over two hours our hospital was going to shut down virtually for the Christmas 'grant' – military parlance for the leave period – and that would be the same for all the other RAF stations. I had to be quick and thought the best way was to alert the medical system.

Chappell turned out to be very sympathetic. He told me he would contact Support Command HQ to tell the principal medical officer there and the PMO Support Command would inform PMO Strike Command.

Most of the RAF stations that we would have to visit were Strike Command stations and we needed to follow protocol to gain permission to make the calls. I phoned all the senior MOs at all four stations we would visit. Leuchars, Leeming, Stafford and St Athan had all sent mountain rescue teams. Luckily, I'd been in the RAF Medical Branch for long enough now to know most of them, which made the task a lot easier. After that, there was nothing else for it but to head home, the strains of Slade's 'Merry Christmas' subsumed by something the mountain rescuer had told me: *people are seeing things – the same things – and the things that they're seeing aren't going away.*

That phrase haunted me, because I knew that this was it. No more theory. No more supposition. This was PTSD writ in giant letters.

People – people I knew – needed help. The adrenaline rush – the thought of the responsibility that was on my shoulders – made me feel light-headed.

It reminded me of the time we landed on Clarence Island during the Elephant Island Antarctic expedition in 1976. We'd been dropped off by two tiny Wasp helicopters from HMS *Endurance*. The Royal Navy ice patrol ship first had to establish the caches of kit we needed at strategic points on the island. Then they dropped off the eight of us. After the helicopters had landed back on their mother ship, the *Endurance* had headed off, with ungodly speed, to deposit the other eight members of the expedition and their equipment on Gibbs Island some distance away. It was the last we would see of them, our mates and the ship, for at least two months.

I remembered sitting on the edge of what was really the peak of a submerged mountain watching as the *Endurance* eventually slipped over the horizon. It had been an awesome moment, because I realized that I was the only medical man in our party. I prayed that all would be well because I was going to have to pull everything out of the medical bag if anyone needed treatment.

I'd been filled with a mixture of apprehension at what might be and the sheer thrill of starting the adventure of a lifetime. The thrill won and we hurried about the task of setting up camp because we knew that, although it was a brilliant day with hardly a wisp of cloud in the sky, the Antarctic weather could be hellishly capricious and we had to be quick.

That was then. I'd been responsible for seven others, none of whom had ended up confronting a life-or-death situation. Lockerbie was different. One hundred and twenty individuals had been involved in the recovery operation. It was all I could do to keep the car on the road.

As soon as I got home, I flicked on the evening news.

Despite the best efforts of the IRA, Lockerbie was the worst terrorist attack to have occurred on UK soil. It was also the worst-ever attack on American civilians: the 189 dead US passengers of Flight 103 was almost three times the number of civilians killed at Pearl Harbor. Britain and America were united in their suffering, but as the details continued to emerge – confirming, in all likelihood, that a bomb and not mechanical failure had brought down the jumbo – the outpouring of sympathy from across the world had been remarkable and moving.

With professional involvement, however, came emotional attachment: the full horror of Lockerbie was drawing me in.

Pan Am Flight 103, a Boeing 747-100, had left Frankfurt in Germany for New York two nights earlier, stopping off at London Heathrow en route to pick up more passengers. The aircraft, full of fuel for its transatlantic flight, clawed its way into the night sky at 6.25 pm. There were 259 people on board – 243 passengers and 16 crew. A considerable number of them were children. It was a damp, miserable, overcast night and they would have had the barest glimpse of the lights of London before the plane slid into low cloud.

Thirty-five minutes later, an air traffic controller at Glasgow's Prestwick Airport saw the moment that the bomb in the forward hold ripped Flight 103 apart. Where, seconds earlier, there had been a single bright radar plot, the screen was suddenly twinkling with a sea of 'returns': the reflections of pieces of aircraft falling earthward. What the bomb had started was finished by the 500-mph winds that tore through the holes in the fuselage. On the ground, a few people out walking their dogs or scuttling home to escape the pre-Christmas cold heard the explosion and saw the sky raining fire.

Then, the main section of the aircraft, still filled with 200,000 pounds of jet fuel, slammed at more than three-quarters the speed of sound into Sherwood Crescent, a suburb of the tiny Dumfriesshire market town of Lockerbie, bordering the A74 to Glasgow. The blast measured 1.6 on the Richter scale, sent a fireball reminiscent of a nuclear explosion into the sky and gouged out a crater almost 200 feet long and 150 wide. Several houses simply disappeared.

For the next minute, major components of the aircraft, pieces of luggage and people, some still strapped in their seats, cascaded down on the town and the surrounding countryside. One young boy had gone round to have a bicycle puncture fixed by a friend in the adjoining street and had a miraculous escape. He lost all the members of his family with whom he'd been having tea moments earlier.

The debris field was scattered across a thousand square miles of northern England and southern Scotland. The nose section of the aircraft – the only major piece of it that was still recognizable – lay in a field bordering a churchyard three miles from the town.

The news brought fresh horrors. The reporter struggled to describe the scene.

An aerial shot of the town showed the blast crater and what was left of Sherwood Crescent. The A74, with cars still slewed across the road, remained closed to traffic. Bodies were still lying where they had fallen: in fields, in trees, in the streets, in people's back gardens. They were still there because the government's forensic experts, mobilized to full strength, could not cope.

I turned off the TV and headed towards the stairs. If David Whalley's team was 'seeing things that wouldn't go away', I hadn't the first idea how we'd cope. I knew only that we were about to confront trauma reactions on a massive scale.

'Daddy . . . ?'

Stuart stood in the doorway. He was wearing his pyjamas and dressing gown and holding his teddy. I bent down and scooped him into my arms.

'Time for your story?'

He nodded enthusiastically and rubbed my cheek with the palm of his hand. He liked the rasping sound.

'What about your brothers?'

He wrinkled his nose and shook his head. 'Iain is too old for stories and Bobby is too little.'

I laughed. This wasn't strictly true. Bobby was three and Iain nine. Stuart, at eight, was the impish one in the middle and usually in the thick of trouble. I looked at him out of the corner of my eye and fingered the tips of my moustache to let him know that I was pondering a big decision.

Then I set him down, raised my arms and growled at him like a bear.

He ran off squealing, straight into the arms of his mother.

Alison looked at me reproachfully for a second – as if she was about to give me a massive bollocking for razzing the kids so close to bedtime. But she couldn't keep it up for long and we ended up laughing, joined by the other two kids, who didn't want to miss out on the action.

After dinner, Ali drifted into the sitting room to watch the TV, but I had too much on my mind to be able to lose myself in the usual diet of movie repeats and comedy shows that constituted the pre-Christmas line-up. Instead, I took my glass of wine into my office, a room in a far corner of the house that looked out over the Wiltshire village where we lived.

The kids' laughter was still ringing in my ears. Rain streaked the window, refracting the Christmas lights on houses either side of the main road.

I took a sip of wine. I was filled with so many conflicting emotions and the Christmas imagery wasn't helping. I had just watched pictures on the news of a scene that looked almost Dantean in its depiction of the carnage at Lockerbie. But in the meantime – here, now, everywhere – life, the world, went on; Christmas, indeed, went on.

Like everyone else, I was appalled by what had happened. It defied belief. Yet, at the same time, I felt a guilty buzz of anticipation. I knew the RAF mountain rescue community well. If I was to accept the standard definition of a trauma reaction, then I also had to accept that what these men were going through in light of events in and around Lockerbie, apparently en masse, must have been caused by a truly overwhelming experience.

I knew, too, that what we were seeing on the television must be a very watered-down version of what it was actually like. Mountain rescuers were very tough. I'd worked with them, I knew many of them extremely well. They must be feeling it very badly. It filled me with a sense of foreboding for the test that was to come – the biggest test of my life.

I sat down at my desk and rubbed my eyes. When I opened them again, I found myself focusing on some lines inspired by Goethe that had sat on my desk for years:

> *Until there is commitment, there is hesitancy,*
> *The chance to draw back, always ineffectiveness,*
> *Concerning all acts of initiative (and creation),*
> *There is one elementary truth the ignorance*
> *Of which kills countless ideas and splendid plans . . .*

For the mountain rescuers, the Lockerbie operation was winding down. As David Whalley had said, there was nothing more they could do – there weren't, and never had been, any lives to save.

If the mountain rescuers weren't already back with their families, they soon would be.

For some, that closeness and intimacy with loved ones would be a blessing, but for others it wouldn't make a jot of difference – it might even prove to be a curse. I had immersed myself enough in the subject of PTSD to have formed my own opinion of the benefits of the proximity of friends and family to a traumatized individual in the days and weeks after the traumatizing event. It was a myth, in my opinion, that the intimacy of family and loved ones in that period helped the trauma sufferer. In both world wars, it might, perhaps, have seemed therapeutic for soldiers traumatized by the horrors of the trenches to be able to describe them to those they were closest to, but the reality was quite different. Family and loved ones couldn't have begun to understand what these people had been through and, partly for that reason, traumatized combatants actively sought to shield them from the reality of combat by keeping it to themselves – bottling it up inside. In this respect, I believed that the PIE process developed for shell-shock sufferers in the later stages of the First World War – sending them to hospitals close to the front that offered

Proximity, Immediacy and Expectancy of a return to fighting – had largely got it right.

My training, everything I had learned about trauma reactions thus far, said that the quicker we got to the mountain rescuers, the greater the chance of a successful 'outcome' – the word 'cure' did not adequately describe the process they needed to go through to come out the other side.

We really needed to get to them as soon as possible – get to Whalley and his teams and help them feel *safe*. Safety was key. Right now, if what David described was true, they weren't in a place where they felt safe at all. While friends and family unwrapped presents or tucked into the Christmas lunch, they were reliving not just what they'd seen but everything that came with it: all the sounds, the smells and the emotions – the horror of Lockerbie in its entirety.

While America had made enormous inroads into understanding post-traumatic stress disorder in the wake of Vietnam, the MoD, six years after the Falklands War, was still living in the Dark Ages. There were few formal procedures within the British armed forces for dealing with trauma reactions. The Royal Navy had its specialist trauma unit at Haslar Hospital under Morgan O'Connell. But that was about it. We were all still feeling our way forward.

Britain was the nation of the stiff upper lip – we stood firm in the face of danger. We'd won two world wars through sheer bloody grit. Veterans of those two conflicts didn't need *help* – or, dare the word even be whispered, *therapy*. They'd pulled up their socks and got on with it.

And that attitude remained prevalent within the ministry today. If it had just remained prevalent within the upper echelons of the fighting cadre, the generals, admirals and air vice marshals who ran the show, then fair enough – it was what I would have expected. But it permeated almost everyone and everything; it was particularly prevalent among my bosses in the military medical community.

Our mission would not start until the New Year – the beginning of 1989. In the RAF, never mind what mischief the Russians or anyone else had in mind for Britain or NATO, everything stopped over the Christmas period. But come January, we'd need to be ready.

As I sat at my desk, staring out across the lights of the village, I felt excited and afraid.

Were we ready?

Whatever you can do or dream you can
begin it
boldness has genius, power and magic in it
Begin it now

Goethe was right, but so was my aunt Norma. When I was a boy, worrying about this or that or generally in a bit of a dither, she'd put her hands on her hips and say: 'Stop fretting, Gordon, and get on wi' it.'

I could hear my aunt Norma telling me to get on wi' it now.

While the family dived into the pre-Christmas festivities, in my head I was already planning the composition of the team I'd need. All in all, we'd be away several weeks. Our first port of call was RAF Leuchars, north of Edinburgh. Leuchars was the closest to Lockerbie. Thereafter, we'd take them in order as we headed back south: Leeming, Stafford and St Athan. But who to take with me? Who to put on the team?

The person who loomed head and shoulders above all others in my mind was Squadron Leader Bert Venman. Bert was a senior psychiatric nurse, an ex-policeman and ex-prison officer, but most important of all in the context of Lockerbie, the most organized person I'd ever come across. This, I knew, was what the operation needed – cool, clear thinking at the centre; a Mr Fixit, which was exactly what Bert was. Bert had been a member of the mountain rescue team in Cyprus a few years back. This was a real stroke of luck – or perhaps, as I preferred to see it, a touch of the 'power and magic' that Goethe had written about.

My mind was going to be taken up with the demands of the 'coal face': formulating an approach for debriefing up to 120 mountain rescuers, applying the principles of the measurements scale we'd put together after Hungerford, and ensuring no stone was left unturned in getting to those who'd been worst affected. It made sense that I, as head of department, should be responsible for this aspect of the operation, and it was equally clear who else should be on the debrief-ing team: Alan Lillywhite, one of the Royal Navy psychiatrists on loan to us, who had worked under Morgan O'Connell and, post-Falklands, probably had more experience in dealing with trauma reactions than anyone; Andrew Salmon, a sergeant psychiatric nurse who was a deep thinker, yet tough enough to deal with the gruelling challenges of Lockerbie; and Pearl Barnes, a talented psychiatric nurse, who'd built up a solid reputation on civvy street before she joined us at Wroughton.

On Christmas Eve, in among some last-minute present-wrapping, I called Bert to sound him out.

'I'm in, Gordon,' he said, without a moment's hesitation.

Inwardly, I breathed a massive sigh of relief. Bert was ten years older than me and his cool, calm, avuncular voice was exactly what I needed to hear at that moment.

'At each of the four bases, we're going to need some kind of head-quarters,' I said. 'And to be honest, I'm not sure how much cooperation we're going to get when we arrive on the scene.'

'What do you mean?'

'Getting the cooperation of the leadership at Leuchars, Leeming, Stafford and St Athan is going to be crucial. I'm not just talking about the mountain rescuers but the senior MOs and, most im-portant of all, the station commanders. As soon as we put in a request to debrief the mountain rescuers, pound to a penny, a lot of people are going to dig their heels in.' We needed support at all levels of authority.

Resistance was not an uncommon reaction. Never mind the fact that we were service personnel; we were shrinks and a large section of the military community looked on us with suspicion. We would have to tread very carefully. I'd need all my skills of diplomacy simply to get us through the main gates.

The long pause told me Bert was thinking about this too. 'How would you feel about a *mobile* command HQ?' he asked.

'I'm not sure I understand.'

'Our mobile home,' he said. 'We could use that. I'm sure Beryl wouldn't mind . . .'

Bert and his wife Beryl lived close by in Malmesbury, where they owned and ran a successful nursing home. The love and devotion they lavished on the old folk in their care, in addition to the demands imposed on Bert by the RAF, meant that they didn't get a whole lot of holiday time. But such time as Bert and Beryl did get off, they liked nothing better than to chunter off into Britain's remoter areas in their mobile home, a fantastic thing reminiscent of those big, elaborate contraptions I'd seen in tourist brochures hogging dead straight American roads.

'Bottom line is this, Gordon: put the logistics out of your mind. You can leave all that to me. You just worry about the mechanics of the debriefing process and have yourselves a very happy Christmas.'

He signed off. With Bert as Mr Fixit, I knew now we'd be able to get the show on the road. What happened when we reached our destination, however, was anyone's guess. One hundred and twenty was a huge number of people to evaluate. I was having to make this up as I went along.

Alan, Andrew, Pearl and I would carry out the debriefings – that part was clear. But I knew we'd also need to take careful steps to ensure that we, the debriefers, were supervised for signs that the trauma wasn't getting to us and compromising our ability to do the job. Bert, I determined, would need to take on that role as well – as secondary debriefer.

I'd picked up the idea of secondary debriefing from an American called Jeffrey Mitchell, who in the 1970s created something called the Critical Incident Stress Debriefing (CISD) system to help emergency responders recover from a traumatic incident. A former Baltimore County firefighter, Mitchell developed CISD into a seven-step process designed to return emergency workers to duty after a traumatic event. There was precious little else in the field to draw upon. Another specialist I'd come across was a chap called Bessel van der Kolk who'd worked with Vietnam veterans in the USA in the late 1970s and had published a book on PTSD, the first I knew of on the subject. Van der Kolk was evangelical on the reality of PTSD, but had met with resistance from the Veterans Association, the VA, which, prior to the identification of PTSD in *DSM-III* in 1980, had refused to admit to its existence. There was another expert I'd heard about, Dr Sandy McFarlane in Australia, who had worked with Australian Vietnam veterans. And there was Morgan O'Connell, the UK Royal Navy psychiatrist, who'd done so much for a number of Britain's Falklands veterans in the aftermath of the South Atlantic conflict. But apart from these four, the field was conspicuously open.

A new frontier – exciting to be on, but frustrating when it came to the search for back-up material.

As soon as the shops opened the day after Boxing Day, I drove into town and ran off four photocopied sets of the CISD. I did the same for the post-Hungerford questionnaires we'd developed and bound them into five briefing packs; one each for Bert, Alan, Andrew, Pearl and me.

We met at Wroughton in the small hours of 3 January and piled into Bert's van. The warm interior, pre-heated during his drive over from Malmesbury, took the edge off the complaints as we headed north.

I knew it would take a good seven or eight hours to reach the Scottish border and probably another three or four before we arrived at Leuchars, the RAF's first line of defence against the Soviet bomber threat. The base lay on a windswept promontory between the Firth of Forth and the Firth of Tay. Bert, of course, had worked out all the logistics. Knowing the rigours of the journey ahead, nobody had questioned the wisdom of an early start.

By the time we hit the M6, I could see how Bert's battle-bus would more than come into its own during the fortnight we would be on the road. It had four bunks, allowing us to get what I knew would be some much-needed shut-eye when we were travelling the long distances between bases – or, for that matter, if we ended up so unwelcome that we were denied lodgings on any of the bases.

It also had a table bordered on three sides by cushioned seating, and as soon as we hit the motorway this area became our mobile ops room. I spread out a map and summoned Alan, Andrew and Pearl to the table for our first strategy meeting, to bring them up to speed on what I'd been up to between Christmas and New Year.

A piece of good luck had happened over that New Year. Very good friends of ours had visited Turnbull Towers to see in the New Year with us: Bob and Sandra Andrews and their two sons, Barnaby and Jeremy, who were great friends of our boys. Bob had been the Anglican chaplain at RAF Rheindahlen when we were on tour there and our two families had become close. With my mind filled with what we were about to embark on, Bob had been in a position to offer something more than spiritual inspiration. He had been very involved in working with the survivors and their families after the

RAF band had been caught up in a terrible accident en route to a performance. He knew a great deal about what I was going to face and had been more than willing to share his experience with me.

When I settled down to brief the team, talking with Bob had helped bolster my confidence.

The most critical and sensitive part of the whole exercise, I explained, would be getting all the permissions we needed to gain access to the mountain rescuers. This wasn't as straightforward as it sounded, because of the deep levels of antipathy towards the PTSD issue that permeated the UK's military hierarchy.

Calls made by my CO, Bob Chappell, had gone a long way towards clearing our path, or so I thought.

But once we were through the gates, we'd still need to tread carefully. For things to run smoothly on the base, it was essential we got each base commander and his senior medical officer on-side. I knew how obstructive these people could be, whatever orders came from on high. Besides, there was a protocol. I'd have been miffed if some cocksure doctor had sauntered into my department at Wroughton telling me what was good for people under *my* supervision.

'You make it sound like a diplomatic offensive, sir,' Andrew said with feeling.

I nodded. At every turn there might be people who would seek to derail us. I could not allow that to happen. This was the best – perhaps the only – chance we'd get to demonstrate to the powers-that-be not only that PTSD was a reality but that it could be treated, perhaps like any other medical condition.

On a more personal note, I'd made a promise to David Whalley that I'd help the mountain rescuers and I wasn't going to let that slide without a fight.

It was early afternoon, the sky already darkening, when we crossed the border and joined the A74 to Glasgow. Fifteen minutes later, we got our first view of Lockerbie. I'd seen countless images over the past two weeks, but being so close to the devastation brought home the immediacy of the tragedy for the first time.

As the traffic slowed and I registered that the gap in the row of bungalows on the east side of the dual carriageway was the infamous 200 by 150 foot crater where the fuselage had struck the ground, I realized how unlucky Lockerbie had been. As my eyes accustomed to the gloom, I could see how the destruction radiated out from the impact point.

The bungalows on the edge of the crater were just shells. Further back, I could see houses without roofs. If the 747 had flown just a few hundred feet further west before the bomb detonated, the death toll on the ground would have been minimal – perhaps there would have been no casualties at all.

This could have been any small town in Great Britain. It just happened to be here.

Chapter 10

The Journey into Hell

After spending a night at a local B&B, we drove to the gates of the base and presented our passes.

Because I was the one who would have to do the talking, I decided that I was going to make it as easy as possible for myself, and one thing that I could do was to wear the right gear, appropriate to the person I was talking to. I had a clothes rail in Bert's camper van filled up with the different rigs that I thought I'd need: my 'No.1s' for the most senior officers such as the COs, my less formal 'woolly-pully' for the MOs and casual clothes for meeting the mountain rescuers. I wanted to avoid any obstacles to the debriefings that might come about from wearing badges of rank.

After impressing upon my team the need for diplomacy and tact, I almost blew my top when an officious corporal at the gatehouse told me there was no record of a visit by any doctors from Wroughton and he was not, therefore, inclined to let us on to the base.

An hour later, after we'd managed to persuade him we were legit, I finally got to see the CO.

Despite Bob Chappell's assurances before I left Wiltshire, it turned out that the tall group captain in whose office I was now standing had received no advance warning of our visit. Worse, when I told him why we'd travelled all the way from Wroughton to Leuchars, he more or less told me that we'd wasted the journey.

'I've received no word of any issues with my mountain rescue team,' he said, studying me through a cloud of cigarette smoke. 'Had there been a problem, I'm sure my MO would have informed me.'

He looked, with his long, sharp nose and piercing stare, not unlike an eagle. Personality-wise, he was every inch the fighter pilot: confident, decisive, almost arrogant. As he was a group captain, he had the edge over me and seemed determined to assert his authority.

My one flicker of hope was that he was curious. He asked pertinent, sometimes difficult questions about PTSD and my own role in researching the phenomenon and he listened very carefully to my answers.

I told him about the call I'd received two days before Christmas from Flight Sergeant David Whalley. I explained that I'd got to know mountain rescue people during my stint at Akrotiri and I understood how their minds worked. I emphasized just how worried Whalley must have been to ask for help from the RAF psychiatric department. I told him that the only possible answer to the request for help was an emphatic 'yes'.

'I know how difficult it would have been for him to make that call,' I said. 'He didn't use emotive language. He simply said something was happening – something he didn't understand. And I knew that for him to say that, especially to a psychiatrist, had taken a great deal of courage.'

I felt moved to explain, too, that this was no reflection on the medical procedures in place at Leuchars. While we were dealing with an age-old phenomenon, it was only relatively recently – certainly in Britain – that PTSD had been flushed into the open. We were inching our way forward, I said. As a race, we were notoriously bad at talking about our feelings. Military personnel, moreover, were expected to keep a cork on their emotions. But, come what may, those self-same feelings always had a habit of working their way out.

I told him of Morgan O'Connell's pioneering work after the Falklands and how, in the Royal Navy, it was often mid-ranking administrators – not medics – who were the first to recognize the altered behaviour patterns of PTSD sufferers: via a case of domestic violence where you wouldn't expect one or because a combat veteran who'd 'seen some things' down in the South Atlantic was now arguing excessively with his peers or brawling down the pub.

These, I explained, were often the tell-tale clues that something was amiss.

The stigma of psychological problems – not to mention the fear that they could lead to your being thrown out of the military – meant that military doctors were often the last to know.

The base commander took a long time to stub out his cigarette.

Until now, he had given very little away, but I felt that somewhere what I'd said had struck a chord. I was nonetheless pleasantly surprised when he cleared his throat and told me that I had his full cooperation. His only stipulation was that his MO and the base chaplain should accompany me and my team during our debriefing sessions. He was keen, he said, to attend as many of them as he could himself.

I met his gaze and shook his hand. A partnership had begun. I knew that this man was as keen to understand what had happened to the men in his charge as we were. For a first foray into the great unknown, it could not have got off to a better start.

We headed off together so that he could introduce me to the MO and the chaplain. I'd have to win them over too. My diplomatic offensive continued.

It wasn't until the afternoon that I finally met up with David Whalley. We didn't have long to talk one-on-one – the 30-odd rescuers on-base, he explained, had already assembled in the mountain rescue hut and were waiting for me to address them.

Talk about coming down to earth. This was the nature of my predicament: how to seem reassuringly in charge, as if I had done this hundreds of times before, when in reality I was out on a wing and a prayer.

Perhaps David picked up on my apprehension, because he added: 'I already told them you're one of us – that you'd done your stint as a mountain rescuer.'

He nodded over his shoulder in the direction of a nondescript-looking single-storey block set amid a small group of administrative buildings.

Finding and retrieving people off mountains was not – and still isn't – the primary job of RAF mountain rescuers. As I'd discovered in Cyprus, all mountain rescuers had 'day jobs' within the RAF in roles such as administration, aircraft maintenance and the other disciplines that make up the daily taskings of the service. No one, however, belittles the pride and professionalism they devote to their secondary duty and this was very much evident in the mountain rescue hut where David's colleagues were waiting for me.

The walls were plastered with maps of the regional topography, from the Angus and Grampian mountains north of Dundee all the way to the northernmost tip of the Highlands. Through the half-open door of a cupboard I could see shelves groaning under the weight of ropes and ice axes. Padded anoraks and waterproof overtrousers hung from hooks. There was no mistaking where I was.

David Whalley led Pearl, Andrew, Alan, Bert and me into the room where the 30 mountain rescuers were waiting. Five austere wooden chairs were ranged in front of our audience. Pearl, Alan, Andrew and Bert took their seats.

'No need for introductions,' David whispered in my ear, before I could sit down. 'Why don't you just tell it like it is.'

I got to my feet. Where to begin? An image of the shattered houses by the crater we'd seen by the A74 flashed into my mind.

'I'm here on Flight's invitation,' I began, 'because I believe that something extraordinary has happened here . . .'

I glanced up. I expected to see people gazing at their feet or their hands or for the room to fill with nervous coughing. But instead I was greeted by silence. Grizzled, weather-beaten faces stared at me.

I pressed on. I explained how stress reactions could occur after a trauma and about the signs to watch for. I emphasized that this, in my view, whatever the prevailing medical opinion stated, was not a pathological condition – not an illness – but a normal reaction to an abnormal event. I also said that my research had led me to believe that in spite of the very real distress experienced by anyone who'd been exposed to a severe trauma, it was in some way designed to be purposeful: by which I meant that it was a condition from which we were specifically supposed to gain knowledge; to learn. In short, it was a lesson in survival.

PTSD, I said, was the mind's way of coming to terms with things seen, heard, smelled, sensed and touched that were often too terrible for it to comprehend.

You get a sense of whether or not people are listening to what you have to say and my strong impression was that the mountain rescuers were listening very hard.

With hindsight, I think that was because they had all been experiencing the flashbacks and nightmares I was describing and they were mightily relieved to hear that these were normal reactions – demonstrations that their minds were trying to understand what they had absorbed by looking at the scenario over and over again; that their minds were not playing tricks on them and, most important of all, that they were not going mad.

Day two, first thing, and Bert and I strolled from the accommodation block to the mountain rescue hut for our first full day of briefings.

It was a filthy morning; low, angry clouds driven in from the North Sea were spitting icy rain at us and I was suddenly thankful for the big fisherman's sweater and anorak for which I'd swapped my uniform. The uniform had been necessary for briefing the brass, but it would have been counter-productive in the one-on-one sessions. The trappings of rank constituted the first of the many layers we needed to peel away when we sat down with the mountain rescuers.

'Game plan?' Bert asked as we strode towards the hut.

We were still in uncharted territory. After the mass briefing yesterday, today was about one-on-one sessions. I'd made it plain to David Whalley that we weren't going to force ourselves upon anybody. If they wanted to see us, then Andrew, Alan, Pearl and I were on hand to talk to them in all the privacy these things required. While my talk seemed to have gone down well, I didn't expect to find a queue around the block for our services.

But throughout the rest of the day, people had come forward and slowly the day – today – had filled with appointments.

There was no great mystery to these debriefings. Each session boiled down to my asking two questions: what happened to you and how do you feel about what happened to you? Thereafter, what was basically required was a good ear and a lot of understanding. I knew that we would hear many things that we would find shocking and it was for this reason that Bert would remain outside the primary debriefing process, a tip I'd taken from Jeffrey Mitchell. Having immersed myself deeply in Lockerbie, and having amassed quite a bit of experience already of individual traumas, I was confident that I would not need to call on Bert's services. But I was keen that he should be there, if needed, for the other members of the team, especially Andrew and Pearl, who'd had far less experience of trauma reactions than Alan and me.

I had no idea how the day would unfold and told Bert that the game plan remained the same as the day before: we'd wing it again and hope for the best.

Until there is commitment, there is hesitancy. Whatever you can do or dream you can, begin it. Begin it now . . .

'You what?'

I realized I'd been thinking aloud.

'Sorry, I was bastardizing Goethe.'

'What the hell has Goethe got to do with this?'

'Good question,' I said. I gave him what I hoped was a reassuring smile. 'The ramblings of a madman.'

Bert furrowed his brow. 'I guess we're all flying by the seat of our pants.'

As if on cue, a pair of Phantoms roared over us, iron grey, barely discernible from the sky. Glasnost or not, Leuchars was still Britain's forward line of defence against the Soviet bombers that continued to probe our airspace.

As volunteers, mountain rescuers were drawn to the mountains and were therefore driven to give something back. As such, I suspected that beneath their weather-beaten skins there was a good deal more sensitivity than a cursory examination of their CVs would credit.

Angus Maxwell, much like David Whalley, a sergeant with twenty-plus years of experience under his belt, seemed to fall into this bracket. His file, which I'd read overnight, told me he'd been born and bred in the Highlands and been one of the first rescuers on the scene.

He was my first appointment of the day.

Maxwell examined his fingers as he spoke. He pinched the tip of each with the thumb and forefinger of his other hand, as if to remind himself that he was here and not there. He was a big man, the kind that spoke softly and only when he had something to say. His skin was the texture of sandpaper. Every time he rubbed his fingers, it was an audible reminder of a life lived in the elements.

We were in a small office, a back room used for training purposes. The walls were plastered with more maps. Boots and crampons were crammed into a cupboard in the corner.

Maxwell could have been reading from a telephone directory. He rarely looked up. It was difficult to catch his words above the wind which was rattling the windowpanes behind me.

He said it again. 'It was like hell on earth . . .'

'In what way?'

A nerve end tugged at his upper left eyelid.

I asked the question again.

'It's the things that go through your mind,' he said. 'Stupid, idiotic thoughts. Yet, when the images of that hillside run through my head, these are the questions that keep coming back to me. For the life of me, I don't understand why.'

'Questions?'

He took a deep breath. 'People with no clothes on. Lying there, in the middle of a field. The fall from 31,000 feet had ripped everything off them. Everything. Shoes, socks, trousers, belts . . . How can the wind rip a belt off a man and leave no trace of it, for God's sake?'

He glanced up. 'Crazy, isn't it? All that death, scattered as far as the eye could see, like those paintings you see of Judgement Day, and I'm lying awake at night wondering how the wind has the capacity to remove a man's belt.'

'Angus,' I said quietly, 'this is about trying to make sense of something that makes no sense. Hell is probably the right word for it.'

It was a long time before he spoke again.

'I see their faces, over and over. It makes it hard sometimes for me to close my eyes . . .'

'It's important that you try to tell me.'

'Some of it I can deal with, like the sleepers . . .'

'Sleepers?'

'That's the way they looked. As if they were sleeping. Some even looked as if they were smiling in their sleep. I can see the look on one woman's face right now. I came across her at daybreak. She was lying in a field, face up. A middle-aged lady . . .'

His voice drifted away. I waited for him to continue.

'I couldn't see so much as a blemish on her body; she was just lying there, smiling . . . Strange as it sounds, I found some comfort in it, because I realized she must have been happy when it happened . . .'

His hands were shaking. He pinched another fingertip.

'. . . like she was sitting there, talking to someone, her husband, maybe, a drink in her hand . . .' he looked up suddenly, 'when, bang, the bomb goes off.'

He told me he'd found quite a few victims like that and for a second I did what I shouldn't have done – I placed myself in the seat next to this woman and started taking in my surroundings: the air-craft cabin half an hour into the flight; hostesses in the aisles handing out drinks, the passengers relaxing as Pan Am 103 slipped into the cruise portion of the flight, knowing that in six hours' time it would be the dawn of a new day in New York, three days before Christmas . . .

I forced myself back to the here and now.

It was good, I told him, that he was able to draw comfort from the fact that these people died not knowing what had hit them.

'Not all of them,' he said, his thumb and forefinger moving more rapidly now. 'The worst thing is the knowledge that a lot of them – too many – knew exactly what was happening; what was going to happen to them.'

He gave an involuntary shudder. Drops of rain started to splatter against the glass behind me.

'The abject terror of finding yourself in a disintegrating aircraft at 31,000 feet and knowing that you're going to die . . . What does that do to someone?' He snatched a glance at me. 'Nobody should live their last few moments on this earth like that, nobody.'

Maxwell hadn't slept more than a few hours a night since the crash. When he closed his eyes, this was what he saw.

Fighting every professional instinct, I started to see it too.

I was falling through space. My eyes were wide open. I was terrified beyond all reason, but somehow I was registering the black-ness, the smoke, the flames and the kerosene; the clothes being ripped from my body and, in the midst of it all, strobe-like images of other bodies falling, a series of mid-air explosions, huge, burning pieces of machinery spiralling into the blackness.

Five minutes, he was telling me. That was the time it took for some sections of the fuselage to hit the ground.

Daybreak on the morning after the crash found him combing the fields above the town. Looking back gave him a clear view of Sherwood Crescent and the smoking crater where the main section of the plane had gone in. Eyes forward and it was another vision, an entire panorama this time: a bank of seats lying in the middle of a field with passengers still strapped into it; one of them, a child, was headless; a woman's body lay impaled on the branches of a tree; a child's dressing gown, caught by the wind, was bowling down the hillside, like there was somebody still in it; and there were imprints in the earth where some of the bodies had been removed by the forensic teams.

Day two was worse, he said, because that was the day the looters turned up: gangs of thieves from Glasgow, Liverpool and Manchester masquerading as rescue workers.

'Looters?' I said. 'But that hasn't come out in the press.'

Not yet, he replied. Perhaps, for once, even the newspapers can't find the bloody words.

Finally, he got to the part that really plagued him.

'I'm standing over this child. She's lying next to her mother. The ground was soft that night, the earth very wet. We pull the mother out first and that's when I realize that the image of them being unharmed is just an illusion. As they hit the ground, everything inside them disintegrated – organs, bones . . . When we pick her up, she's just mush.'

I kept my gaze firmly on his face, letting him know I was there with him. It was hard to tell at first over the noise of the rain, but I knew that he was weeping.

'All the while we're taking her body to the truck, I'm thinking, I've got to go back for the little girl . . .'

He cleared his throat and sucked down some air.

'We pull her from the earth and there's something in the ground beneath her. The impact has driven it into the soil. I think, for a second, that it's part of her, but the poor kid's body doesn't have a scratch on it.'

He shook his head.

'What was it?' I whispered.

'A doll,' he said, lifting his eyes to mine. 'The exact same doll I had bought my little girl for Christmas.'

He called it hell, and perhaps he was right; maybe this was what hell was: a place where thought, emotion, memory, reality itself, became trapped in some never-ending loop.

Every time he closed his eyes, every time he saw his little girl, every time he thought of Christmas, every time he saw a doll . . .

David's words filled my head again.

He sees things, the same things, and the things he sees won't go away . . .

This was what he saw over and over again in his flashback.

Stories like this, many of them every bit as harrowing as Maxwell's, were echoed across the other three bases. I knew that we were making progress when at RAF Leeming, our first port of call after Leuchars, the senior medical officer from RAF Catterick phoned. He told me that he had learned what we were doing and wanted me to come to Catterick to see the RAF Regiment personnel who'd been mustered to go to Lockerbie to act as guards. Many of them were very new to the service, because Catterick was the main training base for the RAF Regiment.

We travelled to Catterick and while I was being introduced to the SMO and his colleagues in the hallway of the medical centre, I was told that there was a call for me. I went to an office, picked up the phone and immediately recognized the voice on the other end of the line: Air Vice Marshal 'Big Al' Johnson, the principal medical officer for Strike Command. I was about to get a first-hand dose of official scepticism from the senior hierarchy of the RAF about the validity of PTSD. Big Al had been my CO at Wroughton before Bob Chappell took over. It was immediately obvious that he had not been pre-briefed either and I knew this was going to hamper our case; it might even jeopardize our ability to get to the remaining mountain rescuers.

'Turnbull,' he boomed, 'you've got exactly thirty seconds to tell me what you're doing on one of my stations and if you can't persuade me there's a very good reason for you being there you'll be going home straight away!'

I told him in very short order.

'You've really got a bee in your bonnet about this PTSD business, haven't you?' Big Al said.

'It's not what I think,' I told him, 'it's what the data is telling us.'

'The data is largely American,' he said, raising, in a heartbeat, the old perception that PTSD was a phenomenon unique to the Vietnam War.

'That would ignore the experience of the Royal Navy in the Falklands, sir,' I replied.

Big Al coughed and spluttered a bit, then said: 'Well, something good might come of it, I suppose, but I want a full report on my desk after you get back to Wroughton.'

I promised I would send him one and put the phone down. We remained in business.

RAF Stafford turned out to be particularly interesting because of a tragic coincidence. A few days before we arrived at the base, its mountain rescue team had participated in another air crash rescue.

On 8 January, shortly after 8 pm, a Boeing 737-400 operated by British Midland came down on the M1 motorway close to the village of Kegworth while its crew attempted a dead-stick landing at East Midlands Airport. The full facts of the crash had not yet emerged, but it later turned out that pilot and co-pilot had shut down the wrong engine when a fan-blade sheared in the left-hand powerplant at 28,000 feet.

The tragedy was compounded by the fact that the aircraft, which effectively was flying unpowered, had glided to within a few hundred yards of the perimeter of East Midlands Airport when its tail section struck the embankment of the M1, causing it to break up. Forty-seven passengers died at the site of the crash; a further 74 were injured, most of them extremely seriously.

The mountain rescuers from Stafford were quick to arrive on the scene and worked tirelessly through the night to pull the dead, dying and injured from the wreckage.

Given that we arrived at Stafford a few days after this appalling incident, logically we should have been confronted by people who were doubly traumatized by what they'd been through at Lockerbie and at Kegworth. In fact, the reverse was true. At the time, we had no explanation for this. It was only later that we began to understand.

At Lockerbie, time and again we heard about the universal feeling of helplessness shared by the mountain rescuers as they'd picked through the debris in and around the town. As was so graphically demonstrated to me by Maxwell and others, the term 'rescue' was a misnomer. There had been no rescuing to be done at Lockerbie. It was a clean-up operation and a desperately harrowing one at that.

The Stafford mountain rescuers experienced that same feeling of helplessness as their colleagues, but Kegworth, paradoxically, turned out to be a safety valve. At Kegworth, there *had* been people to rescue. The mountain rescuers had been able to deploy their considerable paramedical skills to good effect. There had been an outlet for all that pent-up, frustrated adrenaline generated at Lockerbie. This, later, would shed light on the chemical make-up of a stress reaction within the body.

At St Athan, our last port of call, it was a different story.

On our way south, we were suddenly informed that no one was available to see us. This struck me as strange as Bert had gone to great lengths to ensure that the timing of our visit was convenient to everyone. So, instead of going to St Athan, we headed home. Only later did we find out the reasons why they'd not wanted to see us.

It turned out that the St Athan team was in complete denial about Lockerbie.

When we did eventually get to see the team, the guy in charge was quite aggressive towards us. We were made to feel like intruders and that they were only seeing us under duress. To compound these messages, the walls of the mountain rescue centre at St Athan were plastered with more images than I ever wanted to see of the Lockerbie victims; pictures, graphically described by others, that I did not want inside my head. Some of the photographs were deliberately placed in front of us during our debriefing sessions. To see in photographic form what thus far we'd only visualized in our minds was deeply disturbing.

What the St Athan mountain rescuers were saying through the pictures was clear: we don't need any psychobabble to get us through what happened at Lockerbie.

This attitude is healthy to an extent, but in this particular case I could see that it stemmed from the team leader. It told us that junior members of a trauma team will often adopt the attitude of the person in charge.

Immediately upon our return to Wroughton, weird stuff started to happen. I'd noticed that Andrew Salmon, our sergeant psychiatric nurse on the Lockerbie debriefing team, had been off-colour – really down in the dumps, in fact – ever since we'd returned and at first I put this down to an attack of the January blues. Later, when his mood didn't alter appreciably – he was being snappy with everybody – I asked someone in the department if he was all right and was told that he'd been having fierce arguments at home with his wife. I assumed then that his domestic difficulties lay at the root of his problems at work. I also assumed that in time the difficulties would blow over and decided to let him work things through at his own pace – to intervene only if it went on unduly.

But then Alan Lillywhite came to see me to ask my permission to do some locum work at the surgery of a nearby GP, something that he was fully within his rights to do. In passing, he made a comment I barely registered at the time, though I should have. He said he'd be happy to work the longer hours that came with the locum job as it would get him out of the house. He, too, he said, had been having arguments with his wife and the atmosphere at home was unbearable. That was when the penny should have dropped, but it didn't. It didn't even drop when I heard soon afterwards that Pearl had gone completely bananas – a totally uncharacteristic reaction for her. While we'd been away, for almost two weeks, there had been a spell of very bad weather and a pipe had burst in her room in the barrack block and she'd had to move to another room temporarily. Her futon bed would not fit in the new room and she went crazy, had a huge fit of temper. It was only on the fourth day after our return, when Bert came to see me – solid, dependable, stoical Bert – to ask if he could take a few days off that things began to click into place.

'What's up?' I asked him as he prepared to leave my office. He looked utterly miserable.

'I don't know. I'm just tired, I guess.'

I had to agree. Everybody was. The two-week trip had been unrelenting. I wished him and Beryl a happy few days off and asked him where they planned to go. I assumed they'd found someone to look after the old folks' home while they were away.

Bert paused by the door. 'Beryl's not coming. I'm going to jump in the old mobile home and see where the road leads me. Haven't decided anything beyond that. I just need to walk, get some air. Beryl understands. Thanks for the time off.' He closed the door behind him.

Four green bottles, I said to myself. *And if one green bottle should accidentally fall . . .*

That evening, I parked the car in the drive and listened to the sound of the engine cooling.

There's a pattern here. Why hadn't I noticed it before?

Visiting so many bases on the trot, dealing with case after case, writing reports, smoothing things over with station commanders and senior officers who tolerated us but still, I knew, regarded us with suspicion, had left me with little time to think.

I hadn't seen the pattern until Bert, the devoted family man, told me that he was going off on his own for a couple of days to walk in the hills. That led me to wonder: did I have the same problem?

In the few spare moments I'd had in the two weeks we were away, I dreamed of little other than returning home; of being with Alison and the kids again. But we hadn't got off to the best of starts.

Ali and I'd had a row that morning, serious enough to make her eyes brim. It had been sparked by something completely trivial – my forgetting to take the dog to the vet for his inoculation. She'd had a real go at me, but I wasn't having it. Anyone, I told her, can make a mistake. It was unlike her to be so snappy.

I glanced at the freshly wrapped bouquet of flowers on the passenger seat.

I waited until supper before broaching the subject. Everybody was gathered around the table. Stuart and Iain were telling me what they'd got up to at school that day, but only a part of me was paying attention.

'Listen . . .' I cleared my throat rather nervously. 'There's something I'd like to say.'

The room went quiet. When I looked up, four pairs of eyes were watching me very closely.

I glanced at Ali. We'd been married long enough and been through enough for me to know what her look meant.

Where are you taking this, Gordon?

I didn't quite know.

I talked about the team for a moment or two; about my concern for Andrew and Pearl and Bert, and the price they appeared to be paying for the Lockerbie debriefing.

The children were too young to understand. They'd seen the pictures on the news and they knew that Dad was somehow involved. We hadn't said much beyond that, anxious to protect them, as much as anything else, from the fundamental, unanswerable question that had united the civilized world in its condemnation of Lockerbie: what possible impulse could drive a group of human beings to snuff out the lives of 270 innocent people and devastate countless more?

I finally got to the point. 'Have you noticed anything different about me since I got back?'

I expected blank faces followed by a uniform assurance that I hadn't changed one little bit. 'What are you talking about? Of course not. You're the same old Dad/Gordon . . .' That kind of thing.

Instead, there was a clatter from across the table. Stuart dropped his knife and fork on his plate and threw back his chair.

Everybody else stopped eating. Stuart walked from the room without a word. He didn't even look at me.

I got up to follow him, but Alison stopped me.

'Leave him,' she whispered sharply. Over her shoulder, I saw Iain and Bobby staring at me, eyes like saucers.

'What on earth is wrong?' I said. 'What did I do?'

'They're not used to having you around—'

'But that's what I was trying to explain. I've been away, but now I'm back.'

'Perhaps that's what's frightened him.' Ali's expression was pained. 'Us . . .'

'What's that supposed to mean?'

There was anger in my voice and she'd heard it. I clenched my teeth. Here we go again.

'Ever since you got back, Gordon, the whole family has been walking on eggshells around you. The kids don't recognize their own father . . . I'm not sure I do.'

She looked at me long and hard. 'Is this how it's going to be every time something happens? Who counsels the counsellor, Gordon?'

Who counselled the counsellor?

This was not the way it was supposed to be.

Later, after the children had gone to bed and Alison had retired to our bedroom with a book, I sat at my desk, staring at a photograph of us all on holiday together the year before.

I was shocked by what she had said. I must have been in complete denial. Alison was a nurse and had a nurse's practical take on the way the world turns. She didn't make things up. I'd been seeing things the wrong way round. There was a technical term for it: I had been guilty of a paranoid projection. It was something I looked for in my patients; I never thought it would happen to me. Since returning home I'd been wondering why the family seemed grumpy and Alison, especially, seemed to be distant and remote and snappy. Of course it was the other way round, but I'd been protecting myself from that reality. The realization stunned me. We really did need secondary debriefings to protect ourselves and it had to be more than we'd received during the trip after Lockerbie.

I had to find a way of handling this. More importantly, as the head of the inpatient psychiatry facility within the RAF, I had to find a way of dealing with PTSD and its subtle, pernicious and insidious ripple effects. Lockerbie had given me a clear view of the impact of traumatic stress reactions. It had also shown me how ill-prepared we were for coping with it on a sizeable scale.

As horrific as Lockerbie was, its effects had been relatively contained.

What if we found ourselves in the grip of another full-blown conflict?

Would we end up facing our very own Vietnam?

Chapter 11

The Cuckoo's Nest

I sat staring backwards out the window of the RAF VC10 as the southern tip of Greenland slid under the right wing. I'd always found long plane trips a great time for quiet reflection and on this particular journey I had plenty to reflect on. It was September 1990 and I had just been awarded an RAF medical scholarship to study for two months at the National Center for PTSD at Palo Alto in California.

But there wasn't much time. Saddam Hussein had invaded Kuwait a month previously and it looked pretty certain that we were going to war soon. There was a need to sit at the feet of the Americans to find out what they knew – which had led to their setting up the Center.

For the first time ever I felt as if I was heading for the 'frontier of the frontier' – the cutting edge – and I was excited, but nervous, too.

I needed to absorb what the Americans knew and return to Wroughton to set things up in preparation for the battle-shock casualties we were anticipating.

The Center was the world's leading facility for the study of a condition that Lockerbie had told me was not a disease. Instead, I now saw it as the mind's natural response to an unnatural, terrifying event or series of events. Until Lockerbie, even I had semi-accepted the established British view of PTSD – that its attendant symptoms, which included the flashback, were evidence of a pathological 'fault' within the brain. But the mountain rescuers had changed my opinion completely. Had it not been for the fact that I knew them as a breed, a number of them personally, I might never have formed the view that the accepted version was no longer realistic.

Lockerbie propelled me from dealing with the hypothetical and the theoretical into the real world. I simply could not accept that people who had spent their professional lives rescuing others off mountains – people who were extremely resilient by nature – were suffering universally from a mental illness; it defied all logic, not to mention what I knew about them.

But it was a big wrench. I was having to unlearn much of what I'd been taught since entering psychiatry. In 1980, *DSM-III* had categorized the existence of PTSD for the first time, but it had nonetheless characterized it as a pathological condition. But post-Lockerbie, I felt I had cracked a lock I'd been picking away at for years. Suddenly, things were beginning to make sense and I felt I had to tell as many people as I could about it. This was a phenomenon that the military needed to learn about. We could no longer afford to be stuck in the past – we needed to move on from the shell shock and LMF paradigm that still seemed to characterize official attitudes in certain quarters of the establishment. For this reason I'd spent much of the post-Lockerbie period travelling and lecturing: telling as many people as I could what I thought was at stake here.

On the whole, I was pleased with the reaction I'd got; people (with the exception of a good many surgeons, a lot of whom would storm out of my lectures in protest) were generally intrigued. This was not an illness, I told them, and the core clue was the flashback. I felt it was trying to tell the sufferer – and us – something. It seemed to be the brain's natural response to whatever terrifying, unnatural event it had been exposed to. I didn't yet know what it meant, but I was hoping that Palo Alto might unlock some more clues, especially now that there was a pressing reason: the possibility of war.

After Saddam Hussein's invasion of Kuwait, an international coalition led by America and Britain had been dispatching vast numbers of troops to the Gulf in a bid to stop the Iraqi dictator in his tracks. It had also issued him with an ultimatum: get out of Kuwait or face a military response. As yet, the coalition wasn't in a position to put a date on that ultimatum, but most of the armchair analysts seemed to think that it would come in the New Year. It would take several months for the coalition to build troop and equipment levels to the point where they would be able to take on Saddam's army – one of the most formidable, if numbers meant anything, in the region, if not the entire world. I knew that our PTSD team at Wroughton had to be ready then too. With tens of thousands of British service personnel in Saudi Arabia and the Gulf states, our potential for being swamped with trauma reactions on a massive scale had become a terrifying reality. Lockerbie had opened my eyes; now I needed a system to cope with the scale of the fall-out that seemed to be just around the corner. I was travelling to Palo Alto on my own. Ali and the boys would follow in a week or two. The plan was to rent a house and put the children in a local school for a term.

The psychiatric facility at Palo Alto was run by the VA – short for the US Department of Veterans Affairs – and consisted of a sizeable number of buildings of various heights and antiquity laid out in grass and woodland. To begin with I stayed with my old friend Greg Vagshenian, who happened to be working there, although in a different part of the campus – a complete coincidence, but a happy one. Greg had joined the US Navy around the time I joined the RAF, but subsequently had swapped the Navy for the Army. He never lost a chance to remind me of the prediction he had made on our first meeting as students, that I would become a shrink; I joked that it was entirely appropriate that he should be working across the way from the place where they'd filmed *One Flew over the Cuckoo's Nest*.

This was a bad joke, because the VA Center was nothing like the archaic institution depicted in the Jack Nicholson movie. It was way ahead of any kind of established thinking on PTSD in the UK. The VA had set up a programme for the treatment of Vietnam vets but it had grown to encompass others, including, at the time of my visit, a Second World War veteran and a guy who'd fought in the US military's invasion of Grenada in 1983. Its work had been so successful that it had expanded to embrace civilian trauma victims as well. The Americans had struggled with the established model of PTSD ever since Vietnam and this was their response. For once, I was on the same page as officialdom.

I loved working in America. You didn't get all the backchat that you got in the UK; psychiatrists were respected here as physicians. You didn't need to establish your credentials all the time; you were just accepted as another type of specialist.

I was given my own consulting room and told I would be included in any and all sessions. Everyone was beyond polite – they were incredibly deferential and I soon found out why. In the USA, a 'wing commander' – my rank – denoted someone who led an entire wing, and there were only two – the operational wing and the support wing. It was the equivalent of an air marshal back in the UK. Amazingly, when I had to come clean, they didn't seem to think any the less of me.

I had two 'a-ha' moments in Palo Alto. The first occurred during a meeting early on with the Center's director. He drew a picture on a flipchart in his office of a mirror – the kind you found in a gentlemen's outfitters; a tall mirror with three parts, like a triptych, that allowed you to see what you looked like from all angles. This was his PTSD model.

'See, Gordon? It's like going to the barber shop: you can see yourself from the front, the sides and the back. The back represents the individual's back-story – the story that has to be checked out when a trauma is diagnosed. The sides represent the trauma itself and the front represents the way forward. What this is is a—'

'Narrative,' I said, interrupting him. 'A narrative for stress.'

I told him that John Rollins and I had also come up with a stress narrative – the Pint Pot Model – and that ours, like his, also had three parts. At first I thought that his mirror and the Pint Pot were different ways of looking at the same issue. But then I realized that his model was subtly different from ours. 'You go into that system of mirrors, you get fitted up with a suit and you walk out of the shop with a new set of clothes. You've taken a slightly different form, but you're still the same person.'

He nodded. This was at the heart of it. The Mirror Model said that the trauma was something you could move beyond. You came out with a new set of clothes, but you were essentially the same person. You wouldn't go back to where you had been before – you'd moved on.

It was a depiction of the future and a representation of hope; something I'd always felt innately, but had never articulated in quite the same way.

*

Palo Alto was where many of the ideas that I already had running about in my head were able to take root. I realized that I wasn't going bonkers; that other people were thinking along similar lines, and actually doing something about it. Central to this action component was the idea of groups and how effective they could be in the treatment process.

The patients at the VA Center were as enthusiastic as the staff, and were receptive to the wealth of treatments and ideas that the Center had to offer. Nobody was there under duress. Nobody grumbled about being there. People wanted to be part of it, on both sides, and were really excited about the work, because they knew it was important. I think they also knew they were at the forefront of something deeply significant. It was like a melting pot in which everyone's ideas were respected because there were no set camps to be in, no schools of thought to fall in line with or challenge. It was very different from the UK.

Group treatment took the form of a seminar and it would open with a seminar leader giving a talk on a particular topic, then gradually taking a back seat and becoming a member of the group as views from the floor became more prevalent. So, if the topic of the day was anger management, the seminar leader would open by asking for instances of anger in people's lives. People from the floor would open up, but only if they felt 'safe'.

Discussions among the members of the group about their experiences of anger would then take over, allowing you, the seminar leader, to slip into the background and become like any other member of the group – still the leader, but no longer the presenter, because the patients usually knew a lot more about anger than you did, because they had had these experiences. All you were doing was introducing a familiar topic to people who had experienced the issue for real. I liked this idea; of learning from my patients. Again, it reminded me of my time at Ely, where I had been taught by Fred Amroliwalla to listen – really listen – to what my patients were telling me.

When this discussion got going, it created an atmosphere of mutuality and trust and togetherness; of cohesion, and coherence among its members.

I soon realized that they were able to normalize many of the fears that they felt as a result of comparing and contrasting their experiences with the other members of the group. In this way, they felt less freakish or odd about having these things happen to them. They could also normalize the anger and see why it had happened, and where it had come from. Other people would then give them advice about it – hey, that happened to me, too, and this is what I did about it. It was a very rich preparation for the processing of trauma and I saw that it really worked in helping people to get better; processing, of course, being key.

There were about ten different topics which served as introductions to basic psychology to help people think in a more structured way about the things they had experienced. It helped them prepare these experiences for processing in their own minds, and gave them plenty of opportunity to think about themselves through the mirror of other sufferers' experiences. I saw that they found it 'safe' to approach their trauma in this way, and if they felt safe they would open up more. They could then go into processing the traumas with the tools they had already amassed through group discussions.

My second 'a-ha' came in a fabulous moment of synchronicity with a chap called Dudley Blake. Dudley, a psychologist, was actively involved in the therapy programmes. He was very friendly and had an office near to the one I'd been given. He had a huge vacuum flask and in the morning he'd fill it up with coffee or Coke and then wander around campus, settling down cross-legged on the grass with whomsoever he was with at the time – be they patients, fellow psychologists or me – dispensing drinks as he talked and listened to all and sundry.

It was what I loved about the place – there were none of the cobwebs I'd encountered in so many establishments in the UK. It was both super-relaxed and yet clearly the nerve centre of something special. It also sent a message to veterans themselves. There were tough and chronic cases of PTSD at Palo Alto, people who'd been referred by VA doctors from all over the US for treatment. Even if you'd been in the military for a day, you were entitled to VA medical treatment for the rest of your life. It was an inducement to join the military and every major city in the country had a Veterans hospital.

I thought about the way we'd treated our Falklands veterans and then thought about events that were ramping up in the Gulf. While America might be prepared for the return of hundreds, perhaps thousands, of traumatized troops, Britain most certainly was not.

To be able to treat people for trauma reactions on the scale I feared following combat actions in the Gulf, I knew I needed a system. But what kind of system?

And then, one day, I was in Dudley's office and out it popped. 'Wouldn't it be great,' I said, 'if we had a way to measure PTSD. A system.'

Dudley poured some coffee from his go-everywhere flask, then rocked back on his chair and looked at me. 'What would you want from such a system, Gordon? If you could wave a magic wand, that is.'

'Instead of imagining in our heads what's going on in the patient's mind, it would be ideal if we had a form that assessed when people exhibited the cardinal features of PTSD – the points defined in *DSM-III*.'

He arched an eyebrow. 'Why would you need such a thing?'

'Because we're about to fight a war and I'm terrified that we don't have the means to deal with the fall-out.'

'Well, that makes sense, I guess.' He leaned forward and pulled a document from a tray. 'Something like this, then.' He slid the document across the desk.

I picked it up and started thumbing through it. I glanced up.

'It's called CAPS,' Dudley said. 'The Clinician-Administered PTSD Scale. We developed it here. It's brand new. But it's exactly what you just asked for – a front-line instrument for assessing whether people have PTSD.'

I sat there staring at the questionnaire. Up until then, what we had in the UK was far from satisfactory. We had instruments that measured aspects of PTSD; tools like the Beck Depression Inventory, the General Health Questionnaire and the questionnaire we'd devised at Wroughton for the Hungerford victims. There was also the Impact of Events Scale devised by Horowitz a decade or so earlier, which was useful in measuring PTSD but couldn't assess the frequency and intensity of the symptoms. I could see, simply by flicking through the CAPS questionnaire, that this was different. This was a scientific instrument; a measurement device – a scale with numbers, intensity and frequency. Furthermore, I could see that you didn't need to be a fully qualified psychiatrist or psychologist to carry out the assessment; the questionnaire did that for you. Joe Blow could administer CAPS in Palo Alto and Joe Bloggs could do it in the Gulf. All you needed to know was how to administer the questionnaire. It standardized the process.

'How can I make use of this, Dudley?'

'Well, technically, it's copyrighted, but I can't see why that should stop us acting spontaneously with our oldest ally at a time of crisis, do you?' He rocked back on his chair again and smiled.

A few days later, Ali, the kids and I drove across the States to New Orleans, which was playing host to an international conference on trauma. After two extraordinary months, the International Society for Traumatic Stress Studies (ISTSS) conference was my swansong in the US and from the East Coast we would head back as a family to the UK. Professor David Parry-Jones, an eminent child and adolescent psychiatrist at the University of Glasgow, had been one of my Merlins while running the unit at the Warneford Hospital in Oxford when I was on study leave there, gaining experience in child psychiatry ahead of my membership exams back in 1982. He had organized a series of presentations to be given at the conference about the Lockerbie disaster. I presented on the impact of the trauma on the RAF mountain rescue teams involved.

It was November. US, British and other coalition forces were assembling in increasing numbers on the Kuwaiti border, ready to drive Saddam back into Iraq. Had hostilities begun, I would have been pulled out of Palo Alto and sent straight to the theatre of ops. That almost happened a couple of times and I was put on standby. The irony, of course, is that I'd have been no better off than the little Dutch boy with his finger in the dyke. But with Dudley's CAPS, I felt like a soldier armed with an AK-47 after being equipped with a musket. I was going to the Gulf with something that I could exploit very usefully in our war effort. Strange to admit, too, but I was excited. At long last, I knew I had a tool that wouldn't just help serve the people who needed it most, our soldiers on the front line; I also had something I could bash over the heads of the doubting Thomases in the British establishment, who still believed that trauma reactions were evidence of psychological frailty. With talk of weapons of mass destruction in the Gulf – Saddam's chemical and biological weapons – it felt as if we were about to fight the Third World War. But with talk still within senior medical echelons of malingering and of people with PTSD who were going to crack up anyway, it was as if we'd been time-warped back to the First and Second World Wars.

The penny had also dropped about groups. We now not only had a means of assessing whether people on a broad front were suffering from trauma reactions; through the seminar-group sessions, we had a means of treating them as well.

I flew back from the States on a Saturday and jumped on an RAF Hercules transport four days later bound for Cyprus, which was acting as a staging area for British service personnel heading for the Gulf.

Because I was head of the psychiatric department at Wroughton, I needed to delegate what I had learned at Palo Alto, so, before I left, I handed over a pile of material on CAPS to Walter Busuttil, my registrar, and to my pal Captain Jonathan Bisson, who was the Army psychiatrist showing most interest in PTSD. We agreed that we'd continue to liaise as soon as I reached Akrotiri.

We all knew that we needed to establish a way of coping with possibly tens of thousands of combat stress victims and that Wroughton, under the aegis of the RAF, was the right place to focus this effort. We also agreed there was no way we had the manpower to deal with combat stress casualties on a one-to-one basis and that group treatments offered the best solution. With Dudley's CAPS as our diagnostic measuring tool, medical personnel in the Gulf would be able to ascertain who had PTSD and who didn't. It was important, though, for me to get out to theatre as soon as possible to brief them on its existence.

Our trauma programme had been agreed. It would come down to ten working days of treatment spread over two calendar weeks. It was a huge undertaking and everybody at Wroughton had chipped in to make it possible.

We were very fortunate in that one of my Merlins, John Rollins, had come back to help us. After retiring from the RAF, John had gone to the Navy as a civilian, working as a locum. With war imminent, I'd asked if he would come back to help guide our department, knowing that I would be sent out to the Gulf. He'd agreed and his wise old head had been incredibly helpful in putting together the psychiatric war plan in the run-up to the outbreak of hostilities.

After a short stint in Cyprus, I was able to return to Wroughton to help organize the groups and get things sorted at the hospital before hostilities broke out. The clock was ticking. I knew that my call-up to the Gulf could come at any moment.

In recognition of this, my brother- and sister-in-law, Patrick and Sue, put on a full Christmas dinner in November at their house in Buckinghamshire. The whole family gathered for the occasion and I had to shake my head to remember that it was not actually Christmas Day.

The toast was for 'a safe return' and I felt a wave of loving and powerful support from the whole family.

My father-in-law, Noel, was reliving his own memories of the time he had deployed to war in 1939 as a tank commander. He made me feel I was doing something that needed to be done and this helped to quell the anxiety that had been clawing away at my stomach since Cyprus. It was as if the ultimate 'director of operations' was making the point: a new chapter in my life was being opened up, but whatever excitements were ahead, they weren't going to come cheap.

In fact, I was 'called forward' on seven occasions between that Christmas dinner and my eventual deployment. It felt as if the fates were toying with me, but it was much harder on Alison and the boys than it was on me.

The bombing started on the night of 17 January after the coalition's final deadline for Saddam to get out of Kuwait came and went. Like millions of other people, I sat up into the early hours of the morning watching Baghdad being pummelled by coalition air attacks on TV.

After the weeks of inevitability, part of me was relieved that it had started. Everyone knew that Saddam was evil and had to be removed. The question was how – and at what cost? For this reason, the greater part of me was petrified. Saddam had weapons of mass destruction – chemical and biological agents and the means to deliver them via aircraft and Scud missiles – and most people thought that, backed into a corner, he had nothing to lose by firing them at our troops, ensconced on the border with Kuwait and Iraq and at garrisons in Saudi Arabia and the Gulf states.

As the night wore on, an array of pundits paraded before my eyes, extolling the virtues of our 'smart weapons' – TV- and laser-guided bombs that could sail with pinpoint precision down air shafts to destroy targets, avoiding, in the process, 'collateral damage' – an expression that was bandied around in abundance that night. By the early hours, weary through lack of sleep, I watched the first post-strike briefing and saw, with my own eyes, just how accurate those weapons had been. BBC reporters, phoning in excitedly from Baghdad, talked about cruise missiles flying beneath their hotel windows and making turns down streets.

After a couple of hours, there was a palpable sense of euphoria that this amazing technology had worked so well – the first time it had ever been demonstrated on such a scale in anger – and for a moment I lulled myself into thinking that it might all be over relatively quickly. But the following day, as I snatched moments during work to watch the TV bulletins, talk of the first coalition casualties started to build; the more so when, after another briefing, we learned that the RAF had lost a number of aircrew – MIAs: crews missing in action.

A few days later, we were shocked to see a number of these air-crew paraded on Iraqi TV. The appearance of two of them – identified as an RAF Tornado pilot, Flight Lieutenant John Peters, and his navigator, Flight Lieutenant John Nichol – was especially sickening, as it was clear from the bruises on their faces that they had been tortured. Both men read out statements, clearly prepared for them by their captors, about the 'illegitimacy' of the conflict and called upon Western leaders to end it so that they could return home to their loved ones. They said it with such little conviction, their voices barely audible and their eyes averted from the camera, that it simply had the opposite effect: the nation, outraged that PoWs could have been treated in this way, rallied behind the systematic bombing campaign. Even when things looked bad, as they did when Saddam launched Scuds at Israel in the hope of drawing the Israelis into the conflict, and when a large number of Iraqi civilians were killed when a stray 'bunker buster' hit their underground shelter, popular support for the war remained high.

A few days later, we received our first casualty, a Tornado pilot who had been labelled by his base doctor, somebody I knew and respected, as having 'acute melancholia with hysterical features'.

This was the kind of language I'd have expected a doctor to have used during the First or Second World Wars, but not in the Gulf on the cusp of the twenty-first century.

When I read the pilot's file, I could see he was universally regarded as one of the best. His '5000 Series' – the name given to the record of your flying career in the RAF – was immaculate. But a couple of nights earlier, he'd gone berserk at his base in the Gulf, sobbing and screaming as he beat his fists against the walls of his cabin.

The pilot had been taking part in JP233 raids. The JP233 was a munitions dispenser slung under the belly of the Tornado. It was designed to riddle enemy runways with bomblets so as to render their airfields unusable. It had been designed to destroy Soviet runways from a low level, where missile systems couldn't engage. It had not been intended for use against a country like Iraq that relied primarily on good old-fashioned flak. Flying on a JP233 raid meant flying through a curtain of anti-aircraft fire and I'd seen reports on the TV of RAF Tornados returning to their bases looking like pepper pots.

Our pilot, whom I'll call Frank, had known the two captured RAF aircrew, Peters and Nichol, and, from the report I'd been given, the thing that had tipped him over the edge had been his seeing these two men, his friends, battered and bruised on the TV news bulletins.

The doctor who had seen the pilot in the Gulf was a very sensible man. He'd been at Wroughton in the aftermath of Lockerbie and had been one of the biggest supporters of our post-Lockerbie work. So why, I wondered, hadn't he recognized this man's trauma reaction for what it was?

I had a suspicion that it was all to do with contagion and echoed what I'd read about stress reactions during the First and Second World Wars. In the field, combatants don't like to think of people on the same base or in the same unit developing such reactions because they feel, whether consciously or subconsciously, that they might develop them too. And so, in a way, it was perfectly understandable that this doctor would want to deny that the pilot had PTSD – a trauma reaction – because he would prefer to think of it as something extraordinary, unique – a one-off. The doc would be helping himself to believe that the unthinkable couldn't possibly happen to him or anyone else. These, after all, were pilots he was dealing with.

If you're in the thick of it on the front line, which this doctor had been, you might not want to think that this man represented the tip of the iceberg; that his could be the first of many cases that would conspire to overwhelm our medical resources. You might be tempted to brand it as something rare: 'acute melancholia with hysterical features' would certainly have been that.

Our pilot had flown that day; he'd gone back to his cabin, he'd seen stuff on the TV and he'd undergone a dramatic change in his personality. The acute part of the melancholia diagnosis was definitely right. Melancholia implied that he was very depressed and distressed, which he most certainly was; he'd had a whole range of emotional reactions. 'Hysterical features' was also accurate, but it hadn't gone far enough because it wasn't linked to the combat experience. It placed his trauma reaction instead in the realm of an acute psychiatric illness, which by my reading, albeit from afar, it most definitely wasn't.

As I knew from my Atomic Model, it was perfectly possible for steely-eyed pilots to cut through their defensive shields, if the stressors challenging them were powerful enough. I had long suspected there was a dangerous rigidity to the highly developed defence mechanisms within pilots; one that would take a great deal to break. But when they did go, the collapse would be the equivalent of a dam bursting.

Frank arrived the next day, having been driven to Wroughton from the nearby transport base at Lyneham. When I heard that his car had passed through the main gate, I left my office on the first floor and went downstairs to welcome him.

In the vestibule, I found John Rollins and four nurses hanging around by the door, pacing up and down expectantly as they waited for the car to arrive. As I, too, waited for it to swing into view, I reflected on how lucky we were that John had agreed to come back. His wisdom and experience would be invaluable when the shit really hit the fan. I was convinced that the pilot represented the bow wave of the hundreds, possibly thousands of psychiatric casualties who would come to us when the coalition ground offensive started.

The car swept up to the porch, its windscreen wipers working hard against the rain. Two of the nurses ran out to the car. One of thém opened the rear nearside door, giving me my first glimpse of our casualty.

He looked younger than I knew him to be – in his late twenties – had dark hair and hadn't shaved. He was still wearing his olive-green flight suit, a reminder that not 24 hours earlier he'd been flying combat operations. As he stepped hesitantly on to the tarmac forecourt, he glanced up at the front of the building. He then turned round to look at the rolling Wiltshire hills, as if he couldn't quite work out how he had got here.

As he turned, I noticed something swinging from his neck; a piece of cardboard on string.

One of the nurses took him by the arm and pointed him gently towards the main door. I could see now that the cardboard sign had something written on it. I peered through the rivulets running down the window pane to try to see what it said, but it was only when the pilot was a step or two away from the building that I managed to decipher it – and as soon as I had, I felt my blood boil. Somebody, the SMO at his base in Saudi, I imagined, had handwritten 'Acute melancholia with hysterical features' on it. As if this poor fellow hadn't been through enough, he had flown all the way back to the UK with a diagnosis of his condition (a wrong one, I was already fairly sure) scrawled on a piece of cardboard for all to see. It might just as well have said 'Unclean'. Forget the First and Second World Wars, I felt as if we'd regressed to the Dark Ages.

Fortunately, the nurse noticed the sign, too, and gently removed it before the pilot entered the building.

I had rarely seen such a broken figure. He was hunched over and could barely walk. The two nurses had to help him every inch of the way. I looked at John, who shot me an expression of pain and sympathy. We had fully intended to welcome this chap to our hospital, but he looked so dissociated, so unaware of the reality that surrounded him, that there would have been no point. Instead, we watched as the nurses led him past us to his room, where he would be settled in, sedated if necessary, and readied for our treatment, which would begin in earnest the next day.

'Good morning, Frank,' I said brightly as I held out my hand.

Frank stared at it for a moment as he shambled in through the door. He did not offer me his hand. He looked at me, I imagined, much as he might have looked at an Iraqi interrogator. The whites of his eyes were visible above and below his irises, a sign that he was producing too much adrenaline. The nurses had told me that, in spite of sedation, he hadn't had much sleep.

I ushered him to a seat across from John and me. One of the nurses helped him to sit down. I asked Frank whether he'd like a cup of tea or coffee. He said nothing, but gave a minute shake of the head.

'My name is Wing Commander Turnbull and this is John Rollins. We're consultant psychiatrists here at the Princess Alexandra Hospital at RAF Wroughton. How are you feeling this morning, Frank?'

Nothing. Frank kept his eyes lowered. I could see that they were puffy and red-rimmed.

I looked at John, wondering whether he wanted to say anything, but he motioned for me to continue.

'Let me start, Frank, by telling you that you are perfectly safe here. Nothing is going to happen to you . . .'

For a brief moment, Frank raised his eyes to mine. 'I'll never fly again, will I? My career's over, isn't it?' He started to weep uncontrollably.

'We're not making any assumptions about what brought you here and nor do we make any assumptions about your future, Frank,' I said. 'We know that something traumatic happened to you the other day and I'd like to try to understand what it was.'

Frank wiped his eyes and whispered: 'It scared the shit out of me.'

John lightly cleared his throat and said: 'Please. Just tell us what happened.'

Frank looked at him suspiciously.

John, recognizing his hesitation for what it was, held his hands up. 'What you tell us stays with us. I'm not taking notes.' He gestured towards me. 'Wing Commander Turnbull isn't either.'

Frank glanced up. He'd stopped crying. 'Flying is everything to me. My mates are everything to me. I've never experienced anything like this.'

'I know,' I said.

'I'm not a coward. I want to be back with my mates . . .'

'And we want to see that you get back to them,' I told him. 'But the more you can tell us about what happened, the better.'

The surge of anger I'd felt when I'd seen Frank emerging from the car coursed through me again. And then I thought of the Pint Pot.

The secondary shock of the aeromedical evacuation and having that damned sign hang from his neck had done its damage. Never mind the original stressors – this was what he was now obsessing over: the thought that he had been disgraced in some way. This was the fourth component of stress that we'd accounted for in the Pint Pot Model: the stigma of breakdown and its aftermath, depression. In Frank's case, this was what was threatening to keep him in a vicious cycle of PTSD.

'We want to help,' I said. 'And we can help you, Frank. But, like John said, we need you to tell us as much as you can.'

Frank held my gaze for a moment, then sat back and exhaled. 'I don't know. When I saw them on the TV, I just snapped.'

'Peters and Nichol?'

He nodded. 'John Peters and I know each other pretty well. It was the bruises around his eyes. Those weren't from any ejection. I just felt this incredible anger. And then the world started to close in on me. Thoughts, images, everything . . . it just seemed to explode inside my head. I couldn't take it any more. That's when I just . . . lost it.'

'It was a panic attack,' I told him, 'a perfectly normal reaction, Frank, considering everything that had happened.'

At the word 'normal', I saw relief flood behind his eyes. I told him then that what he'd experienced was a stress reaction and that not only was it normal, but as old as the hills. I reiterated that he was safe and that nothing bad was going to happen to him. I told him, too, that he'd be free to speak to his family – he had a wife and young child in Germany, close to the base where he'd been stationed prior to deploying to the Gulf – and that, within a few days, all being well, he'd be able to join them.

In this way, bit by bit, John and I reconnected him to the world Frank had known before his breakdown. This took the form of the psychological debriefing we had used after Lockerbie, borrowing from the technique that had originally been described by Jeffrey Mitchell in Maryland. The next step was to ensure that Frank remained stabilized – that the safe place he now found himself in remained a place of sanctuary.

Two days later, John and I saw Frank again. By now, he was in a much better state. The 'place of safety' routine was starting to have a beneficial effect. He was calmer, was sleeping and had lost the haunted look that he'd arrived with. He'd also been in telephone contact with his family.

I started the session by reminding him where he was and what we were trying to achieve. I told him the truth – that our intention was to try to get him back to fitness; to a state where conceivably he'd be able to return to his squadron, this being his number one priority. But we also told him, as we had to, that this decision was not in our hands; that it would have to be taken higher up the chain of command. I did not tell him, as it wouldn't have been helpful at this point, that the odds of achieving this weren't in our favour. To the best of my knowledge there had never before been a case of an RAF pilot returning to flying duties in the wake of a breakdown during combat operations. I did, however, reiterate what I'd told him during our introductory meeting: that whatever he confided in us would remain confidential. We weren't taking notes. Our sole priority was to restore him as rapidly as possible to full health.

Having made this clear, we started the briefing proper with the so-called 'cognitive domain phase', in which we asked the very simple question: what happened to you?

To give us all the information we needed, Frank had to patiently respond to our 'who, what, where, why and when' questions in order to establish a timeline of events. These started with the night-time bombing raids that began on 16 January, the Peters and Nichol shoot-down the following day, their being paraded on Iraqi TV a few days after that and a string of missions that Frank had flown in between.

The missions themselves sounded unbelievably stressful. I had become used to sanitized images released by the coalition of laser-guided bombs hitting their targets with pinpoint precision – one bomb, I remembered, had even sailed down the ventilation shaft of a bunker.

But these JP233 raids had been nothing like that. Often flown in daylight and at very low level, the Tornados had already suffered a terrible attrition rate, with more than half a dozen aircraft shot out of the sky by Iraqi SAMs and triple-A.

The next part of the process overlaid a simple question on to the answers he had already provided: how do you *feel* about what happened to you? The process itself had changed little from the system we had devised for the mountain rescuers who'd attended Lockerbie.

Two days on from his arrival at Wroughton, and safe in the knowledge that he was now no longer in freefall, Frank was able to describe his feelings perfectly. He told us what it was like to have the flak rush to meet him, what it was like to see mates shot down either side of his aircraft, to watch their planes plough into the deck and explode in a fireball. He was clear, too, on the symptoms he had been left with as a result: flashbacks not only to the missions themselves, but to the moment when he had seen Peters and Nichol paraded on TV and the impact it had had on him. The evidence seemed to suggest that he had been able to handle the stress of the missions up until then. It was seeing Peters and Nichol on TV that had been his trigger moment.

It was, he said, as if a fuse had blown inside his head. One minute he'd been keeping it all together, the next it was like watching a movie that had sped into overdrive. He 'saw' the missions, the flak as it hurtled across the sky towards him, slowly at first, then accelerating as it came closer, before whipping past the cockpit; he 'saw' aircraft getting shot down, described the sickening lurch in his stomach at the sure knowledge that friends and colleagues had lost their lives, yet had to detach immediately from thoughts of loss so as to be able to complete his mission; he 'saw' Peters and Nichol and described the physical revulsion he'd felt at their treatment; he talked about his own wife and child and the fear of what it would do to them if he were shot down.

We were into classic flashback territory.

He went on to describe the acrid cordite smell from the triple-A that worked its way into the cockpit; the chatter of his mates over the intercom as they fought to avoid the flak and the SAMs; how he kept on hearing the voices of Peters's and Nichol's interrogators . . .

Most tellingly, throughout these flashbacks, he felt all the emotions he'd felt during the original experiences: the excitement and fear of the JP233 raids; and the unbelievable anger at seeing what the Iraqis had done to his two mates.

John and I talked about flashbacks being unprocessed memories and how the re-presentation of information in this form, over and over, was the mind's way, as far as we could tell, of trying to find explanations for events that, on a first pass, defied reason. I drew a picture of the Pint Pot for him and pointed to the force – akin to a physical force, with enough power to knock a person off their feet – that moved from the beginning to the end of the stress narrative.

The idea of this force was something that Frank could get his head around. His particular pint pot, we told him, had already been filled to the brim. To anyone else, the sight of Peters and Nichol on the TV, although distressing, would not have had the same impact. That it had such an impact on Frank was down to the fact that he knew them so well.

We told him that the rapid heartbeat and sweats that he had experienced since his original panic attack was his body's natural response to the chemicals it had been producing to help him survive. We also told him that avoidance was another core feature of PTSD and that there were three recognizable types, signs that he should watch out for.

'Such as?' he asked, with almost clinical detachment.

'Consciously or not, you may try to avoid people who remind you of the event.'

'On the squadron?' he said, smiling self-deprecatingly. 'Well, I'm hardly likely to see them, am I?'

This was another good sign. In reversing back out of his shells, Frank had even managed to regain some of his humour – the human being's first line of defence.

'It might also include family and friends,' I told him, 'people who, with the best of intentions, are genuinely sympathetic and want to know what happened to you, thinking that it's good for you to talk about it.'

'Which is why you recommend isolation, I suppose,' he said.

'Yes, at least for the first few days. It may well be easier for some-one who's been through what you've been through, Frank, to be with people you *don't* know for that very reason.'

I also told him about psychological avoidance, otherwise known as dissociation, and chemical avoidance, normally associated with alcohol abuse but often with other endorphin-producing stimulants, such as cigarettes and caffeine. I didn't tell him not to take them – he was a grown man and could do what he wanted – simply to be aware of them and their effect on him. Drinking, the data showed, could delay his recovery by some time. Data was something Frank understood well.

Understanding, I reiterated, was key. The more he understood about what had happened to him, and what was happening to him, the more we, collectively, could demystify the event and hasten his recovery.

Frank understood this. In fact, both John and I were amazed at how quickly he got it.

The original *DSM* definition, that a person had to be exposed to events outside usual human experience, was absolutely in line with what Frank had been through. It was something he could never have been trained to deal with himself. Other people had seen what he had seen on television and had been upset by it. But it was his personal and emotional connection to Peters and Nichol that had caused his fuse to blow.

As soon as he started to understand this, Frank began to make a remarkably swift recovery. He processed the experience and began to lose the flashbacks. The nightmares went too. These are the cornerstones of a PTSD reaction. If you don't have either of these symptoms you don't have PTSD.

The three symptom clusters are intrusive recollections of a powerful, traumatic event; avoidance of reminders of that event; and hyperarousal. If you don't have flashbacks or nightmares you've got nothing to avoid. And with those stressors gone, you shouldn't have hyperarousal.

Air Vice Marshal Alan Johnson – 'Big Al', the principal medical officer of Strike Command – knew that our treatment of the pilot was significant and wanted to come and see what was happening for himself. I was apprehensive about this because of my previous experiences with him. There was the time at RAF Catterick when the progress of our mountain rescue team debriefings was very much in the balance and depended on some straight talking on the phone, but my mind drifted back to one time at Wroughton . . .

Big Al had been the CO at Wroughton before Lockerbie. During his time at Wroughton I had been seconded into the role of OC Medical Wing and was, therefore, present at the morning 'Prayers Meetings' where the CO, matron, OC Admin Wing and OC Medical Wing discussed what was happening in the hospital and this always included talk about the patients who were 'on board' at the time.

'I don't believe it,' said Big Al, when we were discussing the case of a psychiatric patient currently being treated in my department. He pushed his chair back from his big desk and, exasperated, said quite loudly, 'Depressed? Not responding to treatment? What this man needs is a kick up the backside! Tell him to get himself sorted out!'

He was referring to a pilot who was finding it very difficult to deal with a divorce and had developed a deep and dark depression. Before I knew it, I found myself on my feet, pacing up and down in front of my commanding officer, giving him a lecture on depression and the underlying biology, how we had to regard it as a real condition and not a put-on . . .

The memory faded. I comforted myself by recalling that Big Al had taken my outburst very well and had actually listened to what I had to say. I also remembered how his initial scepticism about the post-Lockerbie debriefings had melted away and he'd become a firm advocate of ours after reading our report on Lockerbie.

By the Gulf War, Big Al had become the principal medical officer, the PMO, of Strike Command. In 1991, he was the top doc involved in UK war planning.

I knew why he was coming to see us. He needed to see with his own eyes that this man had made a full recovery, not just in psychiatric terms, but in overall terms; that he could function again not just as a pilot but as a human being. In other words, that he really was back to normal – and we weren't viewing him purely through a shrink's prism.

Frank's case had created a lot of waves within the RAF medical system. At stake was not simply his career but quite possibly ours too. Big Al made arrangements to come and see us forthwith.

Five days after Frank set foot in our hospital, on another cold, windy day, Big Al swept in through the door of the Princess

Alexandra. At six foot eight inches he was an imposing figure. He looked stern at the best of times, but with so much riding on this case Big Al managed to look even sterner than usual. John and I welcomed him, then escorted him up to my room on the first floor where we briefed him on everything that had happened. After listening attentively and firing the odd question, Big Al said he wanted to go and see Frank for himself.

John and I waited anxiously for his return. When finally he reappeared, Big Al's expression was hard to read. After closing the door behind him, he looked at John and me and said: 'Well, this is remarkable; he appears to be fixed.'

From that moment, with Big Al's blessing, the plan swung quickly into action. It was agreed that Frank would go to his home base in RAF Germany where he would be evaluated for a full return to combat operations. This, counter-intuitively, was part of the process of bringing him to a place of safety; of telling him that things were as they should be – both at home and on his squadron. In Germany, he would be re-evaluated on the Tornado and, provided he was able to satisfy the instructors that he could not only fly but withstand the rigours of combat, he'd be sent back to us for a final medical examination. Provided we were happy – and most importantly, provided Big Al was – he would be sent back out to the Gulf and put on combat ops.

Within three weeks of being flown home, Frank passed his flying tests and a further medical examination at Wroughton and went back to the Gulf to fly and fight again; the first time, to my knowledge, that anyone in the RAF had been returned to combat ops after such an experience.

I knew I would be going to the Gulf soon afterwards, when I had to have my inoculations one freezing cold Sunday night at Lyneham. Stripped to the waist, I was told by the medic, as he prepared to inject me in both arms, that he was not permitted to tell me what he was injecting into me.

I stopped him right there. 'Listen, Corporal, I'm not going to have these injections unless you tell me exactly what they are for.'

He stood his ground resolutely. 'You have to have them, sir.'

He relented finally, but just enough to tell me that one of them was codenamed Sabre and that was all he knew.

I hoped my immune system would be up to the assault. 'Just play up and play the game.'

'Pardon, sir?'

Nothing, I told him, before offering him an arm and exhorting him to do his worst.

My immune system showed its mettle a couple of days later when I developed a mild flu-like illness, which was expected, and a lump in my groin, which was not.

The swelling still made it painful to walk when, several days later, Big Al phoned me after receiving the news that Frank had success-fully carried out his first mission since requalification. 'Of course, Turnbull, you realize what this means, don't you?' he said.

I told him I reckoned I did.

Sure enough, the following week I was on my way to the Gulf.

Chapter 12

Prisoners of War

On the morning of my deployment, I drove the boys to school and tried to pass off the departure to the Middle East and the war as being only a short trip away from home but, inside, I felt a real sense of foreboding. Having said goodbye and watched all three sons – Iain aged eleven, Stuart ten and Bobby six – walk into school with a lump in my throat, I drove off to Wroughton hospital to deal with the one in my groin.

The medical officer who looked after hospital staff was a very experienced military medic, a retired group captain. There was pretty much nothing he hadn't seen, but I could tell from the look on his face that something about my case was troubling him. He took the history of the recent inoculations and eventually told me he hadn't seen anything like this since Aden.

With the characteristic conspiracy of silence that develops between doctors when there is bad news, I accepted that I had to go to the surgical ward to see the surgeon, Group Captain Brian Morgans, an old pal.

I reckoned they thought I had developed a bubo. A bubo is an inflammatory swelling of a lymph gland, usually in the armpit or the groin, due to a reaction to the absorption of infected material, such as anthrax vaccine or more probably plague vaccine, because buboes are typically found in bubonic plague – hence the name.

'Don't worry,' Brian said, 'just lie down on the couch over there

and drop your daks.' He walked quickly out of the room and reappeared a few minutes later dressed in gown and mask. He was
carrying a scalpel and a specimen container.

'This won't hurt a bit,' he lied, as he plunged the scalpel into my groin.
'Aha, lots of pus . . . looks like your bog-standard staphylococcus.'

After the pain passed, I breathed a sigh of relief. A nasty infection;
nothing more.

He patched me up with a dressing and left me to wander across
the road to say cheerio to my colleagues at the Psychiatric Centre. I
then went home to say goodbye to Alison.

A staff car arrived after lunch to take me to RAF Brize Norton, the
main transport hub to the Gulf. As I walked out of the house, it
started to snow. Alison and her father were standing at the top of the
drive. As the car pulled away, I turned back and watched them
through the rear-view window, the flakes of snow swirling all around
them. And then they disappeared and I was on my way.

When I arrived at Brize it was all hustle and bustle. I noticed that
most of the soldiers and airmen going out to the Gulf were carrying
arms. I decided I should take the Browning 9 mm that I had only
recently been trained to use. We were authorized to carry the
Browning pistol in the field in the event that we, as doctors, needed
to protect ourselves and our patients.

The bull-necked RAF sergeant who was checking my details at the
desk shook his head. 'You've got no time to go to the armoury, sir.
You've got to get on the flight.'

'I'm not going anywhere unless I have my pistol with me,' I
insisted. I'd been told that if weapons were not drawn at Brize there
was very little prospect of finding one in Saudi Arabia.

The sergeant finally relented and a car was ordered to take me to
the armoury.

It felt much more secure to have that pistol on my belt as I was
driven out to the Tristar waiting on the edge of the airfield, a long
way away from the terminal buildings. When I boarded the aircraft
it became very obvious why. It was loaded from deck to ceiling with
ordnance. Shells wrapped in plastic like flat-packs of giant soup cans
with pointed ends extended from the cockpit bulkhead to the tail,
leaving only enough room – in an aircraft capable of carrying
hundreds of passengers – for fifteen of us.

Soon after I squeezed between the shells to my seat, we lumbered along the runway and groaned our way into the sky, leaving a white landscape behind.

Once aloft, we were cheered by the announcement that it was likely we would arrive at Riyadh under fire from Scud missiles, so once again we went through our NBC drills – protection from nuclear, biological and chemical attack. I thought that if we were hit by fire on landing at Riyadh, then the last thing we'd worry about was getting our zoot-suits on. The shells alone would blow us to kingdom come.

King Khaled International Airport was not the real KKIA. I don't know what I expected – a combination of combat uniforms at the check-in desks and duty-free shops, I think – but we found ourselves in the bare concrete skeleton of an unfinished new terminal on the KKIA site, confronted by vast, open esplanades of rough concrete. The expected Scud attack hadn't materialized. I gave a small prayer of thanks for my safe delivery.

I was supposed to liaise immediately with Squadron Leader Frank McManus, the consultant psychiatrist at the RAF hospital in Muharraq – a short hop away by C-130 transport. Frank was an old mate whom I'd got to know well at Wroughton.

It had been agreed that I would use Muharraq as the launching-off point for visits to front-line bases and units so that I could observe what was happening, with an eye firmly on signs of under-lying combat stress reactions. If the circumstances were right, I'd also brief appropriate personnel about our work. But upon touch-down at KKIA, I was informed that things had changed – that I'd be going instead directly to UK medical detachment 205 at the nearby general hospital. The reasons for this quickly became clear.

Detachment 205, a TA unit, was based on the deserted third floor of what I quickly realized was a half-constructed building. As the lift doors opened, a strange tableau greeted me. In the midst of the vast open-plan floor were two armchairs; each had a guy in combats slumped in it. As I approached, my footsteps echoing off the concrete floor and the bare walls and ceiling, they shook themselves awake and jumped to their feet.

When I drew a little closer, I recognized them. The guy on the left,

Sergeant Dick Hilling, was an experienced psychiatric nurse from the UK; affable and softly spoken. Alvin, to his right, another sergeant, was from the North-East. His mates, perhaps inevitably, called him Stardust.

Both of them stared at me as if the briefcase I was carrying was filled with plague bacillus.

I told them I'd just arrived and asked what was up.

'What's up?' Stardust said. 'You tell us . . .'

The words sounded angry and for a moment I was tempted to put it down to jet lag, but when I saw the look in their eyes I realized I hadn't imagined what I'd heard.

'OK,' I said, dropping the affability, 'is one of you going to tell me what's happening? If you're upset that you've lost Geoff and got me, well, now's the time to get it into the open.'

'Geoff' was Geoff Reid, the RAF wing commander I'd nominally come out to replace as head of the stress management group here in Riyadh.

Attachments develop in time of war and perhaps they were pissed off at the change. If so, then I'd gently remind them that – like it or not – I was here under orders, just as they were, and I was determined to see mine through.

'You of all people should know what the issue is, sir,' Stardust said, hands on hips as he stared at me. 'The recall? You were the one who issued the orders.'

I shook my head. 'What recall? What orders?'

'Our recall from the front line,' Dick said. I knew it wasn't in Dick's nature to raise his voice, but behind his soft southern accent I could sense depths of bitterness. 'Those people needed us. We were doing a good job up there.'

I took a deep breath, counted to three, and asked them to explain from the beginning.

Dick looked at Stardust and Stardust glanced back. Then they both turned towards me. It was Dick who ended up speaking for them. 'For the past month, we've been on the front line, on the Kuwait border, on detachment to the Army. As you can imagine, we've been busy. But it was good work. We were doing what we were trained to do. And we were valued. With the land offensive under way, this is the time we're needed most. Everything was going really, really well, sir. And then we were ordered back to Riyadh.' He gave our surroundings a disdainful look. 'To this place.'

'What's all this got to do with me?' I asked.

'Those orders, we were told, came directly from you,' Dick replied.

'They didn't come from me. I don't know who issued the orders. *My* orders come from Air Vice Marshal Johnson. We're all in the same boat, but since we're in it we're going to do the best job we can. Where are our offices?'

Stardust laughed. 'You're looking at them.'

'But this building isn't even finished.'

'Hardly bloody begun, more like,' Dick said.

Behind the armchairs, I noticed some boxes covered by a blanket. I nodded at them. 'What's the story with that lot?'

'That's what's left of our equipment,' Stardust said. 'TVs, tables, chairs, you name it. Anything we don't actually sit on, they'll nick. We've been here for days, just guarding it.'

'Who nicks it?'

'Anyone and everyone,' Dick replied. 'Basically, because no one knows what we're supposed to be doing here, the quartermaster takes our stuff away and redistributes it.' He pointed to the boxes and the blanket. 'That's all that's left.'

Their numbers had recently been cut, they had no idea what they were supposed to be doing – only that they were meant somehow to be involved in the evacuation of injured personnel. This, compounded by the fact they were convinced I'd been responsible for pulling them off the front line, had led to their sounding off at me.

As the new boy, it was relatively easy for me to grip the problem – it was obvious that what I was dealing with here was a basic issue of demoralization. The unit had been formed in the UK prior to deployment and had become a cohesive group. After arriving in Saudi, it had been moved five times and its consultants redeployed to other units. The quartermaster's raid on their equipment had been the last straw. Colonel Bob Anderson, a retired army consultant psychiatrist, was the boss of the psychiatric component of 205 Squadron. I had known him briefly in his Army days but he had left the Army to go to a civilian job in Perth. It was obvious from our first meeting out in Riyadh that he had become very disillusioned about the way his group had been treated since arriving there. Together we rolled up our sleeves and got to work to rebuild the psychiatric service.

Alvin, Dick and I quickly agreed, once I'd explained the significance of combat stress reactions, of which they'd had very little experience, that the roles of casualty evacuation management and the management of combat stress victims should be combined. I then explained that we were going to brief as many RAF combat bases as we could get to about the work we'd carried out at Wroughton. I told them I'd already secured permission to attend a pre-mission briefing at a Tornado unit, so I could see for myself the kinds of pressures that aircrews were under. Longer term, Dick, Alvin and I were to make our unit's presence felt at other bases to let Strike Command know that we had a resource that could take care of combat-stressed pilots – a resource that had been battle-tested and shown to work.

In essence, I told the two sergeants, the presentations needed to get over three main messages.

First, the reality of acute or combat stress reactions was that they were common following exposure to critical incidents, particularly if they were life-threatening, but that there was solid evidence from past experience of war that application of the simple rules of PIE (proximity, immediacy and expectancy) was frequently very successful in restoring normal function.

Second, that a long-term reaction to exposure to trauma had now been identified and was called Post-Traumatic Stress Disorder – PTSD – and that we were hopeful that immediate intervention would prevent this from developing.

Third, that the acute reactions represented normal survival reactions and did not imply psychiatric vulnerability.

On these points, at least, we were all singing from the same hymn-sheet.

A few days later, I flew from Riyadh to the Tornado unit in a C-130. As I sat in the Hercules's uncomfortable web seating, watching the desert shoot by several hundred feet below, I felt excited. The base had a particular significance as it was Frank's squadron. I was anxious to see how he'd readapted to combat operations after his treatment at Wroughton.

No sooner had I arrived at the admin wing than the CO ushered me outside. A pre-mission briefing was about to begin. The squadron was preparing to go 'downtown', he explained. We touched on a few dos and don'ts as we strolled between austere-looking bunkers in the bright desert sunshine.

In essence, I'd be welcome, the CO said, as long as I kept a low profile. He was sure I understood and I told him I did. Perfectly. I was just extremely grateful to be a part of it all – to see at first hand how the crews were handling the pressure.

Having a shrink sit in on a pre-mission briefing was huge. I tried to imagine how my presence would have gone down at a pre-mission briefing for a Bomber Command squadron during the Second World War. Had the RAF finally exorcized the ghost of LMF? I kept this thought to myself and asked instead how Frank was getting on.

'You can see for yourself,' the CO replied, as we stepped into the dark, air-conditioned interior of a concrete blockhouse. 'We're here.'

The briefing room had two doors. The CO and I entered at the back of the room. No one seemed to notice us – the briefing had been under way for several minutes.

I learned that the target was a command and control centre on the edges of Baghdad and that it was to be hit by laser-guided bombs. The JP233 raids had become, thank God, a thing of the past. They had been replaced instead by medium-altitude strike missions, beyond the range of the Iraqis' deadly curtains of flak.

It was deemed 'safe' to do this, the CO had told me on the way over to the briefing room, because the coalition had achieved almost total air dominance. But that did not mean that these raids were a walk in the park, he'd added, because the Iraqis were still assessed to have missiles that could hit our planes.

What I noticed in that room, therefore, was probably un-surprising: considerable tension, lots of information disseminated by the mission-briefer, very few questions from the floor and brief flashes of humour.

I noticed Frank, quietly scribbling notes at the front. If he knew I was in the room, he didn't show it.

The briefing was short and to the point. Essential data was handed over. There was a curt 'good luck' from the mission-briefer and then everyone walked out.

An hour later, I stood outside the bunker and watched the aircraft take off. I counted them out . . .

. . . and 90 minutes later I counted them back.

They had returned without loss, for which I uttered quiet thanks.

When I re-entered the briefing room, the crews were already there. The atmosphere, I could tell in an instant, had changed completely.

The debriefing was characterized by noise and full, highly detailed descriptions of the mission from the crews. It was evident that not only was a technical debriefing taking place here but a psychological debriefing as well, in which the Tornado crews were ventilating emotions. In this way, they were processing the information of the shared experience they had just been through. This was all good, healthy stuff.

I strolled outside with the CO and talked to him while he puffed away on a cigarette.

'Did you find what you expected?' he asked.

'I don't really know what I expected, but I'm amazed,' I replied.

He inhaled deeply and let the wind whip the smoke from his mouth and nostrils. 'In what way?'

'At their ability to switch their emotions on and off. I don't think discipline or even the rigorous training those boys undergo can give you that. It's something they acquire from each other, I think. It's like a cloak they slip on and off. Remarkable.'

I heard the heavy steel door close behind us, turned and saw Frank. The base commander made his excuses, but Frank stopped him from wandering off; told us both he couldn't stay long – that he'd just wanted to drop by and say hello.

We shook hands.

'It's good to see you looking so well,' I told him.

'I am well,' he said, smiling. 'I just wanted to thank you for everything that you did.'

'I didn't do anything,' I said. 'It was really all down to you.'

There was nothing else to say. With a hesitant smile, Frank turned on his feet and disappeared back inside the bunker.

I knew that the senior RAF brass remained deeply sceptical about allowing psychiatrists on to bases – a view that prevailed all the way to the top.

OC Operations, otherwise known as the 'Warlord', needed to provide an umbrella of protection and cohesion for his aircrew and in the highly charged, tension-laden atmosphere I'd already witnessed, I had no doubt that he saw the presence of a shrink, RAF or not, as a potentially destabilizing influence. My visit here, I concluded, would be a one-off, but it had been invaluable nonetheless. Far from being ostracized by the crews, I felt, in a quiet kind of way, that I'd been made welcome. With the ground offensive under way, we could all hope now for a swift conclusion to the conflict. With any luck, there would be no need to deploy large numbers of psychiatrists to the front line. Our forces had been able to handle the pressure. Resistance, where I'd encountered it, had, by and large, come from the top. In the end, it was agreed that such misgivings could only be overcome fully by discussion and through the interchange of ideas – but that the best time for this would be after the war.

Before I left the base, I met the doctor who had made the diagnosis of Frank's 'acute melancholia with hysterical features'. I didn't have the heart to ask him whether he'd also been responsible for hanging the cardboard notice from Frank's neck. Now wasn't a time for blame or recrimination either. I now knew all about the pressures that RAF squadrons were under, including the medical staff.

In a non-confrontational way, I was able to explain the exceptional circumstances of Frank's case; that it had been the link to another crew – Peters and Nichol – and their appearance on the TV that had acted as the trigger; and this, I think, gave both the CO and the base doctor a level of comprehension about the nature of PTSD that they did not have before. I departed the base feeling that we had made enormous progress, even if we were all still feeling our way forward.

During the last week in February, with the ground campaign well under way, it was clear that the war had entered its endgame and that we would soon be faced with the issue of what to do with British PoWs retrieved from Iraq. Thus far, there were around 20 British personnel held captive – predominantly RAF aircrew and members of an SAS patrol that had been captured in the early stages of the war – the patrol led by Andy McNab that later achieved worldwide fame as Bravo Two Zero.

McNab's eight-man patrol into Iraq had been compromised, prompting several vicious firefights and, in the wake of the failure of

an RAF helicopter to pick them up, a yomp to the Syrian border that
had ended with the death or capture of every man bar one. We had
no doubt that the SAS and the RAF aircrews had been appallingly
treated, but beyond this we were into conjecture. My recommendations, already tabled, were clear. I said we needed to move the PoWs
to a place of safety to accomplish the twin tasks of medical assessment and psychological debriefing.

The idea of a staging post – halfway between the Gulf and home
– was central to the plan. Going home immediately, I warned, would
almost certainly prove disastrous. These people needed to decompress in a place that was both familiar – Akrotiri, with its scrub-like
topography, was not unlike the Gulf – and 'safe'. The psychological
debriefing, I said, should ideally be carried out by personnel who'd
been in the Gulf, who had at least some comprehension of what
these people had been through. I also said that the personnel should
be supplemented by locally based facilitators, such as chaplains and
others experienced in counselling.

The core team, therefore, ought to be composed of myself, two
experienced RAF psychiatric nurses – Dick and Alvin – an Army
psychiatric nurse, two Red Cross and St John debriefers, as well as a
senior RAF psychiatric nursing officer acting as adjutant and organizer.
This last was our very own Mr Fixit, Bert Venman. Bert had been based
in the UK throughout the war, but was now on standby to come out to
theatre and tend to the PoWs at a moment's notice. The debriefing team
ought also to include an RAF community nurse from Cyprus whom I
knew and rated highly, Flight Sergeant Arthur Jones.

The first 24 hours, I said, should be dedicated to rest and physical
medical assessment. The subsequent 24 – 48-hour period should be
dedicated to individual and group debriefing. I recommended that
the security debriefing – i.e., the operational component of the
debriefing process – should be included in this period to save
the PoWs running over the information to two separate sets of
debriefers (something that, if I were them, I'd have found incredibly
irritating); that close associates of the released PoWs should be made
available to facilitate the process of normalization; and last but most
importantly, that a staging post, ideally Akrotiri, should be a *sine
qua non* – a much needed location for decompression, given the huge
media interest in these people. Ideally, close relatives should be

brought out to Cyprus to be reunited with them, not the other way round.

I wasn't sure anyone would have the time to take my recommendations seriously. I wasn't even sure they'd registered. But then, one day, as I was writing a report in our sparse office accommodation on the deserted third floor of the hospital on the outskirts of Riyadh, the phone rang.

Over the receding rumble of a jet departing from the neighbouring airport, I recognized the voice of a very senior RAF medical officer named Chris Bishop. He told me that a C-130 had been tasked to fly us both into the desert the following morning. I was to RV on the apron at 0500 hours. He would only be able to tell me what this was all about when we landed. We were headed for a remote landing strip a stone's throw from Kuwait and not a million miles from the Iraqi border.

'We're going into action?'

'I couldn't possibly comment,' he replied. 'But if this were the Grand National and I were a betting man . . .'

His voice tailed off. I had my answer. This was it.

I told Bishop I'd see him at the allotted time.

That evening, as I sat on the edge of my bed nursing an illicit whisky, half listening for the first note of the air-raid siren that would signal we were under Scud attack again, I started writing an Op Order. The format was standard throughout the military. In a series of short paragraphs and punchy bullet points I had to set out our case in writing.

I handwrote it and it took me several drafts, but by the small hours I was happy with what I'd committed to paper. I folded it up, fell backwards on to the bed and grabbed an hour's sleep before the alarm went off.

The next morning Bishop and I exchanged pleasantries on the tarmac and clambered aboard the C-130. The rear ramp came up and the engines started to turn. We were surrounded by crates of ammunition and supplies heading for the front. Whatever the buzz, there was still a war on.

The loadmaster, a crusty old sergeant with a Jimmy Edwards moustache, watched us with suspicion. Officially, there was no reason for Bishop and me to be there. As far as he was concerned, we were just a couple of medics who were in the way.

What if he was right?

I could only guess what men like John Peters and John Nichol had been through. Did we have the wherewithal to re-equip them for normal life? Had our success with the Tornado pilot, Frank, been a fluke?

I was still grappling with these questions when the C-130 started descending rapidly towards the desert floor, then thumped down on a semi-prepared strip. The props went into reverse pitch, throwing us against our straps. I looked at Bishop, hoping that he hadn't read my thoughts. This was no time to signal doubts to people who'd been harbouring them for years.

As we exited the rear ramp, Jimmy Edwards was barking orders at the crew.

A bevy of trucks had assembled under the tail to transport the crates along the front. The air was sharp with the smell of desert dew and diesel fumes. The sun, a pale disc on the horizon, was climbing into a grey, watery haze.

Bishop set the pace and I followed him. We were some way from the aircraft, far enough for the activity around it to reduce to a hum, when he stopped and turned. Part of me wanted to laugh at the overblown silliness of these precautions, but the Op Order in my pocket reminded me of what was at stake. I waited for Bishop to speak.

What he revealed made the hairs on the back of my neck stand up. As we spoke, he said, two Iraqi generals were meeting with General Schwarzkopf, the coalition commander. The PoW handover was to be a part of the deal.

'HQ wants to know what you plan to do,' Bishop asked curtly.

I told him we needed to debrief the PoWs – that whatever happened, our unit needed to get to the PoWs first. If we could take care of them immediately there was a good chance we could help them come to terms with their experiences early enough to prevent the imprint from causing long-term problems.

'How do you know it will work?'

'I don't. But you saw what we achieved with one Tornado pilot. With the right support, we can help others, too.'

I reached into my pocket and handed over the Op Order.

'It's all in here. The bottom line is, if they go back to the UK, if they succumb to the public relations imperative to reunite them with their families, then we've lost them. This isn't me speaking, Chris, it's the data. It's what the data has been telling us for years.'

The speech must have worked because soon after we landed back in Riyadh I was told to move into the RAF base at Muharraq in Bahrain, where I'd be on standby to go. Where, nobody knew. I was just to remain there and wait. To burn off the nervous tension, I decided I was going to play a lot of squash. After my very first game, against Wing Commander Drew Richardson, one of my oldest and best pals in the RAF whom I'd first met at Ely (and he won!), my shower was interrupted by an announcement that went out across the officers' mess: would Wing Commander Turnbull report in immediately; I had an urgent telephone call.

It was Bishop. 'You're taking off tonight. It's on.'

After thinking of nothing else since our meeting in the desert, I hardly knew where to start. I asked him where we were headed.

'Amman, Jordan. There's been an initial release of prisoners. You'll be part of the aeromed team that'll be heading to Jordan tonight. From Amman you'll be flying to Akrotiri. Your Op Order has been taken seriously, Gordon. This has come all the way from the top. They've accepted your recommendations. The PoWs won't be flown home immediately; they'll be taken to the RAF hospital. You'll be able to spend ten days with them there.' He wished me luck and signed off.

We took off in the mid-evening after waiting for permission for about two hours, sitting on the runway at RAF Muharraq in a VC10. With me were Alvin and Dick, and members of the aeromedical team from Muharraq. As the jet climbed into the night sky, I reran in my mind a speech I'd given myself in the bathroom mirror the previous night.

This was it. No second chances. We had to perform at the highest level. We had to demonstrate that these ideas worked. I looked around me. My team and I were surrounded by the other medical staff and RAF flying personnel. I was braced for action and happy that I had the best possible people accompanying me. But I also felt very much alone. I knew there were still a great many senior officers who believed that Wroughton's formula for treating the PoWs was hogwash; that by far the best thing for them would be to head home as soon as possible and decompress in the company of their loved ones, and to hell with the media. Somehow, for the sake of everyone, the PoWs not least, I had to prove them wrong. For me – and the rest of the team – the template was very clear. Post-Lockerbie, we'd been able to assess the mountain rescuers from two different standpoints.

There was a tradition within the RAF mountain rescue community for family men to spend Christmas with their loved ones; for the 'singlies' – mountain rescuers who weren't married – to take the strain over the Christmas break. When the 747 blew up, the singlies had already been heading for the hills. But because of the horrific nature of the disaster, everyone – singlies and marrieds alike – had been deployed to Lockerbie. When there was nothing more to do, the singlies resumed their trek into the hills. The marrieds went back to their families. The singlies, it later became clear, had decompressed by talking Lockerbie out among themselves; the marrieds, unable to do the same for all kinds of reasons – not least because they did not want to subject their loved ones to graphic descriptions of the horrors they had witnessed – had bottled it up, kept it mostly to themselves, and consequently, as a group, had suffered far worse. I only had to remember the look on Maxwell's face as he'd described the little girl's broken doll – the same doll he'd given his own daughter for Christmas – to be reminded just how badly some of them had suffered.

This was the clue we'd been given: that decompression was best done outside the family first – and I was determined to put the lessons of Lockerbie to the best possible use with the PoWs.

We were in the air for several hours circumnavigating the dodgy parts of the Gulf – peace had only just been declared and we had been ordered to stick to zones that were known to be safe – but eventually, in the small hours, the aircraft started to descend. Soon we were sweeping in to land. No one had fallen asleep during the flight – adrenaline saw to that.

As we pulled off the runway, I spotted a large throng of people assembled around a rickety set of airstairs that had been wheeled out on to the apron.

The aircraft rocked to a stop and I waited for the engines to spool down, but they never did. Instead, the door just aft of the cockpit was opened up. Peering through the window, I saw the airstairs being pushed towards the aircraft.

Through the open door, I could hear shouts of consternation. Then I saw why. There was a gap between the top step and the fuselage. There was some pushing and shoving on the ground, but the stairs wouldn't move.

I saw a blur of colour as three dishevelled-looking individuals in yellow jumpsuits rushed up the stairs.

Inside the aircraft a guy in RAF uniform extended his hand and literally pulled the men on board. The first two I didn't recognize, but the third I did. He had lost a lot of weight and had grown a thick beard, but he was still clearly discernible as Flight Lieutenant John Peters. It was amazing to see him. After the images on the TV, which had turned Peters's battered face, and that of his equally tormented navigator, Nichol, into two of the most recognizable faces in Britain, I couldn't quite believe that I was actually with this man in the flesh. I knew that these men would be in the spotlight and that this would be a first. The mountain rescue workers after Lockerbie had been largely anonymous. I'd been able to treat them without having to worry about the media, because the media had been focused on the victims of Lockerbie – there had been no awareness at all of the plight of those who had staged the clear-up operation. But with Peters and Nichol – and, for that matter, the other PoWs – it would be different. When we had finished with them, a number of them would continue to have high profiles. Some would be interviewed by the press. What would they say about our treatment of them? Would we succeed or would we fail?

As John Peters walked down the aisle of the aircraft to a seat somewhere at the back, I looked up and caught his eye. I smiled and was astounded when he gave me a hesitant smile back.

This wasn't about me, I told myself. It was about them. Forget what the rest of the world thought. I wanted to make this man better. I wanted him to resume his life – with his family and the squadron – and for things to be normal again. What was still scary, though, was the knowledge that I had the power to do this. Now all I had to do was make it happen.

Upon our arrival in Jordan, we learned that another batch of

PoWs would be arriving in Amman shortly. I also learned that Bert was flying out from the UK and would escort them to Akrotiri. Soon afterwards, we took off again for Cyprus.

We were told, all being well, that the other PoWs would arrive in Cyprus just a few hours behind us.

Most of the PoWs accepted that what we were doing was in their best interests even if it did mean a delay in seeing their loved ones back home. Originally, the SAS weren't going to be a part of the debriefing process, but their leadership was so interested in what we were doing that it put in a request to join in.

The only person who vehemently objected to the programme was John Nichol, Peters's navigator, who sought me out as soon as he'd disembarked from the aircraft that had brought him in from Amman. I knew he had been very upset by reports he'd read soon after getting on the plane that his parents had been besieged by the press at their home near Newcastle.

'The only reason I'm going along with this,' he said, his face barely an inch from mine, 'is because we've been ordered to. I want you to know that my colleagues and I think that this scheme of yours is a shite idea and that it won't work. I want to go home. We all do.' He seemed to be acting as the spokesman for the group.

The last thing I wanted was to be confrontational. I told him in as quiet but as authoritative a voice as I could muster that I hoped he'd see the benefit of what we had planned in due course. I added: 'Please, John, just watch this space.'

He spun on his heels and stormed off.

As soon as they'd rested, we split the PoWs into groups. Care was taken to group them according to experiences they'd shared. We were dealing with three sets of people: released RAF PoWs, released SAS PoWs and fast-jet aircrew who had volunteered to come to Akrotiri from their squadrons in the Gulf to support their recently released friends.

Care was also taken to de-institutionalize the PoWs' surroundings. Curtains on windows, rugs on floors, pictures on walls, replacement of typical hospital beds with divans, plus radios and TVs, all helped to make their accommodation more homelike. They were also able to choose their own clothing.

Use of the telephone to contact spouses, partners and friends was positively encouraged. The provision of wristwatches seemed to restore a sense of orientation, control and independence – which is, of course, why watches are among the first items to be removed when a PoW is bundled into captivity. To fill the information gap, videotapes of condensed news programmes provided by the BBC and backdated copies of newspapers proved very useful in bringing them up to date for their imminent return home.

We then got cracking. We'd already agreed that psychological debriefing would become an integral part of the operational debriefing. Alvin and Dick, the two psychiatric nurses, took a group each and I took the third. Each of us was backed up by one of the local facilitators.

We started by telling the PoWs about our work and what, through the experience of Lockerbie and other disasters, we had come to learn about the nature of PTSD: that it wasn't a disease but something that could hit anyone, depending on the nature and severity of the trauma.

A pamphlet that we'd prepared flagged up the fact that they might be afflicted in a number of ways. Flashbacks and nightmares were the most obvious symptoms, but there might be others; numbness, anger, guilt, shame and sadness were just some of them. We then went into the debriefing itself, looking for answers to those two primary questions: 'What happened to you?' and 'How do you feel about what happened to you?'

The first question was usually answered during the operational debriefing. We would have to probe away at the second.

The first operational debriefing I attended was that of John Peters on 5 March. Prior to this, I'd met with the two intelligence officers who'd be handling these sessions, Major Richard Griffin of the Intelligence Corps and an RAF flight lieutenant, Philip Barbera, of the Joint Intelligence Staff, based in Cyprus.

They told me they were happy for me to attend their debriefings and ran over some of their techniques before Peters entered the room. It was a very systematic process. Each point of the PoW's capture was examined in detail, the idea being to build up a picture of his entire incarceration, bit by bit, layer upon layer. For example, at the point of capture, the time of capture was established, the circumstances, the identity of other PoWs taken at the same time and the medical state of both the interviewee and any other PoWs with him. Thereafter, the name, nickname and description of any location encountered by the PoW was recorded, in so far as they could be remembered, and the details picked over. This went for the initial processing point, interrogation facilities, PoW camps and any other installations that the PoW either saw or heard about during the time that he had been held.

As the layers were amassed, the intelligence officers were able to compose a remarkably complex picture of what had transpired during the PoW's period as a captive, often including details that the PoWs themselves were not aware they'd ever known; details such as the names or nicknames of their guards, other PoWs they'd met, clues as to their location and so on.

When Peters entered the room, I was struck by how well he looked after several days of rest and recuperation. He was wearing jeans and a T-shirt that he'd been able to buy in Limassol thanks to the provision of some Red Cross money that had trickled through to us.

He listened carefully to the explanation of the process that he was about to undergo and told his debriefers he was happy to help in any way that he could. If anything, it was difficult to get him to *stop* talking. Griffin and Barbera had to jump in on a couple of occasions just to remind him that all they needed was answers to their questions, nothing more.

As an observer, I wasn't able to intervene. I merely made a mental note that this loquaciousness on Peters's part was his need to ventilate his feelings. The feelings themselves would be explored during the psychological debriefings later in the week. But the details of his story were chilling. Peters and Nichol had been shot down on their very first mission of the war.

John began his story by relating how he and Nichol had been captured by Bedouins at approximately 7.40 in the morning following a direct hit on their Tornado. They had tried to turn for home, but Nichol had seen the fireball that had engulfed the entire aircraft behind the cockpit in his rear-view mirror and recommended, quite strongly, that they eject. When they hit the dirt, the Bedouin stripped them of their possessions and handed them over to an Iraqi officer, who took them under guard to a local airfield. As they were blindfolded, Peters and Nichol were unaware of the location; all they did know was that it was close to the point they'd gone down.

JP, as I thought of him, had hurt his right eye during the ejection and his right knee and lower leg during his parachute landing. JN had suffered a minor leg injury. Both were otherwise OK – glad simply to have survived.

Thus far, their treatment had been relatively benign, their captors, Air Force personnel, treating them as fellow fliers 'for whom the war was over'. They were gently probed for information, but on refusing to give any, were warned that they would shortly be transferred to another location, where their captors 'wouldn't be so nice'.

A few hours later, they were blindfolded, their hands tied, and bundled into a truck. JP's perception of elapsed time had deteriorated by this point, but he felt sure that he had been taken to Baghdad. He was led into a building, knowing only that it was dark outside and that a triple-A installation was hammering away at some coalition aircraft overhead. The building was of prefabricated construction.

I watched as Griffin and Barbera scratched notes.

It was at this second location, as he was held in isolation, that his interrogations began in earnest. When he refused to answer their questions, his interrogators started beating him with what he presumed to be a rubber truncheon on his head, upper torso and legs. When this didn't work, they turned their attention to his injured eye and knee.

I thought about Frank, the Tornado pilot we'd had at Wroughton. Frank had known JP's injuries for what they were. Small wonder it had tipped him over the edge.

JP, thus far, though stressed at the memory of what he had endured, was able to describe what had happened to him without breaking down, which I thought was pretty remarkable. He described how his interrogators pressed him up against a wall and repeatedly banged his head against it. His tormentors were all Iraqi Army officers.

It was a few days into this treatment that he was made to record the 'interview' shown on Baghdad television and subsequently broadcast to the world. He was given lines to learn and beaten when he showed resistance. At this time, too, he was threatened with a gun to his head.

Five days later, JP was moved to a third location. Again, due to a blindfold, he had no idea where he had been taken, but guessed from the strength of the bombing that it was a heavily militarized district in the north-north-east corner of Baghdad.

After a week at this location, he was moved again. The journey took no more than 15 minutes. When his blindfold was removed, JP realized he was in some kind of prison in a residential area of what he still believed to be Baghdad.

On the night of 24 February, the long, narrow three-storey building was hit by four bombs which destroyed the two ends but left the middle section more or less intact. Fortunately, it was this part that held him and other PoWs. At this location, aside from being spat at, he wasn't treated too badly. In fact, he wasn't beaten again from this point onwards. He was eventually released, from the fourth location, on 1 March.

Peters managed to describe it all in a clipped, just-the-facts tone of voice, but it had been unrelenting: night after night of not knowing what was going to happen to him. And, clearly, it had been the same for all the others. I wondered how I would have reacted under the circumstances. Would I have cracked under the pressure of interrogation? I didn't even want to go there. Those years spent in RAF Germany, with Russian tanks supposedly ready to roll against us at any moment, had not, I realized, remotely prepared me for the realities of war. War on the scale that had occurred in the Gulf was something that hadn't been witnessed for an entire generation. And in terms of casualties, we had got away with it – Iraq, with the fourth largest armed forces in the world, had been defeated at the cost of a few hundred killed on the coalition side. And the thousands of trauma victims that at one point I had envisaged being sent back to the UK ... they had not materialized either. Instead, for my Wroughton-based team, it had come down to this group, a handful of former PoWs. I brought myself back to the here and now and determined, as I listened to the rest of Peters's story, that we would do the best we could for him and his colleagues.

Over the next few days, I sat in on all the other operational debriefings of the seven RAF aircrew. Dick, meanwhile, took the second group, RAF friends – aircrew who had taken part in the war but who hadn't been taken prisoner – and Alvin took the third, the SAS PoWs.

Our message was uniform and consistent. In addition to listening carefully to the PoWs' responses to the question of how they felt about what had happened to them, I was also keen to give the clear message that many of the symptoms they had come to exhibit reflected, to use the jargon, 'adaptive mental processes' involved in the assimilation of new information they'd needed to survive over the past couple of months. Their brains had done whatever they'd needed to do to come through interrogation and captivity. Now that those survival skills were no longer needed, I explained that they had to 'de-orbit'.

The whole thing was very much a journey of discovery for me too. We decided to conduct all the psychological debriefings in groups. We assembled the seven members of the RAF PoW group in a room on the first floor. I sat them down on chairs in a semicircle around me.

The first person I looked at was John Nichol, who returned my glance with a scowl. He was still seething about being in Akrotiri, which he seemed to see as an extension of the incarceration he'd endured in Iraq. I'd had a word with him the previous evening, hoping that he'd be more friendly towards me, but instead all I got was a clipped assurance that he'd go along with the debriefing sessions, giving them the benefit of the doubt. But he left me under the distinct impression that he'd 'jump' if at any point he saw any- thing in our techniques with which he vehemently disagreed. This didn't make me feel any more relaxed. At least with the mountain rescuers I'd been called in to help. Here, the group's main spokesman – Nichol – had made it abundantly clear that I was on trial; and if I flunked it, he'd be walking out the door and taking any of the others who wanted to leave with him.

To reflect the fact that I was hanging out on a wing and a prayer I removed my rank bands and placed them on the floor next to my chair. This, at least, seemed to go down well. I then ran through the reasons I felt it was important they were here. I gave them a brief history of PTSD, trying not to make it dry and academic. When we got to Lockerbie, I was then able to describe how men I knew – men renowned for not cracking under pressure – *had* cracked in a number of cases. And because I knew mountain rescuers to be uniformly

tough, I told them I'd been able to be a lot more definitive about
what PTSD was: a normal reaction, just as it said in the *DSM*, to a
highly abnormal event. I was even able to be categorical about what
it wasn't: PTSD was not about a flaw in the character of men who
went into battle. Though I was careful not to name names, I went on
to describe how we'd got Frank, their colleague, back into the fight
again after a programme of rehabilitation at Wroughton. When I
finished telling the story, I heard a number of people who'd known
Frank well murmur their approval.

But not John Nichol. For the most part, he just sat there, studying
his hands or the floor between his feet. Occasionally, when he did
glance up, our eyes would meet and the hostility would still be there.

The following day, when the debriefings began in earnest, I started
with John Peters, asking him how he felt about the various things
he'd described during his operational debriefing. There was a pause
as he collected his thoughts. His face darkened as he recalled the time
he'd spent with his captors.

'A number of things got to me,' he said. He was leaning forward,
his elbows on his thighs, looking at me intently. 'They accused us of
war crimes, which I really resented. They said that our weapons had
killed innocent women and children. I knew this wasn't true, because
all our raids at that stage of the war had been against Iraqi air bases,
but the thought of it got to me, nonetheless. Perhaps, because I
myself am a father . . .'

He looked down, studying the ground at his feet. 'I felt guilty, too,
about letting the side down in the two TV interviews I gave. And I
was worried that I'd given away too much during my interrogations . . .' he looked up and smiled, 'even though, right now, I
can't think of a single thing that might have been operationally
useful to them.'

This comment prompted a big discussion among the group about
interrogation; what it was and wasn't acceptable to say to
interrogators.

I noticed that everyone was contributing to the debate except for
one member of the group, who was silent and withdrawn from his
colleagues.

The next moment I happened to look at him, I saw a single tear rolling down his cheek. Then the dam opened. He sat there, weeping silently. For a moment, nobody knew what to say or do. There was embarrassment, a little morbid fascination and finally deep concern on the faces of his colleagues. I didn't ask, 'How are you feeling?' It was bloody obvious how he was feeling. But then the group stepped in.

'What's wrong?' the bloke next to him asked softly, placing a hand on his shoulder.

His mate wiped away his tears. 'I'm all right. Ignore me. Just carry on.'

Eventually, he was coaxed into telling everyone.

'I feel guilty, too,' he said, his voice barely audible.

'Guilty about what?' the man on his right said.

'About the Big Three. I told them more than my name, rank and serial number. I told them a lot. Like John, nothing that would have compromised operational security, I don't think, but . . . I just feel so bloody guilty.'

What happened next was quite amazing. One by one, all the others confessed to having done the same thing.

I sat there, saying nothing. I was totally spellbound. What, I wondered, would have happened if this hadn't come out? This man – all of them – would have been living a lie and it would have eaten away at them.

After they'd all confessed, we started to talk. I already realized the value of making positives from negatives in trauma work. This, I knew, could be a very positive finding. These men had been trained in escape and evasion techniques and how to deal with interrogation. Standard procedure was to stick to the Big Three. Yet each man had gone against training and told his interrogators things he wasn't supposed to. The discussion became more animated. Wouldn't it be better to come up with a new system, they said; a system where breaking the Big Three didn't matter? Here, after all, was evidence that brave men, under pressure, had all 'cracked' – though that is not a definition I'd have used.

'How would you describe it?' the man who had wept said, raising his eyes to mine.

Where moments earlier they had been lifeless, I now saw something quite else. I thought of the Mirror Model I'd been told about

in the principal's office in Palo Alto. The Mirror Model said that
trauma was something you could move beyond and here was proof
it was right.

'If you regard the fact that you all broke the Big Three as being
"normal"' – I made my fingers do a couple of quote marks in the air
– 'then what this tells me is that it's the system that's flawed, not
you.'

They started to talk animatedly about the US concept of 'trickle-
feed' – how, instead of holding on doggedly to the Big Three, you
offered your interrogators morsels of information that would keep
them satisfied but wouldn't compromise operational security; old
codes, for instance. Trickle-feed had come out of the American
Vietnam experience and had been adopted by US military personnel
as standard procedure in the event of capture.

The group started to talk about the MoD's potential adoption of
trickle-feed and, indeed, later, in the analysis of lessons learned from
the Gulf War, this was something that was adopted. During this discussion, something else wonderful happened. A voice I'd not heard
since we'd started the debriefings was now animatedly engaged – a
voice with a strong Northumbrian accent. I looked up and caught
John Nichol's eye and this time he gave me an almost imperceptible
nod. A positive from a negative.

Yet again, I was learning how, under the right circumstances,
PTSD could be viewed as something life-affirming. Our job was to
ensure that we helped the sufferer get beyond the nightmares, the
flashbacks and high arousal and anxiety states so they could see it in
that light too. And, I realized, if I could win over hard-bitten
sceptics like John Nichol, the guys on the front line who really
mattered, then there was every chance it could work on anyone.

As debriefers, we ourselves were debriefed, another lesson we had
learned – some of us through painful experiences with our own
families – post-Lockerbie. The ripple effect of PTSD was real and we
encouraged the relatives of the PoWs to contact us if any of the
PTSD symptoms we believed we'd dealt with in Akrotiri continued.

To mitigate the ripple effect on us, Arthur Jones, well known to all
the debriefers, and the community psychiatric nurse in Cyprus, solid,
totally reliable and a man with a big reputation in RAF psychiatry,

together with Bert Venman, acted as our debriefers. They became, in effect, the counsellors' counsellors.

Bert was a psychiatric nurse of the old school. He'd been a policeman then a prison officer, which was how, when he joined the RAF, he'd come to deal with behavioural cases. In the old days, psychiatric nurses were all big blokes – they had to be, because that was how you controlled behavioural problems; before the advent of elephant drops. Bert would have fitted into the old regime like a glove, but there was a sensitive side to him, too. We all felt a little better when Bert was in charge.

Their roles were to hear descriptions of debriefing work undertaken that day and impressions gained from the work, and to identify tiredness, 'mirroring' and any over-involvement. Bert and Arthur's professionalism ensured that the system worked. Support debriefing allowed debriefers to vent their emotions, for us all to test new hypotheses for treatment and encouraged the development of new strategies.

The secondary debriefings usually took place towards the end of the day. The day my group had opened up about the Big Three, I'd really felt a need to talk but I couldn't put my finger on why.

We gathered in the dining room on the first floor and sat around in a circle, while Arthur and Bert went around the group asking how our day had gone. Stardust went before me and described a very positive session he'd had with the SAS boys.

The SAS were unusual in that they had minders with them. As these people were dressed in civvies, I had no idea who they were – whether they were also SAS or from the intelligence community – but they seemed to pop up out of nowhere as soon as the SAS touched down in Cyprus. There were five SAS in Alvin's group and each was accompanied by one of these people. This, I imagined, was standard procedure, ensuring that they did not reveal any classified data during the course of their debriefing.

Although I never dealt with them personally, the SAS were curious about our work and very supportive. The whole concept of group debriefings was more familiar to the SAS than it was to the RAF. In the SAS, rank structure means little – under the 'headshed' principle, when the SAS gathers (often in the course of a battle) to discuss next steps, each person's opinion is as good as another's, regardless of their rank. The RAF, on the other hand, is more structured and formal. And perhaps this is why the SAS embraced the process so wholeheartedly, to the extent that they asked if they could bring it back to Hereford so that wives and girlfriends could be there too.

I could see no reason why this shouldn't happen, as long as my team remained involved, at least for the time being. I wanted to ensure that all the debriefing protocols were handed over in the right way. This was medicine that needed to be administered by people trained in the art. But it was all good, encouraging stuff.

When it came to my turn, I told Arthur and Bert about John Peters's testimony and the single tear I'd seen rolling down the cheek of one of his colleagues.

'And what effect did that have on you when you saw him in that state?' Bert asked.

'I thought it was hugely positive,' I replied. 'It was the trigger, the catalyst that prompted his mates to open up and reveal that they, too, had all said things under interrogation.'

Bert looked at me. 'What did you really think, Gordon?'

I took a deep breath. Bert knew me too well; knew that there must have been more. 'I was shocked, I guess. Surprised, because that wasn't something I thought a pilot would do in front of other pilots.'

'Shocked enough for it to have unsettled you?'

'No,' I said. But here was the nature of my dilemma. It had shocked me quite a bit and on the one hand I was keen to be open – to say this – to the group. But on the other, I didn't want to unsettle my colleagues by telling them that the boss had been rattled. I always felt myself being tugged in two directions at secondary debriefings.

'Well?' Bert prompted.

'It made him human and the responses of his colleagues made them human, too,' I replied. It was the truth, but not the whole truth, and I realized it made me sound a little stiff.

Bert moved on to Dick, asking him how it had gone with the other RAF group, and out of nowhere Dick just exploded.

He said he didn't trust me. He said he didn't want to work with me. And all because, he yelled, I'd been the one who'd ordered him and Stardust back from the Kuwaiti border when I'd flown out to Saudi to take over the stress reaction unit.

I sat and listened – we all did – until Dick had nothing left to say.

Afterwards, it felt like a hand grenade had been lobbed into the room. When something like that goes off, you can't just ask everyone to carry on as if nothing has happened; it has to be dealt with. Fortunately, this was where Bert came into his own. He didn't tell Dick to shut up. He acknowledged that he felt this way and invited him to get everything off his chest – as I had on my first day in Saudi. Only Bert didn't give up. He got Dick to vent his feelings and then he asked me for my tuppence worth.

It took the whole session to turn the issue around, but by the end the grenade had been defused. Dick accepted that I'd not been responsible for pulling him and Alvin back from the front line; I accepted his apology. And so we moved on. Only afterwards did I see this incident in a subtly different light. The grenade hadn't merely been defused. It had offered itself up to be defused when I'd not been wholly truthful about my feelings over the pilot who'd wept. This was what the group offered. To Dick it had represented a place of real safety; so much so that this particular issue had surfaced as if compelled to by some unseen force in the room – a good force, not in any way malevolent.

And the even better news about this was, if *we* considered it a safe place, then so did the aircrew and the SAS. It told me that these group sessions really were working.

But perhaps the most gratifying result from the whole PoW experience came in an exchange I had with John Nichol. It was a couple of days after the debriefing in which he and his colleagues had all talked about interrogation protocols – how the rules governing the Big Three had to change; the day John had finally relented and nodded to me – a signal that something inside him had shifted.

'I'm sorry,' he said. 'You were right and I was wrong. We understand what you're doing here and we all see the benefit of it.'

He stuck his hand out and shook mine warmly. 'Now,' he said, 'I'm ready to go home.'

It put me in mind of Archibald McIndoe and the burn victims, most of them RAF, whose faces he'd rebuilt via his pioneering work in plastic surgery during and after the Second World War. What we'd done wasn't perfect, I knew that, but it was something – something I hoped would give impetus to the pioneering efforts of people like Morgan McConnell, the Royal Navy psychiatrist who'd worked tirelessly in the face of enormous bureaucratic inertia on behalf of the trauma victims of the Falklands War.

The group had become a model for processing the symptoms of PTSD, a condition that should no longer be seen as an illness, but, in the context of the PoWs' experience, an adjustment to adversity – a survival strategy. The symptoms – and, most importantly, the flash-backs – were ways and means of adjusting to the experience and learning from it.

Not everyone in the military hierarchy felt this way, however. I could remember, for example, soon after my return to the UK, the time when I raised the idea of continuing to run the group at a consultant adviser's meeting in London.

All the consultants gathered together with the consultant adviser in London every three months or so. One of these meetings fell, quite rightly, after the war, so we could talk about what had happened. People gave presentations; it was a sort of board meeting for consultants in psychiatry. It happened in all the other specialties too.

I was coming back in the train with two other consultants from my unit from Wroughton. By now, I was head of the division.

They said to me, 'This idea you have of running these groups regularly: we think that it'd be far better if you wrote a paper on why you think it would work and then submitted it to the RAF hierarchy and consultant advisers so they could say whether or not you can go ahead with it.'

I said, 'Bollocks to that,' as politely as I could. 'As you well know, I will write the paper and the paper will be criticized and sent back for a rewrite. It's going to be six months down the line before I get the paper accepted. It'll then do the rounds at different levels in the medical world of the MoD, and eventually will be rejected.

'This is too important. I'm not going to let this happen at this par-ticular time. You don't need to be involved if you don't want to be. I'm going to be involved in it, but it won't be my only involvement with the unit. I'll be alive to other things, too. It's going to be part of my work, but I can't pretend it won't be the most important part of my work. I've discovered certain things and I've got to see them through.'

They belted up after that. They couldn't really come up with any objections. I felt I'd covered all the angles, but I was wrong.

Chapter 13

Hostages

It was 7 August 1991. We were in the air, somewhere between RAF Brize Norton (the home of the VC10 fleet) and the Mediterranean. I sat with Bert and the three other members of the team near the back of the aircraft, watching groups of people – many of them huddled in the aisle – talking excitedly.

The news had broken so quickly we weren't even sure which of the hostages was being released. Speculation had ridden high that it was John McCarthy – speculation that appeared to be on the money when I spotted McCarthy's father Pat and his brother Terence on board the VC10. I recognized them from the papers.

The Wroughton team had been on standby for the best part of a year to mount a retrieval of the Lebanon hostages. I'd even written an extensive brief on it. But I'd never thought it would come to this – or that events would move quite so fast.

I'd spent much of my time since the end of hostilities in the Gulf briefing senior RAF personnel about the value of debriefing. The message was no longer falling on deaf ears. This was because we'd now got something demonstrable to show the doubting Thomases. The 'two Johns' had returned to flying within six weeks of leaving Akrotiri. All their colleagues were now back on flying duties. I was being asked up to London every other week. Suddenly, everybody wanted to know about Lockerbie and trauma reactions.

It was in the midst of this whirl of activity that we were scrambled to Brize Norton, the RAF's transport base just down the road from Wroughton, with instructions to prepare for the release of one of the hostages. The flight had been laid on by the Foreign Office and was due to touch down at Akrotiri. From there, we would await further developments in Lebanon and Syria. The Syrians were acting as brokers for the hostages' release. McCarthy, along with a number of other Westerners, including the Archbishop of Canterbury's special envoy, Terry Waite, had been held by Hezbollah for five long years.

In light of the destruction of the Twin Towers in New York on 11 September 2001, since when it has seemed as if the West has been waging permanent war in the Middle East and South-West Asia, the notion of Western hostages in the Middle East being a big news story might seem odd. But the Lebanon hostage crisis of the 1980s was huge. It started soon after the Israelis invaded the Lebanon in 1982 and continued with Americans mainly in the cross-hairs of the hostage takers in the ensuing years, thanks to a strong US military presence in the Lebanon as well.

The original reason for hostage-taking, mainly by Hezbollah, the Lebanese-based Islamic terrorist group, seems to have been as insurance against retaliation by the US or Israel against Islamic militants fighting the Israeli Army. But then, in 1986, US President Ronald Reagan upped the ante by launching a strike mission against Libya, which had been identified as the culprit in a terrorist bomb attack on a nightclub in West Germany. In the course of that attack, a number of US service personnel stationed in West Germany had been killed.

Because UK Prime Minister Margaret Thatcher had supported Reagan by allowing US fighter-bombers to take off against Libya from bases in the UK, there were fears that British citizens would be put in the firing line as well. Those fears were found to be justified when John McCarthy, a British TV journalist, was snatched a few days later. Early the following year, Waite, who had gone out to Lebanon to negotiate the release of McCarthy and a number of other hostages – among them, the Irishman Brian Keenan and two Americans, Terry Anderson and Tom Sutherland – was himself taken hostage. All were believed to be being held by Hezbollah.

McCarthy's plight might not have entered into the public consciousness at all had it not been for his girlfriend, Jill Morrell, who campaigned tirelessly for his release. Jill kept John in the public eye via a savvy, well-orchestrated media campaign that ensured that John McCarthy and his fellow hostages remained household names during their incarceration. McCarthy's fresh face – photographs generally showed a smiling young man in his late twenties with twinkling, humorous eyes – was never far from the newspapers or our TV screens.

And from many of the profiles I'd read on him, I almost felt I knew him. The papers described a very decent, perhaps slightly naive young man who'd been doing no more than his job when Hezbollah came for him and bundled him into the boot of their car. John had been on his way to the airport to catch a flight back to the UK. For most of the five years that he had been held, there had been no news: no one knew whether he was dead or alive. But following the recent release of Brian Keenan, it was confirmed that McCarthy, Waite, Sutherland and Anderson were all alive. Keenan had been held in the same place, a cramped, windowless cell in an anonymous block in a Hezbollah stronghold in the suburbs of Beirut. In the years that they had been held, the world had changed. The Berlin Wall had fallen, the apartheid regime in South Africa had gone the same way and we'd fought and won a major war in the Gulf. On a more poignant note, Sheila McCarthy, John's mother, had died of cancer 18 months earlier, not knowing whether her son was alive or dead.

Bert and I decided that I should try to track down the senior Foreign Office official on the flight and brief him on what I wanted to do. So far, all I'd managed was to blag us on the flight as part of the aeromed team. The aeromed team, as coincidence would have it, was led by Fredoon Amroliwalla, the consultant physician whom I'd worked under all those years ago in Ely. Fred was now a group captain and the senior physician on the medical ward at Wroughton.

If this had been down to the RAF I'd have been able to get my own way immediately – we were still riding high after Iraq – but with the hostages it was different. So many people seemed to have a stake in them it was difficult to know who was in charge. The last thing I wanted was to turn up at Akrotiri only to be told by some government bigwig that they didn't want us along for the second stage – the trip to Damascus.

I was convinced that the hostages' psychological well-being depended on the treatment they received in the hours, days and weeks ahead. But this wasn't part of my brief. As part of the aeromed team, I was here to ensure that the hostages were mentally fit to fly – complementing the role of Fredoon, whose task was to oversee the hostages' physical well-being. But I didn't want to let it rest there. After the successful treatment of the Gulf War PoWs, I knew that the hostages' long-term mental health was at stake – and that the answer lay in their being properly debriefed. But for that, I'd have to get approvals and I didn't have much time.

It took me a while to identify the FO man, longer still to thread my way through the people thronging the aisle as the VC10 cruised south-east towards Cyprus. Everyone was chatting excitedly about the next 24 hours.

I finally took a seat.

'Hello.' I extended my hand. 'Wing Commander Gordon Turnbull. I'm part of the aeromed team. I'd like to brief you, if I may, on certain aspects of the treatment we've been working up for the hostages . . .'

The FO man informed me he had already been briefed by Fred, but I told him that Fred's job by and large was focused on the hostages' physical well-being. My job – how could I put this? – was somewhat more specific.

'We're talking psychological?' the man in charge said. 'You're the psychiatrist?'

I nodded. In the pause that followed I asked him if there was any news on which of the hostages was supposedly coming out.

He gazed out of the window as he spoke. 'The reports coming out of Lebanon and Syria are fairly confused. There are strong indications that somebody is going to be released, but we don't know who. We should know more in Akrotiri.'

He then turned and looked at me earnestly. 'So what can I do for you, Wing Commander?'

I started to tell him about the success of the Gulf operation and how the hostages, in my opinion, should be allowed to benefit from the same experience if they were to be successfully rehabilitated—

'It's got to be done, *got* to be,' the man from the FO blurted enthusiastically before I could even begin to develop a head of steam. He understood, too, the importance of agreeing the debriefing schedule before we launched into it.

My God, the guy had read the brief . . .

One of the lessons we'd learned from the Gulf was that changes in the plan after work had started destabilized the process, since it called the credibility of the debriefing team into question in the minds of the survivors. Restoration of structure and control had a very calming effect. The antidote to being a hostage was to feel that your environment was predictable and that you had a reasonable degree of control over it.

I was so relieved I pumped his hand warmly. If this had been California, I wouldn't have had any explaining to do, but in Britain in 1991 it was still a surprise, and, frankly, a relief when people in officialdom – especially people this senior – didn't treat you like you were completely off your trolley when you brought psychiatry into the mix.

He directed me towards a female member of his team who'd be heading up the debriefing process. It didn't take a size-nine hat to work out that she was MI6. I sat down next to her and we talked. I told her about our work with the PoWs in Cyprus and how we'd added the psychological debriefing to the operational debriefing and how well it had worked. I told her, too, that I thought the same system could work well for the hostages, given that it was pretty obvious that the FO and MI6 wanted to glean what they knew.

I was told that as long as I could structure my part of the proceedings around what the FO needed to accomplish with Waite and McCarthy – a factual debriefing of the whos, whats, wheres, whys and whens of their release by Hezbollah – then they had no objection.

Again, I was pleasantly surprised when they acknowledged that there was real benefit in our working our magic with Waite and McCarthy, given what they'd been through. To be asked a bunch of questions in quick-fire succession, even if they did come from people who looked and talked like you, could resurrect traumatic memories of long hours spent under interrogation, and the FO and MI6 understood this. By the time we hit the tarmac at RAF Akrotiri, we had an agreement. Now all I had to do was get the permission of the people who really mattered: the hostages' next of kin.

In the officers' mess, the woman from MI6 introduced me to Pat and Terence McCarthy. I was full of nervous excitement. They understandably looked worried.

'You're a doctor?' Pat, John's father, asked. He glanced over his shoulder at Fred. 'But I have already met Mr Amroliwalla . . .'

I told him that I was the psychiatrist; that it was Fred's job to ensure that the hostages were physically fit to fly and my job to see that they were mentally up to the journey.

'I see,' he said.

In the conversation that followed Pat did most of the talking. Terence, John's brother, was much quieter, but an interested listener – attentive to everything that was discussed. I was worried that they would find my presence off-putting, but they seemed to draw strength from it, asking me a lot of questions.

They were particularly worried, if John were to be released, about the effect on him of the news of his mother's death. Pat asked what I thought he should do. When did I think he should tell him about Sheila?

'I think you should tell him as soon as possible,' I told him. 'The truth, in my experience, is always best. Besides, if there is anything I've learned in what I've read about your son, I'm certain it is what he would want.'

He gently placed his hand on my arm. 'Thank you, Wing Commander. Sound advice. Let's hope that it hasn't been a wasted journey . . .'

My heart went out to them both. Everyone had been focused on John, but how would Pat and Terence cope with his release? What feelings had they been wrestling with these past five years? A son and a brother whom for a long time they must have presumed to be dead. A wife and mother who'd died not knowing her son's fate.

These were intolerable strains on anyone. And it was with this thought in mind that I sensed my chance and started to tell them about our work at Wroughton.

They both listened attentively, asking questions about the PTSD phenomenon and how it had come to be acknowledged relatively late in the day. There were no easy answers to some of the things they asked, but I was able to stress how successful our work had been with the mountain rescuers and the Gulf War PoWs. In the latter case, I explained how the circumstances of their trauma weren't a million miles from what the hostages in the Lebanon must have experienced.

When I finished, I waited. Had I done enough? Had I oversold the concept? I hoped my own nervous excitement hadn't put them off.

Pat drew breath to speak, but was interrupted by a compact and pugnacious American, whom I'd noticed on the plane. He bounded up to them and told them the news that he'd just been made privy to: it was John who was coming out.

After the excitement had subsided a little, the American turned to me. 'I'm sorry,' he said. 'And you are . . . ?'

Pat jumped in. 'Roby, this is Wing Commander Gordon Turnbull. Wing Commander Turnbull is a psychiatrist.' He turned to me. 'Wing Commander—'

'Gordon, please,' I urged.

'Gordon,' he corrected himself, 'this is Roby Burke.' Roby Burke was the head of WTN in London – the TV station John had been working for when he got snatched. He was the only person from the McCarthy party, other than Pat and Terence, who'd been allowed to make the trip.

Roby shook my hand warily. It was Pat who broke the silence that had fallen on our small gathering.

'Gordon was just telling us about his pioneering debriefing techniques,' he told Roby, before glancing at me. 'And if I read you right, Gordon, you want our permission to spend time with John, to allow him to . . . readjust to life again after what he's been through. Would that be right?'

'Yes,' I replied. 'And not just John. All the hostages. And I think it will be important for you to be part of the process too.'

Roby suddenly held his hand up. 'Hang on there a moment.' He looked at Pat and Terence. 'We don't know anything about this guy.' His tone was punchy, aggressive. He turned back to me. 'I just want you to know,' he said, eyes flashing, 'that we're not going to accept second-best for John. Is that clear?'

'Perfectly,' I told him.

'So, who *is* the best?' he asked, somewhat disarmingly.

'Well,' I said, managing somehow to keep my tone as even as my gaze, 'I'd probably have to think about that for a moment. This is a pretty new field.'

He continued to stare at me.

'Well,' I said, 'there's a chap called Sandy McFarlane in Australia, who's an acknowledged expert in this field, and a guy called Jeffrey Mitchell in America, who has done some brilliant work with traumatized first response teams – rescue workers and the like. There's another guy in the US, too, called Bessel van der Kolk. But obviously none of them works in the UK and that could be a bit of a problem.'

Pat and Terence seemed embarrassed by Roby's outburst, but I understood it perfectly. Roby must have felt responsible for what had happened to John – he was, after all, his boss – and, in jumping down my throat, was probably over-compensating for the guilt he must have felt.

'There are other people involved in trauma,' I said, 'but most of them work overseas. So why don't you think of us? We've worked a lot in the past few years with the Royal Air Force, with released prisoners of war and with people who attended Lockerbie, and I think you should choose us – our team at Wroughton.'

Roby hesitated for a second then shoved his finger under my nose. 'OK, you've got the job. But this had better work. Because if at any moment I don't think it is working, I'm going to jump in and put a stop to it.' He looked at Pat and Terence, explained that there were people they needed to talk to and tugged them towards the opposite end of the room.

I was left with a sense of déjà vu and tried to put my finger on it. Then it came to me.

The last time I'd felt like this had been 1988, when the call had come through about Lockerbie.

Despite Roby's aggressiveness, I knew that he had John's best interests at heart. Pat, Terence and Roby were all asking the same question: what can we do? When David Whalley had phoned me about the things he had seen in the mountain rescuers that had scared him, his question – the same one – contained an unspoken corollary: how will *I* cope? I had sensed the same feeling just now. What I hoped had swung it was the fact that, somewhere within them, they'd felt that I could help not just John but them too.

I turned to find Bert standing next to me. 'What was that about?'

'A timely reminder of what's at stake here,' I replied.

'What's that?'

What's always at stake in situations like these, I replied. It's not so much the techniques that you promise as part of the 'cure' process that are important, but yourself. People won't work with you if they don't trust you. Trust has to have a starting point – a click – and I liked to think I'd felt it with Pat and Terence.

Roby must have been aware of it, too, otherwise he wouldn't have gone along with it. But all this was at a subconscious level. At a conscious level, Roby was putting me on trial and that wasn't a good feeling. When it came to it, would John pick this up and reject me? I suddenly noticed that my shirt was wringing wet with sweat.

We stayed the night in prefab accommodation blocks built for the massive expansion of Akrotiri during the Gulf War. The air-conditioning had been set so cold – and without any discernible means of adjusting it in my room – that I found it impossible to sleep.

This turned out to be a blessing. It gave me a chance to work on our plans for Damascus. It was clear that the hostages were being released one by one, so our post-Gulf War group debriefing strategy had to be rethought. To begin with, it was essential for the individual hostage to debrief with a trusted confidant, so his re-actions to captivity could be normalized and validated before that process became diluted or even imperilled by his speaking to un-controlled groups.

Everyone on this mission felt they knew a man whom few of them had ever met. Everything I had heard and read told me that he was uncommonly decent and that what he had endured was almost beyond description. Nothing could completely undo the torment of the last five years, but with the techniques we had developed at Wroughton we had the chance to make him better. Not a full recovery, perhaps, but pretty close.

The RAF had accepted this; the MoD, too. I had approval from the FO, approval from the McCarthy family – albeit, thanks to Roby, with some qualifications. Now it was down to John himself.

The Gulf experience had taught us that in treating the four people who needed our attention – John McCarthy, his father, his brother and, whether he liked it or not, Roby Burke – the key, as I wrote in a memo after the war, was to 'provide non-directive support, in a non-questioning way to aid ventilation of feelings and impressions without aiming to provoke catharsis or outbursts of emotion'.

We had agreed that I would be attached to John, while other members of the team would be assigned to Pat, Terence and Roby. Bert, with his flare for organization, would play sweeper and watch over the entire procedure.

Of all the possible pitfalls – pitfalls we'd discovered the hard way – the one that worried me most was rejection.

We had to put ourselves in the mind of the hostage and realize that with shattered self-confidence came an inability to judge people – that blink-of-an-eye, first-impression assessment that came naturally to most of us. As a result, any ambiguity, any doubt he harboured towards us, could be translated instantly into rejection.

Too little confidence was bad, but so was too much. Seemingly inconsequential things, like gesticulation, could trigger an adverse reaction. We needed to walk slowly and not wave our hands around. For the past five years, John McCarthy would have come to see hands as instruments of torture.

We also had to use words that were simple and fluid – again, no ambiguity. Latinisms, technical and medical terms – a raised voice, even – were potential stressors. Hostages became very vigilant. They picked up on everything. They'd had to, simply to survive.

Word came during the night that the mission was on and we took off in the VC10 for Damascus soon after sun-up. I felt excited and apprehensive, as I usually did before moments I knew to be pivotal.

As soon as we landed, the Syrians bundled our small team into a cavalcade of blacked-out Mercs, Cadillacs and police cars, which swept, sirens wailing, through Damascus – past open markets, camels, donkey-carts laden with vegetables and fruit, rubbish piled high on street corners and people in unfamiliar, exotic dress, some of whom were staring at us with open hostility. It all added to the sense of a journey into the unknown.

We were ushered through the British Embassy gates by Kalashnikov-wielding guards and drew up in front of the imposing building.

The ambassador, Andrew Green, and his wife Jane walked down the steps to greet us. As I straightened my uniform, I heard the ambassador tell the man from the FO that John was waiting in the garden. He'd been here less than two hours.

I pinched myself, sensing a little bit of history in the making. I also found it extraordinarily hard to visualize that, this time the day before, John had still been a hostage.

Pat and Terence were to go into the garden first, which would give me time to have a chat with Fred and the aeromed sister, Squadron Leader Elaine Proud, about the sequence in which we would each do our bit.

The control freak in me wanted to know exactly what was about to happen. As the senior physician, Fred had to go in first and ascertain whether John was fit to fly. He had been sceptical about the value of PTSD treatment right from the start and I was already regretting an incident that had happened a few months earlier.

We'd had a bomb disposal expert visit us because he'd developed a weakness in his left side and couldn't walk. He'd been sent to us after the physicians at the Princess Alexandra, led by Fred, had been unable to find anything physically wrong with him. Soon after the nurse wheeled this man into my office, I hypnotized him. He hypnotized beautifully and I soon discovered that there'd been a trauma in his life to compound the high-pressure nature of his job.

One day he'd come back from work to find military policemen outside his house.

The MPs would not let him into his quarters and they wouldn't tell him why, so, in a sudden rage, and fearing that something was terribly wrong, he belted one of the MPs – and being left-handed, he'd struck the MP with his left fist. On entering the house, he found his wife crying uncontrollably – their baby of just a few months had suffered a cot death. Some time later, the man developed the weakness down his left side, particularly in his left arm.

The man was weeping under hypnosis as he told me this and I could see that the whole process was very cathartic. I suggested to him that the reason for the paralysis was that his subconscious was telling the world there was something wrong with him – that he needed help. This, after all, was a man with a high-pressure, highly dangerous job, who wasn't routinely used to discussing his emotions. I then asked him, on the basis that we'd discussed and rationalized his paralysis, whether there was any reason why he should still have it. The man said no.

When I woke him, hey presto, he could move his arm – it was stiff but usable. I was so happy about this, I asked him and his nurse, who had remained by his side throughout the hypnosis, whether we might play a little trick on Fred. They both agreed and so we did it – the man pushed the wheelchair, with the nurse sitting in it, back on to Fred's ward. The ward sister was furious and I suspected that Fred hadn't been too happy about it either. Fred just didn't believe in hypnotherapy, full stop.

The irony was that it had been from Fred, all those years ago, that I'd learned the art of listening – and it was via hypnosis that you opened up a world of detail, all of which was ripe for rigorous analysis. But maybe with the wheelchair thing I had gone a bit too far . . .

Would Fred now inadvertently signal this to John and risk things going tits-up?

The Syrians had made it abundantly clear that they did not want us on their soil or cluttering their airspace any longer than necessary. A quick examination would determine whether John was well enough to head straight back to Lyneham. But for his psychological treatment to work, for our involvement to be approved, I knew I had to establish a bond with him straight away.

For once, perhaps because he was in unfamiliar territory, Fred deferred to me.

We barely had time to decide on Elaine doing the introductions when the ambassador appeared and led us into the garden.

As we swept through a set of double doors, I got my first glimpse of the man we'd come to bring home. He was sitting in the shade of a tree, close to a wall at the back of the garden, chatting to his father and brother.

The scene was almost surreal; it looked as if they'd never been apart. I kept my eyes on John, even as Fred was briefing me on what was about to happen next. I tried to concentrate on Fred's words, but it was just so hard. I was overwhelmed with the feeling that this was another of those turning points in my professional life – just as Lockerbie and the Gulf had been – but this time I was terrified, because it all boiled down to that single thing: the click.

Fred stepped forward and moved into the garden, leaving me on the back steps of the residence, still gazing at the scene. Andrew Green introduced Fred and Fred and John shook hands. The whole thing had a rather biblical quality about it: John, quiet and serene in the shade of the tree, like a king receiving dignitaries, while others flustered around him. One of them was Roby, and just seeing him again twisted my stomach into knots. Had Roby said anything about the debriefing process? Had John already considered it and rejected it?

Andrew Green came back and told me that I was next up, which served only to increase my anxiety. While part of me watched Fred giving John the once-over, I gave myself a stern talking-to. If John picked up on my nervousness, it might easily cause him to reject me. I had to be in control without coming across as arrogant. He's been a hostage for five years, I told myself. His vigilance levels are going to be extremely high.

If you're not careful, you'll signal the churn that's going inside you, Turnbull, and you'll blow the whole thing . . .

Andrew Green took my arm and ushered me into the garden. As Fred walked past me back towards the house, he gave me the thumbs-up. John was fit to fly. The butterflies in my stomach went into overdrive.

It was only when I drew closer that I could see everyone's eyes were red-rimmed from crying. I knew then that they had been discussing Sheila and that the grieving process had begun – not just for John but for them all. I suspected that both Terence and Pat had elected at some level to grieve for her only when, one way or another, they knew of John's fate. Through what appeared to me to be little short of a miracle, he had been delivered. Despite the warmth, I felt the hairs rise on my forearm.

But equally miraculous was just how well John looked. For a man who'd scarcely seen daylight for five long years, he appeared to be remarkably fit. His cheeks were flushed and his eyes were bright. The physician in me was fascinated. And, with the benefit of hindsight, I realize now that this was what saved me.

Goethe's observation that *the moment one definitely commits oneself, then Providence steps in too* had been on the money again. I had become so utterly fascinated by John's well-being that my nerves had completely disappeared.

Suddenly, John turned and looked at me. 'I suppose you must be the shrink,' he said, the ghost of a smile playing on his lips.

I smiled. It was a spontaneous thing. But I felt I really did know this man.

McCarthy looked at me. In his eyes I saw it all: intelligence, compassion, sensitivity, loss and, remarkably, willingness – after all that had happened – still to trust. I also sensed that he realized I was juggling a lot of balls inside my head and, astonishingly, that he wanted to help *me*.

'Yes, I am,' I heard myself saying. 'I'll be there to talk things through, if you feel like it, though I get the impression you'll be counselling me before we get very far. You really do look in remarkable shape.'

He reached out and held my hand. It sounded, he said, still with a smile, as if I'd learn as much from the process as he would.

I gripped his hand and nodded. He was right. I could have told him I was learning all the time, but instead I just smiled back and said nothing, because I knew this was it; we were in business. I'd felt the click; and John must have felt it, too, otherwise he'd have sent me packing. There was no need either to ask him whether mentally he felt up to flying. His eyes said it all: he was raring to go home.

There was nothing further to say – we'd cover all the arrangements on the aircraft – and in any case, with the medical examinations over, it was time to get moving again.

Within the space of a few minutes, we were piling back into the cars and heading for the airport. In less than an hour, we were pulling into the clear Syrian skies and banking westwards towards the UK.

While we'd been at the embassy, the loadmaster, acting on a request by me, had turned three sets of seats round (as you can on an RAF VC10) so that three sets of six people were able to sit facing each other, like you do on a train. This enabled Bert and me to sit with John, Pat, Terence and Roby and other groups to form. Throughout the flight, an endless succession of people dropped by to shake John's hand and chat briefly with him. As I listened to him, I again realized what an extraordinary person he was. There was no anger or bitterness in his voice at the way he had been treated and no hint of self-pity.

On the flight home, I realized we had a problem. Despite everything I'd told them about the importance of debriefing, in spite of all

the papers I'd written about the value of de-o\
RAF had apparently signalled that it was ha\
the moment we landed back at Lyneham. I learn\
of the dignitaries on board. John wasn't their respon\
did they need to hang on to him? I forcibly argued th\
be a colossal mistake.

Hostages, it had been determined, along with other v\ ..s of violence, underwent four phases of emotional reaction following capture: initially, shock and disbelief (or put another way, denial); then a range of emotions spanning rage, apathy, resignation, irritability and tension; then the appearance of underlying personality traits – those with high dependency traits, for example, would become depressed and introspective. Phobic behaviours tended to grow from this development and risked the formation of hostile dependent relationships with family and friends after the ordeal. Those with more power-orientated and aggressive personalities tended to show more intensified behaviours, leading to social with-drawal and reclusive, paranoid irritability.

Phase four was only reached when the individual attempted to integrate the traumatic experience, came to terms with it and moved into the future, but not before he or she had sharpened up a few psychological barriers such as defensiveness and increased vigilance.

In the case of hostages held for long periods, these phases could not be processed until after release, some psychologists had written, and I agreed. They remained in suspension until the fear reaction had subsided. After exposure to torture and solitary and group confine-ment, it would inevitably lead to the emergence of complex patterns of behaviour, the resolution of which, I had no doubt, could only be brought about satisfactorily by our decompression procedure.

The top brass remained unmoved.

Halfway through the flight, we were told about the vast numbers of media that had gathered at Lyneham in the hope of interviewing John. Among them was John's friend and former fellow hostage, Brian Keenan.

Keenan, who'd been born in Northern Ireland but had Irish as well as UK citizenship, had been kidnapped a few days before John. After each had endured two months of solitary confinement, their captors had moved them into the same cell.

.. had read interviews with Keenan in which he had described their first encounter. Despite the awfulness of it, it had made me laugh and had again given me an insight into the mind of John McCarthy. Keenan had been thrown into the cell, not knowing, because he was blindfolded, that McCarthy was already in there. McCarthy, also blindfolded, had not dared move a muscle for fear that the person in the room with him was a guard. After sitting together in the silence, each aware of the other's presence, it was Keenan who first lifted the blindfold. He had no idea who John was, of course, but was struck by how well dressed he appeared.

When McCarthy lifted his blindfold, to be confronted by Keenan's unkempt appearance, his immortal words had been: 'Fuck me, it's Ben Gunn.' Ben Gunn was a terrifying castaway from *Treasure Island* – an observation that was lost on Keenan who had never read it or heard of Ben Gunn. The irony was that McCarthy had known who Keenan was because he'd gone out to Beirut to cover the story of Keenan's kidnapping.

After so much time spent in solitary, it had been wonderful sharing news – having someone else to talk to. They, too, had clicked from the get-go.

They were in a room no bigger than a small double bed. The two mattresses had to be lifted to get the door open. To avoid the wrath of their guards, they whispered in the darkness to each other and this served to intensify the extraordinarily close bond that developed between them right from the start.

John learned to stand up to the guards – to battle his fears – from Keenan; and Keenan, in turn, learned to laugh again from John, who, as well as being very funny, was a terrific mimic. I read, in Keenan's accounts, how John had even got some of the guards down to a T.

The humour had undoubtedly helped to keep them sane, but I'd also read how they'd devised extraordinary ways to occupy their time – vital in a place that was often dark and where they had no books, except for an ancient encyclopaedia they were given by their captors in their final year of incarceration. As well as telling each other everything about their lives, they devised mind games to keep them busy. One of these involved escaping via the pages of the encyclopaedia to far-flung places – John was keen on the Caribbean;

Keenan came up with an intricate plan for starting a yak farm in Patagonia, of all places. I could only imagine how much John had missed his company when Keenan was eventually released.

But the news that came to us on the plane had me alarmed. Brian Keenan had teamed up, we were informed, with a British TV channel in the hope of pulling off a bit of a scoop: the first post-release interview with John. John was visibly anxious about this and asked me for my views. He had no reason to trust me – he'd never met me before. But I felt on an instinctual level the bond that had been forged between us the moment we first shook hands.

I advised him that it would be unwise to do any interviews until he had had a thorough rest and we'd been able to think through what he wanted to say.

'But Brian is a friend,' John said. 'It's going to be difficult to say no.'

I nodded. 'I can only really explain this to you in the way the brain works,' I said. 'This may sound shrinkish – it's not meant to – but right now there is a lot of unresolved, unprocessed information in your head and you're going to need time to make sense of it.'

He smiled. 'You're right. That does sound a bit shrinkish.'

'Let me put it another way, John. A decision, I believe, should be made within a framework of safety and control. Right now you don't have that framework, but that's what the coming days and weeks will be all about. If you'll let me and my team spend time with you, your father and your brother, I really do believe – based on the work we've already carried out – that we can give you that framework; that we can help you to get back control of your life far quicker than if you worked on it on your own.'

But I told him it was his decision. I didn't want to direct his thoughts. That would have been contrary to my philosophy. I did believe, however, that talking to Brian Keenan – or giving any media interviews precipitately – would be a mistake.

John looked at me, smiled and nodded. I could see behind his eyes that this was a clear-headed, rational man, who under normal circumstances liked to be in control of things. He shook my hand again. 'You're right,' he said. 'We'll hold off all interviews until I'm ready to do them. You'll know when that time is, won't you?'

I smiled back at him. 'No,' I said. 'You will.'

On the approach into Lyneham, I was staring reflectively out of the window when I noticed lights on the ground shining back at us, even though it wasn't yet dark. The pilot informed us that the lights had been switched on along the flight path by people wanting to welcome John home. The effect was quite magical and I saw John's frame, emaciated by his incarceration, swell appreciably. Almost everyone had tears in their eyes. Soon afterwards, we touched down on the tarmac and caught a glimpse of the assembled circus: the vast reception committee that was waiting for John.

After waving to the crowd from the aircraft steps, the entire entourage disappeared into the officers' mess, which had been con-figured as a welcome centre for John and his party. Fortunately, some time between this moment and John going to bed, the RAF realized that hanging on to this man for ten days of debriefing would be a good thing – not just for him but for them, too. The PR value alone would be enormous.

The officers' mess had a suite of rooms that could be cut off from the rest of the base and which allowed John, his family and friends to choose the level of exposure they received from the outside world.

The first thing that John wanted to do was to fulfil a promise he had made to his captors. He was carrying a letter from Hezbollah for the UN Secretary General, Javier Pérez de Cuéllar. When de Cuéllar heard about this he made arrangements to fly to Lyneham to meet with John.

John needed to discharge this obligation to his former captors before he could begin offloading his own experiences. During his captivity, he had established close relationships not only with Keenan but with the two Americans – Terry Anderson and Tom Sutherland – with whom he also later shared a cell, the four of them all together. After Keenan's release, Terry Waite became the fourth member of the cell. Up until then, Waite, the world had learned through John, had been held in solitary confinement for four years.

By discharging his promise to Hezbollah, John was also being mindful of the fact that he was out and three other hostages weren't – something, inevitably, that had loaded him with considerable levels of guilt.

The day after the de Cuéllar meeting, the FO sent two people down to Lyneham to debrief John. One of them was the woman from MI6 I'd met on the plane. The pattern was almost identical to the routine that had been established in Cyprus: operational debrief first, going over all the details that were needed for a full intelligence picture to be built up; psychological debrief second, with me sitting in on the former so that poor old John wouldn't have to needlessly repeat himself.

During the course of the operational debrief, John gave clipped answers to all the questions he received. There was a distant look in his eye and a remoteness to the way he spoke. No doubt his debriefers put it down to fatigue and disorientation, but I knew there were other factors at play. For me, the operational debrief couldn't have been over soon enough.

The moment the two officials closed the door, John bounded across the room, unable any longer to contain what he'd held back so successfully for the past four hours.

'Is this all right?' he demanded of me.

It was a strange thing to blurt out and it took me a moment or two to understand what he meant. The FO's operational debrief, with its emphasis on timeline and detail, must have put John straight back into his cell. He'd shown no sign of his agitation because he'd contained the flashbacks, but it was a form of dissociation nonetheless.

It was clear to me that he didn't trust the FO and couldn't see the purpose of their questions. His question to me, though, was the beginning of a validation. This was John saying: please ground me. The real world – the one that the rest of us had inhabited in the past five years – felt real enough to us, but it was an alien place to him. Being given an invitation to ground John was a great step forward. I told him that what had just happened was all right; that it was just the way that British officialdom worked. For my part, though, I felt the bond between us growing.

The core philosophy of the psychological debriefing team was to avoid giving the impression to John and his family that they had become patients or that we were their medical advisers. The media interest in them was so intense that it seemed only prudent to set aside time at the outset to re-establish a sense of control and equilibrium before he faced the cameras. Raw impressions of what had happened during captivity, including relationships with other hostages, needed to be thought through and refined before being reported – especially via the media. After the Brian Keenan moment on the aircraft, this was a recognition that John came to himself.

As John's dedicated primary debriefer, I had to sense at what level he wanted to relate to me. For the debriefing process to work, it had to be a real partnership and I'd have to sense shifts in the relationship as they occurred. On one level, I was a doctor checking on his physical well-being; on another I was a father figure, although I didn't feel (and in reality wasn't) old enough to do this any justice. In the end, I was happy that I simply became someone whom John could trust; in the main because I'd sold him on the idea that we had a process that could help him come to terms with what he had been through.

The process was a re-enactment, with modifications, of what we had carried out in Akrotiri with the PoWs, only based on an individual instead of groups. There was still, however, a group element, because family and friends needed counselling, too.

John's re-entry involved reunion with family friends and associates and grief for a mother who had died. In promoting reintegration of the family unit, an effort had to be made to understand the psychological consequences for the family members as well – John's incarceration had made them hostages too.

As with the PoW programme, we knew it was also of huge importance to nurture the mindset in survivors that they had been injured as a direct result of their traumatic experiences, rather than that their experiences had unveiled a vulnerability to a recognizable illness.

Since hostages were exposed to a wide variety of stressors, I was looking for multiple possible facets of the psychological impact of these stressors – PTSD being one of them. The others were depressive disorders, most strongly correlated with torture and loss while being held hostage; cognitive defect states related to weight loss; and central nervous system damage and psychosis, strongly associated with solitary confinement and sensory deprivation.

The following day, I gathered John, Pat, Terence, Roby Burke and all the members of our own team into a room in the mess. We had a game plan of sorts, but I was conscious that to an outsider it wouldn't seem like a plan at all. The plan was to be flexible and adaptable. John's well-being depended on his ability to open up to us – to me, in particular – and that depended on the degree to which he trusted us.

Pushing him into a highly choreographed series of psychological debriefings would be counter-productive and would most likely end up distancing him from us – perhaps driving him and his family away altogether. Fortunately, as I was winging it, an idea came to me. The week ahead was punctuated by a series of medical examinations – X-rays, dental check-ups and eye tests – that John had to undergo. I decided that the best way of maintaining the sense of order and control that he needed was to set out the week's timetable on a blackboard, which would be positioned in the corridor in the mess. Our psychological debriefings would be inserted into this framework, giving a sense of order. Yet they would be dispersed sufficiently throughout the week so as not to become claustrophobic.

To my relief, everyone seemed to think that this was a good idea. I then announced that I'd be John's primary debriefer; Keron Fletcher, an RAF psychiatrist, would debrief Pat and Terence, and Dave Hill, an RAF psychiatric nursing officer, would debrief Roby. There would be occasions, too, when we all came together in a group.

With these arrangements under my belt, I went off to see Lyneham's CO to tell him what we were up to. This was more than mere courtesy; as we were on his base, the CO needed to buy in to what we were doing and fortunately he did – this after I'd told him about my journey into PTSD, what my department at Wroughton was all about and our work during the Gulf War.

The CO was a steely-eyed pilot and we shook hands warmly. 'Keep me informed,' he said. 'I'm wholly supportive of what you're doing.'

On day three, as John and I were walking along the corridor to lunch, I suggested that we might have a drink in the bar.

He looked a little nervous.

'I think it'll be good for you to meet some new faces,' I said, 'but there won't be that many of them – just a few. Trust me on that.'

At this, John whipped round, grabbed my lapels and almost thrust me up against the wall. 'Please,' he said, 'never use that word again.'

I learned that there was a particularly vicious guard in Beirut whose favourite expression had been 'Trust me, trust me' – which is what, in the end, they nicknamed him.

During the McCarthy debriefing the secondary debriefings were held at least once a day and sometimes twice a day, depending on what was going on. The secondary debriefers were John Rollins, Walter Busuttil and Adrian West. Adrian West was a clinical psychologist working at Broadmoor Hospital who had been helping us with the development of trauma treatment programmes and debriefing behind the scenes from the time of Lockerbie. He was a friend of Dee Price, David Price's wife, who had been working at Wroughton for several years and had been one of the first to become interested in the trauma project. Bert was in his usual role as Mr Fixit. In the secondary debriefing I told them about this incident and how upset I was with myself that I'd upset John.

'Gordon, we're all feeling our way here,' Bert replied, using, I remembered, a phrase I'd used during Lockerbie. It reminded me that there were going to be good days and bad – but overall, we were heading in the right direction.

A couple of days later, I felt John was ready for his first drive. We had been confined to the mess for almost a week and everyone was starting to feel the strain, including the debriefers. I felt that a trip around the airfield perimeter would be just the thing to clear the air. It wasn't possible to go further afield because the press were still ringing the base.

Under a clear sky, John and I strolled over to my car: a Maestro with a sunroof. Then, on a whim, I threw him the keys.

'What are you doing?' he asked.

'If you'd rather not be seen in a Maestro . . .'

He laughed and shook his head. 'It's not the car. I haven't driven for five years.'

'I haven't been skiing for five years,' I said, 'but that won't stop me strapping on some planks and spectacularly wiping out next time we head for the Alps.'

He jumped into the driving seat and tentatively placed the key in the ignition. He hesitated before starting the engine, staring straight ahead through the windscreen.

'What is it?'

'I don't know. Something's wrong.' He was looking around him, scanning the cars. I wondered what was going through his mind. The Lebanon, perhaps, when, en route to the airport, they'd come for him with Kalashnikovs and bundled him blindfolded into the boot of their car?

I asked him again, formulating as I did so how we might have to deal with this in our forthcoming debriefing sessions.

John was still scanning the car park warily. 'It's something about the cars,' he said. 'Something's missing.'

'Missing?' It crossed my mind that this was a sign of something more serious; evidence of some psychosis I'd missed in the week we'd been together.

Then he snapped his fingers. 'Cortinas!'

'What?'

'Cortinas.' He was looking at me and grinning from ear to ear. 'There aren't any Cortinas.'

His eyes still searched mine questioningly.

'We call them Sierras now,' I told him.

This could have set a melancholic tone for our trip around the airfield, but instead John muttered under his breath what an ugly-looking beast the Sierra was and how progress, if that was the word, was indeed a funny thing. He turned the key in the ignition, slipped the car into gear and off we went.

Pretty soon he was driving around the perimeter like a pro.

We were wary of being photographed by the media and were thus naturally a little concerned when we had to stop for a guy who was blocking the road ahead while he loaded some planks of wood on to the back of his lorry. When he eventually finished the task, he drove past and gawped down at us through our open sunroof. I caught a glimpse of a mop of thick black hair and a Neanderthal brow. Anything could have been coming the other way and he'd have hit it.

With the obstacle to our rear, John was about to drive off again when we heard the lorry reversing up behind us. I saw a look of apprehension cross John's face.

The lorry drew up alongside and the driver leaned out of the cab window.

''Ere,' he said, pointing a finger, 'you're that McCarthy bloke, right?'

John looked at me, as if seeking approval. Then he glanced up through the sunroof.

'Er, yes,' he said, 'that's right. I am, as it happens.'

The driver stuck his hand out the window. 'Well done, mate,' he said. 'I'd just like to shake your hand and say how we're all behind you. Bless you, John. Good on ya.'

They shook hands through the open roof and the lorry drove off.

We sat there, the car in neutral, the engine idling.

There was no one else around. No press, thank God; no witnesses. I looked at John, who was staring into the rear-view mirror.

As I watched, I saw him grow – his whole stature physically lift. It was a wonderful moment. I knew then that we were ready to start our one-on-one work.

'For several weeks, I thought it was somebody's idea of a joke – I honestly did,' he said. 'I was on my own, in the dark, most probably underground somewhere, in a cell where I couldn't even lie down. And I thought that at any moment, somebody was going to burst in, blow on some party trumpets and go, "Da-da, gotcha, John!" and we'd all go home. Then, slowly, it dawned on me that that wasn't going to happen; that I was a bloody hostage. And that was when it really hit me. I became anxious. About anyone and everything. About my family. My friends. About what was going to happen to me. It was crushing, unbearable . . .'

He paused and looked at me. There was no self-pity in his voice, just a look behind his eyes that I already knew so well from others; the look of someone trying to find answers to events, behaviour, circumstances that were beyond reason.

'These are natural reactions,' I said. 'How long did the anxiety last?'

'Well, that's the thing, not long.' He sucked hard on a cigarette that was already down to the filter. 'Because,' and he hesitated, 'something very strange happened.'

I waited.

'Gordon, you're going to think me mad . . .'

'You're not mad,' I said. 'You've been through, to use the jargon, an exceptional event. One's reactions to an exceptional event can only ever be natural.'

'Jargon? Nothing – I don't think anything – explains this.' I could see that he was still reluctant to tell me what *this* was.

'Part of what we're doing here is filling in gaps,' I said. 'Allowing you to assemble a narrative of the five-and-a-half years you've missed out on. If you don't want to tell me, you don't have to.'

He lit another cigarette and leaned forward. 'No,' he said, 'I do want to tell you.'

It took him a second or two to compose his thoughts. 'Like I said, I was in this cell I couldn't even stand up or lie down in and I'd been there about a month. And I was in this incredibly anxious state. And then, one day, quite without warning . . .'

He leaned forward again, studying me intensely. 'The cell suddenly filled with light. It was a light of the brightest intensity I've ever seen and it drifted down from the ceiling, growing in brightness all the while, until it completely enveloped me.'

'Did it have any kind of form?'

'No. No form at all. But it was completely real. Or so I thought. I don't know how long the light surrounded me for; all I do know is that afterwards I felt better.'

'The anxiety left you?'

He nodded. 'I felt completely calm. I accepted my fate – that I was a hostage – and, amazingly, while I wasn't overly happy about it, I realized that this was it and I had to endure the situation I was in – for everyone's sake; mine not least.'

He fixed me with that intense look again. 'Have you ever heard of anything like that before? I mean, could this have been something going on inside me? Was it God? Tinkerbell?'

Filling in gaps, I told him, wasn't just about Cortinas and Sierras, nor was it about grieving for the mother he had lost; anything and everything, potentially, held meaning.

This was John asking me, desperate to know, in fact: was this somehow significant? What did it mean?

I didn't know. All I did know, and I told him this, was that I'd heard about people seeing this light before. It wasn't understood – certainly not in neurological terms – but it sometimes happened to people who were in great danger; and, when it did, often to those who seemed to be without hope. Explorers who, ill or injured in the middle of nowhere, expected to die; abandoned mountaineers; lone sailors, capsized and thousands of miles from rescue . . . these were the kinds of people who had seen the light. And almost always it had had a calming, soothing effect.

'We do know that with acute stress reactions it can take about a month for some sort of normality to return to the brain-state. If it doesn't then it means that the stress reaction is chronic and will require some form of treatment. What, perhaps, we can say is that you were in some kind of dissociated state when you saw this light – that your brain, in its traumatized condition, distanced itself from your surroundings. It's a safety mechanism, John. Again, as hard as it must be to accept, it is, believe me, all quite natural.'

At this, he looked mightily relieved. Then he told me it wasn't the only time he'd dissociated.

When, finally, he was confined with the other three hostages, Anderson, Sutherland and Keenan, in many ways, he said, he found it more difficult. This was completely counter-intuitive, as the consensus is that solitary is the worst kind of confinement. But this doesn't take into account the unique situation of being a hostage. When John was on his own, he was in control of his destiny. When he was with the others, because group punishment was the order of the day, if one hostage transgressed, everybody suffered. Sutherland was a particularly combative type and used to do things that wound up the guards. Sometimes, he'd stick his tongue out when their backs were turned – it was his way of coping, of letting off steam, perhaps – but the end result was that the others, John especially, lived on their nerves, because it engendered a never-ending raft of uncertainties.

If the guard turned round, they'd all get beaten. If they berated Sutherland an argument would develop and, again, they'd all get beaten. If Sutherland went off the deep end, maybe they'd end up getting shot. When Keenan was released and Terry Waite was put in the cell in his place, in some ways it became even worse. Terry, John had revealed in his operational debriefs, had been quite unwell – he'd had pneumonia and suffered from asthma – when he joined them and at night would splutter and cough. This would rattle Sutherland, who had little sympathy for Terry's condition, and, with harsh words flying around the cell and the constant threat of beatings from the guards, the whole situation placed an almost unbearable strain on them.

So John did something rather remarkable: he started, slowly and deliberately, to reverse his day/night sleep pattern, until, after a week or two, he acquired the ability to sleep during the day and lie awake at night. In this way, he became oblivious to the tensions in the cell, but now encountered a secondary problem: how to remain occupied during the long periods when everyone else was asleep?

He and the others had played a game that involved taking a date – a random, insignificant date – and then internalizing, delving deep down into themselves, until the details of what had been happening on that date came to them. It would take ages – that was the point – and it wasn't rigorously mathematical in that what was recalled was only an approximation, but it was extraordinary how much the brain was able to recall.

This, again, was another form of dissociation.

To while away the long nights, John used this technique and took it further. In the McCarthy household, Sunday lunch had been a big thing. Family members gathered from all over, the food was good and the conversation was always stimulating. They were very happy times and John spent hour upon hour recalling individual lunches. Who was there. What they had spoken about. What his mother had cooked . . .

But when he ran out of lunches to revisit, he started to make up imaginary ones. These, in many ways, were even better, because he could invite anybody he liked and he could talk about anything he wished.

'Through this medium,' he told me, 'I was able to discuss my mother's illness with other members of my family. You see, I knew she was dead. I'd heard it on the radio. This helped me to come to terms with it.'

'How?'

'I gradually excluded her from the lunches. I did it deliberately. We talked about things. We said our goodbyes. Little by little, she disappeared from the room. It was my way of mourning her.'

I sat back. One of the things I'd been most worried about before we met was how John would face up to life back in England without his mother, the most shocking and upsetting reminder of all of the time – the life – that had been stolen from him. But John hadn't collapsed because he'd heard about his mother's death and had built it into his nightly escapes. These escapes were a form of dissociation, a key component of PTSD, and one of a number of tools the brain relied on to protect the self. In this way, John had done a lot of grieving; in fact, I realized that he had processed the grief of his mother's loss much more effectively than his brother and father. Just as I had surmised when I saw them together in the embassy garden, they had put their grieving on hold until John was released, thinking, then, that they'd all need to grieve together. In this way, John was able to take the lead in the grieving process and help Pat and Terence – the opposite of what you'd expect.

Through a number of sessions like these, we watched some semblance of normality return to the McCarthy family. There was no chart on which to tick off or calibrate our achievements. I was flying by the seat of my pants, but I knew, too, that there was a process behind this apparent randomness; a process guided by John's willingness to trust me and my fervent desire not just to make this work for him but to learn from it as well – something he acknowledged the moment we met. When we'd shaken hands in the embassy garden, we'd subconsciously entered into a pact – a contract based on an instinct that we'd be able to work together to our mutual benefit. And we did.

And I knew that one day we'd both know when he and his family were ready to go home.

That day came ten days after he arrived at Lyneham.

John and I said our goodbyes in the mess. We had taken the process as far as we could and had readied him, as far as we were able, for what was to come. It wouldn't be easy, because everything he did would be in the glare of the media. Most pressurizing of all, the press had already married him and Jill Morrell and had them living in wedded bliss, surrounded by little McCarthys, in a cottage hideaway. Of course, it was never going to be that simple, but John was grounded now and I knew that he was prepared for whatever came next.

'Thank you for everything,' he said, shaking my hand.

'No,' I said, 'thank you. Part of the deal was that I would end up learning from you, remember? And I did.'

After leaving Lyneham, John and Jill resumed their relationship, although, as each had discovered, too much had happened to them both for it to survive. Remarkably, they remained together for almost four more years before they parted amicably. During that time, the book that they'd written together, *Some Other Rainbow*, became a bestseller. John eventually married a girl called Anna and they settled in London.

We continue to correspond and my feelings for the time we spent together remain special.

Aside from the friendship we formed, I learned from that instant in the embassy garden, that the 'click' – that moment when, without words, you formed a bond with someone – could become an invaluable part of the healing process between psychiatrist and patient. It wouldn't always be present, but when it was it seemed to act as a catalyst.

But back in 1991, we had demonstrated, I think quite clearly, with both the PoWs and with John, that if you put effort into a re-entry process, people tended to do well. The idea that people who survived in captivity could simply be released and make their own way in free society didn't hold water any more. We'd more or less convinced people in the MoD that it didn't work. It simply wasn't enough to release people and let them get on with their lives. They had been conditioned as captives, hostages or prisoners of war and when they survived in that particular role, you had to conclude that they had been successful – a strange way of describing it, but that's how I saw it. They'd somehow acclimatized successfully to their surroundings and had been able to survive as a result.

But the skills you need to survive as a hostage are quite different from the skills you need in the so-called real world, so there had to be a period of deconditioning and then reconditioning. What I described as the 're-entry phase'.

Some of the American ex-hostages who had been released before John actually wrote about the need for such re-entry work and appeared on television to give their wholehearted support for it. One described how he'd been released from Beirut, flown to an American Air Force base in Wiesbaden, West Germany, been medically and psychiatrically cleared, then flown to Washington DC and been given a Greyhound bus ticket to return to his native California. He went on to describe just how difficult his first post-release year had been. That, for me, was not a coincidence. What

we'd done with John was patently beneficial and a massive vindi-
cation of the work we'd begun at Lockerbie and refined after the
Gulf War.

Soon after John left us, I happened to be watching the TV news at
home when there was a report on Terry Waite. The press was
speculating that he, too, might be up for release and ran a piece of
film in which Waite was boarding an aircraft. It was just prior to his
ill-fated trip to attempt to spring John and his fellow hostages in
1987. Waving a microphone in his face, a journalist asked him why
he was embarking on this mission when there was such an evident
risk of his being taken too. Waite smiled and said that he had a job
to do, that he was confident he could pull it off and that there was
no danger to him personally.

I turned to Ali, who was watching the report with me, and said:
'I'd better start learning up on this chap, because I've got the
strangest feeling . . .'

Alison, used to my ramblings, asked me what on earth I was talking about. 'Feeling about what?'

'That we're about to go through the whole process again,' I said
distantly. Inside, I was intrigued by what I saw: this curious mix of
confidence – or was it arrogance? – and almost childlike naivety.
What made this man tick? I wanted to find out. And I wanted to
know, too, whether it – this core at the heart of Terry Waite's being
– had helped him in captivity or, worryingly, ended up having quite
the reverse effect.

Psychological debriefing was a process of making a detailed,
progressive examination of the events since the identified 'critical
incident' with a systematic review of the feelings and emotions
associated with it. The primary aim was to reconstruct the memories
of the traumatic events without distortions, to allow the survivor to
assimilate the resultant clarified material, to fully integrate its
meaning – to allow the brain to have closure on the trauma, if you
like – and enable emotional ventilation with a view to his or her
restoration to a normal life.

In Terry Waite's case, this was anything but a simple process.

Terry was the Archbishop of Canterbury's special envoy in the
Lebanon hostage crisis. Having successfully negotiated the release of

hostages in Iran and Libya, in 1985 he turned his attention to the hostages being held in the Lebanon. Here, he also achieved initial success – of sufficient magnitude, in fact, for a return trip to the Lebanon in January 1987 in the hope of releasing the hostages their captors considered to be the big prizes: Terry Anderson and Tom Sutherland, who were both American, the Irishman Brian Keenan and, of course, John McCarthy.

In November 1986, the so-called 'Irangate' scandal broke: evidence, reported extensively in the media, that President Ronald Reagan had negotiated secretly with the Iranians – mentors to the hostage takers in the Lebanon – to provide arms, which were embargoed to Iran, in exchange for the release of hostages and funds that would go – utterly illegally, of course – to fund the Contra rebels in Nicaragua. The complex deal was brokered by Colonel Oliver North, who sat on Reagan's National Security Council.

Two months after news of the scandal broke, Terry, against advice, went back to the Lebanon in a bid to secure the release of Anderson, Sutherland, Keenan and McCarthy. It had been reported at that stage that Terry had had dealings with North – it had leaked that he'd taken a secret trip on North's helicopter between Cyprus and the Lebanon – but Terry being Terry insisted on making the journey. To him, it was a matter of honour that he fulfil his promise of getting the hostages back; this, despite the fact that he must have known that Hezbollah and the other Islamic groups with which he was set to meet by then viewed him as somehow being in league with the Americans.

In fact, it later transpired, Hezbollah had grown tired of holding the hostages. It was a relatively small organization and holding hostages was taking up too much of its resources and man- power. So in 1986 the leaders had asked Terry Anderson and Tom Sutherland to write a letter to the Associated Press in New York (Anderson's employer before he was kidnapped) to request a visit to Beirut by Terry Waite, whom they knew by reputation in this field, to organize their release. The letter was sent to the Archbishop of Canterbury's office and was the reason Waite was dispatched.

He was said to be on the point of succeeding in getting them released when Hezbollah began to suspect that he was linked to Oliver North. So they lured him into a trap in which he thought he was going to collect the two Americans but instead, on 20 January 1987, he was taken hostage himself.

. Thus began a five-year period of captivity, the first four years of which he was held in solitary confinement, chained hand and foot to a wall in a darkened room, with just ten minutes' daily respite for eating and ablutions.

'I saw no one and spoke to no one, apart from a cursory word with my guards when they brought me food,' he told an interviewer after his release. This daily pattern of existence, if you could call it that, was only interrupted when he was released from his chains to be beaten on the soles of his feet or subjected to mock executions. A gun would be cocked next to his head, the muzzle placed against his temple and – *click* – the trigger would be pulled on an empty chamber. It took four years of this for his captors finally to appreciate that he hadn't been in cahoots with the CIA.

With the release of Brian Keenan in August 1990, they allowed Terry to take his place in the tiny room that held the three others: McCarthy, Anderson and Sutherland. And that, you would think, would have been a blessing, but, as I had already learned from John, there were circumstances in which group hostage situations could prove just as stressful, if not more so, than solitary confinement.

And this, for various reasons, proved to be the case with Terry.

I flew out to Damascus with the same aeromed team that had gone to collect John McCarthy. We travelled out on an RAF VC10 shortly after it was confirmed Terry had been released. It was a cold November day – a Tuesday – in 1991.

On the aircraft, I had with me the day's papers and press clippings from the day before, when it had been announced that Terry had been freed. There were pages and pages of coverage. I had made a start on my research after the strange feeling I'd got when I'd watched the TV news report with Ali several months earlier, but on the plane I felt a need to review the facts all over again – to try to get under the skin of this man.

TW was around ten years older than me, having been born in 1939, the son of a village policeman. He left school at 16 after he'd managed to learn the prayer book by heart – not the everyday accomplishment of your average teenager. Although not from an overtly religious family, Terry became a committed Christian at an early age. Because he suffered from allergies, he did not see out the two years of his National Service but elected to take a degree in theology at the Church Army College instead.

In the late 1960s, working in Africa for the Bishop of Uganda, he was taken hostage with Frances, his wife, and his two young children. What did this do to him, I wondered? Was it a sign of the recklessness – a thirst for danger and excitement – portrayed in sections of the media? Or was it simply bad luck? From the reports, it was hard to tell.

In 1980 the Archbishop of Canterbury, Robert Runcie, appointed TW secretary for Anglican Communion Affairs to work with churches abroad and to organize the archbishop's foreign trips. It was said that this was the period when he first encountered the media. The implication was that TW had rather fallen in love with his own image – one that from this time on he sought assiduously to place in the spotlight.

How did this square with the man who had sacrificed everything for the release of the Lebanon hostages? I was struggling to equate the two sides of the personality the press were writing about. On balance, though, it seemed that a lot of journalists really had it in for him.

When we got to Damascus, it was tipping down with rain. It was hard to believe that I was back again. Despite the weather, the journey was familiar but the city seemed less exotic than it had in the summer. Soon the cavalcade was pulling up in front of the British Embassy. Andrew Green, the ambassador, met us on the steps again and in we went. Terry, we were told, was waiting in the study – no dreamlike garden encounter this time; there was a feeling of getting straight down to business.

Fred Amroliwalla and Elaine went in first, leaving the ambassador and me to talk for a few moments in the corridor outside.

'This must be old hat for you by now,' he joked as I waited to be shown in.

I smiled, but of course it was anything but routine. I felt pressure, but in a different way from the McCarthy encounter. TW's reputation as a 'big man' – in character as well as physical appearance – went before him. I knew also that he'd assisted in the debriefing of some of the hostages he'd helped to release prior to the Lebanon and that, unlike John, he was bound to have very strong views on the process.

Would we click? It was hard to tell. But fortunately I didn't have time to get worked up about it as, before I knew it, I was being shown into the study.

TW, who was sitting down while Fred took his blood pressure, looked up as Andrew and I entered the room. 'Ah,' he said in a hoarse, rasping voice I did not associate at all with the man I'd seen on the TV, 'this must be the psychiatrist.'

There were shades of the McCarthy encounter here, but it felt a lot more clinical. My subconscious didn't present me with an intuitive response in the same way that it had with John. I just stuck out my hand, smiled and said, somewhat stiffly: 'Yes, that's right. It's very good to meet you.'

In truth, I was rather shocked by his appearance. Unlike John, who really had looked well, Terry was gaunt, had lost a lot of weight and looked drawn, very tired and subdued – in all, it was a far cry from the joyous occasion I had witnessed here three months earlier.

As with John, as soon as Terry was pronounced fit to fly, we were heading back to the airport. As it was night, the plan was to stage through Cyprus, stay there for a few hours, then take off at break-fast time so that we could land at Lyneham at lunchtime. This, I was rather sorry – though not altogether surprised – to learn, had been arranged to maximize the event's exposure on TV. It had been mooted, way over my head, that it might be appropriate for Terry to make a brief statement to the media, who were gathering in force at Lyneham.

After that, I was informed, it was down to him what he wanted to do next – whether, in other words, he wished to undergo the debrief-ing process with us or not.

Soon after we took off from Damascus, I was able to talk to him directly. I found him an eager listener and interested in what I had to propose. As I'd already surmised, the debriefing process was familiar to him, and he'd learned from a radio – a tinny little thing that had been supplied to the Lebanese hostages after John's release – about our psychological debriefing of John at Lyneham. But this placed him in a quandary, because it had been his instinct to debrief with his old friend Richard Chartres, now the Bishop of London.

The current envoy from the Archbishop of Canterbury was Francis Witts. Witts had also been on the first flight to Damascus – the McCarthy flight in August – to be there in case Terry was released too.

Although he had taken no part in the debriefing of John at Lyneham, Witts was not a man to let the grass grow under his feet. He had been very interested in the methods employed for, and the outcome of, John's treatment. I was not surprised, therefore, to see him on the plane. None of Terry's family was on the aircraft. They were all waiting for him to arrive at Lyneham and had already taken up residence in the VIP suite of the officers' mess.

Francis and I did most of the talking with Terry on the flight home and persuaded him that it might be a good idea to make a short statement to the media as soon as we landed. Terry was OK with this and used the pen and the small notebook we'd given him to quickly jot down a few notes. We watched, amazed, at his unflappable, practical approach to his homecoming.

At some point in the flight, it was suggested that TW ought to get some shoes. When we'd left the embassy I'd noticed him wearing what I took to be flip-flops. In fact, his own shoes had long since rotted away. He'd been given some by his captors but because they didn't fit him – he was, I think, a size 15 – he'd had to squash down the backs and turn them into sandals. The result was that he shuffled in a rather undignified way and this didn't seem right at all for his high-profile homecoming. So I went up to the flight deck and asked the captain whether he could radio ahead to Stores at Akrotiri to see if there were some shoes that Terry could appropriate from the military.

When we landed at Akrotiri, we were greeted by a Royal Navy storeman, brimming with pride, who presented Terry with a pair of boat-like 'duty shoes' on the tarmac. It turned out that the RAF had been unable to produce anything large enough, but the Navy had come up trumps. And so Terry got some of his dignity back.

After a quick breakfast, we took off again and within four hours were dropping down through UK airspace to Lyneham. When John had touched down, it had been night. Terry arrived in the full glare of daylight, although as we landed the heavens opened. The crowds of well-wishers were visible even before the plane came to a stop in the dispersal area. From my seat in the middle of the plane I watched as the door was opened, there was a brief kerfuffle and the reception committee stepped on board, among them the Foreign Secretary, Douglas Hurd, and Robert Runcie, the now retired Archbishop of Canterbury. Moments later, Terry stepped out on to the airstairs and I caught a glimpse of him waving to the crowds. We were then all whisked off by car through the rain to a nearby hangar where Terry would give his short homecoming address.

As I stepped inside the hangar, it reminded me of a boxing arena. There was a stage in the middle surrounded by people, most of them media. TW was ushered up to a podium and immediately started to speak. He said it was overwhelming to receive the greeting that had awaited him and how happy he was to see Robert Runcie and the new Archbishop of Canterbury, George Carey. He even thanked the RAF for his shoes – leaving me with a tinge of guilt and hoping that I wouldn't catch it from the Navy storeman next time I was in Akrotiri. He spoke movingly about the four years he had spent in isolation, seeing no one, and how he had found inspiration in a postcard he had been given that depicted John Bunyan, the Christian writer and preacher – and author of *The Pilgrim's Progress* – in captivity. It was wrong, he said, to hold anyone hostage and those who did so fell below the standards of civilized behaviour. He ended by saying that those within the Church, himself included, would continue to work tirelessly to ensure the release of all hostages, wherever they were held in the world. The crowd applauded enthusiastically and, after a short photo session with Robert Runcie, Terry was led back to the car that would take him to the officers' mess for his reunion with Frances and their four children. The media weren't allowed to ask any questions.

As I watched him go, I thought – for a man who had been kept from all human contact for a period of four years – how well he had handled the whole thing. Moments later I jumped in a car, too, and joined the procession speeding towards the mess.

For the next three days I hardly saw Terry at all. The team was on hand if we were needed, but we didn't get the call. TW spent time with his family and time with his old friend Richard Chartres in the mess. I noticed that he tended to avoid eating meals with his family and spent considerable periods of time on his own. To begin with he ate dinner in the middle of the night. We had catering staff who were more than happy to accommodate him but it seemed that his time in captivity had upset his circadian rhythms.

By the weekend, however, it was apparent that Terry wasn't doing so well. The reason was to be found in the media: a number of commentators had launched a series of vitriolic attacks on him – focusing on his 'recklessness' – and this had left him feeling deeply scarred; perhaps 'traumatized' is a more appropriate word.

It was one thing to have endured five years of captivity – his family suffering alongside him – but something quite else to discover that your entire mission, in the eyes of the medium he had once seen as an ally, was being characterized as an exercise in vainglorious foolhardiness. It also seemed he could do nothing right. The impromptu press conference, which he had handled so well, was billed in some quarters as a cruel slight to his family, the people he should have rushed to first. But I had seen how it wasn't that way at all. The circus had been suggested by me and Francis and arranged by others; and once it had been set in motion, how could Terry possibly have said no?

I was not surprised, then, that by the Sunday – four days after his arrival at Lyneham – Terry called us in to see if we could help.

Every hostage debriefing was different but the watchword, we knew, was 'patience'. It was imperative, as we debriefed Terry, his wife Frances and their children at Lyneham, where we would all spend the next 19 days, that we allowed things to unravel at their own pace. As it had with John, the officers' mess at Lyneham proved the perfect decompression chamber between the trauma that Terry and his family had just endured and the real world. It allowed the hostages to choose for themselves, in itself therapeutic, how much exposure they and their families wanted – especially with the media so close.

We'd known from our experience with John that too much media exposure too soon wasn't a good thing. In Terry's case, however, after the scathing reception he'd been given by some commentators, any further exposure would be disastrous. Terry needed to review his incarceration privately, taking as much time as he required, and to make sense of it himself.

There was a lot to make sense of. Some of the articles insinuated that his supposed arrogance had been responsible not only for his own downfall but for the continued detention of those he had come to Lebanon to rescue, including his fellow hostage, the American Tom Sutherland, who had been released a few days after Terry.

Sutherland also seemed to hold Terry partly responsible for the length of time they had been held. His bitter words had been quoted extensively by the British media. I noted that Sutherland was the only hostage who had turned down the offer of debriefing. I also noted that he seemed to be debriefing in public, trying to make sense of his terrible experience through the media – with no safety boundaries, no controls and the real possibility, thanks to the tendency of the media to sensationalize, of creating more distortions and less clarity.

The vitriol in some of these attacks had a terrible effect on Terry, a giant of a man, whose six-foot seven-inch frame seemed to shrink visibly under the onslaught.

The atmosphere in the mess was quite different from the feeling that had been present during the McCarthy debriefings and it soon became clear why. Terry's wife Frances and their children – three girls, including twins, and a boy, all in their teens and early twenties – were with us for much of the decompression period. They all seemed very remote from the man they hadn't seen for five long years. This, I soon realized, was because, unlike John's family, the Waites had come to accept during the period of Terry's incarceration that he was dead. And while they had mourned his 'passing', they had no doubt also felt a swirl of other emotions: anger at his having allowed himself to be taken hostage, coupled with guilt that they felt this way. Although they did not intend to signal any of these things when Terry was released, you can't fake emotions and hence the atmosphere between them was so thick you could cut it.

The first thing I had to do, however, was to get Terry to come to terms with what was being said about him in the media.

'Listen,' I told him. 'The press are just speculating. They weren't in the Lebanon, you were. They don't know the truth, they're just getting snapshots of it.'

Terry looked at me earnestly. His skin was like paper and there were large black rings under his eyes. 'Why is Tom saying these terrible things about me?'

'I believe that he hasn't been through any kind of decompression process himself and is therefore ventilating years of anger and frustration in a random, uncontrolled sort of way. In many ways, Terry, you just happen to be an outlet for it.'

Drawing on what I had learned from John McCarthy, I was able to fill in a good many of the holes in Terry's narrative of his hostage experience. Because he had failed in his attempt to rescue the two Americans, they harboured a great deal of resentment towards him – resentment that was mixed with guilt for the fact that Terry had become a hostage himself. Propped up against the wall opposite the Americans in this tiny space Terry was probably having the same feelings but the other way round – he was resentful that he had been captured trying to release them and felt bad that he had failed to do so. There was not enough space in this tiny cell to set such powerful emotions free, which led to a very unreal environment. Nobody dared vent their true feelings, because any kind of disturbance – any kind of ruckus – would draw the unwelcome attention of their captors and quite possibly lead to punishment, torture or even death. So suppression became the order of the day. People suppressed their feelings and withdrew from their fellow captives. So much for the idea that being held captive in a group was less traumatic than being in solitary, I thought.

Only when we were able to break down the dynamics at work in the cell and explain them to Terry was he able to process them, come to terms with some of the harsh things that were being written about him, and move towards resolution and recovery.

The two questions that had proved integral to the recovery process of the Gulf War PoWs – 'What happened to you?' and 'How do you feel about what happened to you?' – were just as pertinent in our debriefing of the hostages. But we couldn't rush them for answers – we needed to build trust, and that took time.

One bizarre outcome of this process was the degree to which I found myself arguing with my old mentor John Rollins whenever we compared notes on the Waites. We argued about the most ridiculous things and I couldn't for the life of me work out why, because, fundamentally, while we'd always tested each other, we'd predominantly seen eye to eye. While I was responsible for working with Terry, John was debriefing Frances. At first I put it down to the fact that working round the clock at Lyneham was getting to all of us. It was the secondary debriefing team, led by Chris Cook and David Stevens, who eventually pointed out that this was the phenomenon known as 'mirroring'. Not unnaturally, the difficulty that Terry and Frances were having in reconnecting – the children, too – was being reflected on to us. John Rollins and I were subliminally picking up on the difficulties in the family relationship and bouncing them back between us – hence the term mirroring. It was another powerful reminder of the value of secondary debriefing teams – psychiatrists one step removed from the front line – who could guard against the kind of problem I'd first encountered during my sessions with the mountain rescuers after Lockerbie. Somebody not involved in the day-to-day details of the debriefing process needed to watch over the counsellors themselves.

As soon as the problem was pointed out, John and I were able to resolve our differences in a trice.

But we weren't the real issue. The question was, how to get the Waite family to bond again?

On the Sunday, four days after Terry arrived at Lyneham, there was a service of thanksgiving for his release at his local church in London. Terry and his family watched the service on television in their quarters in the officers' mess.

The service was televised nationally and I watched it at home with my family. I had thought I'd be moved by it, but I wasn't. All I could think about was this other family in torment and our inability to get them back to where they'd been before. I felt that we'd failed.

The following morning, back at Lyneham, we were holding our 'start the day prayers meeting' and the main topic of discussion at this briefing was the thanksgiving service. Suddenly, my colleague Dave Hill piped up and asked whether we'd seen the programme he'd watched – one on the Waite family in happier times – that had been on another channel. Dave had switched on that channel first and had become so fascinated by it that he'd stayed with it. The rest of us had all watched the service.

I asked him to tell us what he'd seen.

The programme told the story of Terry's early life; his growing up in the North of England, his commitment to Christianity from an early age, his joining the Church Army, the evangelistic arm of the Church of England, his meeting and marrying Frances and then, in 1969, his moving with her and their four children to Uganda, which he used as a base for travelling extensively. From his office in Kampala he founded the Southern Sudan Project, which was responsible for aid and development programmes throughout the region.

'As the words of the narrator drifted over me,' Dave said, 'I suddenly found myself confronted by an extraordinary scene – the Waite family, Terry and Frances and their four children, gathered round a table eating Christmas lunch. Two things made me sit up and take notice. The first was the setting: the grainy cine film was shot in the lush garden of their home in Kampala, a setting that naturally contrasted with our expectations of what a family Christmas meal should look like. The second was the fact that all the Waites were laughing and smiling, joking and interacting together, just like a normal family; something that had been totally absent from their behaviour in the time that they'd been together at Lyneham.'

Dave and I glanced at each other. I suspected we were both thinking the same thing.

We knew Terry and his family hadn't watched the programme. After we'd discussed the risks and potential rewards, I agreed with Dave and the others that the plan we'd talked through was worth a try. I rang Southern Television and asked if I could get hold of the film footage. The producer was incredibly accommodating. It arrived by courier that same afternoon.

As soon as I'd watched it, I knew Dave was right. We had something very significant in our hands.

I found Terry in the mess and asked him if it would be all right for us all to have dinner together that night, the family and the debriefers, and then to meet in one of the biggest rooms where we held debriefings. I didn't tell him why, only that it was important.

During dinner, I told the Waites about the programme but said nothing about its potential significance.

We then moved through to the debriefing room where there was a

TV and VCR. John Rollins, Dave Hill and all the debriefing team were there; I wanted this to be an experience that we all shared. We settled into our seats, the Waites more perplexed than ever, and the tape began.

We passed the next hour in silence. Then, as the credits rolled, and before anybody had time to say anything, I announced that the team was going to leave the family on their own and that I hoped they would discuss what we had all seen. I hoped that this gesture was not too theatrical but I knew that sometimes a bit of drama can break down defences. We arranged to meet up the following day, all of us, in the same room.

The die was cast and we psychiatrists allowed ourselves to indulge in a little compulsive ritual as we crossed our fingers, withdrew and left the Waites alone.

I arrived early at the mess the next morning and it was as if someone had waved a magic wand. The whole family were chatting and yabbering like they'd never been apart. The film – especially the footage of that Christmas lunch in Uganda – had provoked an explosion of discussion. I noticed it especially among the children. With their father gone for five years, they'd hardly been able to remember a period in their lives when times had been good. But here, in the film, was all the evidence they needed. There had been a time when they had been a normal family and here was the proof. Also, there was some footage of difficult times in Uganda and they realized they had got through those bad times by pulling together as a family. And when I told them about the cooperation I'd received from the TV channel, this had the effect – especially on Terry – of compounding the bond.

The media, the messenger that Terry had come to associate over the past few days with vitriol and vindictiveness of the most vicious kind, had actually come to his rescue. It was the breakthrough moment.

The key with all the hostages had been giving them back their sense of control. We'd demonstrated it with the PoWs in group form and had adopted a more flexible approach with John and Terry and their families. Furthermore, because of all the publicity that the process had received, the MoD had at last sat up and taken notice. We'd demonstrated to the sceptics in Whitehall that if you put effort into the re-entry process, as we had, the people who came through our programme did well. We'd also convinced them that it simply wasn't enough just to release people.

It was Terry Waite himself, in fact, who coined the term 're-entry' as a good way of describing the process of returning from captivity. He drew a comparison with the Apollo space capsule returning from moon shots: 'A bit hot and bumpy at times, but eventually penetrating into clear air and parachuting gently into a calm, rolling sea.' I couldn't have put it better myself.

Prior to our involvement with the PoWs and the hostages, the closest the establishment had come to acknowledging PTSD was in recognizing that some monitoring of their psychological state might be necessary after their release. Now, it was accepted that treatment was an important part of the process.

When I was finally called to London to account for myself, a summons that arrived soon after Terry successfully re-entered normal life, I told them that our experience had demonstrated that a psychological debriefing ought to be an intrinsic part of the return process for any hostage or PoW and that it should be seen as part of the operational debrief that the PoW received as a matter of course; and that furthermore, the psychological debriefer should sit in on the operational debrief so that the released individual didn't need to go through the story more than once but could put all of their energy into telling the story in the natural order: 'What happened to you?' deserved to come before 'How do you feel about what happened to you?'

The result was a better outcome than even I had dared hope. The recommendation that all released PoWs should be psychologically debriefed was incorporated into the Queen's Regulations and Wroughton was formally inaugurated as a PTSD treatment centre in 1991. We weren't alone. The Royal Navy, thanks to the post-Falklands work of Morgan O'Connell, had a trauma unit in place at Haslar Hospital in Portsmouth and the Army had set up a trauma programme at the Queen Elizabeth Military Hospital in Woolwich.

Following a series of major disasters in the 1980s, the civilian world had also started to show an interest in the trauma field.

In what can only be described as one of the worst periods for civil disasters in British history, the mid–late 1980s had not only witnessed the tragedies at Lockerbie and Hungerford but also the Bradford City Stadium fire in May 1985, in which 56 football supporters were killed and 265 injured; the Zeebrugge ferry disaster, in March 1987, in which 193 passengers drowned when a cross-Channel ferry capsized soon after leaving the Belgian port to sail for the UK; the November 1987 King's Cross tube station catastrophe, in which a flash-fire that began under the Piccadilly line escalator incinerated the ticket hall, killing 31 rush-hour commuters and rescue workers; the Piper Alpha North Sea oil-platform disaster that saw 167 oil workers killed when the platform blew up in July 1988; and the Kegworth air disaster of January 1989, in which 47 people died and 74 were injured when a British Midland Boeing 737 crashed on the M1 motorway on its final approach to East Midlands Airport.

As a result of these terrible events, pockets of interest in how to recognize trauma reactions and manage them sprang up in the places the disasters had occurred; for example, in Bradford and Aberdeen, where there was a perceived need to help survivors. The National Health Service began to evaluate the inauguration of trauma units at selected hospitals, but it wouldn't be until the mid-1990s, when a dedicated unit was set up at the Middlesex Hospital, that the initiative properly got under way. It was Stuart Turner, psychiatrist, and James Thompson, psychologist, the men responsible for establishing the Middlesex unit, who also at this time founded the UK Trauma Group, an informal gathering of trauma specialists from around the country. I was included in this group, which would meet three times a year.

To give a sense of where trauma was at that time, there were only 10 of us to begin with at these meetings; now as many as 200 gather for them.

The emergency services – police, ambulance and fire – established a centre in Lincoln during this period, under the leadership of Roderick Orner, a pioneering psychologist, but it was still largely the military – the Navy and us at Wroughton – that were in the van of work in the trauma field, based on our wartime experience of the Falklands and the Gulf. To have achieved this, everyone on my team – the team that had worked so hard since Lockerbie to make this happen – felt on top of the world.

But it wasn't to last. Before I'd gone to the Gulf, it had been announced that the RAF hospital at Ely – my *alma mater* in many ways – would be deploying in its entirety to the war. With the war over, Ely never reopened.

Within months of our debriefing the hostages, we heard that RAF Halton in Buckinghamshire was to close, too. Halton was a general hospital, but it had outstanding, world-class units for renal and cancer care, as well as a sophisticated barometric unit – essential, you would have thought, for treating aircrew beset with some of the altitude-related problems associated with flying.

Nine months after the end of the Gulf War, the Cold War formally ended with the dissolution of the Soviet Union. First Ely, then Halton. What next? I wondered.

I started to feel anxious for the career that I loved and for the programme that we'd built up at Wroughton. Everyone was talking about the peace dividend, but if history had taught me anything it was that peace didn't last for very long. My own research had taught me, too, that trauma wasn't just an affliction that hit combatants. There was evidence in some of the cases I'd treated on the peripheries of the military that PTSD was more pervasive than any of us might have imagined. For these reasons, my thoughts began to drift to what I'd blithely described to my PoW and hostage survivors as the real world, but which to me, institutionalized as I'd become after two decades of military service, right now seemed anything but.

Chapter 14

Ticehurst

The Royal College of Psychiatrists held a conference every year and 1992's was going to be an extra big event as it was the college's 150th anniversary. Hundreds of delegates had gathered in Brighton, from all over the UK. HRH Prince Charles attended. A whole morning had been set aside for presentations on military psychiatry. This was unprecedented, and I felt privileged to have been asked to speak. By the time I arrived, I was relishing the prospect of presenting.

It had been a good summer, and the south coast was catching the best of the sun. The morning of my presentation was one of the hottest days of the year. It was also the day on which the hotel's air-conditioning decided to break down. The conference room was full of red, sweaty faces as I took to the podium. This is going to be a tough sell, I thought. My presentation was one of five given by military psychiatrists representing the three armed forces. They mostly dealt with the Gulf War, but mine was about debriefing the RAF mountain rescue teams who attended Lockerbie.

Despite it being like an oven, I could see a certain level of interest in the room. I was glad. Lockerbie, after all, had been my first real PTSD breakthrough moment. The session that followed included a presentation from Prince Charles, who was very supportive of the military aspects of psychiatric work. But by now the auditorium was packed and I was slowly roasting alive. As soon as HRH had finished, and on the basis that heat rises, I made my way downstairs to the basement, where all the pharmaceutical companies who gather at such events had laid out their stalls. I went from company to company seeing how many pens and pads of paper I could pocket and was wandering out again, feeling happy with my haul, when a couple of nice and enthusiastic young women leapt out in front of me.

'Come and help us celebrate our birthday,' they cried.

The Royal College wasn't the only institution having a birthday. It was also the 200th anniversary of a hospital called Ticehurst House, and its marketing director and manager, Louise Orpin and Margaret Cudmore, were here to advertise its wares. No human being could have turned down the offer of chilled champagne on a day like that, especially if he'd already given his presentation and had no more sessions to attend in the afternoon.

Ticehurst House, Margaret said as she filled my glass, was a 63-bed acute psychiatric hospital for adolescents and adults deep in the East Sussex countryside. It offered a wide range of inpatient, out-patient, day-patient and therapy services. The hospital provided specialist services as well as treatment for a wide range of general psychiatric disorders such as depression, anxiety, panic, OCD, self-harm and schizophrenia. It had a long-standing reputation as one of the most innovative and forward-looking psychiatric units in Britain. By now, I was intrigued.

Ticehurst's specialist services also included treatment for alcohol, drugs and behavioural addictions. What was more, they provided individually tailored evidence-based treatment packages that focused on psychological processing techniques derived from cognitive behavioural therapy.

Margaret replenished my glass. 'We're a multi-disciplinary team – including consultants, staff psychiatrists, specialist nurses, a family therapist, social worker, occupational therapist and specialist teaching staff. Why don't you come and pay us a visit? With your experience, I know the people I work with would love to hear what you've been up to. We're thinking of setting up a trauma unit, too, you know.'

She said it casually – so casually I almost missed it – but her enthusiasm was clear to see and hear. I became even more attentive. Ticehurst, she said, provided intensive, highly flexible care programmes in a safe environment for patients with complex needs that couldn't be met within conventional hospitals or care homes, including detention under the Mental Health Act.

Louise took up the baton. 'And best of all, there are 47 acres of grounds. Lots of walks and other opportunities for outdoor activities. It's a truly spectacular place.'

She finished the pitch by handing me a brochure and a big slice of birthday cake, and I wandered back to the rest of the conference. It took me a while. My feet seemed more navigationally challenged than they had half an hour earlier, but my mind was humming.

One Sunday night a week later, I received a phone call from somebody called Tony Goorney.

Tony was the medical director at Ticehurst and a retired RAF wing commander and psychiatrist. Whether or not he'd been tipped off by Margaret and Louise I wasn't sure, but he told me he had become very interested in the work of the RAF Psychiatric Division at the Princess Alexandra Hospital at Wroughton: the Lockerbie work during 1989; the debriefing of the RAF and SAS prisoners of war in 1991; and, in the aftermath of these events, the formal establishment of our traumatic stress treatment service. It had also come to his attention through the media that we'd treated the Lebanon hostages and that they were doing well in their rehabilitation.

Ticehurst didn't offer any services specifically for psychological trauma at that time, but he confirmed what I'd heard from his colleagues: that he was interested in setting something up. But first, Tony explained, they were organizing a major conference as the centrepiece of their 200th anniversary celebrations. The title of the conference was *Trauma*. Was there any way I'd be able to come down to Ticehurst to help them set up a list of speakers and topics?

Though the call took me by surprise, I did, in fact, know a little bit about Tony Goorney. He'd been an RAF psychiatrist in the sixties and seventies, and John Rollins and David Johnstone, my tormentors, both spoke fondly of him. In military parlance, he 'checked out well'. He was well known for his pioneering work with aircrew, on the stresses involved in flying the jet aircraft introduced into the RAF after the Second World War. He had also written extensively on flying phobias.

I told him I would be happy to help.

The speakers we started to bring together were all prominent in the field of trauma in the UK. There was James Thompson, the man who had worked with victims of the King's Cross fire, which became the first major disaster in Britain to attract an organized response that looked at and treated psychological trauma reactions.

Dr Gillian Mezey was working with the trauma victims of rape and assault. She was very much ahead of her time, because it was only in the early 1990s that PTSD was recognized as being something that could kick in after rape or assault; hitherto it had been considered only possible after major catastrophes such as war, or natural or manmade disasters – mainly on a grand scale.

As I worked on the conference programme, the good feeling I'd had about Ticehurst only grew stronger.

Every time I visited the place, the sun seemed to be shining. There was an army of gardeners who loved the place, and it showed. Besides the acres and acres of magnificent trees, it had a well-manicured, nine-hole golf course. The azaleas and rhododendrons were in flower on the day of the conference, and the rose beds were immaculate. I strolled around the grounds, taking it all in.

In the middle of it all was a stunning white quadrangular building, elegantly proportioned and with a tranquil atmosphere.

Ticehurst had always been a psychiatric hospital. It was built as a private lunatic asylum in 1792. The founder, Samuel Newington, had been in practice at Ticehurst as a surgeon and apothecary. The local stonemasons raced against their colleagues up north, who were building the Retreat for the Quakers in York. At stake was the title of the oldest psychiatric unit in an asylum. Ticehurst won.

I'd done a bit of due diligence before turning up, and knew that the opening had coincided with a stirring of public interest in the care of the mentally ill, sparked by King George III's 'insanity'. The poor man had been confined to a palace room for the duration of his 'treatment'. Dr Newington did not approve. He opened Ticehurst House as an asylum – not a place of custody as the public had come to understand the term, a place jangling with over-zealous use of manacles and chains, but in the correct sense of the word: a sanctuary or place of refuge.

Samuel Newington's patients were initially drawn from within a small radius of Ticehurst. The early records of one set of admissions showed eleven clergymen, one admiral, one ship's captain, one merchant, one surgeon, one druggist and one clerk from India House. At first the hospital admitted a number of pauper patients as well as private clients, but no paupers were admitted after 1838. The clientele came increasingly from the prosperous and aristocratic classes as the century progressed. By the 1820s, a prospectus was being issued with elegant illustrations of the asylum and its grounds, which included a pagoda, a summerhouse and an aviary for gold and silver pheasants.

Ticehurst developed over the rest of the century into a grand estate covering 500 acres. The clientele were now so wealthy that some pitched up with an entourage of servants, who were housed in one of the villas within the grounds. There was regular theatrical and musical entertainment, weekly dances in the winter months and cricket matches in the summer. Two estate farms supplied meat, dairy products and fruit. Vegetables and exotic fruits like peaches and early strawberries came from a walled kitchen garden, where an elaborate system of boilers and pipes provided heat to the glasshouses.

In 1882, a newspaper report described the Ticehurst establishment as 'ducal', with 'horses and carriages, valets and liveried servants, hothouses, greenhouses, and its own pack of harriers'. Patients were increasingly drawn not only from the Home Counties, but from the whole of Great Britain and even overseas. Treatment continued to be benevolent. Patients were allowed pipes, tobacco and snuff, wine and port. It must have been a success: the average stay was just a few months.

Men demobbed after the Battle of Waterloo landscaped over 40 acres of grounds. Two miles of footpaths were laid out through estate plantations, orchards and grounds. The therapeutic walks circumnavigated summerhouses, the pheasantries and a bowling green. The result was said to have been the model for Kew Gardens.

Tony Goorney didn't go so far as to say so, but I got the distinct impression that Ticehurst might be interested in my services if I signalled the fact that my time in the Air Force was running out and I had decisions to make. I couldn't resign without a lot of notice. I had a permanent commission, which meant that I had to announce my intention to opt out – otherwise I would be retained till the age of 65. One of the two option points remaining to me was the 22-year point, and this was due to come up in 1993.

The dwindling support for military medical resources was worsening. After Ely and Halton, military hospitals were being closed left, right and centre, and resources were being directed at reservist medical support, with only a small number of personnel in uniform all the time.

To my mind, it was very useful – necessary, even – to offer sanctuary to people with psychiatric illness, and community services were a valuable adjunct to hospital services. But they should not take over completely. Without inpatient facilities, I believed, RAF/military psychiatry was a lame duck. Worse still, I foresaw the end of our trauma unit at Wroughton, if the trend continued and more hospitals were to close.

We had become excited by the excellent results we were obtaining from our inpatient group treatment programme. It took patients away from their usual environments, which had already proved toxic – why else would they continue to have PTSD if that were not the case? It also involved them in a safe group environment where everyone had PTSD and in which there was a common understanding of what the problems were. The group programme we'd developed for the Gulf War provided normalization of the symptoms and broke the cycle of fear, shame and guilt that so often fed the PTSD and kept it within the survivor in a swirling vicious circle.

Our initial results, though unofficial, showed that 80 per cent of those going through the programme, which was based on the group treatment we'd pioneered with the PoWs, were completely cured of their PTSD within 12 months. What I couldn't understand was why all the enthusiasm we'd racked up for group treatment within the MoD in the initial months after the Gulf War was evidently on the wane.

Ticehurst had a reputation for progressive psychiatry, and Tony Goorney now confirmed that it was adding a highly innovative trauma service to its repertoire – bolstering its reputation as one of the oldest and most respected psychiatric 'asylums' in the country.

Shortly after the conference, on my third or fourth visit to

Ticehurst, my impatience got the better of me and I blurted out: 'Tony, are you ever going to offer me a damn job?'

He raised his eyes to mine. 'Oh yes,' he said, smiling; but then disarmed me completely by adding, 'But I don't expect you to accept it.'

Was this some kind of ruse to make me even keener than I already was to join the staff?

'What do you mean by that?'

Tony said he was concerned that I would be giving up a promising career in the RAF. He was also concerned for the service itself, as we were bringing in new ideas that he knew to be important to its development.

Tony's considerable contribution to Air Force psychiatry had been in the development of treatments for, and better understanding of, flying phobias. He had looked at the work done during the Second World War on LMF and phobic reactions to flying, and the service's understanding of what had happened to bomber pilots particularly, and had taken it further. He was deeply interested in what we were doing because he could see that the concepts that underpinned trauma reactions were really an extension of the flying phobias that could develop in people who'd been exposed to extreme danger during air combat.

I came away needing advice. Chris Sharples was my CO at Wroughton, another man who 'checked out well'. He was an air commodore then and had previously served at Wroughton as the registrar and rugby coach. His very first day as CO at Wroughton was the day that John McCarthy came home. Chris was strongly supportive of the work that we had done with the PoWs and the hostages and of our in-house trauma programme. He went on to become director general of RAF Medical Services. The MoD selection committees may have been composed of old duffers who weren't too sharp when it came to appointing consultant adviserships, but they usually got the big appointments right. This was more than true in Chris's case.

I sat in his office and listened. Again, it was not what I expected.

'Gordon,' he said, 'frankly, you're going to be more use to the service outside than in it.'

'What on earth do you mean?' I said. 'I thought you'd try to persuade me to stay.'

'It's not that I want to lose you. It's just that I can probably see a little further than you.'

'Closures, you mean?'

He said nothing.

'Here?'

He shrugged. 'Who knows? The point is, I think you've gone as far as you can within the service with your research into trauma reactions. Whether the cuts come here or elsewhere, the forces' medical world is about to be decimated.'

'And new ideas and projects will be first for the chop?'

He sighed. 'Wasn't it ever thus?'

We had developed the most extraordinary unit at Wroughton. The work had been hugely exciting. We'd grown it on the back of a war where we had debriefed PoWs – and then hostages – successfully. We were recognized as pioneers in our field, and it wasn't just the RAF that was interested in us. The Army had sent us patients, and so had the Navy – despite having its own excellent facilities. Our group treatment programme was pretty much unique. GPs from all over the south-west of England would try to get their patients into our unit. We were right to be proud of it.

I thought about Ticehurst. It was posh and privileged and I had my doubts about going into a completely independent hospital, but then again there weren't any specialist trauma units in the NHS at the time – and just the barest hints, through the work of Stuart Turner and James Thompson, that the NHS was getting to grips with the problem. I'd have had to take a general psychiatry job and gradually bend it round to doing trauma, which could take decades. If I wanted to continue pushing the cause of PTSD, then it was the private sector or nothing.

But Tony, Margaret, Louise and the staff had also made it clear to me that Ticehurst wasn't just about patient treatment. They were committed to the development of new treatment techniques and the raw science that underpinned some of the mind's most vexing problems, PTSD among them.

The following day, I wrote to Tony Goorney and gratefully accepted his offer.

Chapter 15

When SARA Met Fiona – The Case of the Invisible Girl

From my first day at Ticehurst, I found everything just seemed to come more easily. I contributed chapters to textbooks and articles to medical and legal journals, and gave presentations to everyone from local GP practices to those attending international conferences. None of it was a hardship. On the contrary; I felt I was embarking on a grand new adventure. People were actually listening and not just in the UK.

No sooner had I arrived than I achieved one of my main ambitions: visiting Australia. I was invited by Colonel Wal Hall, who had completed an exchange posting to our Army psychology unit at Farnborough during 1992. There, he had learned about the development of our trauma treatment programme at Wroughton and our ideas on managing hostage and PoW releases. The Australian armed forces had developed services for the treatment of post-traumatic stress reactions as a result of their involvement in the Vietnam War, as had the Americans, and they had their ears close to the wind whenever there was even a hint in the air about new ideas.

I went out to Australia for two weeks in September 1993 to give presentations to Australian Army psychologists and psychiatrists (unlike us, the Aussies had an Army Psychology Corps in uniform, which I thought was especially enlightened), the Royal Australian Air Force and Royal Australian Navy audiences and, interestingly, to Qantas staff as well. Qantas was well known for being the only major airline in the world never to have had a fatal air accident. Australia, of course, was also the home of Dr Sandy McFarlane, who, along with Jeffrey Mitchell and Bessel van der Kolk in the US, had been one of the few people recognized worldwide for working in the trauma field. I'd cited all three when I'd been put on the spot by Roby Burke in my pitch to debrief John McCarthy.

One of my first meetings was with the head of Australian land forces. We were meant to meet for ten minutes, but ended up talking for two hours. He was a Vietnam veteran and particularly interested in our work with the PoWs and hostages. For the Australians, their involvement in Vietnam was the link to our work. They had had a number of PoWs held under long-term detention by the North Vietnamese – experiences that must have matched, in many respects, the hardships endured by the Lebanese hostages.

While in Sydney I stayed in Victoria Barracks. The first thing I did when I got to my room was to fill up the washbasin, put a scrap of paper on top of the water, pull out the plug and see which way the water drained away. As I watched it, something struck me. In my meetings in Australia thus far, I realized that the people most interested to know about our work at Wroughton were clinical psychologists, not psychiatrists. A psychologist studies the mind, whereas a psychiatrist is responsible for diagnosing mental illness and therefore might be seen to pathologize the mental process – branding it as an illness. Australian military psychiatrists, I had learned, had, on the whole, wanted to CASEVAC those who developed post-traumatic stress disorders from Vietnam straight back to Australia because they had seen them as damaged and wanted to admit them to hospital to treat their illnesses.

I hadn't seen either the Lebanese hostages or the Gulf War PoWs in this way at all – far from it. They had acquired PTSD in the process of *surviving* – it had been a strategy designed to help them come through the ordeal; a strategy, one had to conclude, that had been remarkably successful. Our job had been to detune them on their return – to let their minds and bodies know that there was no need for this survival strategy any longer; that it had done its job. This was a far cry from viewing PTSD as an illness and it was something that the psychologists identified with, because their studies had all pointed to the same thing. The psychiatrists, on the other hand, were still by and large stuck in the old paradigm. And they must have thought that I was something of an oddball, or that rare thing: a psychiatrist who had not pathologized PTSD.

The psychologists were now in the van in this particular area of research in Australian military circles. No wonder there had been a meeting of minds.

I went on to give a presentation at the Aviation Medical Society of Australia and New Zealand and spent the middle weekend presenting at the Australasian Psychological Association's annual conference on the Gold Coast in Queensland, near Brisbane. That was where I first met Mark Creamer, an Australian psychologist working with trauma patients in the Melbourne area. Now, as Professor Mark Creamer, he heads up the Australian Centre for Post-Traumatic Health.

The trip demonstrated clearly to me that as post-traumatic stress services were beginning to develop there was a worldwide desire to share information and cooperate. It was almost like a reverse Klondike, where any nuggets that were discovered were shared among all. I found the idea of others working around the world on this same frontier, all of us sharing our thoughts, an exciting notion, one that certainly eased my return to the UK, where immediately upon arrival I took up my duties at Ticehurst in earnest. I knew, too, from the increasing levels of correspondence that we – this small but growing group – shared on the subject, that my colleagues on this frontier, wherever they were in the world, felt the same way.

The key to the immediate future was the establishment of a PTSD group treatment programme, an evolved version of the system we'd set up at Wroughton.

It was determined that the programme would utilize a highly structured initial two-week residential phase of group work as the cornerstone of treatment, supplemented by one year of follow-up, which included three formal group-day reviews at six weeks, six months and 12 months beyond the initial two-week residential phase. The programme was designed for a minimum of four and a maximum of eight patients, with an optimum number of six. The course was run by two dedicated primary therapists/debriefers and one support therapist/debriefer. The primary debriefers became attached to the group and guided them through the entire programme; and while they weren't supposed to become fully integrated within the group they were on hand to foster and guide the group dynamic.

We decided that the groups at Ticehurst should be heterogeneous in terms of trauma, age, gender, religion, ethnicity and so on, but homogeneous in terms of PTSD – that PTSD, in other words, should be the underlying reason for their being at Ticehurst. We found early on that patients consistently reported that sharing traumatic experiences with survivors of different traumas was helpful in reinforcing their growing awareness that reactions to traumatic experiences were stereotypical and universal – this was something that was not unique to them, but shared by others and, we would demonstrate, throughout history. An explanation of the theory of PTSD was found to be helpful in familiarizing patients with this idea.

Group work was carried out in a self-contained, de-institutionalized living and therapy area within the hospital, where geographical separation from the general psychiatric treatment unit within Ticehurst reinforced the process of 'normalization'. The work was facilitated by two primary therapists (or debriefers) who were trained mental health professionals and included psychiatric nurses, psychiatrists and clinical psychologists. A secondary debriefer carried out a systematic review of the group work with the primary debriefers on a daily or more frequent basis.

Each patient was requested to keep a daily journal noting their feelings, emotions and a self-report on progress. These journals were read and discussed by all three therapists each morning before sessional work commenced. Each patient was also interviewed individually by all three therapists on three occasions as part of the course programme. These meetings were intended to give patients the opportunity to bring up any self-perceived problems that might not otherwise surface in the groups. The content of individual journals was kept strictly confidential and was never discussed during group work.

The residential course incorporated five main phases. On arrival, patients met each other informally. The first meeting was seen to be very important because it not only allowed group members to meet other PTSD sufferers – most probably for the first time – but also allowed each of them to understand that they all shared the same symptom pattern, despite a wide diversity of traumatic experience. This in itself seemed to have a dramatic impact, right from the start, on patient anxiety levels.

Introductions to all three therapists occurred in the first work session. The therapists explained the aims of the programme and helped to draw up a list of the expectations of the group members. They also emphasized the voluntary nature of the participation, confidentiality, the absolute necessity of attending all sessions, the prohibition of all non-prescribed drugs, including alcohol, and the closed nature of the group: what was said within the group stayed within the group.

Each group participant then had an opportunity to meet with all three therapists in a private session, the aim being to enforce motivation and offer encouragement. This also allowed each therapist to undertake a relaxed but full mental state examination to screen for current symptoms.

The psychological debriefing or PD phase was then introduced. Group members listened to a 20-minute audiotape in which authentic disaster victims described their experiences and emotions. The tape acted as a template for each group member, who, in turn, described in detail, the facts, emotions and sensory perceptions – the three fundamental components of PD – surrounding their own traumatic experience. The intention of PD is to facilitate reconstruction, assimilation and integration of actual evidence, sensory perceptions and emotions in order to promote information processing and, hopefully, to prevent PTSD in the long term.

Diverse traumatic events, we knew, shared common themes and cross-identification wasn't difficult. The life threat, the loss of control and dignity and the destruction of the myth of invulnerability were just some of them. The group always insisted on highly detailed personal accounts, which prompted a clearer recollection of each individual trauma and restored a sense of being in control. The use of PD seemed to promote strongly cohesive, supportive alliances, with group members often continuing to discuss the information revealed in their own time. We found that fellow sufferers possessed more credibility as empathetic listeners than their therapists. After completion of this phase, re-experiencing symptoms appeared to diminish in intensity and there was a noticeable reduction of anxiety levels and avoidance/numbing symptoms.

We introduced two simple exercises, known as the Lines and Ladders exercises, to encourage group participants to improve the degree of self-control in their lives. In the Lines exercise, group members were asked to plot a time-graph of their lives as a 'home-work' task during the weekend break in the middle of the residential period. Members noted all significant high and low points and plotted positive and negative events on the vertical axis – the horizontal axis representing the span of their lives. The Lines exercise, when shared among the group members, had two major therapeutic benefits. For the first time, the traumatic event was fitted into the context of the whole life experience and was compared with other high and low points. As a result, a new perspective could be gained. Second, the graphic representation allowed therapists to help the individual identify positive and negative behavioural coping patterns brought about by significant life events other than trauma. These patterns of behaviour often proved to have considerable resonance for other group members and became highly significant entries in the journals. The group became increasingly aware of inherent coping styles, and maladaptive patterns could be identified as maintaining factors for the PTSD.

The Ladder exercise allowed the individual to plan his or her future by identifying short- and long-term goals. These goals were then presented to the entire group for discussion and reality testing. Plans needed to be as realistic as possible, in keeping with the individual's coping styles identified in the Lines exercise. Group participants drew a ladder with several rungs on a large sheet of paper. On the top rung they placed their long-term goal and on the bottom rung the lowest point in their lives. The intervening rungs were filled in by the individual as steps to be taken in order to achieve the ultimate goal. Dimensions included family, marital, social, occupational and financial aspects of living. Each individual presented the plan to the group for reality testing, modifying it through positive feedback from other group members.

The final phase of the course was family reintegration, when family members, including spouses, children and partners, attended a session by invitation from group participants. PTSD didn't just have an impact on the survivor but on family members too and we knew that allowing families to see that they were accounted for in our work would help everyone, not merely the patient, to heal.

Following the end of the residential course, the group was reassembled to review progress for one day at six weeks, six months and one year. Each review included group discussion with the emphasis on residual symptoms of PTSD, what problems had been solved and how, and on progress up the rungs of the Ladder exercise.

My colleagues and I were pleased that we now had a formal system at Ticehurst with which to treat the victims of trauma. My clinical observations of what the phenomenon was continued. Thus far, they had tallied closely with descriptions of PTSD in the classification manuals for psychiatric disorders. But I was dealing with a wily beast and all that was about to change.

In 1993, my view, echoed in what I read in the manuals, was that PTSD had four main characteristics. I visualized them as a cascade, like cataracts in a great river, each section of the river pouring into the next, and came up, on the strength of the four, with the acronym 'SARA', which stood for 'Stressor', 'Arousal', 'Re-experiencing' and 'Avoidance'.

I knew there could be no PTSD without a perceived stressor carrying with it the message of threat to life or serious injury.

The impact of the stressor had to be powerful enough to pierce the psychological defences of the mind and to leave an imprint. Lockerbie had been living proof to me of the sheer power of the stressor. It had induced trauma reactions in the last breed of people I'd have ever expected to see them in.

PTSD occurred in individuals who had been exposed to a catastrophic event; on that pretty much everyone, even the MoD, was agreed.

Brand-new thinking in 1994, and I went along with it, said, however, that PTSD went beyond basic exposure to combat stress, rape, childhood abuse and natural or technological disasters. In the latest revision of the *Diagnostic and Statistical Manual* of the American Psychiatric Association – *DSM-IV*, published that year – it was *also* necessary, the manual said, that the individual exposed to the stressful situation should experience a strong *emotional* reaction, such as fear, terror, horror, helplessness or the feeling that they were going to die.

This represented a very important change in the concept of the type of events that could legitimately be described as traumatic. To make this point fully clear, by definition a 'traumatic event' could not simply be judged to have been traumatic by objective description; it also had to be judged to have been experienced *subjectively* as traumatic by the survivor.

The medico-legal significance was that it was not possible for another person to judge whether or not an event had been traumatic – i.e., it could not be assessed from a purely objective viewpoint. A thorough investigation of the impact that the event had on the survivor was required in all cases to discover the subjective element in the process.

This was done by a variation of the CAPS questionnaire given to me by Dudley Blake at Palo Alto on the eve of the Gulf War.

When it was established that a person had been exposed to a traumatic stressor, three major 'symptom clusters' – hyper-arousal, re-experiencing (flashbacks) and avoidance – would need to develop if the victim were to be classified as having PTSD.

This was integral to the thinking that I had put into SARA.

The first cluster of symptoms, 'A for arousal', closely resembled the symptoms characteristic of anxiety states – increased irritability, insomnia and so forth – but the feature most strongly characteristic of PTSD was 'hypervigilance', because most trauma survivors never wanted to repeat the experience and so were on guard against anything like it happening again. Hypervigilance could be so extreme that it could mimic a paranoid state.

The second symptom cluster was the 're-experiencing' set of symptoms in which the trauma essentially continued to have a life of its own, often in the form of untriggered recurrent thoughts, flashbacks and nightmares; or the traumatic memories might be stimulated by cues that reminded the victim of the trauma.

These latter 'triggered memories' were – and continue to be – a very important factor in some of the PTSD treatment models.

The third cluster was characterized by avoidance and numbing. This was because individuals suffering from PTSD found the re-experiencing symptoms so intolerable that they brought a number of behavioural and cognitive strategies into play in order to minimize the intrusive recollections.

Avoidance involved alterations in behaviour designed to avoid reminders of the event. This might involve deliberately avoiding people who would be likely to talk about the trauma, perhaps because they had been involved in it, or even people who belonged to the same organization. A firefighter, for instance, might avoid fire stations. A police officer might avoid police stations or anyone in uniform.

Generally, avoidance behaviours helped victims with PTSD to avoid situations that would predictably remind them of the traumatic event. This strategy, which was consciously controlled, attempted to block out reminders of the trauma from the external world.

Numbing strategies were, by contrast, not controlled consciously and included the shutting down of the emotions, an inability to have, let alone demonstrate, feelings, and social withdrawal.

Because of the internal psychological conflict between intrusiveness and avoidance, PTSD could come to the surface many years after the traumatic event occurred if the suppressive avoidance factor weakened or failed. This phenomenon was known as 'Delayed-Onset PTSD'.

PTSD was described as 'acute' if the symptoms were discovered within three months of the trauma; 'chronic' if the symptoms persisted beyond three months and 'delayed onset' if they only appeared for the first time six months after exposure to the traumatic event.

In the CAPS questionnaire that detected the symptoms of PTSD according to *DSM-IV*, there were 17 core symptoms in the clusters of arousal, re-experiencing and avoidance.

There were also five associated symptoms of PTSD: guilt (over acts of commission or omission), survivor guilt, feeling out of touch or in a daze, derealization (when things seemed unreal, strange and unfamiliar) and depersonalization – the feeling of being outside one's own body, watching oneself as if one were another person. Those last three symptoms are collectively known as 'dissociation'.

Notably, at that time, dissociative symptoms were not mainstream PTSD symptoms, according to CAPS and the *DSM-IV* classification system. This was telling us that PTSD seemed to be a unique anxiety disorder. It appeared to involve many of the cognitive, psychological and psychobiological mechanisms that were important in coping and adaptation.

But there was a missing link. A piece of the picture that I'd missed in SARA. This was the 'dissociation' element.

By 1994, I knew quite a bit about dissociation, but I hadn't come to think of it as a common or frequent component of PTSD – or, for that matter, integral to it. Even *DSM-IV* didn't. Dissociation, it said, was merely an associated feature of PTSD.

All of that was about to change, however, in a case that was ground-breaking for me, because it helped me to understand how key the psychological process of dissociation is in post-traumatic stress states.

I came to refer to the case as 'The Invisible Girl'. It was she who introduced me to the idea that dissociation was a key but as yet unrecognized link in our understanding of the core, raw state of PTSD.

I had known Fiona for just over a year. She was a highly intelligent young woman who had been a university student until lately, but had been unable to complete her course as she had been involved in a nasty road traffic accident eight years previously. She'd been flung off the back of a motorbike driven by her boyfriend when he'd crashed into a tree. He wasn't injured, but she was catapulted through the air and had landed badly on her right leg. It was broken in several places and the intervening years had been filled with multiple corrective orthopaedic procedures.

The leg had healed with just a slight shortening, but the orthopaedic surgeon had become aware that she had a psychological injury as well. He referred her for an assessment, and I saw her.

Fiona had been studying English at university. She had completed her first year of studies but not taken the exams, and she didn't go back to university for the second year. She had become engaged but

there were no plans for a wedding and her fiancé was looking after
her because she was very withdrawn and seemed almost completely
unable to leave their flat.

I found her to be suffering from the characteristic symptoms of
PTSD and we admitted her into the PTSD group treatment programme at Ticehurst. She described herself as 'in limbo', and had
obvious flashbacks to the incident. She was the right sort of patient
for psychotherapy. She was bright and motivated, could work with
psychological concepts, and I was always aware of her trying hard in
the group. For all that, she didn't improve. At the end of the year,
at the final review, she was still quite agitated by the condition.

I took her on as a one-to-one patient, and I'll never forget our first
session. Not long after she walked into the room, she became very
angry with me. It wasn't the first time such a thing had happened,
and it wouldn't be the last. It goes with the territory.

She accused me of not listening to her. I said that I'd like to listen
to her now, and asked her what it was I hadn't listened to. She said
I hadn't heard her telling me about the 'mirrors'.

Mirrors? Had I made a terrible diagnostic error and missed a
psychosis?

I asked her, 'What is it about mirrors?'

She said, 'I've told you several times. I can't look in mirrors.'

'How long's that been going on for?'

'Ever since the accident.'

Things were so bad, she said, she couldn't even go shopping anywhere she was likely to encounter large plate-glass windows.

This was sounding more and more ominous. I said, 'Do you know
why that is?'

'Because . . .' She studied my face nervously, as if she thought I
might react by rejecting her. 'Because I don't know if I'm going to see
a reflection or not.'

It took me a second or two to take that one in. 'How is it possible
that you wouldn't see a reflection?'

She looked down at the floor and then up again. 'Because I don't
know if I'm alive or not. And if I'm not alive, I wouldn't see my
reflection. I don't want to take that chance.'

Nobody had ever said anything like that to me before. The closest
I'd come to anything like it had been with Freddie, the Lancaster

crew member whom we'd diagnosed at Wroughton with Capgras syndrome after he mistook his wife for a Gestapo officer. Since seeing Freddie, I'd become aware of a variant of Capgras, in which the patient believed that inanimate objects, such as furniture, a letter, a watch, spectacles, had been replaced by an exact double – something that had been made famous in the book by Oliver Sacks, published in 1985, called *The Man Who Mistook His Wife for a Hat*. The delusion is most common in patients diagnosed with schizophrenia, although it can occur in connection with a number of conditions, including brain injury and dementia. It was only recently that I'd come to the conclusion that Capgras had probably not been an appropriate diagnosis in Freddie's case. Freddie had been having flashbacks. His form of Capgras, it seemed to me now, must have been some kind of PTSD.

I looked at Fiona. Was this girl psychotic? I didn't think so. I needed to listen very carefully.

She started to tell me about what had happened to her when she was flung from the motorbike. She told me that she had never told anyone else. She said that as she was flying through the air, she seemed to have come out of her body and was flying alongside herself. She could see herself from outside, and felt that she was in a very cold, very dark place. She was terrified, but she sensed that she had to get back into herself before she hit the ground to be safe.

But she never knew that she had achieved that. She was knocked out when she landed.

It was possible I might have remained dumbfounded by her story had my son Stuart not been an avid fan of *The X-Files*. He was so keen he used to get the *X-Files* magazine, and a few weeks earlier he had shoved an article about NDEs (near-death experiences) under my nose.

It was riveting stuff. I wanted to read more, and there happened to be a reference to a scientific article by Susan Blackmore entitled 'Visions of the Dying Brain'. A dedicated researcher of near-death experiences, Susan Blackmore was senior lecturer in psychology at the University of the West of England – as well as being a parapsychologist and Zen Buddhist. She was a formidable sceptic, not only of the afterlife theory of NDEs, but of many other paranormal phenomena.

Susan Blackmore described the NDE as 'an essentially physiological event' prompted by lack of oxygen, the structure of the brain's visual cortex and other factors. She recognized that the experiences were hallucinations – albeit, seemingly, exceedingly real. And she pointed out that one does not actually have to be near death to have such an experience: 'Many very similar experiences are recorded of people who have taken certain drugs, were extremely tired, or, occasionally, were just carrying on their ordinary activities.'

Near-death episodes make up a very small proportion of out-of-body experiences, she said. She had collected many stories of people having an out-of-body experience as they were falling asleep or meditating. Such episodes could also hit at moments of extreme stress, she said.

Stress as extreme as being catapulted off a motorbike and sailing through the air, I wondered?

Blackmore herself had become interested in the topic when, sitting with friends when she was an undergraduate at Oxford, she had had an intense out-of-body experience, including visits to France and New York City's Fifth Avenue. To see whether she had really left her body, she checked the colour of her building's roof tiles to see if it matched what she had seen as she felt herself floating over the building. It didn't.

Some epileptics, she reported, had also had sudden feelings of floating or out-of-body experiences related to their disease. Scientists knew little about the roots of these episodes. Wilder Penfield, a pioneering neuroscientist, published a paper in 1955 that described the strange effects of applying electrical currents to the brain: sudden limb twitching, hallucinations and, in one case, a woman who said she felt as if she had just left her body. But the work was very crude, said Blackmore, because the instruments available at the time did not allow Penfield to determine the specific area of the brain involved or to replicate the out-of-body effect.

To me, all this was dynamite. I actually had a copy of Susan Blackmore's published article on my desk and I told Fiona, 'There is beginning to be an explanation for these things. They don't need to be regarded as paranormal or supernatural. They can be regarded as entirely normal experiences.'

I told her about the mechanisms that Susan Blackmore had described. She was so fascinated she asked for a copy.

I saw Fiona only once more after that, about three weeks later. I hadn't prescribed any medication or done anything more than give her the photocopy, but she had made a complete recovery. She even invited me to her wedding.

She'd never looked in the mirror because she didn't know whether she would show in the mirror or not. If she had, she'd have seen her reflection. But she didn't want to take the risk. What if she wasn't there? She'd spent eight years just going through the motions, fearing she belonged to the class of the undead.

The moment she knew that out-of-body experiences could happen, and that it didn't mean that she had gone off her rocker, that they didn't mean that she had died, it was enough to make the story processable. It got into her long-term memory. It was date-stamped. It had the authenticity of a memory of something that had actually happened in the past. She was no longer in limbo; she was able to move on.

It was an amazing case, and it strongly enforced in my mind the idea that PTSD wasn't a mental illness. It was just mental processing that had been obstructed in some way, prevented from taking its normal course.

There wasn't another traumatologist in the hospital to speak to, so I tended to use my secretary, Pat Young, as a sounding board. She was more than just supportive in a secretarial way; she was genuinely interested in the subject.

Pat could have come back as a very sensible person with her feet on the ground and said, 'This is bonkers, this doesn't make sense.' But she didn't.

Encouraged, I suggested looking at all 50 or so people who'd been in our group at Ticehurst so far. 'Let's look at the ones who haven't been successful, and ask ourselves the question: "Why didn't they succeed?"'

We looked for people who'd been motivated, but who hadn't made progress. We came up with just five names out of 50 treated.

The five had been difficult cases. I contacted them all and arranged one-to-ones. When we met, I asked each of them the same simple question: 'When you were exposed to the traumatic event that we've talked about, did anything odd happen that you still don't understand?'

Each person looked surprised and also alarmed.

'Yes,' each one said. 'I had an out-of-body experience.'

One of them was the manageress of a Woolworths store who'd been taken hostage by an armed robber in a mask. She was taken up to the office and made to open three safes with a gun to her head. When she was opening the third safe, making the final manoeuvres, she heard the hammer being cocked behind her right ear. That's it, she thought, he's going to shoot me now.

She found herself floating above the safe, looking down on herself with the gunman behind her. She thought the gun must have gone off and she'd been killed. She didn't believe she existed, and therefore wasn't in the room when we were trying to treat her. She continued to be dissociated. When she was suddenly convinced that she did exist, that there was a plausible explanation for her experiences, she made a dramatic and speedy recovery.

All five also said they'd never mentioned this to anyone else, not even during the group programme, because they thought they'd be regarded as crazy.

In four out of five cases, the explanation of out-of-body experiences being normal helped them to understand what had happened to them in a new and meaningful way. As with the Invisible Girl, it provided a huge but missing piece of the jigsaw puzzle. At once the experience became real for them, rather than supernatural, and the four of them made rapid recoveries within weeks.

The fifth one didn't make a spontaneous recovery, and he remained a mystery to me. I suspected that something had already happened to him much earlier in his life, maybe as a child, that had been propelled to the surface by the horrific car crash he had been involved in. I suspected the experiences had fused together somehow, and we weren't able to disentangle them. Not just yet, anyway, but maybe in the future. I kept his records, and when the next discovery is made we'll be able to go back and try again with him.

I realized, however, that dissociation had appeared as a key component in the PTSD story. I had also come to appreciate something else – that the period of a month after the traumatic incident was critical too.

*

I gradually became convinced it didn't really matter how long you had PTSD, you just had to find the key to unlock it. People could make a full recovery after extraordinary periods of time. Despite the increasing levels of correspondence on this subject among specialists – myself included – there was precious little in the way of documented evidence, so the following case came as something of a revelation to me.

Soon after the case of the Invisible Girl, we had a lady attend one of our groups – Doris – who'd had PTSD for 60 years.

As a little girl growing up in Brighton during the Second World War, she had witnessed a German bomb crashing through the conservatory of her parents' house and landing next to the chair where she was sitting. The bomb never went off, but she had suffered flashbacks all her life. Her PTSD had been regarded as chronic and unbeatable and naturally I was very interested in her case.

Under the group programme, each member had half a day to recount the circumstances of their particular trauma. Doris, in her late sixties, was far and away the oldest member of the group. Although I wasn't one of her debriefers, I had a chance to talk to her early on when she came to see me for her one-on-one. It was here that she described her flashback to me.

'It's a lovely, clear early autumn day. The kind you can get on the south coast: sharp, with the taste of salt in the air. Sometimes, all I need is to smell that smell and I'm right back there – sitting in the conservatory reading a book.

'I was only eight years old and understood very little about the war. It all seemed a long way off. There had been some air raids further along the coast, but they hadn't affected us. We had a shelter in the garden, but as far as my parents were concerned there wasn't any need for it. What was there to bomb in Brighton?'

She clutched a handkerchief as she talked to me. She was a tall, elegant woman, with thin features and delicately coiffed grey hair. I asked her to continue.

'My mother was in the kitchen, making a cup of tea; my father was out. I can remember hearing the whistle of the kettle. That can set it off, too. If I'm at a friend's house and they have a gas cooker with a kettle with a whistle on it, it takes me right back, triggers what happened next.'

'What did happen next?' I asked.

'I heard another noise. Over and above the sound of the kettle. It was difficult to detect at first. It sounded like a scream. Later, somebody told me that it was the sound a Stuka makes as it dive-bombs its target. Suddenly, there was this crash, and the glass roof disintegrated. The shards of glass flew inwards, showering everything. I had no idea what had happened. It was as if the sky had exploded. Everything seemed to unfold in slow motion.'

She held the handkerchief very close to her chest.

'I opened my eyes to see this thing in the middle of the conservatory – a big, dark green tube with fins on it. I'd seen pictures of bombs and knew immediately what had happened. I started screaming, because I knew the bomb hadn't gone off and it was as if I could hear it ticking. I was rooted to the spot, waiting for it to explode.

'And then my mother rushed in, picked me up and ran with me out of the house. But I don't remember that part. I just remember sitting there, on that chair, surrounded by glass, staring at that bomb and screaming.'

She didn't tell me she had had an out-of-body experience; I heard it through the group. The case of the Invisible Girl had been so recent, and the subsequent revelations that others had also had OOBEs, that we hadn't had time to fully integrate the findings. But the debriefers had known it to be significant and had passed the information along.

You'd expect people like Doris to be very angry – either with themselves or with their doctors – that they'd endured their condition for so long. In Doris's case, she'd suffered from mood swings and anxiety attacks throughout her life; conditions that could be directly attributable to her childhood trauma. There were the flashbacks, too, of course, which were highly dissociative in nature, and nightmares regularly plagued her.

But Doris hadn't been angry. Instead, she'd tried to derive meaning from this experience, particularly the out-of-body part. But she hadn't been able to; it had frightened her. Like the Invisible Girl, there was a part of her that had become convinced she had died that day.

I discussed her case with her debriefers and they soon imparted their wisdom to Doris through the group. What she had experienced wasn't some paranormal event. As she'd sat there, waiting for the bomb to explode, her eight-year-old mind had done the only thing it could; it had transported her out of harm's way by dissociating – the most extreme form of dissociation there was, as it happened: decoupling her mind from her body; transporting it somewhere else, to a place of safety.

As with the Invisible Girl, this information had an almost immediate effect on the patient. Because Doris had lived with the condition for 60 years, I knew that a lot of pennies would be dropping. But the flashbacks and the nightmares stopped and, over time, her mood changes and anxiety attacks diminished; to the extent that they had disappeared completely several months after she left the residential phase of the course.

Doris and a number of other chronic cases we saw at that time got me thinking about the processes at work that fostered these long-term episodes of PTSD. If we could understand what was behind them, we'd stand a better chance of helping more people coming through the groups. For every Doris, I knew that there would be many others suffering from chronic PTSD, who, like her, had been told it was untreatable. How brilliant it would be, if time could be removed as an impediment to treatment.

In these chronic cases of PTSD, I imagined a two-stage rocket, ignited by the traumatic event. You have an acute stress reaction and the first stage blasts off. But in some cases, the whole thing burns out of its own accord before the second stage ignites: the experience is not going to fire up the second stage and go into orbit, the imprint of the trauma is processed and the acute stress reaction resolves. If, on the other hand, after about a month, the second stage of the rocket is ignited, it takes matters up to orbital altitude. The capsule detaches itself and goes into orbit. Then you have long-term PTSD. This will go round and round in orbit for ever, until the capsule is opened.

When you open that capsule, what you find in there is the same as it was when it went into orbit: an acute stress reaction. It's not changed at all from the point of take-off. It remains unchanged until you open the capsule and fix it, and then it gently comes out of orbit and parachutes back to earth. It doesn't change over time. You've got the same flashbacks, the same nightmares. You may have varied avoidances, because your avoidances multiply as you become more sophisticated. The arousal levels are going to be repetitively the same too.

As you go round and round, you're trapped in that orbit until somebody else comes along and helps you open the capsule. I didn't think you could do that on your own, because you're stuck and trapped in that trauma. You've got to have an 'introducer' to bring you back down to earth. That seemed to be consistent with the concept of re-entry; that re-entry was not something you could do successfully on your own. You needed a mission control.

Sometimes people can appear to come back down to earth and re-enter on their own, but they don't really. They've been helped by a partner, friend, family member, priest or confidant – somebody who had the natural capacity to make them feel safe and then continue a discussion that gradually, over time, helps people to process their traumatic experience. But if you've been through something like an out-of-body experience, you have to be careful whom you speak to. A priest, for example, might reinforce the idea that there's a religious quality to the experience.

The two-stage rocket model had explained my clinical observations that people in the group programme – by definition, well past the golden month – could make as good a recovery as those treated sooner. All they had to resolve was what had been encapsulated.

Take Doris's case. She had been just eight years old when the bomb had crashed through the roof of the conservatory. She was in a familiar place; the war a long way off. It was difficult to imagine sitting in a safer place as a child.

To then have the roof shatter above you, all the glass and debris shower down on you, and a bomb embed itself in the floor right next to the chair you're sitting in – it's hard to imagine that that wouldn't have had traumatic consequences for an adult, let alone an eight-year-old. There would have been some compelling, sudden, totally unpredicted realization that this was an extremely dangerous situation to be in; waiting for the thing to go off, wondering if it was a malfunction or a delayed fuse.

Her inevitable acute stress reaction couldn't possibly have been resolved. She was a child, and children are not meant to have acute stress reactions. They're often the forgotten victims of PTSD. People think children are resilient, they'll grow out of it – and that's if they've even noticed. Young people in the back of cars involved in road traffic accidents are often completely overlooked, even by traumatologists. The focus of attention is on the driver and front-seat passenger.

What I was seeing was that there was no limitation on the type of person who could suffer a traumatic stress reaction, or the length of time they could be suffering from it.

The jury was – and still is – very much out on debriefing as something that should be done automatically after people have been exposed to a trauma. The counter-argument is that sitting in a group and listening to other people's experiences could make that individual's own reaction worse over time. But the received wisdom now is that it is beneficial; the pendulum has swung back quite a bit.

To be properly evidence-based, the results of debriefing had to satisfy the criteria for random controlled trials, RCTs. RCTs work via statistics. One group of patients receives a particular treatment and another doesn't. If you can demonstrate strictly via maths and statistics that the group receiving treatment has benefited from it, then it can be proven that the treatment works because it removes subjectivity and ambiguity from the process.

But the counter-argument was that researchers found it difficult to apply RCT criteria to something as complicated as psychological trauma where there are so many variables to control for in a group of individuals. To demonstrate the complexity, we know for sure now that before people get better from PTSD they have to reinvigorate the symptoms. That is, as you break into the box, these symptoms – one, two and three as defined in the *DSM* – would in fact be hidden, encapsulated for some time, since the trauma. In opening up that box, or that capsule, you would bring the symptoms to the surface. They become manifest. If you applied measurement before such a time, you might have low figures, or a no-show, but during the treatment you would have high figures and would hope they would decline as the material was processed –

particularly for things like intrusions or flashbacks or nightmares. These would be manifest at the beginning of treatment, because they have to be. They have to be out there in order to get processed; for recovery to begin.

From the outset, it has been recognized that PTSD is not a static condition and that the symptoms fluctuate in intensity and frequency over time. A useful way to look at this is to see that in PTSD there are two main dimensions, *intrusiveness* and *avoidance*. Avoidance is a regulator, a means of reducing the intensity and frequency of intrusive symptoms such as flashbacks or nightmares. When avoidance is working efficiently, closing down awareness of the trauma flashbacks, then there will be reduced intrusiveness of these symptoms, but, by contrast, when avoidance is not working well, then intrusiveness will be increased so that flashbacks to the trauma will increase. It's a seesaw mechanism – if one is up then the other must be down and then it reverses.

That does not mean that a person is sicker at that point in time, it means they are actively processing the trauma memories (flashbacks) and are beginning to get better. But the psychological instruments would yield high scores (levels of symptoms), and therefore suggest that they were getting worse. This can make the analysis of results based on quantitative research methods such as RCT difficult to interpret.

Yet our experience was that 80 per cent was the enduring recovery rate for patients who had completed the full year of the group programme; that is, patients who had experienced the initial two-week residential programme at Ticehurst and Wroughton and then three day-reviews spaced out at six weeks, six months and 12 months. Of those patients admitted, approximately 80 per cent no longer fulfilled the criteria for PTSD.

Before admission into the residential phase, all patients were clinically assessed in a standard way by a psychiatrist experienced in dealing with trauma and a battery of psychometric questionnaires. The clinical assessment and the same psychometric measurements were repeated at each day-review. When the scores for symptoms decreased we found this was very encouraging for the patients, who had 'hard' evidence that they were recovering.

When people left us and we said they were better, that 80 per cent no longer had PTSD, that was measurable and could be demonstrated with the CAPS, the gold standard for measurement given to me by Dudley Blake in California. But there was another feature too. Most studies, to this day, in terms of treatment efficacy – where you're trying to measure the effectiveness of certain treatments like cognitive behavioural therapy, CBT – tend to take place over a six-month period, with no follow-up. We measured over 12 months. We had a durable fix, a durable treatment effect, plotted over a period that was at least six months longer than the other studies available. We were still getting people with a durable recovery. And we were working with a points system. With the RAF personnel that we treated it was particularly apparent. If they'd deteriorated again after those 12 months, they'd have come back to us. The military system didn't tolerate failure.

Why, then, within the MoD, was there a backlash round about the time I left the RAF? Why had it ignored, or chosen to ignore, that over a medium- to long-term period, 80 per cent of people we saw were no longer exhibiting the recognized criteria for PTSD? Even worse, why did they choose to turn the clock back? Choose to believe that group sessions were quite possibly harmful?

It remains a complete mystery to me. When I left the RAF, the groups that we'd set up at Wroughton ran for a little bit longer under the direction of my very able friend and colleague, Walter Busuttil, but then Walter was transferred elsewhere and they petered out.

I put it down in the end to the energy effect. It needed somebody to lead it, with an enthusiastic attitude towards it, to model it and guide it.

When I left the RAF and Walter was posted away from Wroughton, the driving force behind the PTSD project and the group treatment programme waned, perhaps reflecting the different interests and clinical priorities of the clinicians who moved in to take our jobs. So the only place our group treatment programme continued was at Ticehurst.

After the Gulf War, in 1991, the trauma field was still relatively young and the research had not demonstrated the universal superiority of one treatment for PTSD over any others. Our group treatment work was subjected to the rigours of research evaluation and was shown to have an almost 80 per cent recovery rate at

12 months, which was very good. But one-to-one treatments were beginning to develop too, and these lent themselves more easily to quantitative statistical research methods.

When it came to individual treatment methods, psychodynamic methods such as Freudian psychoanalysis could not offer the same amenity in the treatment of PTSD, because the assumption that developmental anxiety would predispose to reactions following exposure to trauma in later life was anathema to the idea that PTSD was a reaction to an abnormal event of life-threatening intensity that could happen to anyone. Cognitive therapies, on the other hand, in which the therapist re-exposes the trauma survivor to the memory of the event in a bid to desensitize them to it, had been slowly but progressively introduced during the 1980s, eventually becoming known as Trauma-Focused Cognitive Behavioural Therapy (TFCBT). But, in the early 1990s, it was all still front-line stuff and, from what I had read and learned, no more effective than our group treatment work, which to me – RCTs or not – still represented the way forward.

At the end of our two-week residential programme, I had the task of telling the participants' partners, families and friends what we'd been up to. We felt strongly, I said, that if we treated sufferers in isolation, and those at home didn't know what we were trying to achieve, then re-entry, according to the two-stage rocket model, would be difficult if not aborted altogether. If people were returning to an unsafe environment, they were going to close down again. We'd opened them up, and they wanted that to continue.

Typically, the significant others included loved ones who felt guilty that they hadn't been helpful or supportive enough. There were also those who felt that they, too, had been traumatized, and their needs had been neglected. They were the secondary or tertiary victims: those who fell prey to the 'ripple effect'.

The ripple effect was well recognized in the field of trauma. I now see that it is a phenomenon that ought to be recognized much more widely in psychiatry and not remain so closely attached to trauma as it has become. I think it's important to remember that trauma re-actions are at the extreme end of the spectrum of anxiety reactions and that we should not be surprised to find that the extreme level of anxiety spreads out to have an impact on those close to the primary victim. However, that does not mean that we should ignore the impact, perhaps milder but still significant, of less intense anxiety reactions than PTSD on close associates. The ripple effect refers to the stone that is thrown into a pond to produce its biggest splash at the point of entry. Although the ripples might then have lower amplitudes, they still often reach the edge of the pond. Here were the family and friends who had to put up with withdrawal, irritability, volatility and violence. Loved ones who'd never been hostile or shown any harmful tendencies could become quite bruising companions – sometimes literally. Those on the receiving end could feel angry that their loved one who'd turned 'bad' was receiving treatment, while their needs were being ignored. We believed it was a good idea to cast the net wide and haul them in.

The format was that I delivered the essential messages to the significant others on their own for a couple of hours, introduced them to the concepts, and gave them an opportunity to describe how the trauma had impacted on them. Afterwards, our patients came back in so that we could hold a general discussion.

I was talking to my significant others group one day when I realized that I needed a formula to put over the points I was trying to make in a way that would be memorable. That almost always means drawing pictures and the Leaky Sac Model came into my head. As it came to me, I drew it on a board.

The first element was a stick man; a normal smiling person with arms and legs: Joe.

Then came the second element, a bolt from the blue.

To qualify as a lightning bolt, I said, it had to be a very powerful event which happened suddenly, was not predicted and was overwhelming, even life-threatening.

The person on the receiving end of the lightning bolt was usually someone who was normal and who didn't have any psychiatric vulnerabilities – a normal man, woman or child, of any age, race or creed, who was struck by a lightning bolt so powerful it pierced their defences and made them feel very vulnerable, that their life was in danger. An acute stress reaction to the impact was inevitable.

I emphasized the importance of the word trauma. 'In Greek it means pierce or puncture,' I said. 'A traumatic wound was one

THE LEAKY SAC MODEL

Stage 1: the Incident

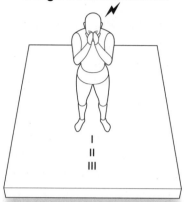

I. Intrusion
II. Avoidance and numbing
III. Hyperarousal

LIGHTNING BOLT
- Characteristics
- Very powerful
- Sudden
- Unpredictable
- Overwhelms all defences – 'punctures'
- Life-threatening

Stage 2: Leaky Sac Stage

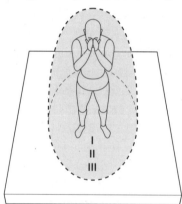

NEGATIVE
ADDS TO STRESS

Negative comments
Lack of information
Isolation/fear
Sleeplessness
Irritability

POSITIVE
LESSENS STRESS

Friends/family community support
Information
Advice
Practical support
'Space' to rest and recover
Critical incident stress debriefing
Access to counselling
Credibility given to reactions

Stage 3: PTSD or the 'Concrete Box Stage'

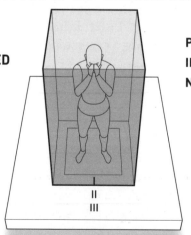

NEGATIVE COPING SKILLS ESTABLISHED

- Flashbacks
- Intrusive thoughts
- Depression
- Anxiety state
- Social isolating behaviour
- Misuse alcohol or drugs

PSYCHIATRIC INTERVENTION NEEDED

caused by such force that it could pierce armour or a shield. A psychological trauma has to have the same power: it will shatter the psychological defences that give the impression that the world is safe and that we are in control of our lives.'

What damage does it do when it pierces and punctures? I asked. 'It has three effects. It produces an imprint of what the trauma was, which the victim re-experiences over and over in a very unpleasant way. The victim then tries to avoid these re-experiences as much as they can – and the third effect is the higher levels of arousal that occur when re-experiencing cannot be avoided, the constantly being on guard for another bolt from the blue.'

These elements, it suddenly occurred to me, could be seen as contained in a sac – sac, that was, in the medical sense of membrane. Inside this sac were all the flashbacks, nightmares, higher levels of arousal, avoidance: the whole horrific shooting match.

'But the sac is leaky,' I said. I scribbled arrows heading in and out of it. 'For the first month after the trauma, things can enter and leave it . . . or the sac can even stay the same. In other words, it can contract or expand; things can get better or worse.'

The first month – the 'golden month', as I called it – was indeed crucial. If there were secondary traumas within that time – if, for example, a fireman was exposed to something nasty and way beyond his usual experience at work, and then told to pull his socks up by the station commander who said he was a wimp – then that could make it worse. There were also things, I said, that could make it better, including debriefing – and I talked about my experiences with Lockerbie and the Gulf War.

This was a crucial stage, I put to them. In the first month, the Leaky Sac could either expand or contract. If it expanded, there'd be more mess to deal with. If it contracted, it could become manageable, or even disappear altogether.

I knew that month to be critically important, even from my own clinical observations. People seemed to need 30 days to come to terms with what had happened. We had a month – that golden month – in which to sort things out. After that, the victim could develop PTSD. Conversely, inside the month, PTSD could not be diagnosed.

'I see that month as an adjustment period,' I went on. 'Some people are not affected; they will have no reaction at all to the trauma. It won't have imprinted. The lightning bolt will have bounced off their defences. It's like the Klingons' laser torpedoes hitting the Starship *Enterprise* but being deflected. All three layers of the defence shields remain intact.'

Once there was evidence it had penetrated – that the traumatizing energy had got in and made its mark so that the same event was re-experienced over and over – then that led to the cascade effect. It went to work like a virus.

'That said, we also know that having an acute stress reaction does not automatically mean Joe here is going to move on to develop PTSD. However, for PTSD to develop, you do need to have had an acute stress reaction. It's a harbinger, if you like – the messenger with bad news.'

I turned back to the board. 'Things then move on to the third phase.' I drew a square box. 'If, after a month, the reactions have not been resolved – i.e., the Leaky Sac still has contents – then the sac becomes a thick-walled box made of a very hard material.'

I rapped the blackboard sharply with my chalk. 'The same three items – re-experiencing, avoidance and arousal – are still inside, but this time they constitute PTSD. From now on, very little spontaneous effusion or infusion will occur. The behaviours will have become hardened in their box – encapsulated, if you like. And someone has thrown away the key. What the victim needs now is someone to find that key again and help them open the box.'

The Two-Stage Rocket Model still applied. There had been a trauma that ignited the rocket, and once it was ignited it had no alternative but to blast off. The first stage lasted for about a month, the time it took to take the rocket up to the end of its acute state. Sometimes the first stage fizzled out of its own accord and the whole thing came back to earth. But if it wasn't resolved, the second stage would ignite and carry on into orbit. The capsule and its contents would go round and round in an unchanged way, a legacy of some-thing that had happened many times previously. And it would stay that way, as objects do in orbit. It wouldn't spontaneously resolve. Round and round it would go until somebody got proactive about it. Somebody had to go on a spacewalk, open the capsule from the outside, and help the victim with the controls to bring it back down.

THE TWO-STAGE ROCKET MODEL:
Acute Reactions 'Fizzle Out',
Chronic Reactions 'Go Into Orbit'

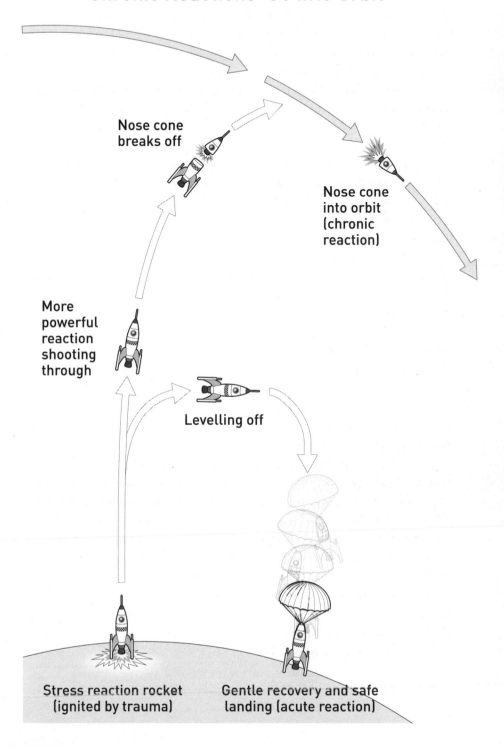

Nose cone breaks off

Nose cone into orbit (chronic reaction)

More powerful reaction shooting through

Levelling off

Stress reaction rocket (ignited by trauma)

Gentle recovery and safe landing (acute reaction)

This model had explained my clinical observations that people in the group programme – by definition, well past the golden month – could make as good a recovery as those treated sooner. All they had to resolve was what had been encapsulated. The keys to what had been encapsulated, in my experience, still resided in those two crucial questions: 'What happened to you?' and 'How do you feel about what happened to you?' They had formed the basis of the PoW and hostage debriefings we'd carried out at Wroughton and they now formed the basis of the group debriefers' work at Ticehurst.

An American professor at Harvard, Ronnie Janoff-Bulman, wisely came up with the idea of looking for something called 'shattered assumptions'. It's not just that you look for something life-threatening, she said, or which causes you physical damage or makes you feel terrified or helpless. It's more about, 'Why did it do that to *you*?'

The work to help victims of trauma to face up to the most significant issues caused by the traumatic experience is directed at helping them to re-evaluate the psychological impact through cognitive restructuring and reprocessing. Affected individuals may re-evaluate their pre-trauma assumptions about their personal worth, how truly kind or malevolent the world is and how to find meaning in their experience.

If successful – and here was the key part for me – personal growth becomes a real possibility.

PTSD is an individual reaction. Not everyone who's exposed to a trauma will develop PTSD. Even though it's the nastiest, the most horrible event you can imagine, some people will not develop PTSD as a result of it. The event didn't get through; it didn't penetrate the sac. The assumptions that are shattered are particular ones that you have a lot invested in. If a person has an investment in an assumption, then *bang*, it will trigger a reaction – and, in turn, re-experiencing, avoidance and arousal.

There are phenomena that we know predispose people to trauma. I didn't realize it to begin with, but the Invisible Girl introduced me to just how important dissociation is at that point in time, and the meaning of the dissociation: *does it mean that I have died?*

In the Invisible Girl's case, her reaction was: 'I've come out of my body, and I know that because I saw it with my own eyes. Something fundamental happened to me back there, so I can't be alive in the way that I used to be alive. Yet I still seem to be here. I'd better not test it though, because I might discover I'm dead. This may be a transient phase I'm going through, some kind of limbo. If I don't test it, it might just wear off. One day, I'll wake up and everything will have gone like a bad dream.'

The dissociation has a meaning for the individual. It's not just the phenomenon, it's the *meaning* of the phenomenon. Therefore, what happened to you is of fundamental importance – and that's what we've got to find out.

When we understand the meaning of what happened to somebody, it's possible to help him or her to process it. Processing, in fact, was fundamental. Without it, there could be no resolution to the underlying trauma.

Chapter 16

Wrestling with the Gatekeeper

Of the six main criteria for the diagnosis of PTSD in *DSM-IV*, the first one, 'Criterion A', is an attempt to define what constitutes a 'traumatic' event, and it isn't an easy thing to do. However, it is imperative that the best possible effort is made to define it because, without exposure to a traumatic event, post-traumatic stress disorder cannot occur. For this reason Criterion A has been called 'the Gatekeeper' – a catalytic event in the PTSD train of events that has certain qualities to it.

In *DSM-III* (1980), which was the edition that introduced PTSD as a diagnostic entity, Criterion A was defined as 'the existence of a recognizable stressor that would evoke significant symptoms of distress in almost everyone'. When *DSM-III* was revised in 1987 (*DSM-III-R*), Criterion A was adjusted and expanded to explain that 'the person [must have] experienced an *event that is outside the range of usual human experience* and that would be markedly distressing to almost anyone.' Such an event, it said, would have to constitute a 'serious threat to one's life or physical integrity; serious threat or harm to one's children, spouse, or other close relatives or friends; sudden destruction of one's home or community; or seeing another person who has recently been, or is being, seriously injured or killed as the result of an accident or physical violence'.

In the current definition of Criterion A (*DSM-IV*), it is recognized that simple exposure is not enough to provoke PTSD; that there had to be evidence of a powerful emotional reaction to the event, demonstrating that it had 'pierced' or 'penetrated' the individual's psychological defences. Specifically, that 'the person has [to have] been exposed to a traumatic event in which both of the following were present: the person experienced, witnessed, or was confronted with an event or events that involved actual or threatened death or serious injury, or a threat to the physical integrity of self or others; and that the person's response involved intense fear, helplessness, or horror (note: in children, this may be expressed instead by disorganized or agitated behaviour).'

All of this suggested that individuals exposed to traumatic events tended to be affected by them in a negative way. But in reality, only a minority of trauma-exposed individuals developed symptoms – a testimony to the strength and power of human psychological defence mechanisms. We are, if nothing else, a resilient species.

I had paid special attention to the work of David Alexander, a traumatologist who'd cooperated with police body-handlers following the Piper Alpha oil platform disaster in the North Sea off Aberdeen in 1988. This was the worst oil platform disaster in history and claimed the lives of 167 people. David Alexander noted in his *International Handbook of Traumatic Stress*, published in 1993, that 'a major trap seems to be that helpers become pedlars of gloom and miserable statistics about the presence of post-traumatic stress symptoms. However awful the circumstances of a disaster are, it is imperative that a positive approach be maintained. People do cope with adversity and even in the worst tragedies one can (and should) find the positive gains.' This simple statement grabbed my attention, because this was what the evidence of some of my recent cases had started to tell me. Yet was this truly possible?

It forced me to go back to basics; to look at what the rule book – and the neuroscience – said.

I needed to gauge to what extent what I was seeing in my patients was in line or out of step with the consensus, starting with Criterion A. This brought me into contact with a Thames Valley policeman called David Kinchin, who had been involved in a terrifying incident while out on patrol in the quiet Berkshire market town of Wantage in 1990.

But his story and its relationship to the Gatekeeper criterion really started two years earlier.

On 19 March 1988, I, like millions of others, had sat in front of my TV as news unfolded of an IRA funeral in Belfast. Like the rest of the world watching that day, I was transfixed and sickened in equal measure by what I saw. It was the funeral of a member of the IRA who had been killed three days earlier by a UDA gunman during another burial service. The gunman had gone into the cemetery with a pistol and hand grenades, and had killed three people and injured 60 others. He was chased to the road and beaten up by the crowd, then rescued and arrested by the police. Catholic Belfast was inflamed.

The news cameras were filming the IRA man's funeral procession. Hundreds of mourners crammed the narrow streets.

Then, from nowhere, a silver VW Passat headed straight towards the cortège. It drove past the stewards, who tried to direct it out of the way. Instead of just turning, however, the Passat mounted the pavement and turned down a side road. It soon reappeared, but by the time it got back on to the main road it was blocked in by black taxis. It tried to reverse, and was then swamped by bodies. In full view of the world's TV cameras the angry mob swarmed all over the vehicle, rocking it and smashing the windscreen.

The driver tried to climb out of his window as more taxis moved to box him in. He fired a shot into the air and the crowd fell back. But only for a moment. The hard core surged again, armed with wheel braces and anything else they could grab. One of them wrenched a stepladder from a photographer and rammed it through the windscreen.

Two men were eventually pulled from the car, punched, kicked and dragged away. We didn't know it at the time, but they were taken to a nearby sports ground where they were stripped and searched. The poor souls were then thrown over a wall and shoved into the back of a black cab. The jubilant driver waved a fist in the air.

They were driven to Penny Lane, off the Andersonstown Road. Two IRA men stabbed them in the back of the neck before executing them with shots to the head and chest.

As the IRA scattered, a priest appeared. Together with the nauseating footage that had preceded it, the image of him administering the last rites to the naked and mutilated bodies was to become one of the most enduring of the 30-year Troubles. Later that day, the IRA issued a statement saying that they claimed responsibility for the execution of two members of the SAS who had launched an attack on the funeral cortège.

The two occupants of the Passat were British servicemen, it turned out, but they weren't members of the SAS. They were signallers, on their way to service a transmitter. For whatever reason, they'd found themselves in the wrong place at the wrong time that day.

From start to finish, the incident had lasted no more than 20 minutes, but that was long enough to etch the episode into the world's memory drum. Probably everybody watching knew that they'd never forget it.

David Kinchin certainly didn't. Two years later, he would be exposed to an event that would go beyond usual human experience – the bland catch-all that the manuals used to describe the onset of PTSD. In David's case, it induced feelings of terror and helplessness; he believed he was at risk of being killed. We were talking a lightning bolt on a massive scale.

The system that comprises our central and autonomic nervous system evolved out of an animal's fight-or-flight response to danger and was naturally transferred from animals to humans when we first walked out of the jungle. In this sense, the brain's primary purpose ought to be considered as a *survival* organ – one that removes us from danger – as opposed to a *thinking* organ.

When we are threatened, a dramatic change takes place in the body, organized by our central nervous system, that transforms us, as a friend and US colleague, Dr Sandy Bloom, put it so eloquently, into a 'different version of ourselves'. There is nothing we can do about this as it is instinctual: an unconsciously controlled reaction that shifts us from the state we are normally in – a state where our unconscious self is absorbed in feeding, digestion, reproduction and development tasks – into a mode where we suddenly have to deal with a life-threatening emergency; one which our ancestors recognized, instinctually, that only gave them two choices: to flee from the threat or stand and confront it.

To become this different a version of ourselves in the micro-seconds we require to get into fight-or-flight state, a number of neurotransmitter chemicals, mainly adrenaline and cortisol, as well as hormones, kick in to trigger huge changes in our bodies – mainly in the functions of certain critical organs. While this is going on, the brain releases noradrenaline, which triggers a simultaneous and instantaneous alerting effect on brain function. Here, the function of the amygdala, two almond-shaped groups of nuclei clustered within the medial temporal lobes in the front of the brain, is very important, along with the hippocampus, the anterior thalamic nuclei and the limbic cortex, which are all part of the limbic system, that is known to support a number of functions within the brain, including emotion, behaviour and long-term memory.

The amygdala is an amazing memory organ and is particularly attuned to danger. Anything that has threatened the individual will be logged by the amygdala, which will continue to remind the individual by constantly scanning for threats. When it receives a danger signal it sends an alert at 150 miles per hour to our adrenal glands, commanding them to release large amounts of adrenaline. At the same time, the adrenal glands release large amounts of gluco-corticoids, particularly cortisol, into the bloodstream, and these ensure that the initial response is maintained for as long as is required – minutes or hours. The brain also releases endorphins and enkephalins, the body's own opiates, that are designed to dull the way we feel pain.

Among a plethora of other hormonal reactions within the body, insulin production is switched off, because insulin promotes the storage of energy – precisely what we don't need in an all-or-nothing emergency. Adrenaline, noradrenaline, glucocorticoids and glucagon overturn the storage process, releasing glucose, proteins and fats into our bloodstream, giving our muscles the energy they need to respond instantly. Heart rate, blood pressure and respiration all go into over-drive to deliver an immediate energy boost to the muscles that need it. To do this, blood is diverted away from the digestive tract so that as much blood as possible is available to our arm and leg muscles. The mouth dries, acid secretion in the stomach shuts down and peristalsis, the movement of food through the intestines, slows.

The endorphins that have been released into the brain help to numb any feelings of pain inflicted on the body, but since traumatic stress is about extremes – either too much feeling or too little – the effect on memory becomes interesting. As a general rule, long-term stress has the effect of eroding memory but short-term stress enhances it, and in my RAF career I had certainly encountered two good examples of this.

I recalled Mr Arun, the MoD policeman I'd treated at Wroughton, who'd come off his shift one morning and crashed his car into a tractor-trailer. We didn't diagnose him as having PTSD because we didn't have the concept of it at the time – it was very new and we didn't see it for what it was. He didn't get better and we fell into the trap of saying, 'We're doing all we can to help this guy improve, but he's not getting any better, and therefore it's his fault.'

'Abnormal illness behaviour' is something that *does* happen throughout medicine and appears in all specialties. But psychiatrists do have the opportunity more often than others to consider a patient who is not responding to treatment in the 'normal' way, that is by recovering from their condition, to have a disorder of personality and to judge that there might be some advantage, however perverse, in maintaining the sick role.

When I say that psychiatrists 'do' have the opportunity to make such a judgement perhaps I should have said 'used to have', because of the new discoveries made about the nature of stress reactions since the research into PTSD began to take off in the early 1980s. Some form of dissociation is much more likely to be considered the underlying cause of such 'abnormal illness behaviour' now and it would be seen as an intrinsic part of the condition and carry 'meaning' rather than simply being dismissed in a blameful way.

Mr Arun had had a few seconds available to him before disaster struck, and he reported a flashed-life event. It got me interested in the phenomenon, as I had also come across it in an Air Force pilot who'd been flying a Jaguar, a jet fighter notorious for going into spins, soon after he got his into one and couldn't get out of it, no matter what he did. He'd tried all the usual procedures and was on the point of having to either eject or go in with the aircraft. It would be dodgy either way.

An image suddenly popped up in his head of a particular page in a manual that he'd read when he was in his early days of training: 'If you are in a spin and all else fails, try this.'

He described how he read the page as clearly as if it was in front of him. He followed the instructions, and he pulled the plane out of its spin.

What's happening when people do that, I came to realize, is that they're Googling their personal web for anything that's happened to them in the past that might save them.

People recounting a trauma will say, 'It was as if my whole life flashed in front of me – like a movie.' Traditionally, people have put a mystical slant on this, but to me it was simply evidence of the brain saying it isn't going to give up yet. It's trying its very best to pull out all the stops. This is the last desperate check: *is there anything that I've forgotten, that's not in the front of my mind but could be in the back of my mind, anything that I could do now to retrieve this situation and survive?*

There may be a page in a book, something you've read, a conversation you've had, some film of John Wayne leaping out of a stagecoach as it's heading towards a cliff, that tells you how to survive. All of those things will suddenly be taken into account, because it's chips-down time.

If there isn't anything, then people report a feeling that it was more a matter of unwinding their lives: *this is my life coming to an end, and therefore I'm remembering everything quickly to remind me of who I am.*

Sadly, in David Kinchin's case, he was reminded of all the wrong things.

David and another officer called Tom were in their patrol car when they drove into the middle of Wantage. Wantage, with its square and monument in the middle of the town, is as near picture-perfect an image of England as anyone could imagine. There were a few public houses around the periphery of the square and it was a hot summer's evening. People were milling around outside the pubs and beer had been taken. Someone approached the patrol vehicle and mentioned that there was a fight going on across the square – could they deal with it? David and Tom drove round the square and spotted the fight. There were two youths drunkenly knocking seven bells out of each other and being egged on by 20 others. David waded in and grabbed one of them, a guy with curly hair, at which point the crowd started to turn on them, maintaining that the Fuzz were picking on them.

The crowd swelled and surged forward. David and Tom decided to make a tactical withdrawal and attempted to arrest 'Curly'. By now, the crowd was trying to wrench Curly from David's grip and were landing some hefty blows on the two policemen. With his back to the patrol car, David found himself surrounded on three sides, clinging on to Curly and trying to defend himself from a rain of blows. He was knocked to his knees, but managed to get up again, reach into the car and send a desperate message to headquarters that they were under attack – by now, he estimated, by more than 60 youths, all of whom had streamed out of the pubs to join the riot.

By the time back-up arrived, just a handful of officers and a lone police dog, the crowd had swelled to 200. They closed in again on the hapless policemen, chanting, 'Get the pigs' and 'Kill the Bill'. It was only when a police helicopter and additional officers turned up that David and Tom, and their two prisoners, were able to make their tactical withdrawal: they piled into the patrol car, surrounded by the crowd, and attempted to start the car and get moving. But the crowd surged forward again and began to rock the car back and forth, attempting to tip it on its side.

It was at this moment that David recalled the television news clip about the incident in Northern Ireland. David, like everyone else who'd seen the news footage, remembered how the incident concluded. He quickly pushed the thoughts out of his mind, but the association had lodged. Both men had been murdered.

By now, David and Tom were in a very dangerous situation. The rocking movement of the car got worse. One of the prisoners started to cry. Somehow, Tom managed to drive the car forward and as a gap opened in the crowd he accelerated away to the police station.

Both officers suffered severe physical injuries. Both needed to be hospitalized. But only one of them developed PTSD and that was David.

I talked to him after reading his book, *PTSD – The Invisible Injury*, because our paths occasionally crossed. We appeared together on a radio programme when Matthew Parris, the journalist and broadcaster, came to Ticehurst to talk about trauma reactions and the treatment we were offering. It was then that I heard, for the first time, that David had been aware of the incident in Northern Ireland and had seen the footage on TV.

When the drunken mob closed in, he believed that he, too, was going to die.

Tellingly, the other officer had not seen those images, and had never believed it possible for a police officer in the UK to be dragged out of a car and killed. But David Kinchin's recollection of the shocking footage from the IRA funeral told him otherwise. He knew it could happen, and he was terrified.

David's book describes the struggle he faced to have his psychological injury recognized. He was dismissed in all the good old-fashioned ways as somebody who was pretty vulnerable for some reason – despite the fact that he'd had an exemplary record as a copper. David, in fact, went on to lecture extensively about his experiences and I know that a lot of people have benefited from them – validation that you can overcome your trauma, as David did, and move on.

Those treating him wouldn't have known better at the time. They wouldn't have realized that if everything possible had been known about him, then they would have taken into account something that had happened in his past, a memory that allowed him to believe he could be killed, that allowed the lightning bolt to get through.

And this is the problem with the Gatekeeper – Criterion A in *DSM-IV* and its antecedents.

There is a strong argument in trauma circles for the abandonment of Criterion A altogether. Does it matter what the event was that precipitated PTSD? Isn't what really matters simply that PTSD happened as a result of the exposure? If you're riding a horse and neither of your legs is broken, and the horse then falls over, lands on one of your legs and it breaks, you can make a direct causal link between the horse falling on your leg and it being broken. The horse has gone and is no longer relevant, but you can see the break on an X-ray.

The problem arises when people want to apportion blame and demand compensation from the horse.

In PTSD, it must be the case that whatever has imprinted as a result of the lightning bolt having struck is the substance of the re-experiencing. The re-experiencing informs you what the traumatic event was.

We can't say that PTSD is a universal reaction. We shouldn't be at all surprised when a collection of people is exposed to the same traumatic event and yet only a proportion of them develop PTSD. This is not the same, however, as saying, as they did in the First and Second World Wars, that the people who develop PTSD are weak and vulnerable in some way, and that the people who don't are not.

It's true only in the sense that the person who interprets the trauma in a traumatizing way is a person who actually has the capacity to make it into a traumatic event – whereas the person the same lightning bolt just bounces off doesn't.

The individual isn't vulnerable, it's the *meaning* they attribute to the experience that ultimately decides whether or not they develop a traumatized reaction. Some events, however, are so terrifying that they would produce PTSD in almost everyone.

Meaning can come from any point in that individual's history. Anything could have happened that has created a fear response or reservation – or indeed it might not even have happened, but the possibility has been feared. What's more, it could be something that's happened relatively recently and hasn't yet been processed, as in a case I encountered shortly after my meeting with David Kinchin: that of a firefighter who had been called out in Bristol on a dark and threatening night.

For a number of years I had been taking on medico-legal work: assessing people who had suffered some kind of trauma and were seeking compensation through the courts. My introduction to this work had come through Morgan O'Connell, the Royal Navy psychiatrist who had done so much since the Falklands conflict to bring the PTSD issue to the attention of the MoD. In the wake of Lockerbie, O'Connell had been approached by solicitors representing a number of Lockerbie trauma victims – citizens of the town mostly – who were involved in personal injury litigation. In a world that was then only just beginning to acknowledge PTSD, O'Connell's pioneering work went before him and he was often sought out to write these reports. Because he knew of my involvement in PTSD, Morgan, who was swamped by this work, approached me and a couple of other specialists in the field to help him tackle it. I wrote these reports with a view to recommending treatments, although I wasn't actually involved in the treatments themselves. Medico-legal work was very demanding and required taking periods of time off from my regular work to see it through. I'd started this when I was in the RAF and continued it when I took up my post at Ticehurst.

It was in this capacity that I came across Trev, the firefighter from Bristol.

Trev was the driver of a six-man tender that had been called out on a particularly nasty night in the Bristol area. These tenders were known to be poor at taking corners, and while Trev was an experienced driver, the conditions that night exacerbated his vehicle's poor handling qualities and on a sharp corner it overturned. Tragically, a car was coming the other way and the tender toppled over on top of it. Trev, who was still visibly shaken by the experience – even though it had occurred several years earlier – described to me what happened next.

'Me and my mates weren't hurt, which somehow made it worse. We were supposed to be the rescuers that night, but we became the perpetrators of another tragedy. It was terrible, terrible . . .'

He hadn't been able to work since the accident and I could see why. The poor bloke hadn't been sleeping. There were black rings under his eyes and a couple of days' worth of stubble on his chin. As he rubbed it anxiously, the rasping sound filled the air between us.

'The car was almost completely crushed by the tender. They had to get a specialist vehicle to lift it off. When they did, it was impossible to see in. They brought in another team and cut the roof off. I was helping – in fact, I was right by the driver's side of the vehicle when they lifted it off.'

He faltered. I waited.

He took a deep breath and carried on. 'Her face was tilted skyward, fully spotlit by the emergency lights they'd brought in to illuminate the scene. She was the only occupant of the vehicle. She was dead, but there was scarcely a mark on her – at least, not on her face. Her eyes were wide open and it was like she was staring at me.'

'How old was she?' I asked.

'Well, that was the thing. She must have been in her early sixties.'

'Was that significant?'

He nodded.

'Why?'

'Because she looked just like my mother. My mother had been in her early sixties when she—' He stopped and composed himself. 'When she died.'

I knew then that we had hit upon the nub of the issue. I asked him when his mother had died and he told me it had been less than a year before the accident. She had developed cancer, but in the end had slipped away quite suddenly. He was still mourning her death when the crash occurred. This was perfectly normal. He had not been depressed and he was perfectly able to do his job. But he had been grieving for his mother and it was his mother's face that he had seen when they had removed the roof of the car that his tender had crushed. It was the hair of the victim, which was almost identical in colour and style to the way his mother had worn her hair, that established this emotional link in his mind. This had been his lightning bolt.

Trev developed a really severe PTSD reaction, even though the other five firefighters were fine. They developed shock reactions that petered out, but his didn't. It was a prime example of a real life event, in this case the death of a loved one, which can occur in all our lives, but which just happens to be lying dormant and can be fired up at any time.

'But for' is the prefix to many a question in compensation cases. 'But for that individual being involved in that accident, would he or she have developed PTSD?'

The answer in Trev's case was very simple. No, he wouldn't have done. He was coping quietly with his grief. His mother had died of natural causes. These things happen. But for the accident, however, he wouldn't have then been catapulted into a new scenario in terms of his mental state, and that was the PTSD. Equally, it could be said, but for the bereavement he might not have been so affected by the resemblance of the dead woman in the car to his mother that he developed PTSD. He was functioning perfectly well up to that point, but then something horrible happened and PTSD was the result.

What if I had found on examining him that he had no intrusive images, no re-experiencing of the event, but instead had re-experiences of his mother's death? I could not have attributed the PTSD to the accident quite so easily. The weight would very much have been on his mother's death as the original trauma. The nasty accident had exacerbated things, brought them out into the open, made it more difficult for him to function. The accident would have had a reinforcing effect, but it wouldn't have been the primary trauma unless he had intrusive recollections of it.

The medico-legal world has often been accused of everything from inventing PTSD as a gimmick so people can get their hands on compensation, to blurring the issues so that a judge might make a ruling on the basis that nobody has persuaded him or her that this person felt he was going to die in this incident, and therefore he or she must take the defendant's point of view, that this is not PTSD. It is, instead, an adjustment disorder.

An adjustment disorder, by definition, means that you can have any package of symptoms you want as a reaction to an event, including reactions identical to PTSD, but if the inciting incident is not something which fulfils Criterion A, then the resulting condition can't be PTSD. It is an argument often raised by people acting as expert psychiatric witnesses for the defence.

My own point of view is that the interpretation of the impact of the event may or may not be complete, but if a person has been involved in an event that doesn't appear to fulfil Criterion A and yet they have experienced intensive recollections of the trauma, avoidance of reminders and hyper-arousal, then it must have actually been a traumatic event, whatever the onlooker thinks.

If the lawyers don't make the case strongly enough to the judge, and the judge doesn't have the information to put into the ruling that this person thought they were going to die at the time of the event, or that they felt overwhelming fear, or that they felt helpless or were in a state of terror, he or she may not by law be able to find them to be suffering from PTSD – because one of the major criteria, the Gatekeeper Criterion, isn't satisfied.

You're up a gum tree in a case like that, but the counter-argument I always use is that we don't know what went on in the person's head at the time of the event. For example, I had heard of people involved in the most horrific accidents who somehow managed to stagger from the wreckage to make a 999 call on their mobile phone. What was going on inside their heads as they made these calls?

From my own experience of the Invisible Girl or the woman who'd seen the Stuka bomb land at her feet, I could envisage these accident victims sitting at the side of the road, thinking, because they're so dissociated, that they're dead. They try to make contact with people, not because they're fully aware of what they're doing, but because they're trying to prove to themselves that they're alive, when they don't know whether they actually are or whether they're like Patrick Swayze in *Ghost*. They'll make a phone call just to establish that they can use a phone, and that somebody will recognize their voice and confirm they're alive.

That would be a difficult point to get over to a judge. The judge would see this behaviour as it appeared on the surface, as being the actions of somebody fully in control, not somebody who is feeling helpless. They're phoning for help, therefore by definition they're not helpless, and they appear to be fully aware of what's happened and what's required. In the judge's eyes, therefore, Criterion A is not fulfilled and the person can't have PTSD.

I try to make the point that there are things going on in people's minds which we're not privy to – and nor are they, because they're dissociated. If you ask them what happened immediately after the incident, they may not be able to remember that they made a phone call.

The whole area of the definition of Criterion A and the significance for the diagnosis of PTSD – critically significant – especially in the precise field of the law where definitions are crucially important, was a minefield and I found myself right in the thick of it. The common meaning, though, is that only the individual exposed to the event is aware of what the experience meant. Therefore, it is not really possible for an observer to decide whether or not an event has been 'traumatic' or not.

Not only did I find myself somewhat out of step with my fellow professionals on the link between Criterion A and dissociation to PTSD and the medico-legal world, but on a far wider definition of what PTSD actually was. I was conscious that the case of the Invisible Girl had opened up a gulf between where my thinking was in relation to other trauma professionals, both nationally and internationally, although thankfully I still retained the full support of the management team at Ticehurst. But I was also beginning to think of chronic PTSD differently. Chronic PTSD, far from being an illness, my accumulating experience was telling me, should be viewed as a survival tool with a curious and unwelcome side-effect; a bit like a piece of anti-virus software: very effective at what it does, but with the corollary of slowing down the hard drive. If you've got something as crucially important to your future life as a survival reaction that you don't understand, then you're not going to make any progress, you're going to stay stuck. This is where my thinking had got to after a couple of years' experience at Ticehurst.

If you can say: this thing happened – a terrible thing – and it was a supreme challenge to my survival, but I now *understand* what happened and I'm going to build it into my database so that I'll be better able to survive in the future, then you'll be in good shape. You can carry on with increased resilience and the confidence that you're going to be better able to deal with things in the future because you know what to do. You know what you've done before and, indeed, you can actually come to *rely* on that experience because you've survived it.

It's like a driving test. If you fail it, you can always do it again. You can regroup and you can say, 'Well, I didn't do that very well, reversing into a parking space, but I'll practise, and I'll pass next time around.' You can go confidently into the future without being too hampered by your inability to understand what happened. But if it's survival we're talking about, you can't; particularly, I was finding, if your experience had happened in childhood.

If you're a child who is being repeatedly traumatized by an abuser, your emotional maturity will cease to develop. The same applies if a child is involved in some horrendous accident in a car. If they aren't able to process it, they won't be able to face the future, to develop into a future form of themselves. That's why we see middle-aged people who behave like children when they're under pressure or stressed. Their defence mechanisms haven't got into a mature phase of development. They can't make progress beyond childhood because they don't believe the world is safe enough for them to poke their necks out and explore further.

It's rather lucky, then, that children are incredibly adaptive. They learn a lot very quickly. They're also inventive and imaginative. That might be why children's brains are adapted towards 'magical thinking', why they have the capacity to imagine their way out of difficult situations.

If a child is traumatized in childhood, he or she usually acclimatizes and gets on with their life. It's only when there's repetition, a drip-drip-drip of unpleasantness or fear, that they give up. If a child is beaten up once by his dad, if his dad is blind drunk and the child gets the worst of it on one occasion, then the child will usually put that down to experience and say to himself, 'When Daddy comes home in that condition, I shouldn't dance up and down and say, "Mummy, Mummy, come and look, Daddy's drunk again."' The child adjusts.

But if the father gets drunk regularly and comes home and beats up the child, and the child feels totally helpless as a result and has run out of ideas of how to modify his or her behaviour, to adapt to this circumstance, then that child will tend to develop a mental state where travelling forward becomes extremely unsafe and they'll tend to rely upon what they've already become. They won't have the confidence to search and discover new things. They'll continue to be like children. It often defines, too, what profession they choose in life.

It's an over-simplification, but, as I'd already seen with Jill, the woman whose shells had so dramatically collapsed in on her at Wroughton, there could be thought to be three main defence mechanisms in childhood: hysteria, paranoia and obsessive-compulsive behaviour. If we look at the types of adult who would best be served by those particular defences, what do we find? Taking hysteria, the dramatic one, the noisy one, it's perhaps no surprise that a lot of actors and actresses are said to be hysterical. They're also often quite vulnerable. Although they're great when they're playful, they can be a real pain in the arse when they're bad-tempered. They're inconsolable, they don't respond to discussion as you would expect an adult to do. They're not problem-solvers. When things are going well for them, everything is great and they're fun to be with. But when things are going against them, they're very difficult to be with. Just like it's great to be with a child when the child is on good form, but difficult to be around them when they're feeling oppressed or upset.

Who would benefit from having a paranoid edge to their personality? People who need to be suspicious. In which case, a legal career might be for them. Becoming a police officer might be another outcome. Can police officers behave in a childlike way when stressed? Yes, they can. There's a well-recognized phenomenon of the police officer wanting to get his man or woman: that if there's a need for somebody to be brought to book for a crime, they sometimes twist the evidence or leave out crucial information in order to make their case.

This happens especially when the public is demanding a head on a platter for a particular murder or crime. Look what happened with Madeleine McCann. The heat was on the Portuguese police and they reacted in a way that people became highly critical of. The neighbour who happened to offer up some telling information became a prime suspect. When that didn't pan out, they turned the spotlight on the McCanns themselves, and although we don't yet know who perpetrated that particular crime, it doesn't look as if it was any of the three of them. The police's paranoia was aimed at them: 'We haven't got enough to hang you with yet, but you're going to have to walk around with this sign round your neck saying "I'm a suspect," until you break down or behave so oddly it's tantamount to an admission of guilt.'

Finally, the people in this world who are control freaks are vulnerable if they rely heavily on obsessive-compulsive defences, just by dint of the fact that we live in such an imperfect world. Things tend to go wrong, and when things go wrong and you're a control freak, you've got a problem.

Who are this type? Who are the controllers of this world? Air Force pilots, for one. When you crack the ostrich shell, the hard exterior, when you get through that, you find there's a lot of childlike stuff inside which makes people act like children, use those particular defences. During the build-up to the air war in the Gulf in January 1991, the pilots I'd seen sitting around waiting for the balloon to go up were very nervous, and they didn't appear to be particularly mature. They were frightened by what was happening and they didn't behave like Tom Cruise in *Top Gun*.

I realized at this time that I had very different ideas about the meaning of PTSD compared with other professionals who were extremely experienced in the field. They, by and large, saw PTSD as a psychopathology – as an illness. Lockerbie had shown me that it couldn't be. I'd known the mountain rescuers before they'd gone to the scene of the crash and assessed them to be some of the toughest people, mentally and physically, on the planet. This was why Lockerbie had been so life-changing for me. It was difficult – impossible, actually – for me to believe they had developed a psychopathology. My whole experience of PTSD in the raw had been with people who weren't really what I termed 'patients'. I saw it as a survival reaction in people who were normal and resilient, who were having a difficult time challenging this particular assault, this intrusion into their lives. They were struggling to absorb new but important information with a high survival emphasis into their understanding of the world. Some other professionals, but not many, saw this the same way I did – which was why my encounter with the clinical psychologists within the Australian armed forces had been invaluable to me.

Why was this? Why, I wondered, was I seeing things differently? Part of the reason, I concluded, was that I was one of the few professionals working with groups.

We saw a broad range of trauma survivors and, by and large, we put them together in the same group. So, someone who had had chronic PTSD for 60 years was likely to find themselves with someone else who had had it for a year or less.

Something about being in a group allowed these people to process their trauma within the same time frame, which was extraordinary. This merely reinforced my view that they weren't mentally ill. If they were mentally ill, their faculties wouldn't allow them to process at this uniform pace. Trauma survivors just needed to feel safe and in control to allow the process to begin, which is what Ticehurst and the groups gave them.

But because Ticehurst was one of the very few institutions around the world that ran groups, this insight was rare. I wasn't surprised, therefore, that I found myself out on a limb.

The non-pathologizing view of PTSD was hugely significant to the military, because if you told a soldier he had a mental illness he'd most likely fall apart. He relied on his mental faculties not just for work but for his very survival. To be able to sell PTSD to someone in the military, therefore, as a natural phenomenon, as a struggle to process new information, enabled soldiers to see it in a totally different light – one that bore no stigma. But on this point I was still in a minority. Other professionals were seeing patients in clinics after they'd been referred, and they were making a diagnosis of PTSD from a clinical point of view. Naturally, they would tend to see them as having illnesses. I was seeing them in a different context: as people who were struggling to come to terms with an overwhelming experience that challenged their assumptions about life.

Chapter 17

Defending the Group

By 1995, the prediction of my former CO at Wroughton that my research into PTSD would be of more use to the RAF outside the service than in had started to ring true. The medical world within the armed services was shrinking. First, the government shut Ely, then RAF Halton, then the Cambridge Military Hospital at Aldershot, then the Princess Alexandra RAF Hospital at Wroughton.

But it didn't stop there. The Royal Navy Hospital at Haslar was the next casualty and even the Queen Elizabeth Military Hospital at Woolwich, the Army's biggest hospital, was under threat. All the British Army of the Rhine hospitals in Germany were shut down. A brand-new, state-of-the-art facility that had been built at Iserlohn was simply handed to the Germans as a gift.

The closures were for political and funding reasons. In 1990, the government had published its 'Options for Change' defence review, which spelled out the savings that the armed forces could reap in the wake of the fall of the Berlin Wall – the so-called peace dividend. After the Gulf War, these cost-saving exercises rippled progressively through the infrastructure of the military. By the mid-1990s, it was reasoned that the Territorial Army, the part-time TA, could take on additional roles, one of which was an increased medical burden via the role of TA-trained doctors and nursing staff. It was rubbish, of course, to expect these people to administer as effectively as full-time, dedicated staff, but then this wasn't about common sense: it was about political expediency. Cuts needed to be made and, as a result, military medical care suffered. It was the start of a slippery slope that has extended into the present day.

Though I let out a private sigh of relief that I'd got out of the RAF when I had, I felt an overwhelming sadness too.

I'd already heard about the diminution of PTSD-related work since my departure from Wroughton. What would happen in the wake of the latest round of cuts? To justify Chris Sharples's faith in me, I redoubled my efforts at Ticehurst to get to grips with the phenomenon – its causes and its cures.

For me, the next three or four years were a period of consolidation. The ideas that I'd brought from the military world into civilian psychiatry were bearing fruit. No matter what the MoD thought of it, the group programme at Ticehurst was acknowledged as a legitimate front-line treatment for PTSD. The trauma community was still divided over whether group or one-to-one treatment was more effective, but I had come to realize that this was how it was going to be – and rightly so: I never saw the group as a panacea for trauma. There would always be circumstances where one-on-one treatments would be right for certain individuals.

It wasn't easy to organize the groups either: it was a nightmare, in fact, getting half a dozen or so people to agree to attend on a certain date, and to be free for a fortnight, but whenever we did, the success rate stayed high. Pat Young, my secretary at Ticehurst, became the high priestess of group organization, and was very much part of our team.

This was doubly encouraging, given the fact we had more complex patients to treat at Ticehurst than I'd ever encountered in the military. The trauma reaction we were attending to might appear to be just to a road traffic accident, but quite often these people had long track records of psychiatric problems. In the RAF, our patients tended to be robust and resilient and had usually experienced a single traumatic event. Occasionally we were thrown curve balls, but on average they were more straightforward patients to treat. Their trauma was normally much more clearly delineated. I was so impressed by the way the new Ticehurst group team worked together. Bo Mills, Ian Dennis, Tosin Clairmonte, Margaret Egner, Stu Johnson, Sheila Davidson and Heather Robyn were fantastic colleagues.

I was by no means complacent about things – there was so much about PTSD we still didn't know – but in many ways it could be said that we'd arrived. The Ticehurst group programme was well known to outside psychiatrists and those writing medical and legal reports, and we got an increasing number of referrals.

I gave quite a few talks on PTSD at this time. These spanned the medical, military and medico-legal professions and reflected my journey into the PTSD labyrinth thus far. Our experiences with the hostages seemed to be of particular interest, the message being that John, Terry and the others had acquired PTSD in the process of survival and that what we had to do was to allow them to find a way of regaining control of their lives by relieving them of the need for it. Central to everything was the idea that PTSD was a condition, not an illness. And I wanted to get over the fact, too, that it wasn't all negative: that that which didn't kill you, as the adage went, really could make you stronger.

As I'd found when I went to Australia, there was a lot of support in pockets of the PTSD community for these ideas. In fact, I was very much enjoying this part of the group dynamic – which really did appear to conform to the 'forming', 'storming', 'norming', 'performing' and 'mourning' phases that had been identified by social scientists when groups or, for that matter, new ideas came to be formed.

The forming stage is when everyone is probing other members of the group to see whether they can be included. Storming is the next phase, when members jockey for position, leadership or their particular role within the group. Norming follows: when the group agrees on ways of functioning so as to guide their collective behaviour towards effective performance. Performing is when group members cooperate with one another to achieve the goals of the group and meet each other's needs. Mourning is the end phase, when the bonds between the group members loosen as it eventually comes to disband.

It seemed to me that our loose affiliation of non-pathologizing PTSD 'experts' was in the very earliest stages, the forming part, and I was relishing the exchange of ideas. I should have known, from the pattern of the model, that there would be turbulence ahead.

I wasn't alone in promoting the idea that dissociation was an extremely important part of the PTSD equation. Indeed, there were people who believed so fervently that dissociation was a part of trauma that they set up their own society, the International Society for the Study of Dissociation, ISSD. They had their own conference distinct from the annual trauma conference organized by its big brother, the International Society of Traumatic Stress Studies (ISTSS). My own feeling was that the two ought to be much more closely linked.

Where I was still very much on my own was on the link between dissociation and out-of-body experience, the breakthrough I felt I'd made with the Invisible Girl. When I brought this up at conferences and lectures, my fellow professionals seemed to respect the fact that I believed I was on to something, but it was just too 'out there' for most of them to engage in meaningful dialogue on the subject.

There was no textbook on trauma yet. The nearest thing to it that existed was a book filled with loose chapters penned by a small but growing community – people like me, Sandy McFarlane, Stuart Turner, Jeffrey Mitchell and Bessel van der Kolk.

But the Invisible Girl was my 'discovery of penicillin' moment. It added a layer of understanding for me that I knew I had to build upon.

Meanwhile, the debate raged: was PTSD primarily an anxiety disorder or a dissociative one, more to do with disconnection?

And what about those who – right at the other end of the spectrum – talked about attachment being a central theme in the development of PTSD? This was a theory championed by Dr Felicity de Zulueta, an eminent psychiatrist and psychotherapist in the field. Human beings needed to have certain attachments in order to mature normally, they argued – and they had to hold on to them throughout their life. A loss of attachment would be a trauma, because it was the loss of something fundamentally important.

Attachment was well understood from work that James Brown did at the Institute of Psychiatry in the Maudsley Hospital in South London, in the fifties and sixties. His papers were classics of their time. One clearly showed that if a person had suffered a bereavement in childhood, they were vulnerable to developing depressions as an adult – particularly if they were female.

Other work in America had shown that if a person suffered a

significant separation in childhood, then if they were challenged in adulthood it would manifest as panic attacks.

The studies also supported what Brown had said: that if a person suffered a loss in childhood – not necessarily a death but that a parent, perhaps, had gone off and developed a new relationship and never visited again – then those people, as adults, were more prone to developing depressions. What happened in childhood left its mark. It might never be unveiled if a person had a comfortable adulthood, but if there were challenges, then there would be repercussions. The implication, I believed, was that a neurological circuit, a behavioural loop, was laid down in childhood, and lay dormant until it was re-excited later in life by a particular toxic stimulus. It was Pavlovian conditioning.

What happened to you in adulthood was related to what happened to you as a child. The lightning bolt's meaning and impact depended on the personal CV of the individual it was striking and puncturing.

By 1980, the general feeling was that PTSD was a universal, normal reaction in normal people facing abnormal circumstances. Flashbacks, avoidance, hyper-arousal: they were all common. You couldn't have PTSD without those features showing themselves, but the development of those features, the traumatization process, was much more individual.

The original studies suggested that people would develop PTSD if exposed to events or provocateurs too big to resist – like natural or manmade disasters. In the 1980s, it began to be recognized that people responded to less tumultuous events like road traffic accidents, assault or rape in much the same way.

The range became so wide that the more sceptical critics began to think that everybody could have PTSD, to the point that PTSD almost became the only psychiatric diagnosis you could make. If somebody losing his or her job can develop PTSD, then why do we bother to call it anything? If it can happen to anybody, is it part of the normal human condition? Why bother trying to diagnose people as being depressed or having other forms of anxiety when PTSD would cover everything?

A lot of it stemmed from the fact that the legal profession had positively embraced the whole subject of PTSD. They could finally

give a name to the psychological injuries people had suffered following exposure to a traumatic event. They could make it 'scientific'
enough to form the basis of a claim. The ambulance-chasing
fraternity was having a field day. The cardinal feature of PTSD is
recurrent, distressing recollections of the traumatic event and this
serves to identify a specific event or events as being the experience
that caused the reaction. A causative link could be identified and this
was very useful in personal injury litigation. Depressive reactions
and other forms of anxiety reaction such as panic anxiety, phobic
anxiety, generalized anxiety and obsessive-compulsive disorders are
less easy to link to definite triggers.

That scepticism continued in some quarters well into the 1990s –
but not at Ticehurst, where we became more and more widely
recognized for our work. We even came to the attention of the BBC,
which wanted to make a documentary based on the group treatment
programme.

On one level, it was good to be able to use the medium of
television to demonstrate that PTSD was a treatable condition and
that it was very possible for people to recover from it even if they
had suffered for years. However, the film-makers really wanted to
film the groups as they worked during the initial two-week residential phase of the programme. They believed that the group
participants would get used to cameras inside the room and the
concept of their work being recorded. They also believed that
the effect of the intrusion would be minimal or even non-existent.
My instincts told me otherwise. The initial phase was designed to
bring people into a place of safety, a sanctuary. It provided an opportunity to open up the PTSD capsule. If the trauma had occurred
some time previously then patients would be bound to feel apprehensive about opening the capsule because they might not know
precisely what the contents were.

Time was dedicated at the beginning of the group session to
facilitate the creation of safe relationships within the group. This
would minimize the apprehension and emphasize the need for
confidentiality.

A major part of recovery was the group participants' re-creation
of feelings of safety and being in control. 'What is said in the room
stays in the room' was a powerful maxim. We realized it would be

impossible for group participants to feel safe, feel that they were in control of what might be a cathartic emotional experience, and to preserve confidentiality, if cameras were in the room. A vitally important part of the group process was to share traumatic experiences and their meaning with other individuals who were less likely to be sceptical and rejecting because of their natural empathy and understanding of the traumatic process.

The creation of a safe sanctuary to open up the individual capsules which contained each unique trapped trauma was a multi-layered process involving place, people and procedure. First, the place itself had to be right and Ticehurst *was* just right, as it ought to be after 200 years of best practice. Group members had to feel safe with each other and also with the dedicated group facilitators. They needed to know that opening the capsule was going to be a private experience within a sympathetic group. Almost all of the group participants had already experienced the scepticism that existed 'out there' in the big, bad world. We were trying to create an 'in here' place that was the opposite: totally sympathetic and impervious to outside influences.

We realized that the sanctuary would be disrupted by the presence of cameras and that the film threatened to blow apart the confidentiality that was essential for the group to work. It would share very personal material with potentially unsympathetic individuals and organizations who weren't in our place of safety.

Eventually, we did go ahead with the film but no cameras were allowed in the room. Filming of group participants was limited to interviewing them after they had opened the capsule and had processed the material inside safely. In this way, the filming became a valedictory record of their progress and was of benefit to their recovery rather than a hindrance.

The film was shown on BBC1 as part of its *Inside Story* series and attracted a lot of interest. Because PTSD was still a controversial subject, not all the feedback we received was positive, but it was difficult to avoid the conclusion that group participants with established PTSD, some of whom had had the condition for many years, could go through a process which did not take very long and from which they emerged with much more confidence in themselves and their relationships. The trauma that had trapped them had been processed and the energy released had provided them with a bridge into the future; a future filled with hope and positivity.

We ran the Ticehurst groups in the same way as we had the tried and tested Wroughton model. A paper had recently been published in the *British Journal of Psychiatry* about the PTSD group programme at Wroughton, which described the process in detail and demonstrated the high success rates we'd been achieving. All of the serving military personnel with PTSD who'd been through the process had returned to their military roles, both combatant and non-combatant. Also, none of them was involved in disruption or loss of important relationships. There were no broken marriages or engagements; indeed, the evidence was to the contrary – that new relationships had developed during the year of recovery.

This was very interesting because it indicated that not only were our group participants healing, but the ripple effect with PTSD that had proved to have a toxic influence on intimate relationships was also disappearing as a result of the group process. A little thought would probably lead to the impression that it *should* do so because the group process was basically about sharing previously undisclosed or unarticulated material with others in a safe environment, but here was the proof of the pudding: real, hard evidence that the group experience had an enduring influence out there – in the big, bad world.

Setting up the group programme at Ticehurst effectively transplanted it from a military setting to a civilian hospital and we were pleased that it could still generate the same good results.

This demonstrated that there was something inherently constructive within the method, as opposed to success stemming simply from the personnel, the hospital layout or the fact the treatment had been military-to-military. To this end, we had to remind people that not all of the patients admitted into the group programme at Wroughton had been serving military personnel. Some of them had been reservists, some were military veterans, some were individuals with no military experience at all and some were individuals who had simply been caught up in trauma and did not belong to 'trauma-seeking' organizations, if you could call them that – organizations such as the armed forces and the police, fire and ambulance services – where danger was a part of the job.

Because we created groups with both male and female patients, we had one male and one female facilitator in each group. This seemed to create a more balanced group environment and also contributed to feelings of safety for the participants.

My experience of debriefing PoWs after the First Gulf War and the released hostages from Beirut in 1991 had taught me that 'secondary debriefing' on a regular basis was absolutely essential for the welfare of the primary debriefers. Group facilitators in the PTSD group pro- grammes were doing the same work as primary debriefers and they needed to be supported. Secondary debriefing allowed them to offload their experiences in the group.

In 1997, my former partner at Wroughton, Walter Busuttil, left the RAF and joined me at Ticehurst. The value of his energy, enthusiasm and experience was inestimable. Sue Pittman, who had introduced me to Colonel Wal Hall and Australia, also came to work at Ticehurst where she was of great help to us. Sue had been a social worker in Canberra, Australia, and had established a debriefing service for emergency service workers.

By now, I felt we'd proved we could take the group programme to the moon if we wanted to. We had a template that could be set down anywhere and it would work. This is not to say that I was opposed to one-on-one methods like CBT for treating PTSD. Far from it. There was still no clear treatment leader for tackling PTSD. Group therapy and one-to-one psychotherapy were not opposing forces but alterna- tives. Furthermore, our group programmes were based on cognitive behavioural principles. But for our part, we just knew that the group treatment programme was successful; that unquestionably it worked.

And then, in 1997, came the bombshell. Jonathan Bisson, an ex- Army psychiatrist working in Cardiff, published a paper on the treatment of burns victims that appeared to blow debriefing out of the water. Bisson, a contemporary of mine and a close ally during the Gulf War in 1991, had studied a hundred consecutively admitted victims to the burns unit at Cardiff Royal Infirmary.

At random, 50 were allocated for debriefing and 50 received no debriefing or any form of extra psychological support at all beyond the usual sensible and human support from the nurses and medical staff. Bisson's study claimed to find that there was no difference between the two groups, that there was no evidence that debriefing was of any benefit and even went so far as to suggest that debriefing might actually do some harm. It did concede, however, that the people who'd had the debriefing felt that they'd benefited from it, and felt that if they had an opportunity to go through the whole thing again they'd prefer to be debriefed rather than not.

I'd had an inkling something was in the air. At a meeting of the UK Trauma Group before the study was published, Stuart Turner set up an informal discussion as usual on a topic of choice. It was a *menu du jour*, a look-in-the-fridge-and-see-what-you-have arrangement, depending on who was there.

I asked if we could debate debriefing. The *British Medical Journal* – not a psychiatric journal per se – had carried an overview article written recently by Sandy McFarlane and Beverley Raphael from Australia. I had always felt indebted to Professor Raphael, who had written about disaster management and whose work had provided much-needed guidance for the debriefing we had undertaken in early 1989 with the RAF mountain rescue workers after Lockerbie. Beverley Raphael went on to publish one of the seminal works in psychological trauma, *When Disaster Strikes*, in 1986. I had also met up with Sandy McFarlane, who had spent some time in my native Edinburgh during his psychiatric training. I held him in great regard for his work dealing with the survivors of bush fires in Australia.

'Everyone's doing debriefing,' the two writers said. 'It's the flavour of the day. It would be good to do some studies on it.' They hadn't said that it did or didn't work; just that it was something that was increasingly being used but hadn't been empirically tested. They offered the opinion that people like to feel they can do something when disaster strikes.

Jonathan Bisson stood up and said that we couldn't study debriefing because it wasn't evidence-based and we only discussed evidence-based topics at our meetings.

That was like a red rag to a bull. 'Of course it's not evidence-based,' I said. 'Nor is treatment of pain with aspirin. No one knows exactly how that works either, but it doesn't invalidate it as a treatment.'

To my surprise, nobody else in the group wanted to discuss it either, so I could do nothing but shrug and leave it.

A few months later, Jonathan published his paper: 'Randomised controlled trial of psychological debriefing for victims of acute burn trauma', *British Journal of Psychiatry*, 1997. He must have had it in preparation at the time of the meeting. It would have taken quite a while to gather together a hundred patients.

The methodology of the paper was apparently well constructed. It was a randomized controlled trial, the gold standard. To demonstrate that something is evidence-based, you have to show in an RCT that the treatment under trial is superior to other treatments and/or the placebo effect. So it becomes an evidence-based treatment, which of course we all wanted to use – no one wants to use something that might be flawed or harmful.

As soon as I started reading, however, I could see that this paper was riddled with errors. The problem was, it was now out there, and the journal was published monthly – it would be an agonizing four weeks before the damage could be undone.

The publication put us on the back foot at Ticehurst. We were using a treatment which depended upon disclosure – the first few days of our group treatment procedure were all about debriefing to get the stuff out into the open: 'What happened to you and how do you feel about it?' Three of us actively working in the PTSD programme at Ticehurst – Walter Busuttil, Sue Pittman and myself – wrote a critique and fired it off to the *British Journal of Psychiatry*.

We opened the next month's issue expecting to find our letter and perhaps a rebuttal by Bisson, but there was nothing. I phoned the editor. He said they were going to publish our letter but wanted to give Bisson and his co-workers full opportunity to answer the questions we asked.

His answer finally appeared three months later.

Our main objection had been the fact that Bisson was testing psychological debriefing without using the same technique we did, which had been devised by Jeffrey Mitchell in the USA and was called Critical Incident Stress Debriefing, CISD. Mitchell's breakthrough work in 1983 had proposed defusing and debriefing as psychological first aid and follow-up tools after an appropriate event.

'Defusing' was the term given to the process of talking it out. It allowed victims and workers the opportunity to ventilate about their disaster or trauma-related memories, stresses, losses and methods of coping, and to be able to do so in a safe and supportive environment, guided by professionals. The defusing process usually involved informal and impromptu sessions immediately after or even during the event, to help people release thoughts and feelings that might not otherwise be expressed. Suppression or repression of this kind of highly charged material might lead to the development of any number of stress-related physical and/or mental conditions. It could be as simple as greeting a victim who is waiting at a disaster centre with a hot drink, or playing a game with a child in an emergency shelter.

Because the allotted time was often very brief, the defusing session was simply a starting point. Further intervention was frequently required and this could be anything from offering ongoing support to scheduling and providing formal debriefing sessions. This was the point at which people like me and places like Ticehurst began to do our stuff.

Psychological debriefing, Mitchell said, was often a good first step for helping secondary victims process their direct involvement with traumatic events. Debriefings were formal meetings, in small groups. The sessions required a block of time that was at least two to two-and-a-half hours in length, particularly if a process such as Mitchell's formal CISD model was used.

The Mitchell process was designed for secondary victims – police, firefighters, paramedics, rescue teams, etc. – to help them overcome the emotional after-effects of critical incidents. Sessions were usually held within the first 24–72 hours after the traumatic event, with follow-up sessions as needed. Given the nature of disasters, we do not always identify all the victims that quickly. Fortunately, Mitchell proved, the debriefing process is still beneficial even when the sessions are held long after the event.

Bisson's researchers only very broadly carried out what could be called debriefing, and yet the conclusions they drew cited it as a technique that didn't work.

Jeffrey Mitchell's research was specifically not about the primary victims, the people involved in, say, a road traffic accident. They were brought together in teams of police officers or firefighters, say, where they knew each other, and they went through a process of debriefing between 24 and 72 hours after the event. That was the way Mitchell said it should happen, yet the people admitted to the burns unit in Cardiff – Bisson's examinees – were not secondary victims but primary victims. They were the people actually injured.

It was the first of many fundamental errors.

The second was that at 24–72 hours after being admitted into a burns unit, victims were very likely to be in pain and receiving major painkilling drugs, probably opiates, which would alter their mental states. They would hardly be in a fit state to go through a debriefing. What was more, as individual victims they'd have been debriefed as individuals, not a group.

It went from bad to worse. The people doing the debriefing in Bisson's study were inexperienced. Jonathan did only some of them himself, and the majority were undertaken by nurses who'd received just half a day's training in the principles of trauma and psychological debriefing. To me, that was like condensing a whole medical degree into a week.

The problems didn't even end there. The next mistake was that the Bisson debriefings could last for anything between half an hour and three hours. Mitchell himself talked about debriefing lasting between two-and-a-half to three hours, and sometimes even double that. Half an hour was just about enough to get to know the person's name and address. And we already knew that time had to be invested and wisely used to establish feelings of safety and control.

Bisson's work measured PTSD symptoms in the same way that we did, with the CAPS scale – but only after the first and only debrief and then once more at 13 months. Bisson demonstrated in his statistical analysis of those figures that the people who were debriefed fared no better than those who had not been debriefed. He also said that, in some cases, it was notable that those who had been debriefed had much higher scores than the average. Overall, he claimed to have proved there was no clear indication that debriefing worked.

Bisson's conclusion was that the practice should be abandoned, and shouldn't be used again until there was clear evidence that it did work.

Our letter pointed out the gaping holes in their methodology: the fact that something that should be a group exercise was applied one-to-one; the fact that it was being used on primary victims instead of secondary; the fact that the people who did these debriefings were not experienced debriefers or even psychologically orientated health professionals; the fact that the victims were probably on pain relief or in pain, both of which would alter their mental state; the fact that they were still undergoing operations, with skin grafts and so forth. You don't know what the end result of a trauma is going to be if it's a burn trauma, until the last operation has been done, until you know what you've got left, what you look like, whether you'll be able to walk. You might not at the beginning know if you're going to lose a hand or an arm. As a result, what they were applying here was not psychological debriefing.

In summary, we wrote, it was unfair for Bisson to say that this particular technique hadn't worked. As sometimes happens in medical science, a single paper had skewed the whole field. What worried me most was the fact that we had psychological debriefing principles at the core of our treatment. If we were treating people sent to us by lawyers who were still going through the process of litigation, I was concerned that the defendants could claim in court that psychological debriefing was invalid, or at least under scrutiny, and that this patient had been treated using discredited methods.

This argument was only applied once, fortunately, and I was able to defend the use of the group treatment on paper robustly, in much the same terms as in the *BJP* letter, and we certainly didn't end up being hauled over the coals for using an invalid technique. There was no litigation on this matter.

But the damage to our group work had already been done.

There were tens of thousands of research papers dealing with individual therapy techniques but, in stark contrast, since PTSD had become a recognized diagnostic condition in 1980, fewer than 20 published studies had evaluated group therapy techniques, including our own from RAF Wroughton – this, despite the fact that positive treatment outcomes were reported in most studies, lending general support for the use of group therapy with trauma survivors.

It wasn't exactly difficult, even for me, to see what was going on. One-to-one treatments were immeasurably easier to organize and study. Groups added a collective dimension, not only in terms of organizing a treatment but also in terms of analysing the results. It was difficult enough to measure the quality of the therapeutic relationship between the therapist and one patient, let alone half a dozen or more. And how did you even begin to measure group cohesion?

Researchers, being human, took the line of least resistance.

Individual treatments, on the other hand, were easier to arrange, did not require an initial inpatient phase (although some groups were composed of outpatients who met regularly) and some had concerns about the element of psychological debriefing in our group, although the disclosure/debriefing part of the group work contained the principles of cognitive behavioural therapy. Group treatments were still recognized as being effective, but were not regarded as front-line.

By this time, the quantity of research into one-on-one treatments was enormous and there was clear evidence-based research that showed that CBT was an effective way to treat PTSD.

Cognitive Behavioural Therapy is based on the principle that a person's mood and behaviour reflect the way they think, or that moods are created by thoughts or 'cognitions'. If thoughts can be recognized and adjusted, then so can mood and behaviour.

Cognitive Therapy (CT) was originally developed by Aaron Beck in 1976 to treat depression and was then further developed as a treatment for anxiety disorders by David Clark in 1986. The basis of the theory is that the interpretation of an event, rather than the event itself, is what determines mood-states. Interpretations that are negatively orientated lead to negative mood-states, and erroneous or unhelpful interpretations, known as 'automatic thoughts' or 'self-schemata', are seen as inaccurate interpretations. CT aims to modify these automatic thoughts.

This process occurs in steps involving the identification of dysfunctional thoughts, challenges those that are considered inaccurate and finally seeks to replace them with more helpful and realistic thoughts. CT is very much a talking therapy designed to modify thoughts via an appeal to the rational side of the brain. These days, when people refer to CT, most are referring to CBT, but there are still people who use CT in its original form. CT is usually folded within CBT to encompass both cognitive and behavioural approaches. It has become augmented by various forms of relaxation such as meditation, reflexology and mindfulness – techniques designed to reach the non-cognitive part of the brain, which, to my mind at least, was where a good many traumas seemed to lodge themselves.

To meet the needs of trauma survivors, a more specifically trauma-focused CBT has been developed to pay attention to the impact of the trauma on their attitudes towards safety and danger, trust and views of themselves (post-trauma issues which closely resemble the shattered assumptions described by Professor Janoff-Bulman).

Using the CBT approach to understand and work through their problems, patients learn how to identify problem situations and themes, emotional disturbances and unhealthy behaviours and replace them with healthier ways to think, act and respond to events. All of these therapies were about improving the inhibiting effect of the pre-frontal cortex on the amygdala, the two almond-shaped structures located within the limbic system on the front and left sides of the brain. The amygdala, we already knew, were instrumental in flagging up life threats and had a profound memory, keeping the brain on high alert for any reappearance of those threats. Each amygdala indelibly lodged all memory events that went through it, imprinting anything that appeared risky or challenging on the once-bitten-twice-shy principle. If you were exposed to that risk again the amygdala would trigger a fear/anxiety response that would get you ready for fight-or-flight mode.

This was all well and good when we were living in the jungle or threatened constantly by sabre-tooth tigers, but less useful in modern life. If you've been hit by a red car in a road traffic accident, not every red car you see thereafter is going to be a threat. But in some cases – most notably where PTSD is present – the amygdala doesn't know this and continues to flag all red cars as threats, putting the victim into a constant and unwelcome state of hyper-arousal – readiness to fight a non-existent threat. The result is that the individual is in a state of ongoing high anxiety. After the very real original threat has gone away, part of the job of the pre-frontal cortex is to inhibit the amygdala – to stop it from remaining in overdrive – but in a good many PTSD cases, the inhibition process seemed not to work. Seventy per cent of people who undergo CBT/CT for PTSD-type symptoms seem to be good at processing and are able to process the threat; 30 per cent can't. This doesn't necessarily mean that they're bad at processing per se, but if there is something bizarre about the traumatizing event, it may be extremely difficult for their rational minds to come to terms with what's happened to them. Take out-of-body-experiences as a pre-eminent example.

Recent advances in scanning techniques – functional magnetic resonance imaging (FMRI), in particular – had shown that the amygdala and pre-frontal cortex weren't the only parts of the limbic system adversely affected by extreme stress. The hippocampus, which acted a bit like a USB cable between the left and right sides of the brain (the left-hand side of the brain in a right-handed person being the seat of rational thought and memories; the right side the seat of sensory perceptions – it's reversed in left-handers), and its associated structures, the anterior cingulate gyrus and the optical cingulate gyrus, seemed to be equally adversely affected by stress. Tests made public in 1995 on US Army Vietnam veterans showed that vets who still suffered from PTSD had an 8 per cent reduction in the volume of their right hippocampus – the hippocampi are structures seahorse-like in shape (hippocampus means 'seahorse' in Greek) deep on each side of the brain – compared with vets who suffered no such symptoms. What this suggested to me was that they would have difficulty passing sensory information – information we're bombarded with all the time – from the right to the left side of the brain via the USB. That being the case, the individual would not, in any real sense, be functioning normally. They would feel disconnected from the world, have problems in retaining short-term memories and difficulty in concentrating. When a patient comes to see me, a simple question or two about whether they're able to remember faces, people's names or lists of things, as well as their ability to concentrate, often tells me all I need to know about whether or not they have a stress reaction.

From the time that PTSD became a diagnostic entity in 1980 the challenge was to find a treatment that would be *generally* effective. Trials of different treatment regimes including pharmacotherapy (based on medications) and a range of different psychotherapeutic approaches were conducted throughout the 1980s and 1990s, and trends were beginning to appear in the mid-to-late 1990s which led to the need to appraise the findings in the literature. From our point of view at Ticehurst, we were confident to carry on using our group programme because it continued to produce consistently good results.

Solicitors, however, started increasingly to refer clients with PTSD for one-to-one therapy, and group work came to be regarded as a treatment for those who didn't respond to one-to-one. The number of people being referred for inclusion in our groups fell off.

At one time we'd been running 14 or 15 groups in a year, which meant full capacity for 30 weeks. They kept running, but by the late 1990s we were down to about five groups a year. Interestingly, they were just as successful whenever we ran them, even though we were mainly seeing treatment-resistant patients who had not responded to a course of individual therapy.

Another factor for the drop-off in numbers was that it was the defendants in personal injury litigation who often funded treatment. Although to begin with our group treatment cost about the same over the year as a year's worth of individual treatment, a gap started to open up between the two. With fewer participants, we became about twice as expensive as individual treatment techniques. Defendants would therefore choose one-on-one as their first treatment option.

As the number of referrals decreased, the gap between the groups increased, which meant that some people could be kept waiting for months. I'd get a referral, I'd see them and I'd say, 'Right, you're in the next group' – only to discover there wasn't a group scheduled until three months down the line. By that time their symptoms might have worsened, which might in turn have led to their being taken on elsewhere for one-to-one.

The answer was not to wait for full-sized groups of a dozen or so, but to run with what we had. We soon discovered that three was too small to constitute a group; it tended to split two to one. If we had three men or three women, that would reduce the likelihood of a split; but if we had two women and one man, or vice versa, that would increase it. If three was an awkward number, then two was definitely not a group, and one was one-to-one. We established four as the minimum.

We also found that if we had a facilitator working with one person, using the principles and steps of the group programme in the same order, then that produced very good results. We used this technique on people who found it difficult to fit into a group.

A good example was when a man came to us who'd been the

victim of a miscarriage of justice. I'll call him Philip. Philip had been released on appeal after 26 years of wrongful imprisonment. His solicitors, worried for his mental health, sent him to us immediately he was set free.

Twenty-six years previously, Philip had owned up to a murder. The police, having got their confession, no doubt congratulated themselves, but Philip's case was complex and had they looked more deeply into his background, they would have had good cause to wonder if they had really got their man. Philip had been physically abused as a child, neglected for much of his life, and, shortly before the murder, had been medically discharged by the Army after just a few weeks' service – a rejection that had thwarted his lifelong ambition to be a professional soldier.

All that neglect and rejection had risen to the surface when he'd confessed to the brutal murder of a young girl close to where he lived. He told detectives he'd dreamed about her and they'd put two and two together when he'd said he wasn't sure whether he'd committed the murder or not. Consciously or not, the way I saw it, he'd been trying to tell people that, deep down, he had a lot of unresolved stuff going on. The confession to murder – an inability, in actual fact, to remember whether he'd done it or not – had been a cry for help. For almost 20 years, he'd said nothing – perhaps it had taken him that long to process all the hurt and rejection that had led to his 'confession'. But then it was as if a switch had flicked inside his brain; he came alive – telling anyone who'd listen that he'd been wrongfully convicted. But by then, of course, nobody believed him. It was only when the forensic evidence was re-examined that the conviction was found to be unsafe and Philip was released. Because his solicitors were aware of the work we'd done with the PoWs and hostages, they made arrangements for Philip to come to Ticehurst immediately.

I was on business elsewhere when Philip arrived at the hospital. It was agreed that a very experienced therapist, Stu Johnson, would be his one-on-one debriefer, using group techniques.

Released, wrongfully convicted prisoners manifested behaviours similar to those shown by released hostages and PoWs. We knew that the re-entry phase into ordinary living would call for significant adjustments to be made. We also knew that released prisoners from quashed convictions would generally find rehabilitation more difficult than released hostages because they had been detained by legal means within their own countries rather than by alien cultures.

Our intention through the group programme that Stu would supervise on a one-to-one basis for Philip was to convert him from victim into survivor.

The aim of the psychological debriefing process, just as it had been with the PoWs and hostages, included reconstruction of undistorted memories of the traumatic events of his arrest and incarceration, the arrival at a 'narrative' meaning for the trauma, which Philip could come to describe verbally and understand, and finally assimilation of its meaning prior to processing the memories themselves. Once processed, we knew, the traumatic experience would lose its intrusive qualities and would no longer have a life of its own in the form of flashbacks and nightmares, which he'd had for much of his incarceration.

When I arrived at Ticehurst in the afternoon, I met Philip in my office. Ironically, I had been in court, testifying in a medico-legal case as an expert witness, and, unusually for me, I was wearing a suit. I told Philip we were delighted he was with us and how we had every hope, based on our many successful cases of treatment, that we'd be able to help him. But Philip wouldn't speak to me – I wasn't even sure he was listening. It was as if I was addressing a brick wall. He stared into space, resolutely refusing to look at me.

Not only was this not normal, it was uncharacteristic; Stu had reported no such problems when I'd touched base with him just before Philip and I had met.

'Philip,' I said, 'is there a problem?'

He nodded.

'What is it?'

'It's your shirt.'

I looked down. I was wearing a white shirt with a blue stripe. I thought for a moment that I might have spilled something on it, but it was perfectly clean.

'What about my shirt?'

'It's almost identical to the one I used to wear in prison.'

I breathed an inward sigh of relief and cursed myself at the same time. Yet how could I have known? 'Would you like me to change it?' I said.

He shook his head. 'No, it's OK. It was just a bit of a shock, that's all. I'm over it now.'

This perfectly encapsulated for me how difficult it would have been for Philip to readapt to life in the outside world on his own. What if he'd been at a bus stop or in the supermarket and had reacted in the same way towards someone who'd then had an altercation with him? What if a fight had ensued and Philip had ended up punching the guy? People would have said, 'There's no smoke without fire,' and Philip would have been judged and convicted in the court of public opinion all over again. He might even have ended up back in prison.

By implementing our group techniques, listening to Philip's account, helping him to process the information and come up with a narrative of that chain of events that made sense to him, Stu was able to reintroduce Philip to the real world and he made a good recovery.

But, overall, the period felt tarnished by what I saw as unjustified attacks on our methods. Inevitably, I felt that research into the causes and effects of PTSD had taken a step backwards, although this was undoubtedly mainly paranoia on my part (oh, yes, even psychiatrists aren't immune to this) – it was, after all, the group treatment process that had been subjected to the fiercest criticism, and the group was the method that I had pioneered. Nevertheless, I felt the need to move things forward again, but I had no idea how.

It seemed to me that the first phase of development of effective treatments for PTSD had come to a natural halt: it was time for an audit. The theoretical basis for identifying PTSD as a clinical condition had arrived in 1980 with *DSM-III*. It was not yet 2000: the trauma field (at least in the modern era) was not yet 20 years old.

It was in June 1995 that Professor Beverley Raphael and her senior research assistant, Lenore Meldrum, from the University of Queensland in Brisbane, and Professor Sandy McFarlane expressed their thoughts about psychological debriefing and its effectiveness in a leading article in the *British Medical Journal*.

Perhaps it was most appropriate that this signal to 'stop and stare' came from Australia. In 1986 Raphael had published the seminal text *When Disaster Strikes*, which championed the concept that talking through traumatic experiences may help the recovery of those who have suffered psychological injuries. This concept had spread throughout the world. It had led to military psychiatrists providing immediate interventions on the front line – interventions that are intended to heal and return soldiers to activity – in the Israeli Army. It had also inspired the work of Jeffrey Mitchell in his development of Critical Incident Stress Debriefing and had been put into practice by Sandy McFarlane in his work with bush fire victims in Australia.

In their article, Raphael, Meldrum and McFarlane considered that the proponents of debriefing agreed that it needed evaluation. Psychological debriefing had expanded rapidly and had begun to reflect a powerful social movement to meet the needs of emergency service workers, disaster victims and those who had been affected by trauma and violence in a wider society and it was important to know that it was a force for good and did not cause harm. This would require high-quality research.

'Getting the story right', by eliminating distortions of perception within a group of individuals who had shared a stressful experience as a team (emergency service workers, aircrew or a platoon of soldiers), seemed intuitively to be a healing thing to do. To incorporate the same principle into a group treatment programme involving individuals who had not shared the same experience but who had all developed PTSD as a direct reaction to their individual experiences of trauma seemed to have the same intuitive validity, because the results showed that 80 per cent of those in the RAF and at Ticehurst who processed their experiences in that way got rid of their PTSD. A similar group strategy had been running in the National Center for PTSD VA programmes in the USA for several years.

Clearly, more research was needed.

It occurred to me then that there actually wasn't all that much difference, in essence, between group and individual treatments for trauma.

On the outside the two strategies seemed very different but, on the inside, each depended on a 'click' between patient and therapist. In one-to-one treatment, the interaction was between the two individuals involved. Processing some very strange, unfamiliar and

unsafe information and impressions depended on the patient knowing that the therapist was safe and trustworthy.

Instincts and intuition help, of course, but a 'therapeutic alliance'
can take a long time to establish. Almost certainly, the communication system depends much more on what is not said between the
therapist and the patient rather than what is said. Things that are felt
and conveyed between individuals are part of the energy flow
between them; an information flow for which, as yet, we have a very
imperfect description, though we know it's much more than body
language. Almost an awareness of another individual's body
memories, the anatomical imprint of experience.

In groups there is the same need to be safe and to 'click' but there
are many more opportunities for an individual within a group to find
a suitable therapeutic alliance, with another patient for example. In
my experience, this was borne out by the swiftness and depth of the
bonds that typically developed in our groups. Remember that
the leaders of our groups were 'facilitators' of a group process rather
than therapists. Members of the groups who did well were those
who were able to identify at least one other member as being safe
enough to confide in. A kindred spirit. Someone with whom to work
out the antidote to the toxin that had brought their curiosity about
life to a halt.

I thought about the 'click' and my mind immediately swerved off
track to Miss Roberts and her belt and the way she had tried to beat
the curiosity out of me and my determination not to let her. I also
remembered that first, magical sight of Salvador Dalí's Christ and
the way that Miss Sprunt was able to lead me to the meaning of the
truly joyous feeling it had immediately created in me. She, through
Dalí, had made me realize I could be free again.

Was that what happened in a therapeutic alliance? Was an individual
who was trapped by trauma able to 'sense' how to escape to freedom
by being with someone who'd experienced it too or needed to be
emboldened to make the move? These questions about groups,
debriefing and one-to-one strategies were very thought-provoking. I
saw this as a staging post: an opportunity to reflect and to refine.

Boldness has genius, power, and magic in it.
Begin it now.

What about those lines inspired by Goethe? I was committed and hesitancy had long since disappeared. Could the 'Providence' described come in stages? Could a natural breathing space following an initial layer of thinking lead to the discovery of a new rich vein or even dimension of thought? When Providence moved in again (when it was ready) . . .

> All sorts of things occur to help one that would
>   never otherwise have occurred.
> A whole stream of events issues forth from the decision,
> raising in one's favour all manner of unforeseen incidents and
>   material assistance,
> which no man could have dreamed would have come his way . . .

And this is how it happened. Another breakthrough was waiting round the corner, and, as was so often the case, it came from one of my patients.

So-called 'body memories', I was about to discover, were as intrinsically part of the trauma reaction as flashbacks, dissociations and nightmares.

Chapter 18

Body Memories

By the late 1990s, I had known for some time that clues presented to GPs and physiotherapists were a way of detecting PTSD in people who might not otherwise report it, because high levels of adrenaline, one of the key signature characteristics of PTSD, could affect any part of the body that was controlled by a muscle, which was just about anything from the head down.

A South African woman was referred to us. She'd fled her own country and been in the UK for two years. Times were hard for her and her family here. They'd been able to bring very little of their own goods and chattels with them from South Africa, and they'd had to start again from scratch.

She'd left South Africa after a horrific incident at her parents' house. She was having dinner with them and her child one night when intruders broke in, stormed into the dining room and shot her mother and father dead at the table. She somehow managed to escape with her child.

These horrors can be difficult for people to take in, let alone make sense of. She didn't appear to be traumatized by the event itself, in the sense that in the context of living in South Africa it was a fairly frequent occurrence. For her, it wasn't beyond normal human experience.

What she had in fact developed a trauma reaction to was something that would probably sound innocuous to people outside the field. She had bought a car. She and her husband had worked double shifts to meet the payments and the rent on their flat. They had just completed the final payment on the car, and it was theirs: the first solid thing that they could call their own since coming to the UK. Everything else was rented and transient.

The event that triggered the PTSD was that the car was bashed into the day after the final payment was made. It was dented badly enough for her to have picked up a whiplash injury in the process. She in no way thought she was going to be killed or die in the accident; she had no sense of foreboding or imminent death or anything like that. It was purely the nature and timing of the insult. I was expecting her to tell me the impact had given her flashbacks to the intruders bursting into the room and killing her mother and father, but she never did.

The trauma of the insult manifested itself in the most interesting way. She was referred to me by an ENT surgeon to whom she'd presented with tinnitus. The surgeon could find nothing physically wrong with her. Her ears were healthy. But he had attended a lecture I'd given about the unusual ways in which PTSD can present. I'd explained that PTSD had a biological signature, which meant that it usually presented to physicians and specialists other than psychiatrists.

I explained this one day soon after I'd come across the South African woman to a group of physiotherapists at a seminar at the Ridgeway Hospital in Wroughton.

High levels of adrenaline, which is characteristic of PTSD, tighten muscles in the body. Starting from the head down, the victim will therefore present to the neurologist with headaches; to orthopaedic surgeons with neck and back pain; to ophthalmologists with altered eyesight; to ENT surgeons with altered voice patterns and tinnitus, because the muscles that connect the bones in the middle ear tighten up under the influence of adrenaline; to gastroenterologists with everything from difficulties in swallowing all the way down to irritable bowel syndrome; to dentists with teeth grinding and jaw ache (the jaw muscles are the strongest in the human body – ask any trapeze artist); to urologists with irritable bladder; to gynaecologists because of all the tubes that can tighten; to cardiologists with palpitations, accelerated heart rates and, of course, chest pain; and to chest physicians with asthma and hyperventilation. PTSD can affect anything controlled by a muscle, in fact, which is just about everything.

'Virtually all of you in this room,' I'd said, 'will have patients with PTSD.'

Physiotherapists see more people with PTSD than most. To them I said, 'If you have a patient whom you know to be genuine, but isn't responding to the treatment you're giving, or if your investigations are not showing the things you expect them to – just think out of the box for a moment. Is there a trauma behind this? Ask them about it. Ask them particularly if anything strange happened when, for example, they had a road traffic accident. They may tell you spontaneously they were out-of-body.'

I got a few odd looks after that last comment, but then that didn't altogether surprise me. How could I possibly explain to this audience the significance of the Invisible Girl or where my thoughts on PTSD were now heading?

Far from being an illness, I had now come to see PTSD, even chronic PTSD, as memory-processing that had got stuck.

This could mean that PTSD could be discovered late, although it might have been making its presence felt for a long time, even decades before its true identity had been recognized. Remember that the mind comes equipped with psychological defences that can deny the existence of emotional changes, but the body has nothing like that. The biochemical changes, such as increased adrenaline, which are characteristic of PTSD will cause psychological anxiety, which can be denied or suppressed to the extent that it will not be noticeable to the affected individual or observers, but will also cause bodily dysfunction, which cannot be disguised.

Professor Jonathan Davidson wrote an article that was published in the *British Medical Journal* in 1992 about the drug treatment of PTSD in which he observed that doctors need to maintain a high level of awareness that patients may have experienced trauma, that PTSD can often account for a variety of common symptoms and that it may also be at the root of a persisting, treatment-resistant depressive or anxiety state.

He also observed that while the hallmark symptoms of PTSD are unique to that condition, especially the intrusive recollections, flashbacks and re-experiencing of trauma through nightmares, PTSD is still a diagnosis which is frequently missed, even by psychiatric professionals. He considered that the reasons why a doctor might perhaps overlook the diagnosis include not asking the patient about experience of trauma; a patient's reluctance to disclose painful material; a physician's discomfort at discussing events which might be gruesome, horrifying or unimaginable; the fact that chronic PTSD often presents with non-specific symptoms, such as headache, insomnia, irritability, depression, tension, substance abuse, as well as interpersonal or professional dysfunction.

Physiotherapists, in particular, people who treated patients with muscular problems, were of great interest to me and ought to be to the wider psychiatric community, I thought, especially after some of the recent cases I'd experienced and wanted to share. The South African woman was a case in point.

So I sat down and wrote a letter to the editor of the British Journal of Psychiatry.

I'd wanted to make the point that we shouldn't see flashbacks in trauma reactions as limited to the obvious sensory channels of what we see, hear, smell, taste and touch. We should also potentially see them as containing emotions, feelings, sensations and pain, on the assumption that absolutely anything that is absorbed at the time of the trauma might replay itself later. Such flashbacks might account for ongoing pain following whiplash injuries of the neck and spine commonly seen in orthopaedic consultations, I said, when patients are not found to have any ongoing tissue damage or inflammation or any abnormality of bone structure or architecture, even though the pain is still there. Pain such as whiplash, I was suggesting, is usually developed in the context of a trauma, and could therefore effectively be described as a flashback – which, in turn, could therefore effectively be managed using PTSD treatments.

I got a reply from the BJPsych's editor acknowledging receipt of the letter, but saying he wouldn't be publishing it. The notion that these phenomena could be flashbacks was plain as plain could be to me; it was what clinical observations were telling me, and yet there were people in authority who wouldn't listen. I felt, for the first time in ages, that I was being confronted by some of the same barriers I'd run up against at the MoD.

*

This is where I was at when a girl called Erica came to see me. Erica was a model and her looks were so picture-perfect that when she smiled she literally dazzled me with her teeth. She reminded me of a Barbie doll, wore lots of make-up and was very theatrical in the way she spoke and acted. She had been branded a bit of a drama queen by her previous physician, who doubted the substance of her story – that she was being brutalized by her husband. She had gone to her doctor, desperate for advice, because her marriage was falling apart and she was in a bad, hyper-aroused state. She'd been treated for anxiety and depression, and was regarded as 'hysterical' with personality problems. Her previous physician said in her notes that she was probably making too much of what she'd declared about the violence in her marriage. It couldn't have been as bad as all that, he'd told me, when I'd spoken to him on the phone. The language he'd used smacked of something I'd have expected to see in a shell-shock report from the First World War.

'Tell me a little about your childhood,' I said to Erica, as soon as we'd gone through her history.

'I'm an only child and was left on my own quite a lot,' she said. 'My father was a workaholic and wasn't around much and I think my mother felt neglected, because she used to drink when she was on her own, which was most of the time. She was cold and distant, not motherly at all. I wanted to be close to her, but she had a lot of anger inside and it was always better to stay out of her way. Eventually, she left and divorced my father. Because of my mother's drinking, my father won custody of me in the courts. He had quite a lot of money and I ended up being looked after by a succession of nannies – I didn't really get on with any of them.'

'What about your mother?'

'I hardly ever saw her. She moved abroad. She lives in Australia now. We don't even exchange Christmas cards.'

'And your father?'

'He married a terrible woman with a violent temper. She used to lock me in my bedroom for hours, sometimes days, at a time. My saving grace were my dolls and my doll's house. I used to create this fantasy world that I could retreat into. Then, when I was in my teens, I joined the local beauty queen circuit. At first it was a means of getting away, of escaping the situation at home, but I came to like the fact that people paid me attention. I never got any at home – not the right kind, anyhow.'

I could see that what had happened in her childhood probably meant she relied on childhood defences, and when she developed problems in adulthood – after her encounters with her violent husband – these defences became evident and the hysteria shone through. Though a natural defence mechanism, a form of protection, hysteria is annoying for other people because you can't argue against it and it doesn't respond to reason.

Erica needed some intensive care in a sanctuary so I admitted her to Ticehurst into the daily care of one of our new psychotherapists, a woman called Heather Robyn. Heather had one of the widest repertoires of therapy skills that I knew. She had a very engaging smile and a bright personality and had recently arrived in the UK from New Zealand. Having trained in both group and individual psychotherapy, she was particularly interested in working in trauma. We all liked Heather immediately and didn't hesitate in offering her a job at Ticehurst.

One day, Heather and Erica got to discussing some aspects of Erica's marriage, and they talked about some significant injury she'd once received after her husband kicked her on the back of her calf. The following day, she presented to Heather with a big bruise exactly where she'd described the earlier injury caused by her husband. It was difficult to imagine the injury to her calf being self-inflicted, but it wasn't completely out of the question. It would have been easier to think along those lines, but Heather and I didn't. I examined her leg and it was definitely a bruise. I couldn't be sure she didn't have a deep vein thrombosis, so I sent her off to the local hospital for tests. They excluded DVT, though there was definitely a soft tissue injury.

When Heather and I discussed the results of these tests with Erica in my office, she was shocked by the bruise's appearance. 'This is exactly what it looked like when I was hit by my ex-husband – same shape and everything,' she said.

Very hesitantly, not even knowing the language to use, I said: 'This looks like a sort of body memory of the trauma.'

'Which is precisely what it is,' Heather said.

'You've come across this before?' I asked her.

After Erica left the room, Heather told me it was not an unusual occurrence. When a person was processing some traumatic memory, it would often be accompanied by a transient manifestation that resembled the original injury.

It wasn't altogether a surprise to me that I hadn't witnessed the phenomenon myself until now. Psychiatrists don't usually get involved in psychotherapy. They usually diagnose a condition and then design a strategy for therapy, which might or might not include psychotherapy. The psychiatrist will tend to remain involved in the medication side of things, but will otherwise hand over the day-to-day treatment to the therapists. You wouldn't sit in on therapy sessions – that would be an intrusion – but you would keep in close contact so you knew what was happening.

Because Erica had assured us that she had not injured herself in any way whatsoever, that this thing had arisen spontaneously, Heather and I were left with the firm conviction that this was a body memory. It was the very first time I'd ever encountered the phenomenon.

Women can get a nervous flush on the chest as part of a warning mechanism, a sort of 'back off, you're making me feel nervous' kind of thing. And redness in the face can actually denote anger.

But this was different and Heather – someone for whom I had an enormous amount of respect – said that it wasn't the first time she'd seen these so-called body memories of actual trauma. Here, we agreed, was a lady with a leg injury that was a total replica of something that had happened to her before. It was real. It didn't just go away the next day. It was a bruise, which meant that a blood vessel had burst, with an escape of blood into the surrounding tissue.

I remembered reading how women who had been raped could experience abdominal pains and bleeding as they recounted the assault. Marks could appear on their legs and elsewhere, where they'd been grabbed. They re-experienced the pain, but it was not something you could actually see or detect in an objective way, so much of the research had been dismissed.

Because none of this had ever been reported in the psychiatric literature, I said to Heather that we really needed to write a paper on it. But of course, as with so many other things, we never got round to it.

I remained intrigued though. Here there appeared to be a direct connection between visual flashbacks and physical flashbacks, the link being the emotional trauma suffered at the critical moment of distress. It seemed related to another phenomenon – one that was widely reported, but, like so many areas I was now finding myself in, not well understood.

After amputation of a limb, an amputee often continues to have an awareness of it and to experience sensations from it. Phantom limb pain – pain appearing to come from where an amputated limb used to be – is often excruciating and almost impossible to treat. To make matters worse, patients whose limbs have been lost traumatically are much more susceptible to the development of phantom limb pains than patients whose limbs have been electively removed.

Ever since a neuroscientist called Weir Mitchell first coined the term 'phantom limb pain' in 1872, researchers have been trying to figure out where the mysterious sensations originate. When a limb is removed, the severed nerves in the remaining stump (nerves that formerly carried messages of touch, temperature and pain from the skin) form nodules called neuromas on their cut ends. The classic explanation for phantom limb pain is that these truncated nerve endings continue to send impulses up the spinal cord to the brain. Cutting the nerves just above the neuromas or where they enter the spinal cord does seem to bring some relief, but only temporarily. Within a few months or years the affliction of the ghost limb returns.

These phantom sensations are also present in children who are born without limbs, suggesting that our perception of our bodies is hard-wired into our brain and that sensations from the limbs become mapped on to these brain networks as we develop.

Neurologists now believe that the sense of touch, and the physical world it brings into existence, has much more to do with what is going on in our heads than at our fingertips.

There has been a shift in emphasis away from the site of damage – the stump – to the centre of pain processing – the brain. It appears that disordered inputs from the limb's sensory systems, combined with disrupted motor signals back to the limb, generate a mismatch between the brain's built-in map of the physical body and what is actually perceived. For some reason, this mismatch results in pain.

In some ways the phenomenon resembles reflex sympathetic dystrophy, RSD, in which the autonomic nervous system goes out of control following a wound or amputation. The wound can be surgical, but only, it seems, if it's a repair to something that has been traumatized.

Neurologists see RSD as a dissociative phenomenon. It is thought to arise as a result of abnormal nerve healing following trauma, although the exact mechanism still remains a mystery. Because of the long-term nature of RSD and its symptoms, a depression often develops.

If identified early, RSD is treatable. Treatment is aimed at controlling pain, enabling the person to regain or improve the function of the affected limb, and providing emotional support.

I'd once treated a police officer who had badly injured his knee while apprehending a burglar. When he had surgery to trim the cartilage, the skin around the wound site became exquisitely tender and sensitive. There was also marked discoloration and abnormal hair growth. Nerve blocks – injections of local anaesthetic into the affected nerve – can be effective, but they weren't in his case. Medication may also be used to relieve symptoms, including painkillers and drugs most commonly used to treat depression.

What worked best for him, in the end, was something called 'micro-current'. Micro-current is a natural current that courses through the body at almost undetectable levels – around a millionth of an amp. When the flow of the body's natural current becomes disrupted, micro-current technology can be used to normalize it. The technology has been around for 50 years, but it's only since the advent of the computer chip that it has been packaged in a form that's small enough for it to be carried for sufficient time to promote adequate healing.

Micro-current has parallels with *chi*, acupuncture and reflexology, although in the late 1990s I wasn't ready to publicly make those connections because they weren't thought of as being 'scientific'. Micro-current *is* scientific, however; it's measurable. Achilles tendons heal in half the time when micro-current is applied. The implication is that it normalizes the function of endocrine (hormone-producing) organs as well as tissue, so if someone is producing an excessive output of adrenaline or cortisone, say, in the wake of a traumatic accident – a snapped Achilles tendon being the perfect example – it will normalize the levels, allowing natural healing to begin. Micro-current seems to optimize the function of the immune system, hence acceleration or stimulus of healing.

But the actual reasons for phantom limb pain and the strange bruising suffered by Erica at Ticehurst remained baffling. The break-through came, as it so often did, when I least expected it.

In the summer of 2000, we were going away on holiday and as usual I gathered up all the journals I hadn't read. At the airport, I also visited the paper shop and bought a copy of every British broadsheet to see me through the next fortnight. I liked to browse through them and cut out coupons and readers' offers. My garage is full of a life-time's worth of paintbrushes that cost me just £10.99, and other wonderful bargains – all of them useless.

In the *New Scientist*, I caught up with the work of a Swiss neuro-biologist who had published a series of case histories that suggested a part of our brain harbours the potential to make us believe a double of ourselves exists. Peter Brugger of the University Hospital in Zürich had come up with a new theory on ghosts and doppel-gängers (a doppelgänger is the ghost of a living person, usually the viewer). Brugger suggested the viewer was experiencing a 'phantom of the entire body' in just the same way an amputee might experience a 'phantom limb'. The limb is no longer there, but the brain still tells the amputee it is. Brain damage can cause this effect, but people with normal brains may have the effect triggered by intense emotions such as fear, sadness or euphoria. Brugger reported that mountain climbers who have experienced oxygen deprivation at about 18,000 feet have reported feeling a 'presence' or having an out-of-body experience. All of these things, given my experiences with PTSD, interested me greatly.

Some people, Brugger said, actually see their double, often as a mirror image. This may be the result of damage to visual areas of the brain that affect the way we sense our body, he concluded. Others merely feel the presence of a double without actually seeing one. He believed that these doubles are generated when the parietal lobes, the regions responsible for the distinction between body and surround-ing space, are damaged.

Out-of-body experiences, where a person 'sees' their body from the outside, may be caused by temporary over-activity of certain brain regions. 'Excitability of the temporal lobes seems to be a plausible explanation,' said Brugger. These regions are connected to the parietal lobes and are sensitive to visual signals, low levels of oxygen and emotional arousal.

Brugger believed the brain could account for other paranormal experiences: 'Ghosts are probably nothing more but also nothing less than phantoms of the body.'

Brugger had even reported at the recent Federation of European Neuroscience Societies meeting in Brighton on a unique series of cases of a rare and peculiar delusional disorder called the Doppelgänger syndrome. Patients could suffer several bizarre experiences, but the primary sensation was a visual hallucination of seeing themselves – but not just as if seeing themselves in a mirror. There was also a strong accompanying sense that the other person really *was* yourself. Some sufferers even believed they were gradually being replaced by their own double.

The classic doppelgänger experience is a common theme in fiction where the appearance of the double often announces the hero's death by suicide. Dr Brugger argued that some of the fiction's authors are known to have suffered from epilepsy, one cause of the doppelgänger delusion. It could be their own personal experiences that inspired these intriguing stories. Dr Brugger reported seeing patients who'd become suicidal after developing the doppelgänger delusion. Their understanding from folklore was of the double as a harbinger of death. In one of his cases, a man felt so persecuted by his double that he shot himself to get rid of it. In another, a patient felt dizzy when he woke in the morning. Turning round, he saw himself still lying in bed. He got angry about the man he knew was himself and who would be late for work. He tried to wake the body by shouting at it, then by trying to shake it, but the recumbent body did not react.

He began to be puzzled about his double existence and became more and more scared by the fact that he could no longer tell which of the two he really was. Several times his bodily awareness switched from the one standing upright to the one still lying in bed; in the latter case he would feel quite awake but paralysed and scared by the figure of himself bending over and beating him. His only intention was to become one person again. Looking out of the window from where he could still see his body lying in bed, he suddenly decided to jump out 'in order to stop the intolerable feeling of being divided in two'. At the same time, he hoped that 'this really desperate action would frighten the one in bed and thus urge him to merge with me again'. The next thing he remembered was the painful awakening in the hospital with multiple fractures from having jumped out of a high window.

Brugger had also interviewed several otherwise normal world-class extreme high-altitude climbers who had not used supplementary oxygen, and found a particularly high rate of doppel-gänger-like experiences when above 6,000 metres – usually of the nature of a felt 'presence'. All but one of the climbers reported bodily illusions and hallucinations, of which the doppelgänger hallucination was the most common.

Brugger argued a combination of hypoxia, social and sensory deprivation plus acute stress played a role in the genesis of these experiences, which are also shared by single-handed sailors and cast-aways. He suggested the neurological mechanism was probably similar to that underlying phantom limbs, only in the doppelgänger delusion sufferers felt the presence of their whole body in another space. This all suggested that an inner model of the body is represented in a part of the brain, which will then not match the physical reality of what has happened to the real body.

Brain disturbances caused by tumours, head injuries, migraines or epilepsy can then upset this internal representation of the body, leading to the belief that another version of the same body exists 'out there' in space. This could also explain transsexuals who believe they have been born into the wrong body sex, and people who want limbs amputated because they just don't 'feel right' with the normal limb.

Exactly where this representation of the body resides in the brain was unknown, but Brugger's collection of cases provided a clue. Most doppelgängers were 'felt' to exist on the right side of the body. I found this interesting. Phantom limbs tended to occur more often after right-sided amputations.

Most people tend to be right-handed, so it could just be that the brain's representation of the body is more extensive for the right side, leading to a higher chance of distortion because there is more brain devoted to the body image on that side.

Maybe, I felt, the answer lay in the fact that our brains consist of two hemispheres, right and left, often specializing in different activities, like language based in the left and spatial skills in the right. Maybe they both had representations of the body within them. If there was a disturbance in the connection between the two hemispheres which meant that they didn't communicate properly, then perhaps one hemisphere felt that the representation of the body in the other was actually another person, but also the same as the original person – a doppelgänger.

Brugger's findings suggested that our own understanding of ownership of our bodies was so much a part of conscious experience that we took it for granted. The doppelgänger delusion pointed to the fact that a part of the brain had to be devoted to telling us that our body was our own, and that when it malfunctioned, truly strange things could happen; strange, that is, if you were a conventional person of science.

But everything I was now beginning to discover about PTSD defied convention. Most doctors, just like the editorial staff at the *BJPsych*, would have dismissed the bruising on Erica's calf as a medical irrelevance – even though they would have seen it with their own eyes. I realized I now faced a choice.

Either I stopped where I was, refusing to be led by my curiosity – as Miss Roberts would have had me do at Lorne Street School – or I followed the path pointed out to me by evidence gathered by my own eyes: the Sprunt school of learning.

Needless to say, after not much deliberation the route to take was obvious.

EMDR (Eye Movement Desensitization and Reprocessing) was a relatively new form of psychotherapy that was beginning to challenge everything we believed or had assumed about emotions and the nature of change. Where up until then it was accepted that psychotherapy often took a long time, depending on the nature of the problem – and even then, there were no guarantees of success – with EMDR, therapists and patients were reporting that problems that had been resistant to years of psychotherapy were being resolved in a very short amount of time – sometimes within a few sessions.

Very much a behavioural technique, EMDR was believed to facilitate the processing of difficult memories such as those found in trauma reactions and depressions, anxiety states, and a whole range of conditions which we know involve problematic memories that are difficult to process. The technique involved, it was believed, stimulation of the two sides of the brain alternately, sometimes by inducing eye movements, by asking the patient to follow your finger with their eyes in sweeping movements across the front of the face – so-called saccadic movements. These saccades involved stimulation of first one side of the brain and then the other. This wasn't New Age mumbo-jumbo; there was a neurological basis to it.

Sometimes the stimulus was aural. People had sounds played through earphones into alternate ears. Or eye movements and sounds were combined to increase the stimulation of the two different hemispheres alternately. The back of people's hands could be tapped, or their knees. I had also read about very small electric shocks applied to the ankles.

The technique was discovered by accident. Dr Francine Shapiro was a hard-boiled, highly esteemed neuropsychologist working in Palo Alto in California. All her work was solidly research-based. She demanded evidence. She was currently working on the different functions of the two sides of the brain.

The story went that in 1987, she was walking through a park as she thought about something that was troubling her. She tended to go out for a walk at lunchtime; on this occasion she went out into a new area with no paths and lots of saplings. In order to avoid bumping into these little trees, she had to keep darting her eyes from side to side. When she returned to her thoughts she noticed that they weren't as disturbing. Her problem seemed to have resolved itself – or at least, she felt a lot calmer about it. This intrigued her and she tested it out on herself by thinking of something unsettling, then thinking of it again while purposely moving her eyes back and forth. The results were the same.

Most people would probably have left it at that, and put it down to fresh air blowing away the cobwebs. But she was studying laterality at the time, and the function of the two cerebral hemispheres. She hit on the notion that the movement of the eyes might be connected with the processing of memory, ideas and thoughts. She started to experiment on people in her institute with minor personal problems. She found that the simple technique of inducing eye movement with her finger – a way of simulating walking in those trees – was very effective in helping them to process their problems.

Encouraged by immediate successes, a clinical trial was done of people with problematic memories that were repetitive and couldn't be processed – war veterans suffering from PTSD. Some of these men had been in traditional therapy for 15 to 20 years and yet they continued to have nightmares and flashbacks that felt as if they were reliving the horrors of war. In some cases, it was found that just a couple of EMDR sessions eased their symptoms. The American Psychiatric Association and the Department of Veterans Affairs and Defense placed EMDR in the highest category of effectiveness in the treatment of trauma.

In another study of 22 participants who had also been diagnosed with PTSD, a comparison was made between EMDR and another form of treatment called 'prolonged exposure'. In this, the patient revisits the memory of the trauma and, via steady exposure to it, processes the information until the symptoms diminish or disappear altogether. It was found that of the two groups, the EMDR participants appeared to improve far more quickly; 70 per cent reached a level of clinically significant improvement in PTSD symptoms after just three sessions compared to 17 per cent in the prolonged exposure trial.

These apparently significant results were repeated when EMDR was tested with rape victims and victims of other types of trauma. What was remarkable was that Dr Shapiro found that not only did EMDR desensitize painful memories, but people began spontaneously to view themselves and the event in a healthier and more positive way.

Exactly how EMDR worked wasn't really known, but it had a reputation for being the Heineken of treatments – reaching parts of the brain that other therapies couldn't reach – and this made me very interested in it. We did know from memory and brain research that painful or traumatic experiences were stored in a different part of the brain from pleasant or neutral ones. Normally, if we're troubled by something, we think about it, talk about it, perhaps dream about it and eventually we are able to come to some sort of adaptive resolution. But when we experience a trauma or painful event, something happens that interrupts this process. Instead, the traumatic material gets 'stuck' in the brain and remains in its original form, with the same thoughts, feelings, bodily sensations, smells and sounds – classic flashback territory. It's as though it is sealed off – encapsulated – from the healthy, functioning brain. The dysfunctionally stored material doesn't get processed. The stereotypical way of reaching into the conscious mind was through CBT. But for material that had become stuck in the unconscious mind another tool was needed – and that's where EMDR came in.

The protocols were very precise, and to get to grips with them I asked Heather Robyn whether I might sit in on a session with one of her patient-clients to get a better sense of how EMDR worked. I asked the patient-client, too, and he agreed.

Andrew was 43 years old and came from a broken home, though not one that would be classically recognized by most social workers. His parents were both very well-to-do, but his mother had upped sticks and left when he was five years old. His father hadn't been able to cope and so Andrew had gone to live with his aunt and uncle, who already had children. When he was eight, his father had remarried and he had gone back to the family home. His mother at that stage of his life wasn't around – she had moved abroad and he had only sporadic contact with her. She came back into his life much later.

Andrew had wrestled with self-esteem issues for a long time and had complained to Heather of high-anxiety states, undoubtedly brought on by stress, that were affecting his work as a financial analyst in the City of London. From time to time, the stress and anxiety came out in the form of bodily pain – stomach cramps that were so painful they could double him over.

To begin with, Heather and Andrew just talked. Andrew had been to Heather a number of times already. In these meetings, she had taken his history and described what she hoped his EMDR treatment would achieve. Andrew had been convinced that his anxiety stemmed from the time his mother had left him, but in the course of a number of EMDR sessions it had emerged that it was his overbearing stepmother who had exerted more influence on the way he currently felt. Andrew's target was to rid himself of the maladaptive beliefs that fed his anxiety and were responsible for, he felt, the physical pain he often experienced.

I sat back on my chair in the corner of the room, making myself as unobtrusive as possible, and listened.

Andrew talked about what he had been up to since his last session the previous week, and what changes he had noticed in himself. He said that, thanks to the EMDR or not, he had felt a little less anxious, but that anxiety still gripped him for much of the time. He was wearing a suit – it was the end of the working day – and he looked and sounded at ease with his surroundings. He had been public-school educated and was set to return home after the session to his wife and two small children. They lived in a large and beautiful sixteenth-century manor house just outside Maidstone – Andrew had done very well in his career. He had already made clear to Heather that he was happily married and loved his family very much. This was significant to the session in that, prior to the commencement of the eye movement therapy, Heather had asked him to think of a 'safe place' that he could 'go to' if he started to feel distressed at any point during the coming EMDR session. Andrew had chosen his home.

'Are you ready?' Heather asked, when they had talked everything through.

Andrew nodded.

To begin with, Heather asked him to focus on a negative image and asked what that image might be. Andrew described the home where he used to live with his father and stepmother. He was then asked about a so-called 'negative cognition' of himself when he thought of that image and he told her about the inadequacy he felt as a parent; how he felt unable to protect his family, because of the crippling anxiety he experienced. He was worried it would do him in completely, that he would be unable to function at all and that they'd lose everything – the life he had worked so hard to forge for them all. He was then asked to think about a 'positive cognition' – something he would like to be in preference to the negative image he held of himself. Andrew told her he wanted to feel confident, self-reliant and responsible; and above all, to be rid of the anxiety and physical pains that were besetting him.

Heather asked him to sit back and look at her. She sat around four feet in front of him and asked him to focus on the negative image – the image of his childhood home – the negative cognition and the pain that often went with it: his stomach cramps. She then asked him to follow her finger as she moved it from side to side, like the pendulum of a clock, in front of his face. Keeping his face still, Andrew followed her finger for about 45 seconds, at which point Heather lowered her hand and asked Andrew whether anything had bubbled up – a thought, an emotion, a physical sensation, an image . . . anything. Andrew, his eyes now closed, looked suitably blank. He shook his head slightly, as if to say, 'Nothing.'

Heather asked him to open his eyes and she went through the routine again. When she stopped her finger movements, she asked Andrew a second time. Now, as he closed his eyes, I saw a momentary look of pain – a wince – cross his face.

'What's happening?' Heather asked.

'I'm in the house,' he said. His speech was flat and monosyllabic – a tone of voice I knew from the hypnotherapy sessions I'd carried out on my own patients. Andrew, it was clear, was 'under'.

'What do you feel when you're in the house?' Heather asked.

'It's cold and dark in here,' Andrew said. 'It's a dripping wet winter's afternoon. I'm afraid.'

'What of?'

'I don't know. There's something here with me. A presence. It's malign. Evil. Not good. Not good at all.'

'How old are you?'

'I'm nine and a half.'

'Do you want to come out of there?'

Andrew appeared to think about that for a second or two, then shook his head.

'Do you feel anything else?'

'A buzzing sensation in my stomach – just above my stomach, actually.'

He touched a point between his stomach and his diaphragm.

'Are you happy to go on?'

He set his jaw and nodded. 'Let's continue.'

Heather asked him to focus on the feeling, then instructed him to open his eyes and follow her finger again. When she stopped, she asked him again what he felt. Andrew clutched his solar plexus again.

'The buzzing's getting worse. It's like an electric current. It's to do with the house. The feeling in that house. I'm in the dining room and I can hear my father and stepmother in the kitchen. They're arguing. Screaming at each other. It's about money. They don't have enough of it. My stepmother is smashing plates. I can hear her yelling at my father that they're going to lose the house . . .'

'On a scale of one to ten,' Heather said, 'how distressing is that feeling?'

'Eight, nine, maybe.' He held his hand over the pain. His face was contorted. 'The buzzing is getting stronger. It's like somebody's pouring 50,000 volts into me.'

'Do you want to go to your safe place, Andrew?'

Andrew shook his head. 'No. I'm OK. I can handle it.'

'Do you understand, Andrew, where your anxiety comes from now? Your anxiety about money? Your anxiety that you're going to lose everything?'

'Yes. It was nothing to do with my mother leaving at all. It was from listening in to those arguments. They went on all the time. I thought we were going to lose the house, everything. And the vehemence, the anger behind those arguments – it seemed to permeate the walls, the floor, the ceiling; every single room in that house. I couldn't get away from it. It was as if the place was haunted. It made me feel sick and afraid . . .'

'And now you understand where that feeling comes from, is it necessary to hang on to it?' Heather asked.

Andrew shook his head. 'No,' he said. I noticed that he had let go of his stomach.

'And when you say goodbye to it, Andrew, what do you feel?'

'That the pain goes away.'

'Completely?'

'Not completely, but almost.'

'On a scale of one to ten?'

'It's now about a three or a four.'

'That's much better,' Heather said, in her softest, most reassuring antipodean accent.

The session went on. Heather asked Andrew to hold the thought of the negative image together with the positive cognition; the positive image of himself that he aspired to. After a few moments, she then asked on a scale of one to ten how the feeling in his stomach now registered. Andrew told her that it was now one; two at the most.

A short while later, Heather brought him round from the trance. She smiled as Andrew opened his eyes and Andrew smiled back. They talked for a while about the session and Heather made sure that Andrew was OK before he left – some of the EMDR sessions, she told me later, were so powerful that the patient-client needed to ground themselves before re-engaging in the real world. Fortunately, Andrew wasn't driving home; his wife was coming to collect him.

He and Heather agreed a time for next week's session. We all shook hands and, with a cheery wave, Andrew walked from the room. The session had left me a lot to think about.

Researchers, Heather told me, thought that EMDR was in some way able to nudge the 'stuck' material so that it reconnected neuro-logically with the healthy brain, and was then reprocessed and integrated at an accelerated speed. The most popular theory was that when the eyes moved back and forth it created brain activity similar to that which occurs during REM (rapid eye movement) sleep. It's during this REM phase, when we dream, that we process inform-ation, consolidate learning and memory, and resolve conflicts. By creating similar brain activity while thinking about the painful event, it appeared that EMDR was able to help the brain finally process the stuck material. The painful event or trauma remained a memory but devoid of emotional pain.

I checked with Heather from time to time about Andrew and, within a few months, I was told that his anxiety had left him altogether.

But EMDR itself, although formally approved as a treatment for PTSD (along with CBT) by the National Institute of Clinical Excellence, NICE, remained controversial. Dr Shapiro had had the audacity to come up with a treatment which was apparently very effective and durable, and sometimes one session was enough to sort things out. Most cases didn't seem to require more than about 15 sessions.

In the late eighties and early nineties, psychoanalytical therapy was still the most influential branch of psychotherapy in America. So a turf war had broken out.

This young whippersnapper of a girl, as the establishment saw it, was trying to introduce this very brief therapy that wasn't just a challenge to their techniques – which of course involved 50-minute sessions, five days a week, for 50 weeks a year, for five years or ten years – but also was a challenge to their income. As a result, the mother and father of all rows erupted in the therapy world and has been bubbling away ever since.

I had many discussions about EMDR with Walter Busuttil, my major supportive colleague in the Air Force when I'd been setting up the unit, and now my right-hand man at Ticehurst. My view was that there had to be something in it, based on all the positive things I'd read and the fact that Heather, whom I trusted implicitly, said that she'd seen rapid and positive results with her own eyes.

Walter's view was that the evidence wasn't there yet – that it wasn't scientific enough. The role of the eye movements was especially speculative, according to some critics, who pointed out that there were a number of elements to EMDR – exposure to the traumatic event being the primary one – and that no one mechanism could yet be held to be responsible for its apparent success.

Originally, EMDR was used to resolve the after-effects of psychological trauma: assaults, natural disasters, traumatic grief and other acutely painful situations. It was seen to work with unusual speed, and to achieve a degree of relief that was uncommon, to say the least. In recent years, however, it has been seen that EMDR can do wonders with a wider range of psychological disturbances than had originally been thought. Many accomplished therapists found that EMDR was helpful in treating other problems besides PTSD. These included other anxiety disorders, sexual abuse issues, work-related problems, low self-esteem, acute stress disorder, generalized anxiety disorder, depression and depressed mood (subclinical depression), sleep disorders, nightmares, phobias – and also substance use, addictions and impulse control disorders, anger management problems, chronic pain management, bi-polar disorders, panic attacks, dissociative disorders and personality disorders.

Furthermore, some EMDR therapists found that EMDR could even enhance the performance of athletes, artists and writers.

It was important to understand that EMDR was not merely a technique using eye movements, but a complex, integrative method that utilized very precise protocols. Nor was it a 'miracle cure', as some had – and still have – been led to believe. Most long-term problems are not cured in three sessions, though treatment is generally much shorter than traditional talk therapies – which is an advantage in the age of managed, solution-driven care.

With EMDR, however – to my mind, at least – we appeared to have found that a psychotherapy that seemed focused on trauma resolution actually helped with, and could heal, a wide range of problems not previously thought to be trauma-related.

Many times we cannot know if use of EMDR will help or not until we try it. Often it does. Our understanding of why this is so is currently limited. But this is not particularly a problem. There is very little that happens in psychotherapy that we can fully explain. It's simply far more important to understand that EMDR can help than it is to know why or how.

I had a patient, a young man, who was referred to me by his GP for anxiety and depression. Peter had had an episode of trauma in his young life; he had been knocked over in the street by a bully in his local town when he was 16, and had hit the back of his head on the pavement. Transiently blind, he was taken off to hospital, where he didn't regain his sight until the next day. He was a bright lad, but though he'd started sixth-form college he didn't complete the year and never took the exams. So he'd left school and drifted between a number of unskilled jobs. He was now 22 and this pattern of starting and quitting had gone on for quite a long time. I knew his parents, whom I'd met, were very worried about Peter – as any parent would be. Here was a kid who, through no fault of his own, was finding it difficult to adapt to life in the real world. Being punched by a bully, hitting his head and going temporarily blind must have been a very frightening experience. I was in territory where I felt very much that I ought to be able to help.

Although psychiatrists usually refer patients to a therapist for treatment, as I was trained in hypnotherapy, and more recently I had been shown how to carry out EMDR, I didn't feel that on this occasion there was any need to send Peter elsewhere. I ushered him into my consulting room and sat him down in the chair opposite my desk. He looked nervous and suspicious, casting worried glances around the office and picking at his fingernails as I asked him about his mood-state. When I tried to talk about his parents he remained just as taciturn, answering most of my questions with monosyllabic grunts. I could see that he wasn't dissociated – that he was 'in the room', so to speak – but I knew, too, that I wasn't going to get very far with him on a level of conscious thought. And it was for this reason I decided to employ EMDR on him.

I had a laminate of the protocol on my desk. Although I hadn't been fully trained in the technique, I knew enough to know I'd be perfectly safe. I'd practised hypnotherapy for a long time and could get people back out of hypnotic trances. I would follow the manual to the letter and see what happened.

I did the sweeps, and he went into a blank stare. His pupils dilated. In Scotland we used to call it 'yon look' or 'glaikit' – empty and vacuous.

I asked him to think about the troublesome experience, which was, I thought, being hit by the bully in the street when he was 16. I asked him to conjure up as clear an image as he could of that experience, not to talk about it but have it in his head, and follow my finger with his eyes.

Eventually I said, 'What's happening?'

He replied, 'I'm a year old, a little older, perhaps, and I'm falling down the stairs.' He reached up and rubbed the front of his head.

There was an innocence, a lightness in his voice. 'Are you OK?' I asked.

He nodded and smiled. 'Nothing broken. In fact, I pretty much bounced. I bumped my forehead, but it frightened me more than anything else. I'm sitting in a heap at the bottom of the stairs, crying my eyes out. I guess I'm crying for attention.'

'Are your parents there?'

His expression darkened. 'Yes,' he said. 'Now they are.'

'What are they doing?'

He said that his mother and father were yelling at him for having fallen. It was a little bit difficult for me to accept. I couldn't see his parents shouting at anyone, least of all their one-year-old child. But when people are frightened, they often react by overreacting. And with Peter being so little, they must have been terrified out of their wits that he'd damaged himself, or might fall again.

The fascinating thing for me was how far I'd been able to regress him. Most people have difficulty thinking of anything before they're three or four. But here was Peter recalling a memory from his first eighteen months of life.

I got him to do the eye movements again.

'What's happening now?'

He said, 'I'm now about three, and I've snuck out of the house.' He told me he was quite a mischievous little boy. He'd gone to the local shop and come home with a chocolate bar. 'It was a Topic or a Kit Kat – no, it was a Mars bar.'

His parents were angry with him and berated him for being a naughty boy. He'd eventually had to take it back to the shop.

Again, we did the eye movements.

I asked him, 'Where are you now?'

'I'm now seven.'

He was riding his scooter, and had bumped the front wheel up against some obstruction. He'd gone head over heels and hit his head on a tree. He was knocked out. When he came to, he was lying on the ground, and his mum and dad were standing over him, berating him again.

He suddenly snapped his fingers. 'That's it,' he said. 'That's what this is all about.'

'What what's all about?'

Still in an EMDR trance, he looked at me and said, 'It's all about being blamed for things that aren't my fault.'

The trauma for him when he was 16 wasn't so much that he'd been beaten up by the bully, nor was it really about being transiently blinded. It was more about the expectation of being wrongfully blamed by his mother and father again for something that wasn't a wrongdoing per se, just infantile high jinks. And sure enough, he said, his mum and dad got very upset with him for having got into that situation in the first place.

What had effectively happened here was that a young man of 22 had been thinking about an event which had obviously had a major impact on him. With EMDR, I'd been able to open up the other trails in his memory that carried the same theme, as far back as when he was one. I could imagine how, with each subsequent event, the impact of the first traumatic incident had been reinforced and compounded.

This, I realized, was the beauty of EMDR. A 'penny dropping' isn't just an arbitrary thing; for the brain, it's a neurological process. You can't have a new thought without some accompanying new circuitry in the brain. Peter had had memory fragments that were not meaningful or part of a narrative before EMDR. Following EMDR, those fragments, the strands of the narrative, had all been pulled together and in neurological terms had formed a new pathway; one that cleared the block that had previously disrupted his thinking – the block that had caused his anxiety and depression. The formation of new neural circuitry is what any successful therapy has to achieve. CBT, a verbal, logical therapy worked on the left-hand side of the brain, the cognitive side; EMDR, on the other hand, worked on the right, the sensory part; the part that verbal reasoning couldn't touch. In Peter's case, the new circuitry laid down by EMDR would help the pre-frontal cortex inhibit the amygdala on the right-hand side of the brain. The amygdala, it will be recalled, are the two almond-shaped sensors within the limbic system that are highly attuned to danger. In the wake of a traumatic experience, the inhibiting role of the pre-frontal cortex can go badly awry; something is needed to detune the amygdala's hyper-sensitivity to danger – and this is what effective therapies do. In Peter's case, a verbal therapy wouldn't have worked, because the 'penny dropping' moments had been locked in his subconscious and it needed a therapy that unlocked the subconscious to reach them.

For about a year afterwards, Peter was free of his PTSD. He was doing his studies at home and considering going back to college to complete his course. He was doing fine. He had a job, he was saving money, his behaviour had settled down, his mother and father were very pleased with him.

He was working as an under-manager in a retail premises in his local town and a South African girl who worked there was having problems with her work permit. She was about to have to go back to Cape Town, which she didn't want to do. She invited Peter out, and they did a lot of drinking together. He escorted her home. There was a bit of kissing on the doorstep but nothing more, and then he went home.

The following morning, the family were woken by the police beating on the door at 6 am. They carted Peter off, accused him of rape, and he spent a week in the cells before being taken to court. He denied all charges. Her story was fragile and there was no forensic evidence. Regardless, the magistrate committed him for trial in the crown court.

While he was awaiting trial, the local newspaper published his photograph and made him appear to be guilty. He was basically witch-hunted out of his home. It was yet another event in his life that made him resentful of the unfairness of it all, and, not surprisingly, it had a massive impact. It brought his PTSD reaction flooding back. Maybe if he'd had longer to desensitize and live a normal life, he'd have been all right. But if I'd been writing the script for a movie on the subject I couldn't have thought of a more powerful way of bringing back his original themes of unfairness.

The case took a year to come to court, and the jury took all of ten minutes to reach their unanimous verdict. He was completely exonerated. As importantly, his PTSD disappeared.

I got a letter from him a few years later to tell me that he'd got a first-class honours degree in English from Durham University, which I thought was absolutely fantastic. He'd got there in the end. We remain in touch. He's still doing well and has developed quite a talent – the poetry that he's shown me is outstanding. Although he is still finding it difficult to settle down to 'life' – he hasn't yet got a full-time job – I know he's going to be all right. The poetry is a sign that he's 'bedding-in'; the career, perhaps in an area that will employ his writing talents, will come.

He was the first person I'd ever used EMDR on, and the technique had provided a breakthrough. So why don't I use it on everyone I see? It's hard to answer that. I think it's partly time, and partly that I still believe I ought to be fully trained in it before I'm let loose on the public. I've used it only two or three times in clinical settings, when there's been a special reason.

Someone who has been very influential on my career, a clinician,

researcher and teacher called Bessel van der Kolk – a man who had
been at the forefront of PTSD research for 20 years – once asked me
if I liked taking a patient's history. Bessel was one of the handful of
early PTSD professionals, alongside Sandy McFarlane, Morgan
O'Connell and myself, who'd found themselves on the 'frontier of
the frontier' of PTSD research.

'Yes, I do,' I said. 'It's an aspect of the job that I enjoy very much.'

'Then do yourself a favour,' he said. 'Learn how to do EMDR
properly. You'll feel you're taking the story for a purpose. You'll
never look back.'

Bessel was absolutely right.

As well as being a remarkable trauma specialist, Bessel had by now
become a good friend – we had met on a number of occasions and,
while sparring on the issues that separated us, I had always enjoyed
his company.

I admired Bessel because he wasn't afraid of controversy. He was
a big advocate of EMDR, even though it hadn't at that stage been
clinically proven or approved, and this had set him against much of
the psychiatric and neurobiological mainstream, which said that new
techniques shouldn't be used until they'd been established under
laboratory conditions. Bessel's point, and I agreed, was that psychotherapists – people like the remarkable Heather Robyn – had been
using EMDR on their patients for years and had been witnessing
astonishing results. Why wait years for clinical trials to take place,
when suffering could be alleviated in the meantime? This was the
sort of proactivity that characterized Bessel's work. He even ran a
theatre group, located at the trauma centre he'd set up in Boston,
dedicated to working with violent, traumatized teenagers.

A Dutchman by birth, Bessel first came across trauma professionally when in the late 1970s he was working in America with the
Veterans Association – before the phenomenon had been properly
recognized in *DSM-III*, the version that appeared in the 1980s, soon
after I arrived at Wroughton. Bessel's arrival at the VA was only
shortly after the end of the Vietnam conflict and the VA's official
posture was that there was no such thing as PTSD – a position that
made it impossible for Bessel to do the one thing that he really
wanted to do: research the condition – a condition that he could

clearly see in the anguish of returned combatants, many of whom, in their own minds, were still fighting in the jungles of South-East Asia. Not put off by the VA's then position, Bessel and his colleagues did their own studies on Vietnam vets and soon realized that the PTSD they were witnessing contained twin characteristics of hyper-arousal and dissociation. Quoted later, Bessel described this as the 'paradoxical conundrum' at the heart of trauma. Traumatized people, he said, either saw and felt their trauma – as if they were experiencing it for the first time – or saw and felt nothing at all. Soon afterwards, he wote a book, *Post-Traumatic Stress Disorder: Psychological and Biological Sequelae*, the first book to be published on the subject. Still frustrated by the VA's refusal to admit to the phenomenon, he took his research to the Massachusetts Mental Health Center, a state hospital and psychiatric teaching institution associated with the Harvard Medical School. It was here that he saw first-hand something that I had also witnessed, not just in the process of treating patients, but in courtrooms where traumatized litigants were forced to go over their trauma again and again, making it worse, not better, as a result.

But it was in his witnessing of the deep psychological scars inflicted by a natural disaster, a hurricane that ravaged Puerto Rico in 1989 – Hurricane Hugo – that Bessel was the first to recognize what I also knew to be true: that helplessness after a trauma was as much responsible for its lingering persistence in sufferers as the impact of the original trauma itself. I had seen it in one-on-one cases. The mountain rescuers at Lockerbie. Frank the Tornado pilot. Trev the fireman. But Bessel had witnessed it on a grand scale. Accompanying US Federal Emergency Management Agency officials to the disaster area, Bessel noticed the inhabitants busily trying to rebuild their shattered lives – getting on with the business of survival. But then the FEMA officials stepped in and ordered all reparation work – the rebuilding of houses, shops, schools and so forth – to cease until official permission to begin the reconstruction process was given. The result, Bessel noticed, was pandemonium. All the energy with which these traumatized people had been pitching into trying to make things better suddenly had nowhere to go. The result was an upsurge in violence, looting and rioting.

'The brain is an action organ,' I'd seen Bessel quoted as saying years later in an online article in the *Therapy Networker*, 'and as it matures, it's increasingly characterized by the formation of patterns and schemas geared to promoting action.' If this can't happen, or is blocked, as was the case in Puerto Rico, the people to whom the trauma has happened cannot re-create their place of safety and often develop PTSD, he believed; and this, too, gelled with my own experience. But what Bessel went on to articulate was also remarkable, because he realized that the traditional therapy process – usually characterized by one-on-one treatment sessions between patient and psychotherapist, often using CBT to process the trauma – wasn't working. Words, he realized, couldn't articulate the depth of the trauma – a trauma that was as much about something being stuck in the body as the brain. I remember him saying, 'The trouble with trauma is that you can't keep your body out of it.'

In 1994, in a paper called 'The Body Keeps the Score', van der Kolk explained how traumatic memories were, in effect, staying locked in the brain's non-verbal, non-conscious, subcortical regions – the amygdala, thalamus, hippocampus, hypothalamus and brain stem. This was verified shortly afterwards by MRI scans carried out by the neuro-imaging lab at Massachusetts General, where eight trauma patient volunteers were scanned while they remembered their traumas. The result was unequivocal. As they recalled their traumatic events, the left pre-frontal cortex, particularly Broca's area, the part of the brain where speech and thought processing occur, closed down. Speech therapies, therefore, would not have the effect they were supposed to have on the trauma – something deeper was needed; something that accessed not only the deeper reaches of the brain where the trauma had become 'stuck', but possibly the body as well.

Van der Kolk had become impressed by the work of a body therapist called Peter Levine, who argued that trauma became locked in the body and it was thus in the body that it had to be located and treated. Levine explained that the flee, fight or freeze response to danger, if thwarted in humans, resulted in undischarged energy in the central nervous system that eventually developed, once the actual danger had passed, into PTSD. Verbal therapies, body therapists like Levine argued, would not be enough to reach and unblock the trauma, and Bessel agreed, which was what had led him to be such an out-and-out proponent of EMDR. However, some strange phenomena came with it.

*

The next patient I used EMDR on was a woman in her mid-forties called Sally who came into my clinic one day as an urgent referral. She'd recently had surgery for breast cancer.

A routine mammogram had detected some suspicious-looking calcified tissue in both breasts. The surgeon wanted to remove this tissue, but wouldn't be able to see it with the naked eye. He needed to have it marked by the radiology department. The way they did this was by inserting metal rods to triangulate the positions of the calcified tissue.

Already anxious, Sally went in for the mammography, but the radiologist insisted on pushing the rods in without any local anaesthetic. They were the diameter of small knitting needles, and they weren't pointed. There wasn't even a nick made in the skin first to facilitate entry. The radiologist had to push hard to puncture the skin. My patient had had that done to her three times. She pleaded with the woman either to give her an anaesthetic or to stop. She was completely ignored. She was traumatized and she was trapped.

The hospital refused to apologize and maintained that this was standard practice. Indeed, at the annual conference of radiologists, when asked the question: 'Do you use anaesthetic when you push these rods into the breast for mammograms?' only 50 per cent said yes. In other words, half of Britain's radiologists didn't feel anaesthetic was necessary.

Sally's ordeal wasn't over. On the operating theatre table, biopsies of tissue are taken under what's called a frozen section. They're looked at by a pathologist immediately, and a decision is made there and then to remove the breast or not, depending on whether it's malignant. A woman who consents to a frozen-section biopsy is consenting to go under an anaesthetic, in the knowledge that she may or may not wake up with a breast removed.

Small wonder, perhaps, that she developed PTSD. She was referred to me in distress. She'd developed acute PTSD. She had flashbacks to the radiologist, to what she'd said, and to the needles and the pain, and the feeling of being trapped and helpless.

This lady was extremely hyper-aroused and I knew that she would need powerful tranquillizers to bring her anxiety levels down. She was too highly aroused to pay any attention to being taught breathing exercises to relax her and I decided to try EMDR. Just one session had a major, beneficial effect. The frequency and intensity of the flashbacks faded, and though I prescribed some medication, she went on her way.

I did not see her again for a few weeks. In the meantime she had been suffering from ongoing symptoms of PTSD but at a much less intense level. She had tried to find out if the way that she had been treated, inserting the needles into the breast tissue without any local anaesthetic, was the conventional method. No straight answers were forthcoming and she had decided to take the hospital and the radiologist to court.

She implored me to write her medico-legal report. She explained that she had been advised by her solicitor that it was a better idea for another psychiatrist, who was not involved in her treatment, to write the report on her behalf because the court would see it as being more objective. Sally explained that she could not bear the thought of having to describe what had happened to her to another psychiatrist because it would remind her so powerfully of what she had had to go through and it would be unbearable. I believed it was right for me to do the report, so I agreed.

The report was duly prepared and the wheels of the litigation process rolled on, but typically very slowly. Sally remained vulnerable and there were some relapses in her PTSD symptoms, which is usually what happens in the countdown to trial. There is no closure and the adversarial nature of personal injury litigation tends to have a negative effect on claimants with psychological injuries. The ideal would be 'therapeutic jurisprudence', where the actual process of litigation would be therapeutic by giving claimants a better opportunity to understand what has happened to them and how they have reacted to it. In effect, such a process of litigation would be a form of psychological debriefing. This did not happen to Sally. Without doubt, Sally is the worst example I've encountred of how badly retraumatized a person can be by the litigation process, but there have been many, many more examples of how inappropriate and inhumane the present system is.

The defendants, the NHS, did not accept my report as being objective enough because I was treating Sally, and they wanted a report from their own expert. They chose a female consultant psychiatrist from Cambridge. My patient was still very vulnerable and she was apprehensive about being examined by a female psychiatrist. The consultant radiologist who had inserted the needles without anaesthetic was also female. There was no question of the psychiatrist coming to her home, so she was going to have to travel to another person's domain, quite a long way away, in Cambridge.

As she was waiting to see the lady psychiatrist I was aware of Sally's mounting tension. In our weekly sessions she described her mental anxiety, but she also began to tell me about pains in her left breast, the side the needles had been inserted into.

About two days before making the trip to Cambridge, the receptionist broke into a session I was having with another patient at my clinic at the Ridgeway and told me she was very sorry but she thought I should take this particular call. She was dead right. Sally was screaming down the line, unable to control her fear. Eventually, she calmed down enough to tell me that she had come out of the shower and noticed three red marks on her left breast exactly where the needles had been inserted. Her anxiety had affected me and I could hardly believe what I was hearing.

She said, 'The marks are where the rods went.'

I said, 'Do you have a camera? Could you get your husband to take photographs of these marks? Would you come and see me tomorrow?'

They brought the photos in the following day. The marks on her breast were clear. She told me that they coincided exactly with where the needles had gone in. Not only had they started off red and raised, but also when I saw them a day later they were slightly cratered, red and black. She was checked by the GP, who couldn't explain the injuries. He referred her to the surgeon, who did some special X-rays and tests to rule out a recurrence of her growth. She was clear.

We were left without any physical explanation for these marks. After Erica, the chocolate box lady with the bruise on her leg, I was tuned into body memories, but this was something else. I rang Heather Robyn and asked whether she could offer any explanation for what was happening.

When Heather asked me what they looked like, I found myself struggling to find the right words. Somewhat embarrassed, I told Heather that the only word I could come up with that might describe such a thing was 'stigmata', the Christ-type wounds that are occasionally reported by ultra-devout Christians.

As soon as she saw them, Heather agreed. 'These *are* stigmata, physical sensitivities, memories of an actual injury, of a trauma.'

The idea came to me to canvass pals around the world, the people I knew to be actively treating people with PTSD, and who would see complicated cases. Bessel van der Kolk and Sandy Bloom were on the list, as were Sandy McFarlane in Australia and various others in the UK. I outlined the case, and said, 'These marks appear to be body memories of the original injury, without any other cause. Have you ever seen anything like this before?'

I can't remember how many I sent out, but I remember the number of responses: zero.

Not a single person responded. Not even Bessel said, 'No, but this is very interesting – have you had any further thoughts?'

I got the impression I was lifting the lid on a taboo.

I thought, how can it be that people who share the same patients can have very different insights into what these things are? How can one be so accepting and not the other? But of course, a therapist isn't really concerned with evidence-based stuff, or proving that something is there. They see it day in, day out, and just accept that it exists. Medics, on the other hand, have a tradition of demanding evidence-based proof and labelling phenomena as accurately as possible. Even leaving aside the litigious aspect that had crept in all over the world, especially in the States, where people wouldn't want to speculate for fear of legal repercussions, there was a wide discrepancy between the attitude of therapists and doctors. Doctors didn't seem to want to acknowledge that this phenomenon existed.

I wouldn't take it lying down. I went to the American Psychiatric Association convention that year, where there was a section of the meeting about trauma. A panel of experts gave presentations and took questions from the floor – but not directly. The questions were filtered. Instead of the chairman asking for questions from the floor and someone running round the hall with a microphone, we had to fill in a small slip of paper. They were gathered together and the chairman sifted through until he found what he considered an interesting question. I wrote a very brief description of body memories, and asked if any members of the panel had experience of this in the context of trauma.

I could see that the chairman didn't exactly have a barrelful of questions to get through, and he seemed to ask the panel as many questions as there were in his hand, but he didn't ask mine. It was plain as day to me that medical people were trying to avoid the issue. They didn't want to acknowledge that these things happened.

When I flew back, it was time for Sally's case to go to court – and I was in for a pleasant surprise. The female psychiatrist turned out also to be a psychotherapist. She was aware of body memories, and was able to support my views in court. She just gave the story the way she saw it, and it largely coincided with mine. Sally walked away not feeling a crank, her version of events was upheld and she was vindicated. She won her case, but, more importantly, her PTSD disappeared – at least to the extent that she could lead pretty much a normal life.

Once again, this demonstrated to me that PTSD was infinitely more complex than the textbooks indicated. What seemed so utterly bizarre to me was that I was part of a fraternity that was operating on a frontier, yet the frontier itself had a frontier – a place beyond which a number of my colleagues, it appeared, were not prepared to go.

Following 9/11, President George W. Bush declared his 'Global War on Terror' and was joined in his crusade by Tony Blair. We were told, following the attacks on the Twin Towers, that fresh terror attacks of equal if not greater magnitude were possible, perhaps inevitable. If the world had seemed like a reasonably safe place in the last few years of the twentieth century, it didn't feel that way any more.

I felt, to a degree, back where I'd been before Lockerbie. We had made so many strides since, but there was still so much about the brain and the way it reacted to trauma that we did not understand, and yet now, it seemed, we needed to get to grips with it as never before.

Chapter 19

The Man Who Disappeared from Himself

A patient whom I will call Jack was referred to me by his GP. A tall, good-looking man of about 35, Jack was a software expert who'd left the Army about five years earlier after 17 years in uniform.

The story was that he'd received a head injury on a skiing holiday in France. He'd been admitted to an intensive care unit, where he was in a coma for 48 hours. A brain scan had revealed some bruising. He then regained consciousness and was discharged a few days later. Since that time, he'd had increased mood swings. He was feeling very anxious when he came to see me.

He was a nice chap, but vague about things: not vague about himself, or being avoidant, he just wasn't quite sure what had happened. He said he couldn't really understand why he was thought to be in a coma. His friends had told him he'd got up from the snow after falling and hitting his head on a mogul. It bled profusely, but he was talking to them on his way to the ambulance that took him off the mountain.

To begin with, I thought he was suffering from a post-head-injury anxiety depression, which is quite common. I prescribed Prozac and intended to review him, but before I had a chance to do so he underwent an adverse reaction to the medication. He had a high temperature and became very confused. I saw him as a matter of urgency and we stopped the Prozac.

I probed more deeply into his background. 'Is there anything in your past,' I asked, 'any event that you feel had a powerful impact on you and you haven't fully come to terms with?'

He said no, he couldn't think of anything. Then his brow creased. 'Hang on, when I was three, I was on holiday with my mum and dad—' He paused and added: 'No, that can't be significant, that's far too far away.'

'Go on,' I prompted. 'What happened?'

'I fell into a swimming pool. I couldn't swim, of course, at that age, and I was drowning. I could actually see myself drowning. I remember that quite vividly. And then I can remember seeing, as if I were a bystander, my father diving into the pool and rescuing me, and then taking me out of the pool and resuscitating me, mouth to mouth.'

He paused again as the memory played out. I could see how upsetting it was to him. It was another minute at least before he continued.

'I remember standing by my father's side wondering how this could be possible – because I was actually standing next to him, and yet that was me he was resuscitating on the poolside.'

I nodded. A decade earlier, before the Invisible Girl, I'd not have recognized the signs. This man had had an out-of-body experience at the age of three, and he'd never felt that he'd got back in. He disappeared from himself, and this had had a major, traumatizing effect on his life.

The family had lived in Malaysia for a while, and one day his brother lost control of his bike and careered on to the main street. He was hit by a passing truck and suffered severe injuries. Jack, the disappeared one, felt that he should have done something to prevent that from happening, but was immobilized. He couldn't explain why he didn't react.

Jack had gone on to join the Army at the age of 18, and had found it a good place for him to be. He felt safe there. There were boundaries. People wore things on their shoulders that told you what rank they were and how to react to them.

His problems had only begun after he left the Army and had to adapt to civilian life. He became accustomed to doing extraordinary things to prove that he was real. He would do extreme sports, and drive his car at outrageous speeds through country lanes. He did things like kite surfing. He got dumped on a pierside in Poole and was badly injured, but was totally undeterred. He felt the exhilaration, and he felt that if he got through it he must be alive. These activities were the mirrors that he dared to look into to demonstrate to himself that he was still here.

By the time of the skiing holiday, he had not that long been hired by one of the software giants. He'd been working like stink, yet his appraisal was lukewarm. It made him feel that, if he couldn't judge his performance, then maybe he didn't have a good grasp of who he was. It was on the ski slopes that he tested himself this time. He admitted that he pushed himself harder and harder until he took on an impossible mogul at speed and crashed.

I went to visit a colleague in Winchester not long afterwards. Robert Oxslade was somebody I knew from afar but admired a lot. A Brit who'd lived in Canada until a few years ago, he was now doing occupational psychiatry work with the Navy and the Metropolitan Police. I was interested in his ideas about the connections between sleep and PTSD.

Robert told me about some work that had been done in Canada on 'opiate antagonists'. Dissociation, which was of interest to both of us, was linked to endorphin flooding, and he had written some papers on the subject.

Opiates/opioids are similar to morphine in structure and are commonly used for their potent painkilling properties. Illegal opioids such as heroin have similar effects, but are more likely to cause dependence or addiction. High doses, excessive intake or abuse or overdose with these drugs can cause reduced lung function and respiratory depression, which can be life-threatening.

Opiate antagonists bind to certain receptors in the brain, but instead of activating them, they prevent the binding of the opiates themselves. In fact, if the receptors are already occupied by, for example, heroin molecules, an opiate antagonist like naloxone (administered by injection into a vein, muscle or under the skin, or via a drip into a vein) will quickly push off the heroin molecules and rescue the patient from a drug overdose. A 'cuckoo molecule'. Another, naltrexone, which is an orally administered opiate antagonist, is used to help recovering heroin addicts stay drug-free.

Endo-rphins are the opioids from within; *exo*-rphins are the opioids from without. The original *exo*-rphin – opium – is actually, therefore, the *endo*-rphin of the poppy plant. Endorphins make you feel good in the same way that opiates do – they take away pain and they make you feel calm. It is interesting to realize that we make these chemicals ourselves in our own bodies and have discovered, through history and by accident, that nature provides analogues of these chemicals which are often more powerful than the ones we make ourselves. For example, we have our own morphine and we have our own Valium. Our own inbuilt Valium (the generic name for the group of chemicals is benzodiazepines) is called GABA. Endorphins weren't discovered until 1972.

When I was a medical student, we learned that the nearly 300-year-old Cartesian paradigm, which teaches us that the mind and body are separate, was one of the most sacrosanct and enduring in all of science.

I was taught that gamma-amino-butyric acid (GABA) was an intrinsic tranquillizing substance, but that was about it. Long after I'd left, oxytocin came to the fore. Another intrinsic tranquillizer, oxytocin was tagged the 'bonding hormone'. It was the hormone that makes women feel so strongly attached to their babies and their husbands. The person who isolated the brain's opiate receptors in 1972 was an American postgraduate student named Candace Pert, and it won her a Nobel Prize.

A receptor is like a chemical lock on a cell, into which a particular substance, or key, fits. A typical nerve cell has millions of receptors on its surface, each waiting for another molecule to flow past and bind to it. When the two join into one, the receptor changes shape, and that shift sends a message into the cell itself.

Candace Pert's discovery that the brain is hard-wired to respond to the body's internal morphine opened up an entire new field of research and led to the discovery of endorphins. Eventually, a class of tiny proteins known as peptides, including the opiates and serotonin, were found to regulate our behaviour, mood and general health.

Our bodies are studded with peptide receptors. 'Information molecules' or 'information substances' communicate across systems which were for the most part traditionally considered separate. The new neurology demonstrated communication between the neurological, immune, endocrine and gastrointestinal systems. The traditional neurotransmitters, such as dopamine, histamine and GABA, comprise only a tiny fraction of nervous system communication. The peptides, carriers of emotion and other information, make up 95 per cent.

Candace Pert said that this means consciousness operates at a cellular level, involving each receptor and the particular peptide that binds to it. Another way of putting it: your subconscious mind is really your body. Peptides, she postulated, are the biochemical correlate of emotion. She has even stated subsequently that our white blood cells, which contain many of the same receptors and chemicals as the brain, are bits of the brain floating around the body. She talks of a kind of molecular psychology, a true biology of emotions.

Pert first spoke about the mind–body connection in a keynote address at the 1985 symposium for the Institute of Noetic Sciences, an organization that supports studies in consciousness. A version of her talk was published in the *Journal of Immunology*, entitled 'Neuropeptides and Their Receptors: A Psychosomatic Network'. It detailed her view of emotions and health.

According to Pert's talk, peptides provide our body's most basic communication network. To study the molecules' specific function, Pert and colleagues began taking wafer-thin slices of rat brains and mapping peptide receptors in the brain. Thick clusters were recorded in parts of the brain long associated with emotion.

According to Pert, the hippocampus is the brain's emotional gateway. Almost every variety of peptide receptor is found there, she said. The amygdala, the brain's highly attuned sensors to danger, and their inhibitor, the pre-frontal cortex, are also densely populated with peptide receptors.

Since emotions are regulated by neuropeptides, and the brain's memory centres are filled with receptors for these peptides, it's likely, she proposed, that emotion and memory are intertwined. What's more, the peptide network reaches into all the organs, glands, spinal cord and tissues of the body. According to Pert, this means that emotional memory is stored throughout the body. Emotions from anger to pleasure trigger a mass of bodily changes, of which facial expressions are simply the most obvious.

She quoted the example of her never getting a cold on a skiing trip. She loved to ski and it made her happy and excited. The peptide norepinephrine (noradrenaline) is the chemical that stimulates excitement, and the cold virus uses the same receptors. When you're happy, the virus can't lock on to the receptors. That's why, she suggested, depressed people get sick more often.

You can access emotional memory anywhere in the network, she said, and that had now become obvious to me. How else could therapies based on therapeutic touch, or EMDR, engender profound transformations? Her theory is that repressed emotions and memories might actually be stored in receptors throughout the body. In other words, body and brain are not separate. Scrap the Cartesian model.

In the Pert model, emotions travel in both directions, from the brain into the body and up the body into the brain, where they are integrated and expressed. She has called herself a 'molecular Reichian', after the theory of radical psychotherapist Wilhelm Reich, who believed that body 'armouring' and muscular tension were a result of emotional repression, and led to illness. Breathing deeply, as in yoga and meditation, may alter the flow of peptides. To be sure, changes in the rate and depth of breathing produce changes in the kind of peptides that are released from the brain.

Perhaps the connection between emotions and health is more than folklore. Even the immune system may be a different kind of emotional brain. Could being in touch with our emotions facilitate the flow of the peptides that direct our immune system's natural killer cells, she asked. Might that explain why women with breast cancer live longer when they participate in support groups?

I found her work exciting. Babies' brains develop in the womb, bathed in chemicals like serotonin that can make you feel calm, or dopamine and adrenaline that can make you feel afraid or hyper-alert.

Dr Margot Sunderland, director of the Institute of Child Mental Health, and somebody else I'd come to respect hugely, also said that: 'Relationships change brains, not just minds.' She was saying that persistent emotional states became personality traits.

Candace Pert has shown that our brains (and our bodies) are full of chemical messengers and that they basically carry one of two messages – the first being to be wary, and the second to relax and have fun. She said in her book *Molecules of Emotion* [1997] that: '[In our brain], each of us has his or her own . . . finest drugstore available at the cheapest cost – to produce all the drugs we ever need to run our body-mind . . .'

If a child is brought up in a world where it senses that it is in persistent danger and threat, then it is the stress hormones such as adrenaline, noradrenaline and dopamine that will become dominant. These chemicals govern behaviours that actually help 'avoidant-attached' or 'ambivalent-attached' children to survive in adversity.

If a child is brought up in a world it perceives to be safe, then optimal emotional chemical activation will be via a different set of chemicals such as oxytocin, endorphins, prolactin, GABA and natural benzodiazepines. Such children are described as 'secure-attached', and they have the advantage of being able to dip into this treasure trove of chemicals denied to less securely attached children. In this way, a securely attached child lives in a completely different world from a traumatized child.

Endorphin flooding linked to dissociation was the chemistry that underpinned the faraway, daydream-like states that promoted the not-being-in-the-room type of scenario, and treatment resistance.

I put Jack, the man who disappeared from himself, on an opiate antagonist and within days there were quite dramatic changes in his behaviour. His perception of the world jarred at times, but he felt more comfortable, more connected; ready for therapeutic treatment, which was key. I referred him for a course of psychotherapy and he did really well. By putting him on an opiate antagonist, I was able to block the endorphins that produce dissociation. Because he couldn't retreat into dissociation any more when faced with difficult situations, he learned to deal with everyday life in a grounded way. Even if confronted by awkward issues in his psychotherapy sessions, he couldn't retreat into dissociation. He was determined and bright and gradually became more expert in the thrust and parry of everyday situations and is now a successful executive in the software industry.

The big breakthrough in my thinking stemming from his case – and the role Robert Oxslade and Candace Pert played in his treatment – lay in the fact that I could now visualize the brain as a 'plastic' structure. It wasn't static; it was dynamic and could change. If the hippocampus (the part of the brain that played major roles in short-term memory and spatial navigation) changed as a result of acute trauma, then you had to depend on that part being restored to normal before processing could occur properly and fully. Was it remotely possible, I wondered, for the hippocampus to be restored to full function in this way?

My journey thus far had shown me that PTSD was not an illness, but a survival tool; one that had been created by nature to see us through events of maximum danger and distress. PTSD, unlike cancer, wasn't a case of the body 'going wrong'. It was a natural response to highly unnatural events.

If PTSD was a 'normal' reaction and reversible – and our group therapy techniques had demonstrated that in four out of five cases it was – then my intuition told me that damage to the key components in the complex, interlocking machinery of PTSD, the hippocampus being one of them, was reversible too.

I'd seen three people already on this particular day, and, unusually for me, I was ahead of time and had a quarter of an hour to kill before the arrival of my next patient. Sebastian was somebody I'd known for years and I always looked forward to his visits. He was highly intelligent, very amusing, good company and, despite the seriousness of the issues underlying the reasons for his visits, we usually managed to find time for a catch-up and a bit of a laugh. He was also a challenger; upfront and robust if I said something he didn't agree with. I liked that. It meant we had a proper dialogue. He was in his late thirties, but had been in his twenties when I first met him at Ticehurst. He'd been suffering from complex PTSD – the condition that develops when, instead of there being a single trauma, it's been a relentless drip-drip-drip.

When repetitive trauma hits children and adolescents, as was well known, it can have a significant impact on their developing personalities. Individuals can only respond to trauma with the defences at their disposal and for children these were mainly hysteria, paranoia and the obsessive-compulsive defence. The capacity to use cognitive, problem-solving defences forms later in the development of the brain structures that underpin behaviour, thought, mood, emotions in general and style of memory.

If children and adolescents are traumatized over and over, it makes them reliant on those defences, and this can block their ability to mature. People with complex PTSD as a result of a trauma in childhood or adolescence tend to go on to use those defences in adulthood if they're reminded of that trauma or if they come across challenging situations. They tend not to respond with humour or more mature, cognitive defences. It's not in their make-up.

The impact of trauma on psychological and biological functioning following exposure has been a major focus in clinical psychiatry and in research for the past three decades or so. This may seem to be a long time but, in reality, it is not compared with other areas of psychiatry such as schizophrenia, and it certainly represents a very brief time compared with some areas of physical medicine.

The diagnostic criteria for PTSD focus on the intrusive memories and disordered arousal that are the typical, distinguishing characteristics of post-traumatic changes in function. Within this framework, the remaining symptoms of PTSD are understood as avoidant strategies, an attempt to minimize the stimulation of trauma memories and impressions which will cause the individual to re-experience an inherently unpleasant event.

'Simple' or single-event PTSD had three main distinguishing characteristics that made it unique: persistent distressing recollections of the trauma; persistent avoidant behaviours to minimize reminders of the trauma; and persistent hyper-arousal and hyper-vigilance. In essence, exposure to life-threatening trauma switched on biological and psychological survival mechanisms that would naturally persist until the trauma was understood, the sensory images were processed, there was a sense that it happened in the past and that lessons had been learned and it was safe to move on into the future.

When recovery and resolution occurred within one month – 30 days or thereabouts – the traumatic stress reaction was called an 'acute' stress reaction. When symptoms persisted beyond one month, the traumatic stress reaction became 'chronic' and could persist for months or even years or until resolution took place. Chronic reaction to a single stressor in adulthood led to the development of 'simple PTSD' with the three persistent characteristics already documented and, untreated, would eventually lead to enduring changes in personality and behaviour.

Chronic reaction to multiple stressors in childhood before the personality has reached its adult form, on the other hand, led to the development of the three characteristic features of PTSD *and* the seven characteristic features of DES (disorders of extreme stress). This could also happen in adulthood following periods of prolonged captivity or extreme over-control. The combination of PTSD and DES was known as 'complex PTSD'.

Complex PTSD was central to Sebastian's case. I'd referred him for psychotherapy with different therapists and assumed all was going well, but he'd emailed me recently to say he was thinking of coming to see me at my London clinic.

'I'm all right,' he'd said, 'but I think we need to talk about medication.'

I worried about what might be happening to make him consider going back on his meds.

In that spare quarter of an hour before our appointment, I'd picked up that month's *Journal of Traumatic Stress*, the organ of the International Society for Traumatic Stress Studies. There were two or three articles on the front page that caught my eye, but one in particular grabbed my attention: 'Tonic immobility mediates the influence of peri-traumatic fear and perceived inescapability on post-traumatic stress symptom severity among sexual assault survivors' (Bovin, Jager-Hyman, Gold, Marx, Sloan).

It couldn't possibly have been more on the money relative to Sebastian, who was the survivor of a sexual assault that had taken place while he was at his preparatory boarding school.

'In response to life-threatening circumstances that are both inescapable and elicit intense fear (e.g. capture by a predator),' I read, 'animals often exhibit a set of unconditioned responses that include gross motor inhibition, motor tremors, analgesia, suppressed vocal behavior, fixed and unfocused stare, and periods of eye closures.' These behaviours, the article said, were known collectively as 'tonic immobility'.

Tonic immobility was thought to be the ultimate response of an animal where escape was impossible. Because predators were less likely to attack or kill immobile prey, tonic immobility was seen as an evolutionarily adaptive strategy that increased the animal's chances of survival.

Up until this moment, I had known that phenomenon as *freezing* – and something that had always worried me about it was the sheer range of the spectrum. Freezing wasn't always freezing. Sometimes it could be a state in which people were hyper-aroused, their senses highly vigilant – the initial phase of response to perceived danger, 'stopping and staring', taking in as much information as possible before making a move. This type of 'freezing' led to a decision to 'fight or flee'.

I thought of the Invisible Girl. She had known the danger she was in as she flew through the air. She'd dissociated, but she'd been aware enough to think she had to get back into herself before she hit the ground. She didn't know what would happen if she didn't: she just sensed the outcome would be highly dangerous. She wasn't frozen, however: she couldn't have been in a state of complete and utter immobility or she wouldn't have thought those things. She'd have been totally numbed.

But tonic immobility was different from the freezing behaviour that occurs early in the encounter stage of the defensive reflex. Freezing, the article stated, was an initial response during which the animal stopped moving to avoid detection and shifted its resources to locating the predator. In other words, the highly aroused senses pick out the predator. They sense the danger, the prey freezes, and all its senses scan the environment for the predator.

The writers were saying that when a person was in freeze-state, they had the capacity to jump out of it if the situation demanded it. But tonic immobility resulted in nothing but motionless posture and unresponsiveness – a big fat zero.

I found the most riveting nugget right at the end, in the wash-up at the bottom of the paper: results of trials suggested that tonic immobility might be an important factor in determining whether sexual assault survivors developed PTSD. Research on tonic immobility, the writers concluded, might also inform our ability to treat sexual assault survivors who experience post-traumatic symptoms. Reminders of the original trauma could produce the same effect – suppression of the body's autonomic nervous system.

This was interesting because the classic concept of PTSD was that when reminded of the trauma there was autonomic *hyper*-arousal – in other words, if the actual experience of trauma involved physical fear responses like speeding up of the heart, dry mouth, butterflies in the stomach, then when you re-experienced the trauma you re-experienced those too. Yet what these authors were talking about was reminders causing *hypo*-arousal, i.e., suppression – quite the opposite. They were saying that if tonic immobilization set in at the time of the trauma, then you would experience the same immobilization when reminded of it and experiencing a flashback. It would, they said, be like going into a black hole, into nothingness.

Their final point was that traditional CBT-type treatments for PTSD wouldn't work in rare cases where tonic immobility had occurred; shades of the teaching espoused by Bessel van der Kolk and Peter Levine. But this went even further.

The traditional assumption, the *Journal of Traumatic Stress* authors went on, was that a patient had to have been hyper-aroused when they re-experienced their trauma, and thus the strategy, via CBT, was to desensitize that to reduce the level of arousal. They concluded that although these strategies might effectively treat many cases of PTSD, they might not be appropriate for all trauma survivors, particularly those who had experienced tonic immobility and did not display autonomic arousal to trauma cues.

Cases of PTSD in which clients responded to trauma with reduced physiological arousal (such as in the case of tonic immobility) might, therefore, need an alternative treatment strategy, such as increasing arousal to trauma cues. 'Importantly,' the authors stated at the end, 'these alternative treatments have not yet been empirically established through independent replications.' In other words, none of this was yet evidence-based.

To my mind, however, all of this fitted perfectly with other pieces of information, such as a film I'd seen recently on TV of a polar bear being shot with a tranquillizer dart so vets could tag it for research purposes.

The polar bear went into a state of tonic immobility. It fell flat on its face the moment the dart struck – far more quickly than the tranquillizer could have acted. It stayed face-down on the ice, limbs splayed, seemingly immobilized. Later, when the vets had done whatever they'd needed to do and the animal was waking up, it rolled on to its back and, for all the world, appeared to shadow-box vigorously with all four limbs in the air. It was simulating running away, completing the manoeuvre that it could have employed at the time to utilize its adrenaline.

Once again, nature had provided me with a set of clues. The polar bear had gone into a state of tonic immobility. But when it was coming round, as an animal ruled by its instincts, not its head, it reran the mobility into a state of freeze, and then into fight or flight – it was 'decoupling' and coming back out of its most tonic immobile state in stages. When the outburst of energy was finished, the bear had discharged the chemistry of the attempt to flee, had returned to a state of chemical balance or 'homeostasis' and was no longer trapped in its trauma.

This put me in mind of Paul MacLean and Stephen Porges' work on the psychophysiological basis for emotions. An *emotion* is defined as a mental and physiological state associated with a wide variety of feelings, thoughts and behaviour and is a subjective experience. A *feeling* is what is felt within and an *emotion* is what is expressed outwards. There is a distinction between *emotion* and the *results of the emotion*, principally behaviours and emotional expressions: people often behave in certain ways as a direct result of their emotional state, such as crying, fighting or fleeing.

Paul MacLean (1913–2007) was an American physician and neuroscientist who made significant contributions in the fields of physiology, psychiatry and brain research at Yale Medical School and the National Institute of Mental Health in the USA. His evolutionary *triune brain theory* proposed that the human brain was, in reality, three brains in one: the *reptilian complex*, the *limbic system* and the *neocortex*.

Paul MacLean served as a medical officer in the US army during the Second World War and belonged to the generation of American doctors who had seen action in that war and contributed to the first edition of *DSM*. He believed that learning how your brain works is a most important aspect of emotional control. His idea was that emotions are largely an automatic function of the human brain and this is the key to begin to control them and that personal growth and collective growth (evolution) is mostly a matter of exerting more control over our reflexes. He considered negative emotions to have a biological usefulness, but that they are largely destructive in modern humans living in our artificially enhanced environments.

The evolutionary triune brain theory emphasized the importance of evolution as an organizing principle that shaped both the structure of the nervous system and adaptive social behaviour. Paul MacLean was the first to identify the limbic system and recognize the important role of the sensory fibres of the vagus nerve in the regulation of brain and body function. As a result of his work, in the truest sense, it became understood that what affects the body affects the mind and emotions – and vice versa.

Stephen Porges, currently Professor of Psychiatry and Director of the Brain-Body Center in Chicago, is a neuroscientist with particular interests in understanding the neurobiology of social behaviour. His work crosses many disciplines and he has researched and published in the fields of anaesthetics, intensive care, ergonomics, exercise physiology, old age medicine, neurology, obstetrics, child medicine, psychiatry, psychology, space medicine and substance abuse. In 1994 he proposed the *polyvagal theory*, which extended the triune theory and linked the evolution of the autonomic nervous system to the emergence of social behaviour.

Porges had studied the evolution of the central nervous system in the animal kingdom and had identified three stages of evolution, each with its own inherent defence mechanisms.

The first stage of evolution generates the most primitive defensive behaviours, the so-called 'Level One' defences. This is a simple input/output reflex arc based on two different nuclei of the vagus nerve. The vagus nerve starts in the brain stem and extends down to the neck, chest and abdomen, where it contributes to the innervation of the viscera – the lungs and the stomach.

Besides output to the various organs in the body, the vagus nerve conveys sensory information about the state of the body's organs to the central nervous system. With Level One defences, therefore, the input is sensory and the output is motor. The tonic immobilization referred to above is the only defence mechanism available to more primitive animal forms.

Level Two defences are more highly evolved and take the form of a limbic system which produces the chemicals responsible for fight or flight. The limbic system first appeared in reptilian brains. This helps to explain where fight, flight and freeze come together. If the animal tries to fight or flee, but cannot because these responses are not going to be effective, then it will go into a state of helplessness – utter immobilization – and call upon the most primitive Level One defence.

I had this in my head when Sebastian came in. He hadn't changed at all. He appeared confident and smiled warmly as we shook hands. I couldn't help noticing that his right hand had a nasty-looking cut on it.

'How did you get that?'

He looked down. 'Oh, that's nothing,' he said. 'I got it from a swift.'

'A what?'

'A swift. The bird. We've got them nesting in the eaves of our house. Fascinating creatures. Did you know that the swift is the only bird in the world with an asymmetric wingbeat? You know what that means, don't you, Gordon?'

Sebastian knew that I was a polymath like him; into anything and everything, which was one of the reasons we got on so well. I hesitated a fraction too long. Sebastian knew a lot about animals.

'All other birds flap like this.' He raised and lowered both arms together and flapped for a second or two. 'A swift, on the other hand, flaps like this.' He lifted his left arm and lowered the right. Then he alternated the move and carried on flapping. I started to laugh.

'What?' he asked.

'Well,' I said, 'I'm a psychiatrist and, to somebody walking past my door, this might just be construed as a tiny bit mad.'

Now it was his turn to laugh. 'Good point. Hadn't thought of that.'

'You still haven't told me how you got the cut.'

'Our swifts have a habit of crashing on our lawn. It's the young ones. They haven't quite got the knack of flying yet. They're not supposed to land because their wings are too long – they can't take off again. My wife refuses to touch them and so do the kids, so I have to go out there, pick them up and chuck them back into the air.

Occasionally, they'll give me a bit of a nip. This one got a bit infected. But it's on the mend now.' He chuckled to himself again. 'That does all sound a bit bonkers, doesn't it?'

The rapport was still there. It was like two old friends reconnecting, even if they haven't seen each other for years. They just pick up from where they left off.

Sebastian's PTSD had prevented him from having a formal education following the trauma, but he'd never let the condition defeat him. He was still doing well at work, he said. He'd worked his way up as a journalist on a well-known home improvements magazine. He still thoroughly enjoyed the profession, and knew he was good at it. He was intelligent and had picked up a lot during his 18-year career.

We talked a bit about the early days, and laughed about the first time we met. He'd sat in a chair with his legs folded under him, staring into space. He was as unresponsive as it was possible to be.

His father had been in the Army, his mother was a research scientist. They were both bewildered by his condition. So was I, until eventually he began to tell me about the sexual abuse.

I thought it very unlikely he'd made any of it up. His story was consistent throughout. We didn't go into the details in great depth, but we did talk about his life afterwards and how difficult he'd found conversation and interaction.

He said he'd been participating recently in a group run exclusively for people who'd been sexually abused in childhood, and had found that extremely useful. 'It's not just what you talk about when you go into a group,' he said. 'Most people have similar experiences. It's more about just being there, the feeling of understanding, of camaraderie.'

I eased him towards telling me why he was here.

He said, 'It happened in April. I went to the Far East on a writing assignment.' The trip, he said, had only been for a week.

'I was very excited about it,' he continued. 'I worked like crazy for a few days, and then came back to the UK. But since that time, it's been a big effort to go away anywhere on my own. I feel vulnerable. I didn't feel that way when I was there, I was working most of the time. But when I came back, so did some of the old feelings.'

Some days, he said, he felt so wretched he couldn't get out of bed in the morning. 'People might describe it as depression, but it's not. I don't feel depressed as such – I know what that feels like. It just feels like a complete loss of energy. Like I'm totally numb. Immobilized. It keeps happening. I suppose it'll never go away.'

Immobilized. He used the word himself. I sat up and studied him more closely.

He said he knew it was linked to his trauma reaction, and if it was coming back now after all the treatment and discussions he'd had, with so many different people, he didn't see how it could ever be sorted.

He sighed. 'I'll probably have to learn to adapt to it. Do you think that's right? Is it going to continue for the rest of my life? Should I just somehow learn to accept it? That when I can't get up in the morning, I don't try to beat it?'

I didn't answer immediately. I sensed he had more to say.

'You know . . .' His eyes welled. 'If only I could learn how to re-experience what happened to me, but in a more active way, I think that would do the trick. I think I'd be able to recover then.

'I don't have a proper memory of what happened at the time. That's what the problem is. If I could recall what happened to me, and understand what happened, I truly believe that that would be what I need to be able to move on, that would be the fix.'

I let my gaze fall on to the article I'd been looking at just before he arrived. 'Sebastian, I can't explain to you fully why this is happening, but I have an inkling. I was reading about it just before you came in . . .'

I described to him what I thought I'd understood from what I'd read so far, and we talked about the freeze. He could identify hugely with tonic immobility as being the state he was in when he was traumatized. People in his group had mentioned exactly the same sort of paralysed inability to do anything about what was happening to them. They were totally and utterly immobilized. And knowing what had happened but not understanding why they'd allowed it to brought with it intense guilt and self-recrimination. *Why didn't I fight? Why didn't I flee?*

I told him about the polar bear, something that interested him greatly because of his love of animals. I also told him about Bessel van der Kolk's theatre group in Boston. It was a bit like the setting for the show *Fame*, I explained, the New York Drama School, but for people who'd been abused and had developed complex PTSD. In the course of putting on plays and things, they role-played their interactions with other people: they acted out what they would have done had they not been immobilized.

The guilt thing they felt was more theoretical, I said, at one remove because of the drama. They acted the guilt, but it was hypothetical guilt. I wondered if I might try it, but how does one set up a drama group? And on a one-to-one basis, how would one get people to re-enact safely?

'I suppose you discuss it with them,' Sebastian said. 'You'd ask: "What do you think you should have done at that particular time? What would have been more appropriate?"'

'The point would be to emphasize that the immobilization was an absolutely natural reaction, and one which they didn't have any control over.'

'The legacy of our animal ancestry,' he said.

'You're right. And until about an hour ago, if someone had asked me, "What happens if people are confronted by trauma?" I'd have said that they fight or they flee. I knew about freezing, too, but didn't understand that it could lead to a completely different type of flashback reaction, one of *hypo*-arousal or complete dissociation – total suppression rather than arousal.'

It wasn't mentioned much in the PTSD literature. PTSD literature was, after all, about treating people with hyper-arousal states. It wasn't really about treating people with hypo-arousal states. It was, however, a major interest in the animal behaviour literature and the article I had read provided evidence that the two areas of research were beginning to converge. This was going to have a bearing on cognitive behavioural therapy, as it said in this paper.

CBT was geared up to treating flashbacks and nightmares. It wasn't quite so good at treating dissociation.

Sebastian smiled. 'You've told me before that people who are dissociated are known as treatment-resistant. It's going to be important for those people to have something to help them penetrate that dissociation, and for them to come out into the open and remember what happened to them.'

I nodded. Yet again, I was learning as much from a patient as I did from a textbook. 'All this might take us into a new era of treatments where we focus much harder on what happened to the individual at the time of the trauma, and the meaning of that experience for them. Then, out of that understanding, will come a treatment model that will best suit them.'

'So how do we go forward?' he asked.

'I'm going to use a drug called naltrexone on you,' I said. I told him about the opiate antagonists I'd used on Jack, and how that had helped him to turn the corner.

The key with Sebastian, as with Jack before him, was that he was endorphin-flooded. In most PTSD cases, it was necessary to suppress the hyper-aroused state of the patient. In Sebastian's case, he was hypo-aroused and I needed to bring him 'back in the room' to treat him. Verbal therapies wouldn't get through unless, like the polar bear, I could bring him out of the dissociated state of numbness – the human form of tonic immobility – he'd fallen into since returning from his exhausting business trip. The naltrexone would have the effect of grounding him by temporarily blocking the endorphins. Grounded in this way, his therapist could treat him normally – in Sebastian's case with CBT.

But the implications of his case were extraordinary. They told me that the people with the most severe forms of trauma reaction didn't *technically* qualify as suffering from PTSD – whereas, in fact, they were really suffering from the worst form of PTSD. Immobility. They were already firmly in the capsule.

In one very important area – the medico-legal sector – it helped to explain why a hostile defendant barrister could so easily put someone in a position where they became immobilized again and had no recall of what had happened to them.

It also explained, perhaps, reports I'd read of young men, soldiers returning from the fighting in Iraq and Afghanistan, who'd run amok – gone berserk – when they arrived back home, beating up strangers in pubs or supermarkets under the slightest pretext. Like the polar bear coming round from tonic immobility, these dysfunctional combat veterans seemed to need to vent the stored energy that remained in their bodies from the moment they'd experienced the trauma and it had become blocked – stuck in their minds and bodies.

There was a precedent for this, although not from the animal king-dom but from human history. The word 'berserk' came from the word 'Berserkers' – Norse warriors who were supposed to have fought in a blind rage, almost as if they'd been in a trance of fury.

After 9/11, the world had been plunged back into an era of combat operations, first in Afghanistan, then in Iraq. I came to hear about Iraq first-hand via the testimony of a young Grenadian who had come to see me after suffering terrible head injuries while serving there. During a patrol in the backstreets of a town called Al-Amarah, the Warrior armoured fighting vehicle he'd been driving had been ambushed. The rocket-propelled grenade that had been fired at the vehicle had detonated six inches from my patient's head, crushing the front part of his skull like an eggshell. Somehow he'd managed to save the men in the back of the vehicle by reversing the Warrior out of the ambush area. For this and a previous example of outstanding bravery – when he'd led his entire Warrior platoon out of an RPG ambush, saving the lives of 35 men in the process, includ-ing the boss of his vehicle, whom he'd dragged unconscious, under fire, from the turret hatch – my patient had been awarded the Victoria Cross, Britain's highest award for gallantry.

Johnson Beharry VC had received first-rate treatment for the physical injuries he'd sustained but was still suffering from terrible headaches, backache and muscle pain long after his doctors had said there was little physically wrong with him. It was at this point that he was referred to me, and thank God, because I could see that his problem was about trauma that was locked for the most part in his body, not his head.

Chapter 20

Soldiers

When I met up with Johnson Beharry VC in 2007, I knew that the right hemisphere was the more important side of the brain to look at in terms of the trauma process and was directly relevant to his case. The right hemisphere in a right-handed person is the non-dominant side, the sensory half of the brain rather than the cognitive. It processes sensory information from the outside world including what we see, hear, smell, taste and touch, as well as sensory information from the inside world – what we feel emotionally and physically, like movement or pain. The right hemisphere is, therefore, the part of the brain where most of the information relating to an emergency will be lodged, and where the reactions are going to be instinctual rather than thought out, unconscious rather than conscious.

On our first get-together, Johnson and I spent a considerable amount of time trying to establish the context of our meeting. He hadn't come to me by the classic route. He had just written his book, *Barefoot Soldier*, which gave his account of his time in Iraq, as well as the story of how he had come from a deprived childhood in Grenada to join the British Army. His literary agent, Mark Lucas, had met me through my work with John McCarthy, Terry Waite and John Peters and John Nichol, all of whom he represented. Mark could see that Johnson was still in a great deal of pain and approached me to see if I might be able to help. I was concerned because Johnson was already seeing an Army psychologist and was being treated with CBT for the flashbacks and nightmares he was experiencing.

The nightmares and flashbacks weren't about the encounter, the 'contact', that had led to his head injury, but the relentless day-in, day-out combat ops that his battalion had experienced during their fight against the insurgent enemy in Al-Amarah. The problem was, CBT worked on the cognitive side of the brain, the left side, but I felt – from everything I'd heard and read about his case – that Johnson's trauma was locked up in his body; and that it was held there by processes at work in the non-dominant, sensory side of his brain, the right part.

The conventional way to see Johnson's headaches, backache and muscle pain was to regard them as pains from the scars in those areas which would, hopefully, fade away over time. My experience was telling me not to regard these symptoms in such a passive way. They needed to be approached in a much more active way, because they were directly related to the trauma that he had experienced. They were 'stigmata' – no other word had occurred to me for these body memories – and powerfully reminded me of Erica's calf bruise and Sally's breast craters, which were all indications that the trauma was still trapped inside the body. A more body-focused type of treatment was needed, in addition to the CBT.

When that RPG had exploded inches from his head and crushed the front of his skull, it had wiped out any memory of the event itself. Unprocessed, the trauma appeared to have become trapped in his subconscious and was now coming out in the form of physical pain – pain that the physicians and surgeons had no explanation for. Fortunately, when I spoke to his psychologist, he was happy for me to investigate and see what I could do. Now I just needed to convince Johnson himself.

It was summertime, and we met in my large, airy consulting room at the Capio Nightingale Hospital in central London where I'd held a practice since 2005. Johnson was dressed in civvies. He was with his girlfriend, but I asked to see him on his own at first. She joined us for the second half of our two-hour meeting. I'd picked up signs that she wasn't wholly convinced by my approach.

We soon locked in on the handful of things we had in common. One of these was the fact that we'd both served – he was still in the armed forces, but no longer on the front line. He told me how much he still wanted to be with his mates.

I asked him what he missed most. 'Whisky Two Zero,' he said, with a smile – a smile, I could just tell, that attempted to mask a lot of pain.

My brow furrowed. Johnson spoke with a strong Grenadian accent.

'She was me Warrior – me armoured fighting vehicle.'

Johnson, I discovered, was passionate about vehicles of all descriptions, from sports cars to main battle tanks.

We laughed about some of the things that had got to us about the military, one of which was the discipline. I'd never been much good at taking orders and nor, it seemed, was he.

'During our training, we were at Catterick,' Johnson said. He shook his head at the memory. 'If one person needed the toilet, our instructors used to make the entire platoon go. Fifteen guys all jogging on the spot outside the bogs, but only one guy needing to go. I never did see the point of that.'

I told him about my efforts at learning how to march.

'No disrespec',' he said, 'but I can' see you doin' no marchin'.'

He sat opposite me in a chair turned at a slight angle to avoid the 'headlamp effect' as he told me about the injury that had caused extensive splinter-fractures to the left frontal area of his skull, as well as ricochet shrapnel wounds to his right shoulder.

He had been CASEVAC'd from the field to intensive care in Kuwait, where he remained in a coma for two weeks. When he regained consciousness he was transferred to the military hospital unit in Birmingham, where he had surgery to repair his skull with a titanium plate.

Since that time, he had been unable to return to active military service. He was receiving a programme of treatment, with rehabilitative physiotherapy at the MoD's Defence Medical Rehabilitation Unit (DMRC) at Headley Court in Surrey and psychiatric treatment with a consultant psychologist, a retired army colonel.

An RAF facility, Headley Court had been set up after the Second World War as a rehabilitation centre for pilots and aircrew injured during the conflict. It is now open to personnel from all three armed services who are undergoing treatment for injury or illness. It remains under the administrative umbrella of the RAF, but the command of the unit can be either Army or RAF on a rotational basis.

Though not having much memory of the trauma, Johnson did have memory of what it was like in Iraq. He also told me about the pains in his head, back, arms and shoulders.

'How bad is it?' I asked.

'The pain in me head can get so bad sometimes that I just have to lie down and hope that it goes away. Other times, it's like I've got an army of ants inside me skull. Sometimes, I find meself tryin' to reach in with the tips of me fingers jus' to try an' itch it away.' There was something approaching a plea in his eyes. 'I worry sometimes that it'll drive me crazy.'

When I asked him about the pains in his back, arms and shoulders, he said it was just as bad. The shrapnel wound in his shoulder was particularly painful. He'd ripped most of the muscles in his back when he'd pulled his unconscious 15-stone commander from the turret of their blazing Warrior.

The doctors and physiotherapists at Headley Court couldn't understand why he should keep having these pains when there was no ongoing tissue damage. The critically important thing for me was that the pains he was experiencing in the present corresponded to the wounds he'd received in the past.

With my growing awareness of body memories, I talked to Johnson about the possibility that the pains were part of a sensory flashback to his original trauma. I suggested to him that things could be re-experienced following exposure to an event that wasn't necessarily accompanied by memories of sights and sounds that indicated you were consciously aware of what was going on at the time.

'You don't need to have sight of an event, Johnson, for it to be a traumatic event,' I said.

He was no longer experiencing daytime flashbacks of the first incident, when he had led his platoon out of ambush and rescued his commander, and he had no memory of the second, when the RPG exploded in his face; so he never did develop flashbacks to this incident. But he was still experiencing nightmarish dreams with the theme of being exposed to extreme personal danger. During April and May, they had had RPGs fired at them almost every day. He'd seen colleagues killed and firebombed with Molotov cocktails and the enemy ripped apart by machine-gun and cannon fire at close quarters. And this was after combat operations were declared 'over' by President Bush.

The most striking feature of his presentation was that he was recurrently experiencing pains in his head, mainly on the left side, and his right shoulder and back, none of which responded to painkilling drugs. He also described a fairly isolated life and the break-up of his marriage after the award of the VC, and features of ongoing hyper-arousal with inability to sleep on his own, exaggerated startle reflexes, increased lability of mood, increased irritability, difficulty in concentration and impairment of short-term memory.

He had the typical symptom clusters of PTSD: recurrent and distressing re-experiencing of the trauma, avoidance of reminders, and emotional blunting and hyper-arousal. The fact that these symptoms were now chronic and persistent meant that the havoc created in his nervous system by his stress hormones had prevented him from processing and integrating trauma memories into conscious mental frameworks so that he could construct a trauma narrative.

Because of these complex physiological processes, his traumatic memories had become trapped in the non-verbal, subcortical regions of the brain where they are not accessible to the frontal lobes – the understanding, thinking, reasoning and cognitive parts of the brain.

The additional factor that would lead to problems in memory processing was his head injury. The left side of his brain had been concussed in the second incident, when the RPG exploded by his head. In a right-handed individual, that would be precisely the part of the brain that needed to be working properly for satisfactory narrative-building from the sensory fragments of his traumatic experience. This evidence alone seemed to confirm his PTSD as more a body-orientated phenomenon than a psychological one.

I was pretty sure, therefore, that the trauma had become locked in his body; and that the link to tonic immobility made his PTSD fundamentally a highly activated, incomplete, biological response to threat, frozen in time.

Recovery depended on successful completion of the highly charged state of biological readiness when the traumatic emergency had originally been faced. Johnson was like the polar bear clawing at the air after being hit by and recovering from the tranquillizer dart. He had been knocked out by an RPG and had gone into a coma. When he'd come round, he was still fighting the war. All that nervous energy, arrested in a moment by the blast that had stoved in his skull, had had nowhere to go but inwards.

I told Johnson about these theories and that I thought I had the perfect person to treat him: Heather Robyn. I told him, too, about EMDR and how I hoped it could unblock the unprocessed memories that were stuck in the non-cognitive part of his head; memories that were coming out in his body in the form of pain in the wounds he'd suffered in the original trauma.

I worried that he would think I was completely crazy, and that he would therefore not go along with the idea of being referred to Heather because he'd assume that if I was crazy then she would be too. My main concern was his girlfriend. Johnson wanted her there as support and to listen to what was being offered, but I didn't feel she really understood what I was saying and in some ways was against it. I worried how influential she would be on him and his treatment. This was why I had asked to speak to Johnson alone.

I had a feeling, an intuition, after our meeting that he and I had been able to understand each other. There was nothing dismissive about his manner or behaviour. I really believed that it was very important for Johnson's sake to go down this new therapeutic route – one that he was naturally worried about, because it had not been tried on him before.

Reputations don't matter once you're in the room together. No matter how highly you've been set up, it all comes down to your performance and how well you click.

'How long you been doin' what you do?' Johnson asked me.

Around 25 years, I told him.

'An' you enjoy what you do, right?' he asked.

'As much as you enjoyed driving that Warrior,' I replied.

He nodded. 'Then let's do it.' He held his hand out. 'I trust you to get the job done.'

It helps if you can convince someone that something can be done and you can get them enthusiastic about it. People go into therapy expecting positive things to happen. They seldom go in paranoid and questioning. Call it a placebo effect, but either way it's probably underpinned by endorphins, and that's not such a bad thing when you're dealing with people in pain.

As Bessel van der Kolk had discovered and made plain, the right side of the brain was the area that offered itself up as the target for treatment via EMDR. The trick is to integrate the impact of an event on the function of the right side of the brain into some sort of narrative, and it is during the process of making it into a narrative that it becomes meaningful. When it comes down to it, the translation of a somatic experience – a body, sensory experience – in the right side of the brain into a left-brain experience – a narrative, a verbal story – so that the patient can grasp it at a conscious level is what the treatment of PTSD is all about. In other words, it is about the implicit becoming explicit.

We also knew from functional magnetic resonance imaging (FMRI) scans that people who were reminded of their trauma shut down the left side of their brain, and this was certainly relevant to Johnson. The FMRI machine portrays a dynamic view of the brain as opposed to a static one, by revealing relative activity as it measures the rate of uptake of oxygen from haemoglobin in the red blood cells. The effect can be dramatic. When somebody who has had a traumatic experience is linked up to a Functional MRI machine, the blood flow to both sides of the brain will conform to their usual pattern. If you then talk to that person about the trauma, the blood flow in the left hemisphere shuts down.

Talk to a person about their trauma and Broca's area, the part of the brain where speech is generated, vanishes from the FMRI. This, as van der Kolk and Levine had made clear, has huge implications for conscious, cognitively based therapies. It means that patients must be made to feel relaxed, calm and safe if Broca's area is to remain open for business. Only then will they understand what you're saying and be able to articulate their thoughts and feelings.

A patient can go through the motions of being in the room, but you'll notice that behaviourally they may be frozen. They'll be holding themselves stiffly in the chair: their eyes will be open and aroused; their posture will be that of somebody who's braced, ready for action. They may be very polite and speak to you in a normal voice, but they'll go around the houses when it comes to discussing their problem. They'll talk about the weather, the news, anything that's not related to the trauma or the main business of them being there. Sometimes, patients can become so good at it that you don't notice these characteristic features of freezing. It's difficult to believe it's not consciously determined behaviour and that it's actually automatic.

It's like going to your dentist for a filling, and engaging him or her in a conversation about sailing because you know the subject interests them. I've done it myself. As the physician, you should be aware of these things happening in interviews: you can see they're not in the room. If the purpose of the session is to use cognitive therapies directed at trying to eliminate distortions in their recollection of what happened, you're going to be aiming for the left hemisphere and you're going to fail. If the left hemisphere is switched off, so are the lights: no one's at home.

This isn't just a theoretical nicety. It has huge significance, for example, when a person who has been in a road traffic incident goes to see their general practitioner. What Professor Jonathan Davidson wrote about in his seminal paper in 1992 gives the impression that not talking about the trauma is a conscious avoidance, both ways, by the GP and the patient. Both are often unconsciously avoiding the psychological issues – both are going to have to carry on driving and will want to avoid the possibility of further crashes. Since 1992 neuroscience has yielded up some more of its secrets and we should suspect that the avoidance among GPs and specialist doctors leading to missed diagnoses of PTSD has a mainly unconscious explanation. This can lead to real difficulties in medico-legal work if the GP's notes do not mention psychological phenomena such as flashbacks and they only appear in psychiatric reports for the court, sometimes several years later. It is fertile ground for the defendant's barrister to suggest that if a psychiatrist works in the field of trauma then it will be diagnosed even when it obviously doesn't exist because it has never been mentioned in the GP records.

It linked in to what I'd learned from polar bears and Sebastian's case about tonic immobility, the ultimate response in a series of defence reflexes that I now knew went beyond fight, flight and freezing; reflexes that have been elicited by imminent danger where escape is impossible.

Predators are less likely to attack an immobile prey. It might be diseased or poisonous. Tonic immobility appears to be an evolution-arily adaptive strategy that increases the chances of escape. Tonic immobility is different from the freezing behaviour that occurs early in the encounter stage of the defensive reflex. Freezing is an initial response when the animal stops moving to avoid detection and shifts resources to detect the predator. It is associated with an alert posture and increased responsivity to sensory stimuli. Fear itself is not sufficient to produce tonic immobility: restraint is also necessary. This was certainly true in Johnson's case. His injury had incapacitated him and the undischarged energy of his trauma had had nowhere to go.

Cognitive behavioural treatments for PTSD generally aim to decrease physiological arousal to trauma-related cues through strategies such as exposure, relaxation and cognitive restructuring. Although these strategies may effectively treat many cases of PTSD, they may not be appropriate for all trauma survivors – especially those who have experienced tonic immobility and do not display autonomic arousal to trauma cues. Such cases, as I had discovered with Sebastian, may require alternative treatment strategies, such as increasing arousal to trauma cues, sometimes through the use of drugs like naltrexone.

These alternative strategies usually involve tracking physical movements to complete the cycle of movement interrupted by the tonic immobility – hence the body-focused therapies that were relevant to Johnson, whose life had been so brutally interrupted by the RPG explosion inches from his face.

In some ways, Johnson's trauma shared characteristics with people I'd encountered, mostly in medico-legal cases, who'd re-experienced the pain of a surgical procedure, even though they were meant to be under general anaesthetic at the time. It was assumed, therefore, that the anaesthetic had been inadequate and that they had 'woken up' during the procedure, and lawsuits often winged around against the anaesthetists for not having calculated correctly how much anaesthetic that person had needed. This was not always fair, however, because we know that pain and also hearing and the sense of smell remain as sensory cues, sometimes some considerable time after the individual's other senses have been knocked out.

The paralysing substance administered during operations is a derivative of curare, the stuff that South American Indians tip darts with and shoot through blowpipes. Curare paralyses the neuromuscular junction, with two beneficial results: the patient is relaxed, and the surgeon can cut through tissue much more easily if muscles aren't going into spasm.

Curare won't induce cardiac arrest, even though the heart's a muscle. The muscle of the heart has an intrinsic rate of about 40 beats a minute, and provided the heart tissue is healthy, it's hardwired not to beat any slower. Even if you remove a person's heart, it will continue to beat 40 times a minute for a while. What they show in horror movies is true. But you can paralyse the respiratory centre, and if the ribs don't rise and the muscles between the ribs don't work, then the only thing standing between you and certain death is the anaesthetist's expertise.

Most patients don't have the ability to see during an operation because they have patches on their eyes, and for good reason. If the anaesthetic didn't work fully and their eyes opened, they might witness some horrific sights and not be able to do anything about it.

Hearing is the last sense to go. Many patients have told me that when they were passing out, for every cause from fainting to having been shot, the last thing that went was their hearing. So when people were traumatized by the things they heard in the operating theatre, it might not have had anything whatsoever to do with the level of anaesthetic, it might just have been because they were in a hyper-alert state. It didn't seem to me, therefore, that the anaesthetists had done a bad job in the small number of anaesthetic awareness cases I'd come across, and my reports were not usually what the courts expected to receive. The people asking me to do the reports weren't usually the NHS, who were trying to defend the position; they were the claimants. Quite often, as a result, these cases didn't go to court. This period marked the beginning of my realization that the sensory awareness of the impact of the trauma could run very deep, to the extent that people could be left only with sensory impressions of a trauma and no conscious awareness.

That related directly to Johnson. The source of his dissociation wasn't psychological but physical: he was rendered unconscious by the shrapnel that had hit him in the head. Johnson had been concussed by the RPG to the point that he had no memory of what had happened; but that is not to say that his subconscious mind hadn't absorbed the sounds and smells of that truly terrifying experience.

The brain is a jelly inside a closed, hard box. If there's a bash to the skull on one side, then the jelly will wobble and bash against the box on the opposite side. The effect is known as *contrecoup*. Thus, brain injuries can be paradoxical. Somebody can be hit on the right and you'd expect the damage to be there – but if the contrecoup collides with Broca's area on the left, there could be a profound effect on speech.

This has relevance for injuries like whiplash. If you're travelling in a car and another vehicle rams into you from behind, your head gets pushed back and then it goes forward, then back again and forward. There can be an acceleration/deceleration injury to the brain. If you're facing forward and it's a head-on collision, you can have damage both to the frontal and rear occipital lobes. The result can be deficits in executive function: the ability to have a conscience, to behave in a normal adult fashion.

To the neurologists who looked after Johnson, the actual point of impact of the shrapnel on his skull would have been very important.

From my specific point of view, here was a man who'd been involved in an event that he could not remember. He'd lost consciousness, and he had every reason for doing that because of the blow to the head. But he had these persistent recurring pains that seemed to me to correspond very closely with the injuries that he had received at the time of the trauma.

I knew you could have sensory flashbacks as well as visual, auditory and, most vivid of all, olfactory ones. The smell-brain is very closely linked to emotions. Women talk about the smell of a man's aftershave, and men often associate a perfume with someone they were madly in love with. I'd often come across olfactory flash-backs. The nastiest occurrence can be with firefighters who can no longer eat roast pork or other roasts – the smell reminds them so much of a particular tragedy at work. Smell can be one of the most evocative of the sensory imprints in combat veterans too.

Johnson's flashbacks were of an entirely different type. They were of the impact of the event on his body, including the pain that they caused. He wasn't having flashbacks about what he'd heard, seen, smelt, tasted or touched; he was having flashbacks of what he'd felt in a physical sense in his body at the time he became unconscious.

Heather and Johnson quickly developed a therapeutic rapport and worked very hard together, with a particular treatment emphasis on EMDR.

Heather was soon reporting progress. These sensory treatment methods were helping Johnson to incorporate the 'trauma fragments' which had split off from his consciousness. He hadn't seen them as being connected with his trauma; he thought of them as being the result of shrapnel wounds, and therefore permanent.

We were interested in the variability of his pains and the fact that they tended to come on at certain times; evidence, as we saw it, that they were indeed flashbacks, rooted in physical reality as scar tissue in various parts of his body. They were sensations every bit as real as phantom limb pains; in this case relics of an old event that needed to be brought back into play so they could be dealt with.

Heather's job was to shepherd them back, to help Johnson re-integrate them into himself so he could articulate them and make a story, a meaningful narrative, of what had happened. The story needed to include acceptance that these body feelings were a legacy of the trauma, and that because they were in the past they didn't need to be in the present. They were no more than a talisman of his trauma, a remnant – and once he recognized that, he could leave them where they belonged.

Johnson had been experiencing a lot of pain, which naturally pre-occupied him. It was a vicious circle: pain would remind him of the trauma, and then he would be reminded that something had happened to him in the past that he didn't fully understand. The integration of a body memory had not in fact resulted in him gain-ing further memory of the event. That was never going to happen, for the simple reason that from almost the moment the RPG exploded and the shrapnel struck him, he'd been unconscious.

Pain immediately after a trauma can be dulled by the protective barrier of endorphins, the body's onboard opioids. Casualties may not recognize that they are in pain for some time after the blow is dealt. In Johnson's case, he would have been aware of the thud of the impact, but perhaps no more. Inevitably, it would have caught up; the pain would have been linked to the thud and the body memory rooted as PTSD.

In Johnson's case, Heather worked wonders and after several con-centrated EMDR sessions, he reported that the intense pain in his shoulder, back and head had all but disappeared. To this day, and by his own testimony, our youngest surviving VC-holder is able to lead a near-normal life.

*

People with chronic or complex trauma will come into a clinician's office for one of two reasons. The first is that they used to enjoy a normal life, but following a trauma have never had the opportunity to get their brain back to a more normal function. Their lives are characterized by fear and all the debris that goes along with that: paranoia, wrecked relationships, an inability to study and maybe a hundred and one other things besides. They walk into your office because they don't feel they're performing as normal human beings. They're not able to hold down relationships, friendships, marriages, jobs. They get angry, they may even be criminal; maybe they've been in jail.

The other reason is that the person already had a brain tuned into trauma or threat. Their attachments are insecure, usually stemming from problems in childhood, so they want different attachments: of belonging to an organization where there is potential for real attachments, for camaraderie. They want to feel strong boundaries and clear-cut rules. To be told what you can and cannot do is consoling for victims of childhood trauma. Perhaps unconsciously, therefore, some people join the Army because they feel angry and want to take it out on people – but perhaps, more commonly, they are simply seeking greater security.

What, then, if there is a further trauma, perhaps on the battlefield, and out it all pours? Instead of getting just a middle C in reaction to a trauma, what they get is the whole of Tchaikovsky's 1812 Overture, complete with cannons and trumpets. The whole orchestra starts up.

A person who has an unresolved trauma – a road traffic accident, for example – can be left never being able to sit in a car again, let alone drive it. If somebody who is persistently anxious or paranoid has a road traffic accident and can never go back into a car, they classically become described as 'maladaptive' or 'dysfunctional'.

My problem with this is that I don't see where maladaptive comes in. If the person has an unresolved trauma and maintains this fear of getting into cars, then that should, in my opinion, actually be perceived as pretty adaptive. I don't like to see these traits as maladaptive or personality disorders; to me they are the ongoing impact of unresolved trauma, either of the whole trauma or of residual remnants of the trauma.

How should we then view people in society who are classically branded as having personality disorders, or maladaptive dysfunctions? They are actually adapting in society – they're only avoiding something as part of their defence mechanisms; it's part of the way they function. And this is as true of soldiers as it is of anyone else.

The key that should make even the most illiberal in society sit up and take notice here is that an alarmingly high proportion of the prison population are military veterans. Homeless charities have reported that a very high proportion of the homeless in London – perhaps as much as 50 per cent – used to be in the armed services. It has been shown, too, that many weren't able to readjust to ordinary society after combat; they either mutated into vagrancy or found themselves locked up.

These people came out of the combat zone, having killed or seen people killed: that became their conditioned behaviour. If they're not allowed to readjust back into society where the rules are different, if there's no rite of passage for coming back in, then the potential for trouble in their life is high. They're going to be lucky to get away with the odd shouting match with their neighbours. At the very least they may beat up their wives or husbands. At worst, they'll commit violent acts and murder.

I was once asked to take on a medico-legal case in which an undercover soldier in Northern Ireland, a man exposed to constant danger, had returned on leave to his native Manchester and, while in his local pub, had killed somebody he didn't even know. It turned out the unfortunate bloke had brushed against him, spilled his drink, and the soldier had gone berserk and throttled him to death with his bare hands. I didn't take the case on in the end, but it remains locked in my memory.

We live in a time of war. Life for the modern serviceman or -woman consists of more or less constant exposure to intense counter-insurgency conflicts. It could be said that we're breeding a generation of soldiers who are going to be forever exposed to that high level of trauma, and many more will be damaged. What is that going to inflict on society when they're out?

British Falklands War veterans recently commemorated their 25th anniversary victory celebrations. About 300 men who came home were missing from the parades. They had killed themselves. Many more were battling suicide, and veterans of Iraq and Afghanistan are now swelling their ranks.

From 2003, active servicemen with trauma were treated by the Priory group of hospitals – until recently. It had a contract with the MoD to provide all inpatient psychiatric care for personnel. The bill soon skyrocketed. Older veterans did not qualify for Priory care, because the prevailing government view was that they didn't suffer from long-term mental health problems any more than the rest of us.

Psychiatrists have reported that soldiers coming back from Iraq developed PTSD symptoms earlier than in past conflicts, partly because it was such an unpopular war. 'Many have been on back-to-back duty,' one told me. 'Northern Ireland, Falklands, Kosovo, Sierra Leone, the Gulf, Afghanistan, Iraq. They are being sent back without significant rest periods between. This has left soldiers feeling alienated, confused and abandoned. Some are left feeling downright suicidal. Like many veterans of past conflicts, they will suffer emotional torment. The lessons of the past are being ignored again.'

A major problem is the nature of today's military duties. Troops are becoming involved in peacekeeping duties as well as in full-blooded operational duties. There is a clear conflict of responsibility for such troops, who have to swap one set of rules for an entirely different set, sometimes within one theatre of engagement. This can be very confusing emotionally, especially if troops are attacked during so-called peacekeeping duties by a faction within the community they are seeking to protect.

The new insights into vulnerability for developing PTSD provided by advances in neuroscience help to explain the increased vulnerability that goes with peacekeeping duties. If you can fight or flee you are less likely to leave the chemical imprint of the emergency activity behind than if you are rendered helpless and immobilized.

Many returning service personnel have secure enough attachments to draw upon to be able to rehabilitate largely by themselves. If they have developed PTSD, these are the people who tend to do well in treatment, because they have the basis for getting better. Those people will either detect a change in themselves or have a partner who may accuse them of being hot-headed or warn them about their behaviour, and they change of their own volition because of that insight. Others, however, hopelessly lost in trauma, will beat up a partner who complains about their behaviour or drunkenness. If they have children who are then exposed to violence in the home, either directly or indirectly, those children grow up in an atmosphere of fear, and they develop different brains from others. The cycle perpetuates itself.

The paradox, of course, is that children who've been brought up with insecure attachments or come from broken homes have brains that are attuned to fear, threat, danger, risk and suspicion. They themselves have become ideal candidates for the front line. And so it goes.

I received a letter a few years ago from an ex-soldier who'd suffered from PTSD since returning from Bosnia with the British Army. Today, it sits staring at me on my desk. It doesn't require any action on my part. It's a summary of one man's 15-year battle with his trauma reaction.

Despite feeling suicidal, drinking excessively, having flashbacks and being unable to focus on his job, this ex-soldier, whom I'll call George, was told by the UK MoD that he didn't have PTSD and that the cure for whatever it was he did have was 'to pull his socks up'. Convinced, because the 'experts' had told him so, that he wasn't suffering from a trauma reaction, George left the Army and went on to make a lot of money running his own business – this despite the fact that the depression that had gripped him in Bosnia never actually left him. His drinking continued and so did the flashbacks. He knew something was wrong, but had no idea what it was; no one had given it a name.

It was only a decade later, when he was in Baghdad after the Second Gulf War, working there as a private contractor, that he happened to hear a retired Canadian Army general, who had been the Director General of Medical Services to their military, describing all his own symptoms for what they were: classic PTSD, and praising the humane and effective way he had been treated. It was then, George said, that some mental switch engaged. Just knowing that what he had had a name was in itself 'transformational', he wrote. 'I decided to change my course and get better.' His treatment took several years, but he'd wanted me to know that he was now as near fully cured of the condition as anyone could be.

'Recovering from PTSD is the most difficult thing I have ever done and the most rewarding thing I have ever achieved. It has highs and lows and there are lots of false peaks. I am not sure you ever can become 100 per cent fixed and you are for sure never going to be the person you were before . . . but I am constantly improving myself.'

He had taken legal action against the British Army; not for the money, he insisted, but to challenge it on one fundamental issue: 'that since the recognition of shell shock in the First World War, the British Army is not much further forward . . .' He subsequently received a formal apology from the MoD for its failure to treat his psychiatric problems.

George's story has a happy ending, which is why his letter sits on my desk – alongside photos of my family and the Goethe quote. But its purpose goes way beyond the feelgood factor. It sums up much of the history of PTSD thus far, and my own journey in trying to understand it.

'The attitude at the time was to think that anyone having this was mad anyway or weak in some way,' George wrote, and he was right. The problem is this is still the attitude in certain quarters of the military – that PTSD is evidence of some intrinsic fault line within the individual; that it is a sickness.

My view, of course, is quite the reverse: that PTSD tends to develop in people who are strong-willed or in those who are unable to come to terms with a life-threatening event because it just doesn't make sense. It is the impact of an event which, for some reason or other, the survivor has not been able to process, not because the mind can't do the processing – because it's flawed in some way – but because it hasn't had the opportunity.

Until the trauma imprint has been processed, then the three symptom clusters will continue.

I agree that it is possible to see these clusters as evidence of illness because they will certainly cause torment, but it is different if the symptoms are seen as evidence of ongoing need to process the traumatic event that provoked them. In that event they provide reminders that there is still work to be done and that it is perfectly possible to resolve PTSD, even if it has been in existence for decades. Chronicity does not mean non-resolvability.

The first attitude shift that needs to be made is from the 'accept it ... it's an illness' position to the more optimistic outlook of seeing PTSD as something that can occur in anyone: to run with the spirit of *DSM*.

Further moves include finding out why the PTSD has become treatment-resistant. Sometimes I come across cases where there has been no attempt to treat: the assumption being that it would passively melt away over time. Would that have happened to our PoWs or our hostages? I don't think so.

If the symptoms are resistant to therapies of proven value such as Trauma-Focused CBT then is that because the resistant fragments of the reaction are of a sensory or a body-focused nature, in which case they may yield to body-focused treatments such as EMDR or Sensorimotor treatment or Emotional Freedom Technique (EFT) – 'tapping' – or Gestalt therapy?

Let us remind ourselves of the three symptom clusters that are the principal components of PTSD.

The first symptom cluster are the *re-experiencing symptoms* in which the trauma essentially continues to have a life of its own in the form of untriggered recurrent thoughts, flashbacks and nightmares, or the traumatic memories may be stimulated by cues that remind the victim of the trauma. The latter, triggered memories, are a very important factor in some of the PTSD treatment models. These re-experiencing symptoms are at the very core of PTSD and make it unique.

My experience strongly suggests to me that they will stick around until their meaning is discovered and when that happens important lessons about survival will have been learned.

The flashbacks are the seeds that will germinate into improved resilience and post-trauma growth.

The second cluster is characterized by *avoidance and numbing*. It's hardly surprising that they develop because individuals suffering from PTSD find the re-experiencing symptoms so intolerable and so difficult to deal with that a number of behavioural and cognitive strategies are brought into play in order to minimize intrusive recollections. They are protective.

There are *avoidance symptoms*, such as behavioural changes to avoid people and places that are likely to evoke trauma memories.

There are also cognitive changes, such as reduced mental capacity or the use of psychological defences such as obsessional thinking or compulsive activity and *numbing symptoms*, shutting down of the emotions, dissociation, psychogenic amnesia, inability to have feelings and social withdrawal, many of which depend on changes in *endogenous* substances such as endorphins and, if that is not enough, augmentation with *exogenous* substances such as all the drugs of abuse. These avoidance techniques disappear when the core trauma memories are processed because they are not required. Addictions that may have developed are found to be much more amenable to treatment.

The third cluster of *hyper-arousal symptoms* closely resemble the symptoms characteristic of anxiety states – increased irritability, insomnia and so forth – but what is most strongly characteristic of PTSD is *hyper-vigilance*, because those who have been traumatized never want to repeat the experience and so are 'on guard'. Hyper-vigilance can be so extreme that it can mimic a paranoid state.

Progressive sensitization of the central nervous system, the CNS, requires both repeated exposure to reminders of the trauma and the preliminary establishment of the neurobiological features of PTSD. An example is the repetition of startle responses. This process is called 'reiterative stress' and may explain why depression is such a strong predictor of chronic PTSD because it is a mechanism for repeated exposure to the trauma memories by rumination.

Research also indicates that structural changes to certain parts of the brain's memory pathways occur in chronic PTSD, including reduction of the volume of the hippocampus. This change does not only appear in PTSD, because it has also been noted in depression and schizophrenia. Even this does not imply irreversible damage to the brain. The research has shown that the brain should be regarded as a 'plastic' structure with a turnover of cells. Stem cells are produced in an area near the back of the brain and it is estimated that about 10,000 are released into the brain tissue daily which have the capacity to repair the damage to the hippocampus, for example, caused by the toxic levels of stress chemicals.

On the grand scale, evolutionary psychologists have considered that there is an 'adaptive' quality or heavy survival emphasis in the development of PTSD symptoms. For example, PTSD symptoms express a common response across populations that enhances communication and recruits support, which leads to an enriched environment for assimilating the 'meaning' of the trauma and its implications for those traumatized individuals who require to come to terms with its after-effects.

In effect, PTSD seems to be a unique anxiety disorder. It appears to involve many of the cognitive, psychological and psychobiological mechanisms that are important in coping and adaptation. If it is a disorder rather than a survival 'condition' then it seems to be making its presence felt so that it can be fixed.

Recurrent flashbacks, although extremely distressing, are faithful memories that give repeated opportunities to learn precisely what happened – and in a group setting, where those experiences can be shared, my own observation has echoed George's: that not only is recovery likely, but that you can grow from it as well.

There is extensive literature covering the fact that PTSD victims use alcohol to boost markedly reduced endorphin levels to make them feel more normal, which is how George himself described his excessive alcohol intake. He wasn't looking for a high; he just wanted to feel normal. American studies of Vietnam veterans clearly demonstrated that approximately 80 per cent of PTSD sufferers were also dependent upon opiates and/or alcohol. It was like Jill, the woman whose shells had collapsed in on themselves, leaving her close to death. One of those shells was her obsessive-compulsive defence, something we all acquire from childhood and which most of us grow out of, or, at least, hold in reserve. To the doctors who'd treated her initially, her OCD was the problem and needed to be fixed. In fact, her OCD was a survival tool, a distraction from her core condition. By 'fixing' her OCD they were adding to the problem, not curing it.

In the same way, you could say that George's reliance on alcohol to make him feel normal was also a survival tool.

This is controversial, I know, but excessive alcohol consumption shouldn't always be taken at face value as evidence of 'bad behaviour'. It should instead be regarded with suspicion – even, dare I say it, with curiosity. It might perhaps represent a clue to something deeper: a change in biochemical functioning. In George's case, it was a clear pointer to his PTSD.

For me, George's letter remains a symbol of hope. His experience of PTSD by his own admission had been 'transformational' – that in processing the terrible things he'd seen during his time in Bosnia, his journey to recovery was the most rewarding thing he had ever achieved.

Post-traumatic growth is now an accepted facet of the PTSD condition. Studies by experts in the field have focused on the fact that only a minority of people exposed to traumatic events develop long-term psychiatric disorders. Richard Tedeschi and Lawrence Calhoun, both professors of psychology at the University of North Carolina at Charlotte, have reported that 'positive growth' experiences in the aftermath of trauma far outnumber reports of long-term psychiatric disorders. 'Reports of post-traumatic growth have been found in people who have experienced bereavement, rheumatoid arthritis, HIV infection, cancer, bone marrow transplantation, heart attacks, coping with the medical problems of children, transportation accidents, house fires, sexual assault and sexual abuse, combat, refugee experiences and being taken hostage,' they wrote in a 2004 article in *Psychiatric Times*.

This is indeed the reality of PTSD. It isn't just an experience that affects people who have served in the military or in the emergency services. Trauma can affect each and every one of us – it is the lightning bolt that can strike out of the blue. It is the shatterer of assumptions. Work into a deeper understanding of PTSD continues – my own included – but whatever it is or isn't, I know that it isn't an illness.

It is evidence of something that has been hard-wired into us for a reason.

The military is at long last starting to absorb these lessons. There are pockets of real success. The Defence Medical Rehabilitation Unit (DMRC) at Headley Court, for example, is a fantastic facility, set in 85 acres of rolling Surrey countryside. It was here, when I was treating Johnson Beharry, that the MoD was handling many of the casualties coming back daily from Iraq.

You didn't hear much about it in the papers in the mid-2000s, because not many people outside the military and the government were aware that we were still engaged in fighting a war in Iraq. The war was supposed to have started and ended in 2003.

But some of the wounds I saw when I visited Headley Court were terrible: soldiers who'd lost limbs, their sight or who were otherwise dreadfully disfigured.

By 2007, when Johnson's case was referred to me, the military had closed down all its mental health hospitals, forcing it to send serving soldiers with PTSD to the Priory and longer-term, battle-traumatized veterans to an organization called Combat Stress. Combat Stress is the UK's leading charity specializing in the care of veterans' mental health. It offers specialist clinical treatment at three short-stay residential centres in Shropshire, Ayrshire and Surrey. It also has an expanding community outreach service.

With origins going back to 1919, Combat Stress is a remarkable institution and does a fantastic job, but it struggles to cope with the demands that are being made upon it. Combat Stress has enjoyed top-class medical support to take it through these turbulent times, with Morgan O'Connell pulling at the oars for several years since retiring from the Navy. More recently, my old friend and partner in the RAF and at Ticehurst, Walter Busuttil, went on to become the director of medical services there.

Headley Court is a world away from a normal hospital. The buildings are imposing and contain several large gymnasia and a swimming pool. The first time I went there, it reminded me a little of a SMERSH camp you might see in a James Bond movie: squads of people led by the rehabilitation physiotherapists running through the grounds in same-coloured tracksuits. The only thing that was missing was the cadence chanting.

It stuck out a mile that people felt they were getting better here – people in recovery, with expectations that they were going to pick up the pieces and return to their lives. The air of organized recovery was almost palpable. These were people who knew they were there as the last stage in the recovery process before going back to work – soldiers recovering from back injuries, for example, who were regaining their confidence and learning how to avoid future problems. I could feel in my bones that the place and its atmosphere would be perfect for anyone recovering from a depression or an anxiety state, but most of all from PTSD and other post-traumatic developments.

Feeling safe, secure and optimistic about recovery is half the battle, and Headley Court, as a highly regulated medical environment, was a safe haven for the people rehabilitating there. It remains the perfect place for servicemen and -women to recover from complicated and traumatic physical injuries and often, by happy coincidence, patients there who have suffered psychological injuries recover as well.

But, when I visited Headley Court, the official position was that the Cartesian gap between the mind and the body should be preserved. For all that, the doctors made me feel very welcome. Here, at any rate, I felt that my specialty, PTSD, had become accepted within the UK military establishment.

Out of my conversations with the doctors at Headley at this time came at least one tangible success: I was able to persuade the authorities there to take people who'd recovered from their physical injuries but who'd been left suffering from depression.

I told them, by way of example, about people who'd had heart attacks and been treated successfully with bypass surgery. These people usually did really well physically and could return to full active duty, but they often developed a depression after the operation. With soldiers suffering from similar mood-states, I told the doctors, Headley Court would really come into its own: the staff and environment would help to restore their physical confidence, which in turn would go a long way towards helping their depression.

Physical movement is a particularly good treatment for depression: it not only boosts the physical ability of people to be what they were before, but it also seems to have a direct effect on mood-state.

What I was seeing at Headley Court, indeed, led me to my first brush with the notion that the human heart may be – literally – at the very heart of mood-state. Poets have been saying it for centuries. To them, the heart has historically been given a particularly high status as an emotional involver, the container of emotions.

We see this reflected in a lot of the language that we use daily: *He had the heart for it. She died of a broken heart. Come on, have a heart.*

The heart is controlled by the right side of the brain, which, as I was beginning to fully appreciate, is the hemisphere that takes more of a pasting than the left in PTSD (in a right-handed person; the opposite if you're left-handed). The right side of the brain also controls the autonomic nervous system. The ANS manages the organs you don't need to consciously control. You don't need to think about your heart beating, it just happens. It's the same with breathing.

If the heart is controlled by the ANS in the right hemisphere, and something happens that affects the function of the right hemisphere and has an imprint on it, then it will, in turn, potentially have an effect on all the organs that the right hemisphere controls. We know about irritable bowel. We know that people develop chronic inflammatory conditions like ulcerative colitis when they have been stressed or shocked. We know that people can develop chronic types of arthritis when their auto-immunity is disturbed. This is more about the inflammatory response that is an intrinsic part of the stress reaction which becomes chronic and will alter immune responses until switched off: the stress reaction produces surges of adrenaline, the hormone that induces freeze/flight/fight responses, and cortisol, which initially improves the inflammatory response and healing of any tissue damaged in the traumatic event, but if there is no actual tissue damage then the immune reaction can start to attack our own body tissues. The skin and other membranes are common targets. The relatively new discipline of psychoneuroimmunology has led to a new understanding of how the mind and the immune system work. Stress that triggers changes in brain chemistry is now known to cause further change in body function through changes in hormone control.

These conditions are diagnosed in surgeries all the time – not just in soldiers but in people who experience normal, daily civilian existence. PTSD is a fact of life. It can strike out of the blue, which is why it is often described as a ticking time bomb that's waiting to explode across Western society. It's also why I find myself progressively probing the frontier of the frontier.

The more I learn about the mind and our reactions to trauma, the more I'm convinced of two things: the keys to our understanding it may well be stranger than we can imagine right now; and, despite everything, we have strong reasons to be hopeful.

Chapter 21

Follow the Data, Theory Be Damned

Driving to Ticehurst early one morning from home, I heard the astronomer Fred Hoyle being interviewed on the radio. It was all good stuff, but the most interesting part was when they asked what advice he'd like to pass on to his successors.

He said, 'When you come across something that doesn't fit the present state of knowledge, don't throw it in the bin. It is, more than likely, a valid result – it's just that it probably doesn't fit the present state of knowledge. Keep it on a shelf somewhere, because it may fit with something you discover down the line. Things that happen by accident, that don't fit, that come by surprise – store them all too.'

I found myself nodding in agreement. Fred Hoyle had put his finger precisely on the very thing I didn't like about random controlled trials. Whatever was found not to obey the rules of an RCT was discarded. It wasn't put on a shelf like he recommended, or stored in a physical or mental library for later excavation. The researcher herself might remember it, but for all others it was lost: knowledge that didn't fit with present-day thinking would one day have to be rediscovered.

Fred was then asked what he thought was the meaning of his life. He said, 'That's easy. When I was very young I realized I'd been born into a wonderful place. I decided that before I shuffled off the mortal coil, I'd find out as much about this place as I possibly could, because it's all so fascinating.'

It was probably from that moment that I made sure I never closed my mind to certain possibilities just because they weren't evidence-based.

Fred Hoyle's words came back to me soon after 17 January 2008, a day when our TV screens were filled with dramatic scenes after a British Airways Boeing 777 crash-landed at Heathrow short of the main runway. All 136 passengers and 16 crew escaped from the aircraft. Eighteen people were taken to hospital with minor injuries.

Early indications were that the plane had suffered a catastrophic double engine failure on its final approach. Just 20 seconds from landing, the captain and first officer suddenly found they had no power. So sudden and dramatic was the emergency that they had no time to put out a radio alert or even warn passengers to assume the brace position.

Eyewitnesses on the ground described the plane gliding in very low as the pilot fought desperately to keep the Triple-7 on course and high enough to miss nearby houses and the busy road beside the airport. As they watched in horror, the jet cleared the airport's perimeter fence by just a few feet and smashed on to grass just short of the runway.

The impact tore off part of the landing gear as the plane slewed across the grass on its belly, gouging deep tracks in the rain-softened soil. Both wings and an engine were badly damaged before it finally slid to a halt on the edge of the runway threshold.

As fire engines raced to the scene, then smothered the plane with foam, cabin crew deployed the emergency evacuation chutes and passengers slid to safety. Incredibly, just 18 of those on board were hurt, only one seriously.

One passenger on the flight said it was a miracle everyone had escaped with their lives. Another told of the terror as screaming passengers ran through a smoke-filled cabin, fearing they would die before they reached the emergency exits. He said: 'People started screaming, kids were crying, we thought we were going to die. We thought the plane was going to blow up.'

It was lucky that the plane was not engulfed in a fireball, an expert said, as a significant amount of fuel leaked from ruptured tanks.

The truly terrifying nature of the emergency facing the crew was revealed at a press conference the next day. The pilot said the jet was two miles from Heathrow when the engines failed. The Boeing 777 was descending and had reached 600 feet when there was a catastrophic power failure.

As the plane slowed it began to plunge towards the densely populated West London suburbs. Senior First Officer John Coward, who was at the controls, had to nurse the stricken plane over the rooftops for almost a minute as he glided towards the runway. He finally cleared the airport perimeter fence by five feet before crash-landing on the grass.

At another press conference a day or two later, 44-year-old Peter Burkill, the jet's captain, paid tribute to John Coward's immense skill. He told the assembled media: 'He did the most remarkable job.'

A few days later, I was at Chester University, where I was teaching a course module, when a call came through from the medical director at the Civil Aviation Authority. She asked me if I'd be available to assess the pilots. 'You must realize I'm not asking you to see these people on behalf of British Airways,' she said. 'I'm asking you on behalf of the CAA to assess their fitness to fly. What has happened to these people? What do we need to do to make them fit to fly, if they're not fit to fly?'

Before I got to see them, I'd also treated a passenger on the flight, at the request of BA. He was in his twenties and had flown a lot, but had never experienced anything like this before. It meant I was going to have two insights into what happened, one from the cockpit and one from the cabin.

'I was aware there was something very badly wrong,' the young man told me. 'The ground seemed to be rushing up very quickly – but instead of there being a runway beneath us, there was a lot of grass. I was absolutely terrified.'

Something happened to him then which he was never able to express to me. He later discussed it with a psychotherapist, but it was given in confidence so I've never been privy to what it actually was. It was something to do with a change that he observed in his girlfriend, who'd been sitting beside him.

As the aircraft started plummeting, he perceived this alteration in her, and he felt that something had happened to him too. He was talking about things that he didn't feel he could discuss easily; things that he didn't understand. All he would say when I pressed him was that he felt as if he wasn't really there; that somehow he wasn't himself.

I can only speculate, but my strong belief is that he had an out-of-body experience.

Out-of-body experiences, OOBEs, as I now knew, were powerful dissociative phenomena associated with PTSD. People who have them – as was the case with the Invisible Girl – feel that because they have 'left their bodies' they no longer exist. When people have this experience it is so odd, so alien to them and so frightening that in most cases they don't want to talk about it. They worry that on top of everything else, they will be perceived as mad. But they're not, of course. It's further evidence to me that PTSD is an evolving phenomenon and that we need to keep an open mind when dealing with certain aspects of it.

Fred Hoyle was absolutely right.

When it comes to PTSD, there's a wealth of data out there – and the data is still coming in. A good deal of that data remains beyond our current understanding. That doesn't mean, however, that it's invalid.

We need to put it on a shelf and, when we're up to it, have another stab at working out what it means.

A pilot, as I knew well from my Air Force days, is an individual with a vested interest in being in control of things, which sometimes gets them into trouble in their personal relationships. They can be very controlling. They're usually fascinated by technology, so even if they appear to be haphazard and happy-go-lucky people, they throw that off as soon as they get into the cockpit. Then they're completely focused.

Angus Black, my consultant adviser when I first started psychiatry, was a group captain, a very solid, balanced bloke, who had been scrum-half for Scotland and a British Lion. He commanded a lot of respect. It was Angus who taught me why pilots were such an interesting breed. Very conveniently, they converted from being extroverts in the mess to being introverts at the controls of the plane. He didn't believe you could use the extrovert/introvert dimension of measuring personality very easily with pilots. They disobeyed that rule. They could be both.

I found the two BA pilots to be very individualistic. Neither had a military background. They had not flown very often together before the Heathrow incident, but they did know each other; and they appeared to get along well.

I knew that what I had to do, as usual, was to help them feel safe.

I set out the ground rules. 'We're going to have to tell the CAA about your fitness to fly,' I said. 'We're going to have to come to that conclusion together. You can see me together or separately – how do you want to play it?'

They opted to be seen together. It was almost as if they needed to be seen together to get a full picture of what had happened to them. Neither of them could individually support the idea that they had done something to bring about the deliverance of passengers and crew. It wasn't an 'I' situation, they were telling me; it was a 'we' situation.

They were keen to sit together and work out how, isolated in the cockpit, they'd pulled this off. You expect from the movies that there would have been a rat-a-tat exchange of dialogue like machine-gun fire going to and fro, so that what they were producing was something they were both involved in – and understood – as they tackled their allocated tasks.

But it wasn't like that at all. As I was to discover, inside that cockpit they had hardly said anything to each other.

I had the preliminary report into the crash-landing by the Air Accident Investigations Branch in front of me. It had found the jet's engines had failed to respond to demands for increased thrust during its final descent towards Heathrow.

'At approximately 600 feet and two miles from touchdown, the auto-throttle demanded an increase in thrust from the two engines but the engines did not respond,' it reported, matter-of-factly.

Key to any investigation is the action of pilots and co-pilots. Even if they are not responsible for the initial problem, their responses can avert or spark a tragedy.

Forty-one-year-old John Coward was quick to admit that, when disaster struck, he believed there was going to be a 'catastrophic crash'. He told me he feared everyone on board was going to die before he steered the plane to safety. He said that after the crash 'there was no sound at all. No sound from the engines; no sound from behind. I turned around and composed myself and heard a lot of commotion behind me. I realized that staff were trying to carry out the drills to evacuate all the passengers.'

Coward, who lived in France with his French wife and three children, said he had been left haunted by the incident and was unable to sleep. He was credited by his captain for averting a major crash, but said he was humbled by people calling him a hero: 'I was only doing my job. The crew, the passengers and everybody else acted heroically. Flying is definitely all about teamwork and that is what we all displayed.'

Our first meeting had established that although they were haunted by the incident, neither of them had been psychologically traumatized by it. But both said they needed some time to come to terms with what had happened, and to be with their families.

I thought a month would tell – the golden month, in which reactions would fizzle out, diminish, not change or even expand.

They were in a situation where the leaky sac could easily expand. It wasn't like the pair of them had been in a small aircraft and had saved their own skins – this was a major international airline, where something very dramatic had happened out of their control. They had averted a disaster of enormous proportions. There were going to be inquiries; people might be critical of them. There were all sorts of things that could happen in that first month that might make the situation worse rather than better.

The pilots were very open with me. They both realized it was important for them to have an opportunity to share with each other what they had been thinking at the time. None of it had been verbalized during the emergency, and they were astonished at how well they'd worked together without words.

It had happened very suddenly. John was already at the controls, so he took charge. All he managed to get out was, 'Something's wrong.' They knew they'd lost all power, but they didn't know what had caused it. Yet despite not another word being exchanged, they'd worked together as a unit to bring the plane down.

Now, in my office, they both reported a remarkable thing. Both said they had the very real sense that had either of them spoken, some sort of spell might have been broken.

Individuals have demonstrated this, on many occasions – heroes have performed acts of valour for which they can give no explanation. They do what to others appear to be impossible deeds, often beyond human endurance, but they do them. It suggests to me that, under certain conditions, human beings have the capacity to communicate without speaking – and in a very coordinated way. Training, in the way that pilots are trained to deal with emergencies, is unquestionably a part of it. But what these two pilots were describing went beyond training. This, to me, was animal, instinctual – beyond that even: a sixth sense.

Somehow or other, these two pilots had pulled off something that one of them probably wouldn't have been able to do on his own – yet neither knew what the other was doing.

It brought me into the area of 'Group Think', a very interesting phenomenon in which the sum of the thoughts produced between two or more people is greater than the sum of individual contributions. There's a sort of distillation effect, a processing, a thinking through, that the individual contributions cannot account for.

There is a suggestion that, way back in our existence when we were crawling out of the jungle, we had this ability to be intuitive. We had to be on super-receive to understand the threats that might face us behind trees and bushes from tigers or whatever else. When we were out of the jungle, that intuition was sometimes interchangeable between groups and individuals, probably in much the same way you see wildebeest all stand to attention when they sense a predator nearby.

When man left the jungle and became increasingly urbanized, we lost that capacity. The transmitter and receiver either got turned off or turned down so low it wasn't usable any more. But occasionally we enter a state where it's switched back on again.

I believed that these two pilots had entered that state. The shock of what had happened had pitched them into a state of initial freeze, where people remain vigilant – frozen but not immobilized. In primeval terms, they were thinking about where the predator was. Their senses were working at a high level to try to define the territory, to see where the risks were so they could decide whether to fight, flee or freeze.

As we spoke, the pilots checked out between them what had happened and began to make some sort of sense of it. They knew they'd done the right things. They listened intently to each other's descriptions of what had gone through their heads. Both described being focused and very much in control. Nothing else in the world mattered once they realized they'd lost power. They knew what they had to do. It was almost as if they willed the aircraft to get over the perimeter fence.

They realized they hadn't verbalized anything during those final 20 seconds, but the communication they did achieve was just as articulate – probably much more articulate and more direct than words could ever have allowed.

Words can be metaphorical, and they can be misheard or mis-understood. But this stuff wasn't misheard. They communicated perfectly together. And now they needed to understand what had happened. Because with understanding came processing; and with successful processing there could be no PTSD.

At the end of it, they felt they'd been through an experience that showed that when the chips were down they'd done what they needed to do – and in a way that no amount of training could ever have taught them.

'No simulator could possibly have brought about a real feeling of wholeness, of confidence in our ability to fly that particular aircraft,' they said. 'We now know that we can do it, and we'll carry that into the future.'

None of it was overblown or arrogant; it was just a statement of fact about the way they felt, given in a quiet and unassuming manner.

They both described how they were oblivious to each other in terms of sight and sound and this, in my view, was because they were picking up communications from some other channel. They were plugged in together, working as one, against a common foe.

I felt, as I spoke to these two men, as if I'd suddenly come full circle. The term PTSD wasn't coined until 1980. I was still a psychiatry student at the time, and in no position to question the status quo. It took all my concentration and energy just trying to get a handle on concepts that had already been established by other people. It wasn't a time for anything but sitting at the feet of the masters and learning as quickly as I could. I soaked it up like a sponge and I accepted every word I was told.

In the years immediately after I qualified there were probably many occasions when I encountered PTSD but didn't recognize it.

Then Pan Am Flight 103 fell out of the sky and a lot of my assumptions had to change. I could no longer accept a flashback as a symptom of a mental illness, which was how it had been described in all the journals I had ever read. I knew some of the mountain rescue guys, and I couldn't believe they had become mentally ill. I had gone back to the drawing board and it had been an extraordinary journey.

It had taken another air crash – this time, thank God, one with no fatalities – for me to realize that the PTSD field remained replete with tantalizing conundrums. The BA pilots had demonstrated once again how nature had provided us with a set of survival tools, some of which transcended our current scientific understanding. The elusive ones were still out there, waiting to be discovered, and it was up to us to unlock their meaning.

Epilogue

In 2001, Chris Brewin, professor of psychology at University College London, published a paper postulating that the human brain contained two separate memory systems: SAM (situationally accessible memory) in the right hemisphere, and VAM (verbally accessible memory) in the left.

Brewin saw VAM as the set of pathways that connected our speech centre, both hemispheres, and, to an extent, our limbic (emotional) system, so that we could voluntarily recover a piece of personal history when we needed to. We could replay it for our own consumption and explain it to others, and do so without suffering anxiety, rage or depression. VAM was coherent; it contained autobiographical memory.

While the VAM system used the verbal mode and contained easily accessible information that could be communicated to others and integrated in one's autobiographical memory, the SAM system contained perception-based information received from the different sensory channels. Perception-based information was not verbally encoded, and was therefore harder to communicate to others and to integrate in autobiographical memory.

Since the VAM system depended on good hippocampus functioning, he said, and as this functioning may deteriorate under high levels of stress, memories of trauma may become fragmented and less time-ordered. The SAM system, on the other hand, is less affected by levels of stress, and so sensory-based memories may be strong while not easy to put into words. However, to be effectively integrated into autobiographical memory, the sensory memories must be transferred to the VAM system.

Much of Freudian psychology is based on similar theory: unconscious 'memory' drives neurotic behaviour. Making the unconscious conscious breaks the chain. But post-traumatic therapy was not typically Freudian because most of our patients had memories that were all too conscious. These memories burst into awareness and shattered one's assumptions and sense of security. This was classic PTSD.

Flashbacks, I now knew, were one way of gradually allowing SAM memories into the VAM system, where they could be integrated in memories of past and present. Maybe Brewin's model explained why therapy was a quicker way to help this process. Debriefing – early intervention – might speed this integration or information transfer by forcing sensory memories into words.

Brewin's theory suggested that memory was absorbed in SAM form into a temporary store rather like a floppy disk. SAM is about what you see, hear, smell, taste and touch from the outside world, coming in through your eyes, ears, nose and skin. The response to it from the inside can be sensory and emotional in type. What comes in might make you feel happy, scared or under threat, and those things get imprinted too.

Memories are laid down with a situation and a reaction to that situation. Flashbacks are imprinted at that level, and if the stuff that comes in is ordinary and nondescript and familiar, then the floppy disk contains it for a day – experienced while you're awake.

Then when you go to bed at night and sleep, you relive it during REM (rapid eye movement) sleep.

We have five episodes of REM sleep within one night, each lasting about 15 minutes. REM is when you dream. We know also from various types of FMRI scanning that the two hemispheres are inter-relating furiously at this time.

Brewin's surmise was that normal memory processing is in a SAM form, which then gets pushed across the network into the other side of the brain and converted into VAM. The 'journalist' is on the right-hand side of the brain, getting all this information together, and is trying to wire in his copy. He sends it via a USB cable, which, in the brain's case, happens to be the hippocampus.

The copy goes into the left hemisphere and lands on the 'editor's' desk located in Broca's area, i.e., Speech HQ. The editor will look very carefully at the information that's trying to get into the left hemisphere. If the editor looks at it and it appears to be OK and makes sense – familiar things stand a much better chance of making sense than unfamiliar things – then the editor will go ahead and publish it. When this has been done, you can talk about it, effectively placing it in a filing cabinet. It's when things hit you that don't make sense that the system breaks down.

Imagine that during the day you're seeing a lot of grass, and the grass is green. You won't have too much difficulty persuading the editor the grass is green. But say you went to certain parts of New Zealand or Kentucky where the grass is blue (which, incidentally, is how they discovered lithium: cows eating blue grass were calmer than the ones on regular green stuff). In the Brewin model, you're going to have to persuade the editor to let that information in by proving that grass can be blue sometimes. The editor is going to say, 'Grass is green, you've got this wrong,' and send it back. You then say, 'It's because the lithium in the ground turns it blue.' That might be enough, but if the editor is a stickler he'll send it back a few times before it gets into your filing system, the database of your life's experience. It's got to be accurate; it's got to fit in with your previous store of knowledge and be stuff you can iterate and make a story of.

A flashback, therefore, was an attempt to re-present the information taken in at a particular point in time, to see if sense could be made of it in the here and now. Once it's accepted and firmly logged in the filing cabinet on the left side of the brain, then it is a different quality of information. It has a stamp on it that says, 'I happened in the past.' All the time it stays in the right side of the brain, it doesn't have that stamp. It feels as if it's happening now. There is a degree of urgency to get the material across, because people don't like to have flashbacks to things that happened a few days ago, particularly if they're unpleasant.

That had been my big breakthrough post-Lockerbie: flashback as re-presentation of information to the editor. 'This is unprocessed information I don't understand, I'm giving it you again to see if you can make sense of it. And I'll do it again and again, until you do . . .'

Sometimes, when that information became stuck in the right side of the brain, it took a special process – like EMDR – to send it across to the left side. But this presupposed that the pathway to get it across was intact.

Stress, as I already knew, badly affected the hippocampus, the USB cable that allowed information to pass from the right hemisphere to the left. I recalled the tests that had been made public in 1995 on US Army veterans with PTSD who exhibited an 8 per cent reduction in the volume of their right hippocampus compared with vets who suffered no such symptoms. This explained how information that needed to pass across the USB cable would remain stuck and how flashbacks were the brain's conditioned attempts at getting it to where it was supposed to be: the journalist's copy approved for press, given a big green tick by the editor, and eventually filed away, processed and understood, as old copy, complete with a date stamp.

Pre-1980, the symptoms later associated with PTSD were regarded as a sign of mental illness. For people who came back from Vietnam mentally scarred, that was the name on the tin. For me, that all changed after Lockerbie.

Having been taught that symptoms of illnesses were pathological, I then began to see them differently – as normal features or phenomena which, given the circumstances, were non-pathological. These were normal reactions in normal people to abnormal events that they were tussling with in their heads. And the way of doing that was perfectly understandable: the mind was giving them repeated opportunities to make sense of the material. This was – is – the essence of the flashback.

Debate nowadays is towards PTSD being a non-pathological reaction, but it's still a very live question.

My point of view is that flashbacks, nightmares and all the other symptoms of PTSD are 'adaptive' if you look at the world through the eyes of a trauma victim: attempts to assuage, minimize, optimize performance. I think that people who hold on to the idea that PTSD symptoms – 'features', as I prefer to call them – are evidence of an illness are holding on too tightly to a medical model in which they want to preserve, for some reason or other, the fact that they are the doctors and the patients are the patients. Illness is a vehicle, a dynamic, that they use to preserve distance. The term 'maladaptive' as applied to someone who has PTSD preserves this paradigm.

It's much more accurate scientifically, and possibly therefore more therapeutic, for patients to believe they have reacted normally to an unusual event, and that the symptoms they have are not pathological: they are not, in other words, behaving maladaptively; they're doing their best to come to terms with their trauma.

The argument against that is that when people retreat into drink, for example, they do so as a maladaptive way of avoiding having flashbacks. But if you find that drinking is the best way for you as an individual to get rid of your flashbacks, as George did after Bosnia, then maybe that's just the price you pay. If the flashbacks disappear, then maybe the risk of becoming an alcoholic is worth it. If you've tried everything else and you haven't had the opportunity to face down your flashbacks to process them, then alcohol might be the only thing you try that works. To regard that as a maladaptive mechanism doesn't really cut the mustard with me.

The beginning of my divergence from medical orthodoxy was when I saw the reactions that some of the people in the mountain rescue teams displayed. Not all of them, by any means, but some of them, and I knew that you had to be a resilient character to get into MR teams.

I believed that this was a major medical topic, not just for traumatologists. All medical specialists, including GPs, would see people with PTSD. It was a bit like syphilis, which we used to describe in the old days as 'the wily treponeme' (the Latin term for syphilis is *treponema pallidum pallidum*, and it's a long, snake-like bacterium). It's insidious in its development. You don't know you have it until you have it, and it takes so many different forms. It's capable of masquerading as just about any other illness. I felt PTSD was similar. It seemed to have so many different types of manifestation. But after everything I'd seen, I couldn't possibly describe it as an illness. All my research, all my years of clinical experience, had led me to believe it was a survival tool; perhaps our ultimate survival tool.

Discoveries since 1995 – when those findings were published about the diminished hippocampi of the Vietnam vets – had demonstrated that the hippocampal fuse could be both 'nibbled away' by high adrenaline levels over a long period of time or – and this was the killer – blown instantly by extremely high levels of adrenaline generated in a sudden emergency. To preserve us from the most unimaginable horror, in other words, the brain had a mechanism – the USB-like hippocampus – that blew like a fuse to remove us from the full impact of that horror. Very high cortisol levels, it was found, killed the hippocampal fuse nerve cells, which are called neurons.

Given the way nature worked, I couldn't imagine that that capacity had been given to us by accident. It looked very much to me as if we'd acquired it as an evolutionary defence mechanism. But I had no proof of this. It was simply an intuition.

Whether it blows quickly or slowly, the damaged fuse causes a depression of mood, increased anxiety and deterioration of memory and concentration.

In trauma survivors, PTSD, flashbacks especially, could be viewed as part of the repair process; the mind-body's attempts at fixing itself. The key was to get the trauma survivor to a place of safety. Once that had been achieved, with the help of drugs, therapy, counselling or simply by getting them to a place of sanctuary that might include sympathetic friends or relatives, the condition would eight times out of ten – at least in my experience – improve.

This observation was endorsed, and my intuition validated, when, eleven years ago, it was discovered that the hippocampal fuse had the ability to repair itself. Contrary to previous thinking, the adult human brain is capable of growing new neurons, a process called *neurogenesis*. Provided the trauma survivor could be stabilized – made to feel 'safe' (free from the adverse effects of an abnormal adrenaline attack) – this process could, the scientists said, take place within 30 days.

The 'golden month' that had appeared time and again to be so significant in my research had suddenly been underwritten by science. To me this came as no great surprise. I'd always found it hard to believe that Mother Nature would have created us with a major in-built flaw: an inability to fix ourselves.

We now know, therefore, that acute stress reactions involve *reversible* damage to a certain part of the brain, the hippocampus, that is responsible for acquiring new knowledge, memory formation, concentration and mood.

In 2000, Jacobs, van Praag and Gage wrote a seminal paper published in the journal *American Science*, entitled 'Depression and the Birth and Death of the Brain', describing their discovery that although until then there had been no evidence of the brain's ability to grow new nerve cells (neurons) in adults in a process called neurogenesis, their research showed that *some* areas of the brain were constantly remodelling and they suggested that alteration of these processes may be involved in some neuropsychiatric disorders.

In 2001, Manji, Drevets and Charney published their paper in *Nature Medicine* entitled 'The Cellular Neurobiology of Depression', which provided a new model offering a unifying hypothesis for environmental and biological factors in the development of neuropsychiatric disorders, especially in depression.

Their model suggested that clinical depression might arise from the brain failing to grow new neurones in a specific area such as the dentate nucleus of the hippocampus, which is in a state of constant flux as it processes and stores new information.

Both sets of authors found that stress leads to the release of glucocorticoids (steroid hormones related to cortisol) which inhibits neurogenesis in the hippocampus, leading to changes in hippocampal volume in chronic PTSD and depression caused by atrophy of cells in the dentate nucleus, cell endangerment and cell death. The inability to produce new brain cells was thought to be linked to the failure of new cognitions in both of these conditions which were considered critical for recovery from PTSD and depression.

It was thought that understanding mechanisms of release of stem cells to produce new neurones could benefit a range of conditions, among them PTSD, depression and ageing, by including fluoxetine (the serotonin-boosting antidepressant drug Prozac), which increased cell division (in rats) by 70 per cent in the dentate nucleus in three weeks.

These findings were very exciting and strongly supported early intervention in the treatment of PTSD and depression so that serotonin-boosting drugs might be considered to enhance the environment for neurogenesis. Reduction in stress levels would diminish the intoxication of the dentate nucleus cells by stress chemicals and thus prevent cell death.

After the hippocampal dentate nucleus was demonstrated to be at the centrepoint of the stress reaction's impact on the central nervous system, I started to call it 'the fuse'. Antidepressants and lithium were shown to modulate several cell survival pathways controlled by BDNF (brain-derived neurotrophic factor), which have promised a new generation of drugs for major depression and PTSD.

The fuse, nature tells us, is meant to blow to protect the brain if it is working under great strain. It will repair itself given the right conditions and if it blows it should be regarded as a temporary fault.

What, I wondered, if military medics had known this during the First World War? Would they have still sent men designated as personally inadequate – as character-flawed – to death upon death by firing squad?

There *was* no character flaw. This was designed into us – into us all – as a safety mechanism. We were functioning exactly as nature had intended us to.

That the damage to the hippocampal fuse was reversible endorsed, too, an emerging view – a view that I shared – that positive elements could emerge from the horrors of PTSD. Once the fuse was repaired, the brain could gradually make sense of the huge amount of information it had absorbed at the time of the trauma – and the survivor could move on.

It filled me with hope that a full cure for the condition and others related to it – depression, anxiety and panic attacks, to name but three – was a lot closer to being discovered than many people dared to think.

I still think this. To a very large extent, it's what drives me on.

Recently, some 50 years after I left Lorne Street School, I found myself in my study at our home in Wiltshire preparing a series of reports on a court case involving 30 adults who as young children had been serially abused by the Roman Catholic Church in Ireland – or that, at least, was the allegation.

The reports were filled with graphic accounts of the most terrible abuse: children beaten and molested by priests, nuns and the Christian Brothers, in some instances year after year, on a scale that beggared belief. To prepare for the case as an expert witness, I had to write extremely detailed reports and, inevitably, I would find

myself becoming immersed in the world of the victims – a world
filled with fear, repression and the ritual infliction of suffering on a
systemic level.

One moment I was at my desk staring out over the village, the next
I was gone – transported back to the bedroom that I shared with my
brother Derek in our tenement apartment in Leith. In my mind's eye,
I was six or seven.

For a reason I couldn't explain, I found myself gripped by the old
familiar feeling – the exact same feeling as when I turned the corner
at the top of the stairs at Lorne Street School and, holding the Wee
Red Box that had been given to me by Miss Roberts, found myself
thinking about the chipped, peeling paint on Miss McGregor's door.
Only here I was, lying in my bed, staring at the ceiling, listening to
the low moans of ships' foghorns in the port.

When I examined this feeling, I became convinced that the Wee
Red Box, with its coiled belt inside, was under my bed and that it
had been placed there by my parents.

This was a truly unsettling thought because home had always been
a safe haven and my parents had never been other than loving and
supportive to me and my brother. Why, then, had they entered into
a pact with Miss Roberts and Miss McGregor and placed the Wee
Red Box, this thing that terrified me more than anything else, under
my bed?

I let myself be carried along by the memory.

My brother was not in the room. It must have been during the
time when he had had polio and was in hospital. I squeezed my eyes
shut, hoping the feeling would go away, but it didn't. I couldn't bear
to be alone with the box. I knew I had to get rid of it.

Tentatively, I climbed out of bed, got down on my hands and
knees and walked my fingertips along the floor until they touched
something metallic. Fighting back tears, I forced myself to take hold
of it. I pulled it out from under the bed and there it was, dimly
visible in the light of the street lamp outside my window: the Wee
Red Box.

Trembling as I picked it up with both hands and feeling all the
revulsion I'd ever felt when I'd been forced to carry it from Miss
McGregor's office to Miss Roberts's classroom, I opened my bedroom door, ran into the bathroom, opened the box and hurled the

contents out of the window. I heard the clatter of the belt as it landed on the paving stones in the yard below.

At that moment, I 'woke up', expecting to find myself staring at the grey stone façade of the neighbouring tenement block, but instead I was back in Wiltshire, confronted by nothing more threatening than a tractor laden with hay trundling down the hill towards the centre of the village. I dropped my gaze and there was the abuse report staring back at me from my computer screen.

I was so convinced that this memory was real that I immediately called my father to ask him if Miss McGregor or Miss Roberts had ever given him the Wee Red Box so that he could continue to administer punishment to me at home. My father laughed and made some passing remark about my spending too much time at the coal-face.

Only then did I see this 'incident' for what it was: a moment in which the imprint of a memory, replete not just with sight, sound and smell but also emotion, had been thrown at me so graphically that it was as if I was actually there. I'd dissociated and had some kind of flashback – only it wasn't an actual flashback. The Wee Red Box hadn't been under my bed. My parents had never had any pact with the headmistress of Lorne Street School. But the emotional imprint – the terror – that *had* been real.

In my flashback experience, I had rooted out a symbol of my feelings and I'd flung it out of the bathroom window. It had made my home a safe place.

Why, I wondered.

The flashback had been triggered by the abuse report; that was for sure. The abuse allegedly suffered by those adults as children had been ritualistic and there had been something ritualistic about the Wee Red Box. That was the connection. But why now? Was I hoping to 'transmit' to those 30 abused Irish children that it was possible to throw off oppression? Or was the flashback for my benefit alone?

I'd never acknowledged the Wee Red Box in all the years I had worked in the trauma field. Its memory had lain there, unprocessed, working away at me – until this moment when, spontaneously, I'd been forced to confront it.

'Untreated', so to speak, how had this trauma manifested itself in my life?

Well, for a start, I could see that it had acted as some kind of driving force.

I'd always reacted against bullies and ultimately had ended up in a field where, for years, the system had been the bully: it had sought to impose a set view that people who 'crack up' in the face of a life-threatening experience – or at least, one they perceive to be life-threatening – had been marred from birth by some kind of character flaw.

When that was no longer deemed to be the case, it was stated instead that the trauma reaction was an illness.

Neither of these things, we knew now, had been true. But without Miss Roberts or, indeed, her successor, Miss Sprunt, I doubt I'd have gone on to do what I'd done. Miss Roberts had galvanized me to confront bullies; Miss Sprunt had told me it was all right to be curious. Had I not had these two talismans as my guides it was conceivable, I suppose, that I'd have gone on to become a doctor, but I couldn't see myself entering, much less staying with, the confrontational area of psychiatry that had marked my career.

So out of this traumatic experience, albeit insignificant compared to some of the traumas my patients had faced, perhaps some good had come.

My gaze drifted across my desk, past the picture of Salvador Dalí's *Christ of St John of the Cross*, until it rested on those Goethe-inspired lines about commitment.

I read a little way down until I came to the part that interested me.

> *Concerning all acts of initiative (and creation),*
> *There is one elementary truth the ignorance*
> *Of which kills countless ideas and splendid plans:*
> *That the moment one definitely commits oneself,*
> *Then Providence moves in too.*

Science that will eventually rid us of the lingering effects of trauma is out there, waiting to be discovered. All it needs is courage and commitment – characteristics I see all the time in my patients.

And for that, every day, I utter a small thank you to Providence.

Until there is commitment, there is hesitancy,
The chance to draw back, always ineffectiveness,
Concerning all acts of initiative (and creation),
There is one elementary truth the ignorance
of which kills countless ideas and splendid plans:
That the moment one definitely commits oneself,
Then Providence moves in too.
All sorts of things occur to help one that would
never otherwise have occurred.
A whole stream of events issues forth from the decision,
Raising in one's favour all manner of unforeseen
Incidents and material assistance which
No Man could have dreamed would have come his way.
Whatever you can do or dream you can, begin it.
Boldness has genius, power, and magic in it.
Begin it now.

My copy of this poem, which sits on my desk to this day, cites Goethe as the author. In fact, it seems that only the last three lines are based on a loose nineteenth-century translation of *Faust* by John Anster, while the rest appears to be taken from W. H. Murray, *The Scottish Himalaya Expedition*, 1951. For a full explanation of the poem's complex history, see <http://www.goethesociety.org/pages/quotescom.html>

Men go abroad to wonder at the heights of mountains, at the huge waves of the sea, at the long courses of rivers, at the vast compass of the ocean, at the circular motions of the stars, and they pass by themselves without wondering.

Saint Augustine

Select Bibliography

Books and Periodicals

Alexander, D. A., 'The Piper Alpha Oil Rig Disaster', in J. P. Wilson and B. Raphael (eds), *International Handbook of Traumatic Stress Syndromes*, Plenum Press, New York, 1993

Blackmore, Susan, 'Visions of the Dying Brain', *New Scientist*, No. 1611, 43-6, 5 May 1988

Beharry, Johnson, *Barefoot Soldier*, Little, Brown, 2006

Bovin, Michelle J., Jager-Hyman, Shari, Gold, Sari D., Marx, Brian P., and Sloan, Denise M., 'Toxic Immobility Mediates the Influence of Peritraumatic Fear and Perceived Inescapability on Post Traumatic Stress Symptom Severity among Sexual Assault Survivors', in *Journal of Traumatic Stress*, vol. 21, 4, 402-9, August 2008

Brewin, Chris, 'Memory Processes in Posttraumatic Stress Disorder', in *International Review of Psychiatry*, 13, 159-63, 2001

Brewin, C. R., Dalgleish, T., and Joseph, S., 'A Dual Representation Theory of Posttraumatic Stress Disorder', *Psychological Review*, vol. 103, 4, 670-686, 1996

Busuttil, W., Turnbull, G. J., Neal, L. A., Rollins, J., West, A. G., Blanch, N., and Herepath, R., 'Incorporating Psychological Debriefing Techniques Within a Brief Group Psychotherapy Programme for the Treatment of Post-Traumatic Stress Disorder', *British Journal of Psychiatry*, vol. 167, 495-502, 1995

Davidson, J., 'Drug Therapy of Post-Traumatic Stress Disorder', *British Journal of Psychiatry*, vol. 160, 309-314, 1992

Kinchin, David, *Post Traumatic Stress Disorder – The Invisible Injury*, Success Unlimited, 3rd edn, 2001

Lewis, David, *The Man Who Invented Hitler*, Headline, 2003

McCarthy, John, and Morrell, Jill, *Some Other Rainbow*, Bantam Press, 1993; new edn, Corgi, 1994

Manji, H. K., Drevets, W. C., and Charney, D. S., 'The Cellular Neurobiology of Depression', in *Nature Medicine*, 7(5), 541-7, May 2001

Morris, Desmond, *The Naked Ape*, Cape, 1967; new edn, Vintage, 2005

Pert, C. B., Ruff, M. R., Weber, R. J., Herkenham, M., 'Neuropeptides and Their Receptors: A Psychosomatic Network', *Journal of Immunology*, supplement 135, 820S-826S, 1985

Pert, Candace, *Molecules of Emotion*, Pocket Books, new edn, 1999

Raphael, Beverley, *When Disaster Strikes: How Individuals and Communities Cope with Catastrophe*, Basic Books, New York, 1986

Sacks, Oliver, *The Man Who Mistook His Wife for a Hat*, Picador, 13th edn, 2007

Sassoon, Siegfried, *Memoirs of an Infantry Officer*, 1930, new edn, Faber and Faber, 2000

Tedeschi, Richard G., and Calhoun, Lawrence, 'Posttraumatic Growth: A New Perspective on Psychotraumatology', in *Psychiatric Times*, vol. 21, April 2004

Van der Kolk, Bessel, 'The Body Keeps the Score', in *Harvard Review of Psychiatry*, 1(5), 253-65, 1994

Van der Kolk, Bessel, 'The Long Shadow of Trauma', online article in *PsychoTherapy Networker*, 13 April 2010

Van der Kolk, Bessel, *Post-Traumatic Stress Disorder: Psychological and Biological Sequelae (Clinical Insights)*, APA Press, 1984

Van der Kolk, Bessel, McFarlane, Alexander C., Weisaeth, Lars (eds.), *Traumatic Stress: The Effects of Overwhelming Stress on Mind, Body, and Society*, The Guildford Press, New York, London, 1996

Van der Kolk, Bessel, *Psychological Trauma*, APA Press, 1987

Van Praag, Henriette, Jacobs, Barry, and Gage, Fred, 'Depression and the Birth and Death of Brain Cells', in *American Scientist*, vol. 88, no. 4, 340, July-August 2000

Television programmes

'The Hostage Retrievers', Thames Television, 1991

'Military Trauma', *Panorama*, BBC 1, 2005

'PTSD Treatment Programme – Within Walls', BBC 2, 1992

'Rescuing the Rescuers', BBC 2, 1994

'Survivors', *Inside Story*, BBC 1, 1994

Index

ABOUT THE AUTHOR

Gordon Turnbull went to medical school at Edinburgh University, and then joined the RAF where he gained experience in General Medicine, expedition medicine and neurology. He then trained in psychiatry and was drawn into the field of psychological trauma after the Lockerbie air disaster in 1988. After active service in the Gulf War of 1991 as an RAF psychiatric adviser in the field, he conducted the first-ever debriefings of British prisoners of war and British hostages released from the Lebanon. He developed new treatment strategies for trauma at the Princess Alexandra Hospital, RAF Wroughton, and post-RAF has concentrated on trauma services for police officers, emergency service personnel and military veterans and civilians. He is currently Consultant Psychiatrist in Trauma at Capio Nightingale Hospital in London and the Ridgeway Hospital in Wroughton, adviser in Psychiatry to the Civil Aviation Authority, visiting professor to the University of Chester and one of the world's leading experts on PTSD.